IRON HAND

Smashing the Enemy's Air Defences

IRON HAND

Smashing the Enemy's Air Defences

ANTHONY M. THORNBOROUGH & FRANK B. MORMILLO

with

TONY CASSANOVA & KEVIN JACKSON

Patrick Stephens Limited
AN IMPRINT OF HAYNES PUBLISHING

First published in 2002

Reprinted in 2002

British Cataloguing-in-Publication Data:
A catalogue record for this book is available
from the British Library.

ISBN 1 85260 605 3

Patrick Stephens Limited is an imprint of
Haynes Publishing, Sparkford,
Nr Yeovil, Somerset, BA22 7JJ.

Typeset by Sutton Publishing.
Printed and bound in England by
J.H. Haynes & Co. Ltd, Sparkford.

CONTENTS

ACKNOWLEDGEMENTS

In compiling this work, interviewers Tony Cassanova and Kevin Jackson, photographer Frank B. Mormillo and I were all extremely fortunate in being able to draw on many first-hand experiences of aircrews, and to these men and women we owe our heartfelt thanks. Many people in US Navy/Marine Corps Iron Hand and US Air Force Wild Weasel units – intelligence, maintenance, engineering and public affairs – also lent a hand. To everyone, a big thank you for your considerable help, but in particular the following: William Ackerman, Deborah Aragon, Bill Bagley, Bruce M. Bailey, Daniel Barry, Bruce Benyshek, Robert Besal, Chris Burgess, Scott Bymun, Glenn W. Carlson, Charlie Carr, Lester Carroll, James Chamberlain, John Chapman, Larry Clavette, Pete Costello, Robert Crumm, Chris Eagle, Bob Egan, Mike Gilroy, Doug Glover, Scott Guimond, John J. Harty, Heather Healy, Paul Hollandsworth, Edward Hubbard, Pete Hunt, Kolin Jan, George Jernigan, Joe Kilkenny, Gerry Knotts, Paula Kurtz, Louis P. Lalli, Matthew Leahey, John Leenhouts, Judith S. Lewis, Don Logan, Mike Loughran, Francis 'T.R.' Marino, William C. McLeod II, Barry Miller, Scott Moore, Mark Morgan, Rick Morgan, Edward Navarette, Mike Nervik, Alan Palmer, Sam Peacock, Joe Pepper, Kim Pepperell, Mike Pietrucha, Celia Rakestraw, Mikal Rasheed, Ed Rasimus, Eric Rine, James E. Rotramel, Philip J. Rowe Jr, Joseph Schvimmer, Charles G. Simpson, Gerald Stiles, Sandy Terry, Philip J. Walters, George Walton, John Weber, John D. Weides, William White and James Uken. Many thanks to you all.

Many thanks also to the following individuals who proved instrumental: Guy Aceto, Ted Been, August H. Bickel, Todd H. Blecher, Gina Ceron, Dr Boyd L. Dastrup, Peter E. Davies, Steve Dumovich, Dixie Dysart, Robert J. Egioff, Andy Evans, Mark L. Evans, Phil Evans, Michael France, Ronald Fry, Larry Furrow, Eric Hehs, Kevin Helm, Carolyn C. Hodge, Brenda L. Hogan, Alan Howarth, Ellen LeMond-Holman, Judith S. Lewis, Lois Lovisolo, Todd Merrill, Michael J. Nipper, Paul Osborne, Mick Roth, Dr John Sherwood, Doug Siegfried, John T. Smith, Troy Snead, Joseph Snoy, Bettie Sprigg, Kathy Vinson, Richard L. Ward and Bill Watkins.

Anthony M. Thornborough,
with Tony Cassanova, Kevin Jackson and Frank B. Mormillo
Bristol, England, February 2002

INTRODUCTION

A handful of books have been compiled in the past on the subject of Suppression of Enemy Air Defences or SEAD, the current all-embracing term for Iron Hand. These were published over a decade ago, and for the most part comprised picture albums or heavy-duty official theses. I have endeavoured to provide as up-to-date an account as possible that reflects recent combat over the Middle East, the Persian Gulf and the Balkans, and takes advantage of the wealth of new material describing operations in Vietnam, where missileering electronic combat really came of age. Some of the information vital to the research has only recently entered the public domain, allowing a more accurate overall picture to be painted, including a more candid dialogue with the aircrews.

This book charts all the chief technological and doctrinal milestones in American electronic combat since the early 1960s, while saluting the operational exploits of the flying units – in combat.

Author Tony Thornborough being familiarised with the F-4G's cockpit by Weasel pilot Bruce Benyshek. (Author's Collection)

Scooters on the deck of USS Bon Homme Richard *in the Gulf of Tonkin, being readied for ops over North Vietnam.* (Richard L. Ward Archives)

O N E

ROLLING
THUNDER

V ietnam had been a divided country, geopolitically, since its split across the Central Highlands under the Geneva Accords of 1954. The agreements had ended nearly a century of French colonialism in the region. The North was communist, while the South was nominally pro-western but under constant threat from within by communist-sponsored Viet Cong guerrillas, as well as infiltration activities by regular army units from North Vietnam who kept the guerrillas stocked with ammunition. The United States intervened in an effort to stop the spread of communism throughout South-East Asia, seen to be inevitable under the 'domino theory'. While the US had maintained an advisory presence in Vietnam since the early days of the Kennedy administration, including US Air Force reconnaissance and counter-insurgency aircraft under the Farm Gate venture, in 1964 under President Lyndon Johnson's management the low-key brushfire war suddenly erupted.

The first firelighter into the tinder was Operation Pierce Arrow, initiated on 5 August 1964 in response to North Vietnamese naval torpedo-boat attacks on the US Navy destroyer USS *Maddox* three days previously, infamously known ever since as the Tonkin Gulf incident. Pierce Arrow dispatched jets from the aircraft carriers USS *Constellation* and USS *Ticonderoga* to bomb North Vietnamese patrol-boat bases and oil storage facilities at Vinh. Viet Cong guerrilla action became more commonplace and included a heavy attack on barracks in Pleiku on 7 February 1965. The United States replied with Operation Flaming Dart, comprising reprisal strikes in direct response to each Viet Cong transgression. Two separate air strikes were carried out during February. Then, on 2 March, the Johnson administration initiated Rolling Thunder, replacing the piecemeal Flaming Dart campaign with one intended to be a programme of limited and measured action against selected military targets.

The first strike was against Quang Khe naval base and an ammunition depot at Xom Bong.[1] The idea was that the strikes would gradually work their way – roll, so to speak – towards the Hanoi–Haiphong conurbation at the heart of the North, thus putting increasing pressure on the Ho Chi Minh regime so that it might see fit to leave the South alone, but with the original intent that the bombing would never reach downtown Hanoi. At the same time, US Army troops and US Marines would be stationed in the

Republic, notionally to protect the expanding air bases that would conduct the air war. In reality, it had the opposite effect and led to an escalation of the conflict as North Vietnam turned to China and the Soviet Union for sophisticated air defence equipment and know-how, prepared to sit it out indefinitely. For the United States, embroilment in what became an increasingly politically unpopular war thus endured for almost a decade. For the troops involved, as since time immemorial, it was just another series of battles punctuated by good and bad memories.

THE ALPHA STRIKE

Prospective targets in North Vietnam were placed on an Alpha list created by the Joint Chiefs of Staff (JCS) and strikes on those targets were made only when directed by Washington. In US Navy parlance the strikes thus became known as Alpha Strikes, and were launched from US Navy aircraft carriers cruising in the Gulf of Tonkin, hence the moniker 'Tonkin Gulf Yacht Club' used by combat aircrews operating with Carrier Task Force 77 (CTF-77). Because of the geography of the region, there were just two suitable cruise locations for Line Periods of Action with CTF-77: Dixie Station, off the coast of South Vietnam, was used as a springboard for Armed Reconnaissance (ARREC) strikes over Laos, hunting enemy supply convoys and other authorized targets of opportunity infiltrating South Vietnam, and for theatre familiarization for new pilots and Naval Flight Officer (NFO) aircrew; and Yankee Station, south of Hainan Island, was the launch and recovery spot for Alpha Strikes against North Vietnam.

Alpha Strikes comprised up to forty aircraft flying to the target in waves, all carefully launched in pre-planned formations based on scheduled times-over-target, fuel capacity and speed. The sledgehammer strikers at the heart of the package, and usually the last to join it, were piston-powered Douglas A-1 Skyraiders or Spads, quickly supplanted during Rolling Thunder by Grumman A-6 Intruder all-weather interdictor jets that offered a payload of up to 16,000lb. Douglas A-4 Skyhawks or Scooters were the chief choice for flak suppression, and these bantam-weight bombers would precede the main strike force. In front of them and flying top-cover were Vought F-8 Crusaders or McDonnell F-4 Phantom IIs on Target Combat Air Patrol (TARCAP), primarily there to keep enemy fighters at arm's length, though also occasionally assigned flak suppression duties. Heavyweight Douglas A-3 Skywarriors were also employed for strike duties, but principally acted as pathfinders, and later as jamming platforms and high-volume aerial tankers for the thirsty jets. All of these aircraft were also expected to conduct search and rescue Combat Air Patrol (RESCAP) to help downed colleagues, something few complained of accomplishing.

A host of other aircraft and crews supported the Alpha Strike force in turn, notably RF-8 Crusader and North American Aviation (NAA) RA-5C Vigilante reconnaissance jets which aided with pre-strike targeting and post-strike damage assessment; Grumman E-1B Tracer (later E-2A Hawkeye) airborne early warning (AEW) patrollers, working with

TARCAP and Barrier CAP fighters; and EA-1F Electric Spads which provided jamming support. Adding to the jostle on deck were Sikorsky or Kaman helicopters to retrieve men who had ditched in or ejected over the sea.

Alpha Strikes set the whole aircraft carrier into frenzied motion. Before long, any kind of large strike mission, whether assigned to a target on the Alpha list or not, became synonymous with the Alpha Strike concept, and the term endured until the early 1980s.[2] The USAF similarly put up strike packages from its bases in the Republic of Vietnam and Thailand, mixing aircraft from its various homogeneous wings, each of which tended to operate just one key type of aircraft.

For administrative purposes, in December 1965 North Vietnam was divided into hypothetical strike sectors known as Route Packages (RP). In early April 1966 the exchange system of target allocations between the US Navy and Air Force over the various RPs was replaced by permanent assignments, with the result that 'pilot familiarity with defence location improved substantially and reliance on the relatively inaccurate published AAOB [Anti-Aircraft Artillery Order of Battle] data was reduced'.[3]

At the same time, Commander-in-Chief of the Pacific (CINCPAC) Adm Ulysses S. Grant Sharp added a seventh RP by splitting into two the most heavily defended sector, RP VI, which straddled the Hanoi–Haiphong conurbation. Thus, while crews from both services did operate over all of North Vietnam, they tended to focus on their own turf: the US Air Force pitched their aircraft against RP I, next to the Demilitarized Zone (DMZ) separating north Vietnam from the Republic, plus RPs V and VIA in the far north, which were all readily accessible from their land bases in Thailand, and near the DMZ in the Republic at Da Nang; while CTF-77 focused on RPs II–IV and VIB, which arced around the Gulf of Tonkin. This artificial division pertained throughout the remainder of the United States' involvement in Vietnam. The North Vietnamese, however, did not oblige by locating their expanding air defence system in this convenient pattern, and saturated defences at will, concentrating them around Hanoi and Haiphong, with numerous tentacles.

DVINA: THE 'FLYING TELEGRAPH POLE'

What really threw the cat among the pigeons was the introduction by the Kong Quan Nhan Dan (Vietnam People's Air Force) of the Soviet-supplied V-750 Dvina Surface-to-Air Missile (SAM), code-named SA-2 Guideline by NATO. It possessed a maximum velocity of Mach 3.5, a slant-range of some 25 miles and was effective up to 60,000ft. First publicly shown in the 1957 Moscow Parade, the Dvina was confronted by Francis Gary Powers in his Lockheed U-2 Dragon Lady spyplane over the Soviet Union three years later and subsequently by US reconnaissance jets flying over Cuba in October 1962 (where a second U-2 was brought down). The first Indochina SA-2 battalions, initially manned by Soviet troops, were spotted around Haiphong and Hanoi by a Strategic Air Command (SAC) U-2 on 5 April 1965. By October there were two SA-2 regiments operational, with over six batteries moving between thirty-two confirmed sites.[4]

The SA-2 Guideline was designed for strategic defence but could be relocated by articulated truck in only a few hours. (via Barry Miller)

Initially, US aircrews were not allowed to attack the SA-2 sites. The rationale provided by Washington was that Ho Chi Minh and Premier Pham Van Dong would not escalate the conflict by employing these weapons unless ground forces physically invaded North Vietnam. Thus aircrews watched the SAMs being transported, erected and fielded in classic Soviet-style star-shaped patterns (providing instant virtual 360-degree missile launch coverage) and could do nothing. When the sites neared operational readiness, they suddenly became dispersed, heavily camouflaged and buzzed into action. With Soviet help, the surveying work had been accomplished for over a hundred potential SAM site locations, and operational batteries could soon move between them, fielded in less obvious arrays. Some might be positioned in a fan pattern behind a ridgeline, for example, and comprise only one or two launchers hidden beneath thick foliage. Moreover, dummy sites were abundant. Carpenters worked around the clock creating mock targets, and timber was plentiful.

The SA-2 Guideline was, nonetheless, a large missile and was ferried about on a ZIL-157 trailer hauled by a truck. At its destination it slid back on to a rotatable launch rail. Using Early Warning (EW) radar and visual sightings of inbound aircraft reported over landlines, it would be elevated and turned in the direction of the target, and fired once within range. It relied on command guidance – 'merge the dots' technology – based on steering instructions supplied after launch, using elevation and azimuth angle-measuring Target Tracking Radar (TTR) troughs. These emitters, NATO code-name Fan Song, which were co-located with the SAM launchers and installed atop the trailer vans that housed the operator consoles, would track both the target and the SA-2's progress. UHF guidance signals would in turn be transmitted to fine-tune its intercept trajectory. The missile thus had to be within the guidance beam within 6 seconds of launch, otherwise it would lose control. With a flight-time duration of some 22 seconds, it delivered a 300lb warhead that would be detonated by impact, proximity or command fusing. It was utterly deadly.

SAM sites were typically fielded in a Star-of-David array permitting rapid firing at targets approaching from any direction. (via Barry Miller)

If confronted by a SAM launch, evasion was possible. The SAM could be sighted in Visual Flight Rules (VFR) conditions by a puff of smoke on the ground followed by a dirty, fiery streak that quickly transformed into a white streamer. One tactic was simply to dive down and hope to get out of reach of the missile while it was in its initial, awkward acceleration stage of launch, as early SA-2Bs were seldom effective below 3,000ft. The

The SA-2 was directed using command guidance. Target bearing and range were derived from the SA-2B Fan Song radar system mounted atop a trailer wagon. (via Barry Miller)

second was the high-*g* break. Fast jet veteran Jim Chamberlain explained the tactic:

> Manoeuvring against an SA-2 was always recommended procedure, but to do so one had to see the missile. Never fly above an undercast was always good advice. The game was to put the threat at either the ten or two o'clock position and, as the missile closed, initiate a 4*g* climb and watch for the missile to change course to intercept at the higher altitude. Then, as the missile closed further, dive and watch the missile self-destruct as the proportional guidance tries to turn to the new intercept point. It took some pretty steely nerves, but it worked.

However, avoiding these tenacious missiles in such manoeuvres invariably meant pushing the jettison button to unload the attack jet's payload, leaving nothing to hit the target with. To evade the SAM umbrella, crews were soon forced down into the clutches of the comparatively short-reaching 37mm and 57mm Anti-Aircraft Artillery (AAA, or triple-A), which was directed in turn by Sino-Soviet-supplied SON-9 Fire Can radar. In an effort to mitigate the dangers from both, crews began flying terrain-masking flight profiles, obliging them to negotiate the craggy karst landscape, carpeted with lush arboreal obstacles, that dominates much of Vietnam's topography.

Pilots took advantage of every nook and cranny in the terrain and soon devised nicknames for obstacles that might hide them during their target ingress and egress. US Air Force Republic F-105 Thunderchief pilots, for example, mostly ingressing from the west, used the karst near Hanoi as a radar shield, one particularly expansive mountain outcrop north-west of Hanoi being nicknamed Thud Ridge. US Navy pilots flew eastbound over mostly flatter terrain, and some chose the unauthorized route that hooked through Chinese airspace, rather than the usual northerly back door approach via Cam Pha. This caused diplomatic embarrassment at best, and at worst upped the ante by permitting the two countries to justify joint Sino-Vietnamese interceptor defence duties to cover the Chinese Buffer Zone, where the North Vietnamese had access to more powerful MiG-19 Farmer jets; these interceptors were far more effective than their domestically based MiG-15 Fagots and MiG-17 Frescoes, and were guided by Chinese Ground Control Intercept (GCI) radar.

Thus radar-directed fire was plentiful, and something had to be done about the emitters if strike crews were to be able to go about their Rolling Thunder tasks without incurring unsustainable losses. A gradual escalation of the bombing had brought with it a measured bolstering of the enemy's defences, and the aircrews were caught in a bind.

SKYHAWK: THE SHRIKE PIONEER

Capt William Clark green-inked his logbook (denoting combat) while flying A-4Es with VA-23 on USS *Midway*, when pilots introduced the AGM-45 Shrike Anti-Radiation Missile (ARM) to defeat North Vietnamese radars:

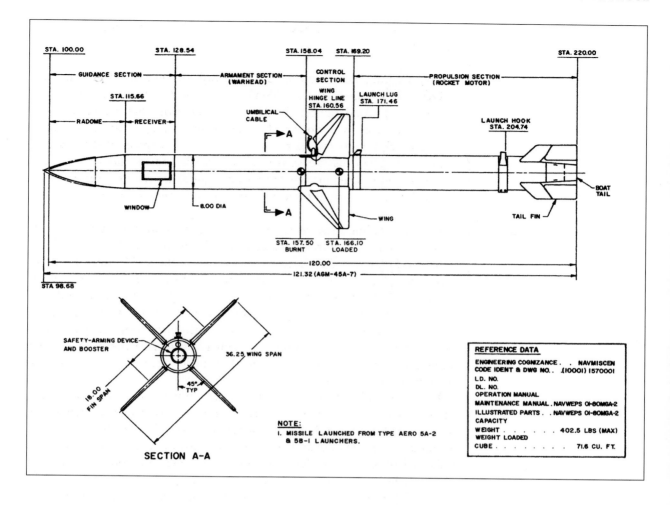

Shrike AGM-45 general arrangement. (US Navy)

Come back with me to the Wonder Years. It is the spring of 1964. A place called Viet-Nam – did you know the words mean South China in Cantonese? – and Laos are getting some press, but we weren't really thinking about them as potential enemies. Air Wing Two (CVW-2) and USS *Midway* had just returned from a deployment to the Western Pacific. Our squadron, VA-23, was the first to be equipped and deploy with the A-4E Skyhawk. Lots of improvements over the A-4B and C versions: bigger Pratt & Whitney J52 engine versus the Wright J65, five wing stations versus three, faster, and longer range.

Our primary mission in 1963 and '64 was the delivery of Special Weapons (Nuclear) under a war plan called the Single Integrated Operational Plan (SIOP). We weren't allowed to even mention the letters, let alone what it meant. We could deliver the Mk7, Mk28, Mk43, Mk105, and Mk57 weapons. They ranged in yield from 20 kilotons to 2 megatons. Anything over 350 kilotons was a thermonuclear or H-Bomb. We practised conventional deliveries about thirty per cent of the time, while seventy per cent was on the total elimination of the 'godless commies'. SIOP called for a process called Roll-Back. The Navy and TAC [Tactical Air Command] were to hit targets starting on the coastline to 150 miles inland. We were to hit things like ICBM [Intercontinental Ballistic Missile] sites, airfields and command centres. We were to open holes for Buffs [B-52s] to get through to their targets deeper inland. In the Pacific we had three CVAs [attack aircraft carriers] to cover areas called Alpha, Bravo and Charlie. Alpha covered everything from the Kamchatka peninsula to about Vladivostok; Bravo went from there to Shanghai, and Charlie from Shanghai to the southern China border. Usually we had two carriers on station and one in port. Each area had a launch point and all our planning started from that point, day or night. The carriers would rotate areas of responsibilities during their seven- to nine-month deployment.

It took a while for each pilot to get nuclear qualified. There were some very special schools, a totally separate and very secure building for mission planning (each qualified pilot had a primary and back-up target) in each of the three areas. Lots of tests and critiques on your planning and a big red tab on your medical file stating 'Any changes in personality, attitude, or habits must be reported immediately to the Commanding Officer and Chief Flight Surgeon'. We sometimes flew with real ones strapped to our bottoms. Our flight profile called for a Hi-Lo-Hi mission from the launch point to target. We penetrated at 100ft when 100 miles from the coast and 50ft from 50 miles to the beach. This was to avoid their EW radar. The overland portion was at 50ft (day) and 500ft (night). We flew at 360kt until 10 miles out, then up to 500kt.

Delivery was normally a loft manoeuvre at 500kt. We had a wonderful piece of gear called LABS [Low-Altitude Bombing System] that enabled you to get very close to your target. After weapon release you continued on over to your back and unloaded the aircraft and beat 'feet out' the way you had come in. It's called a Half Cuban Eight. We called it an idiot loop. The whole point was to gain separation from the nice little present you had just dropped off for your friends. We were very good; lots and lots of practice. I figured out once that I had performed over 2,000 4*g* loft deliveries. We were dedicated, and I had absolutely no doubts that I could reach my target, and would deliver the weapon without a trace of remorse or compassion.

In the spring of 1964 the boys from China Lake (Weapons Development and Test) came and talked to us about Redhead and the AGM-45 Shrike ARM for the first time. Shrike was designed to take out the coastal EW radars for SIOP missions. A separate piece of gear was the Melpar AN/APR-23 Redhead radar threat receiver. It consisted of a display that replaced the APG radar. It was the same size, and looked almost the same. It had no launch warning lights like later Shoehorn gear, but it did allow you to monitor three separate ranges of enemy radar Pulse Repetition Frequency [PRF]. You did not need a Shrike onboard to hear one if you had the '23 gear. You did receive a visual signal on the replacement scope but it did not give direction, only intensity. It was a long way from sat. but a lot better than what we had before, which was nada.

Shrike was to be loft delivered, similar to a nuke, with a weapon release at about the 45-degree point. The missile would fly a high arcing trajectory to hit an envelope in the sky about a mile wide and 4 miles long at 20,000ft. If you put it in that 'basket' it would hit its target. We thought that was a piece of cake. Initially, four aircraft would be wired for Shrike and AN/APR-23. With an A-4E, Shrike could be carried on stations 1 and 5 (outboard wing), leaving you room for two 300gal drop tanks on 2 and 4, and one 'big one' on station 3. We practised with the initial Shrikes all that summer and actually fired some over at China Lake. The only concern was that the warhead wasn't big enough. It was designed to take out the antenna only, not the control van. This was done to keep the overall weight down, so that it could be carried on our outboard stations. We worried that the enemy might somehow replace the damaged antennae. Actually, I think we were hoping we would kill them all with one hit. That was how Shrike began.

In the fall of 1964 a definite shift toward training with conventional weapons was under way. The standard delivery in those days was a 30-degree dive attack with a release around 2,500ft AGL at 450kt. We didn't have release computers, just dumb bombs and rockets and a fixed gunsight with an adjustable reticle in miliradians (mils), a miliradian being defined as the arc of 1ft at a range of 1,000ft. Hence dive-bombing was a game of SWAG [scientific wild ass guesses] as far as compensating for errors in your run, i.e. dive angle, airspeed and release altitude. It also made dive-bombing an art form. Some pilots were really good, others not so hot. Everybody had to meet a certain criteria.

After the Gulf of Tonkin incident, everything became very serious regarding our conventional capabilities. The boys across the mountains at China Lake (we were at NAS Lemoore, California, near Fresno) had come up with the Snakeye tail fins as well as Sidewinder and all the 'Eye' family of air-delivered stuff.[5] The Shrike was their baby and they wanted to use it against missile and AAA radars, and obviously lofting was not the preferred delivery method.

We had a weapons officer named Dick Macke, who was very bright and a good stick, who later went on to become a Four-Star Admiral as CINCPAC. We knew him as 'Macke-Mouse'. He and the China Lake guys developed a high-altitude triple dip-dive delivery. The only Shrike available then had a disable feature, to prevent it from homing on a 'good guy' radar. It wouldn't arm until coming downhill and passing 20,000ft. That eliminated the low-altitude snap-shot option until they designed new missiles. We would pick up the PRF on either Shrike or the '23 and turn till the vertical azimuth needle on our AN/AJB-3A main gyro centred up. Now all we had to figure out was range – not easy as a passive receiver can pick up a radar signal at 1.5 times the range of the threat radar. We used the horizontal needle of the AN/AJB-3A to look for a dip down; at this time you are at 30,000ft, level. When the needle got to 30 degrees below the horizontal you pulled the throttle to idle and pushed over into a 30-degree glide dive. Next you waited for the needle to dip again. This time it had to be either 20 or 15 degrees below your nose. You then pushed over to centre the needles. When you got a third dip you would steepen the dive, centre the needles, pull up 15 degrees on the gyro and fire. By now you would be around 15,000–20,000ft and between 30 and 45 degrees nose down.

It wasn't pretty but it actually worked. Our first ten combat shots were done using this technique against Fire Can AAA radars. The Fire Can controlled 37mm, 57mm and sometimes 85mm AAA sites. I seem to remember five hits out of ten shots. I know we hit one as I followed it down. The early Shrikes had lots of problems. They were somewhat dim as far as smart weapons go. If you had two sites emitting, guess what? Yep, it tried to get them both, and would land equidistant between the sites, much to the delight of the 'rat-eating gomers'.

The timeframe for all these fun and games was April to late July 1965. In those days Hanoi and Haiphong were off limits with regards dropping anything on them. I mean, why fight a war full out when you can do it half ass and drag it out ten years, lose lots of really fine people and assets, and then lose the war to a third-rate bunch of bad guys. *But* . . . we could fly over those places all day with relative safety as the enemy cut their 85mm fuses to detonate at 30,000ft. If you were at 32,000–35,000ft it was just a lot of black puff clouds going off below you. We knew they were building the classic star-shaped SA-2 sites all around Hanoi; they began in June. We had lots of tapes to listen to on the SA-2 Fan Song radars but no one had heard a peep. That is why we were shooting Shrikes at Fire Can radars. When the question was raised with our Intel types, 'How about portable sites? Do we have a problem with that?' 'No problem,' was the answer. 'We know it would take them 36 to 48 hours to set up, align, and be ready to fire.' The bad guys obviously weren't as smart as our brilliant Intel pukes because they figured out a way to do it in about three hours.

The US Navy's first confrontation with SAMs occurred in August 1965, as Bill Clark recalls:

The first SAM strikes were conducted by the Air Force in reply to having had an Air Force jet lost to an SA-2 in late July.[6] One of our A-4s led the mission using the APR-23 as a means of finding the site. On the night of 11 August Lt Cdr Francis D. 'Dee' Roberge and Lt (jg) Donald H. 'Brownie' Brown from our unit were conducting an ARREC mission north of Thanh Hoa and east of Hanoi, outside the missile range of the sites circling Hanoi. We did not have the Shoehorn gear at that time. In fact Dee was not even flying a Redhead-equipped bird. He stated he saw what appeared to be two Mk24 flares low off his left wing. He called them out to Brownie and they did not observe any apparent movement in the flares (as in closure, or turning). Dee stated he watched them for about 15 seconds. They were around 15,000ft and looking for truck lights. Brown was on the left in a loose formation position, a couple of hundred feet out and aft.

Dee watched and suddenly the lights started to split apart. He said he knew instantly what they were. He called 'Break left!' but he added 100 per cent and pushed over instead. He was afraid he would have turned right in front of Brown, ruining their day. He saw a bright flash behind and to port and then his bird was rocked by a violent explosion from below. Some of his ordnance, either flares or ZUNI rockets, was ignited by the proximity of the impact. He cleaned everything off the bird with the emergency jettison handle and got control. He turned left and could not see his wingman. He did see a fireball descending. The first missile had obviously nailed

An A-4E from VA-212 safely back on USS Bon Homme Richard, *complete with an Iron Hand patrol load of AGM-45 Shrike, expended ZUNI rocket pod and, on the port wing, AIM-9 Sidewinder for self-defence. ZUNIs were frequently used to feign a Shrike attack, which got the enemy to shut down their radar. The A-4 pilot thus kept the Shrike unless a live site shot at him.* (Richard L. Ward Archives)

Brown and the second went off about 200ft under Roberge. I was the LSO [Landing Signals Officer] when he returned and he handled the landing quite well. He stated the aircraft flew almost normal. It had over 500 holes in it, some very small, others a bit bigger. The next day we were sent out to get them back. It was one of the most memorable Chinese fire-drills in history.

The next day, 12 August, Adm Sharp CINCPAC ordered Operation Iron Hand into being, with the initial aim of reprisal attacks against the offending SA-2 batteries. For two days running, 124 carrier jets combed North Vietnam for the SAM sites. By sunset on the second day, known as Black Friday, none had been discovered. Bill Clark elaborates on this inauspicious start to the US Navy's counter-SAM operations, which nonetheless represented the inauguration of Iron Hand strikes:

The orders from on high were to knock out the site that bagged our birds, and any other portable sites – not the hard sites around Hanoi; God forbid we might kill some Russian advisors. The search area was north of Thanh Hoa, south of Hanoi and just north of Haiphong. The terrain was flat and mostly rice paddies, with a small village every few miles. They all looked the same: red tile roofs (French built), a clearing in the centre of town not unlike a town square, and lots of thatch roofed houses forming the perimeter. There were clusters of tall palm trees everywhere. We had some Shrike birds along but mostly we all carried 500lb Snakeye [bombs] and 5in ZUNI rockets. The fighters came along to save us from the MiGs, if they could find them, but they didn't want to get anywhere near where we were going, so they were just off the coast. It was a two-carrier strike with multiple launches of two-plane A-4 attackers.

I was the Air Wing Commander's (CAG) wingman for the entire cruise. He was an ex-fighter jock who couldn't navigate from LA to San Diego below 20,000ft VFR; but he knew it and asked for a seasoned A-4 type to keep him out of trouble. I volunteered – big mistake. He was a true follow-me leader and everyone loved him. Naturally he was on the first strike, so was I. Our plan was to fly a series of long rectangular search patterns at 1,000ft and 400kt. Ours was about 30 miles long and 2 miles across. Our total grid was maybe 30 miles by 8 miles, so we had to go north 30 miles, do a 180, go south 30 miles, four separate times. While we were doing that at least twenty other A-4s were likewise searching, albeit in other areas.

The problem was the weather: at the coast the ceiling was about 800ft, and by the time we got 30 miles north it [had] dropped to around 300ft. Then the kicker of the entire failex was that the spot where Dee thought the site was actually located was about 40 miles north and covered by weather. It was like the old joke of the cop asking the drunk why he was crawling around on the sidewalk under the lamp post. 'I'm looking for my keys' was the answer. The cop replied, 'Are you sure this is where you lost them?' 'Oh no,' said the drunk, 'I lost them up the block, but the light is better here.' So there we were, looking where the light was better.

To say that we did not catch them unawares would be charitable. I have never been on such an intense flight in my life. We were flying abeam one another, 1,000ft separation, about 500ft AGL to start, 50–75ft at the north turn point, with lots of weaving turns en route. The tracer fire was near horizontal, and nearly continuous the entire leg. Our first turn was to the left, 4g, with CAG on my left. My turn carried me right over one of the scenic villages and I had a clear view of maybe a hundred people in the central clearing shooting small arms at CAG. On the southern leg I kept seeing big splashes in front and to the side, in the rice paddies. We later figured them to be 85mm fired horizontal and hitting the water – better [it] than us! Each leg seemed to take about an hour rather than the 5–6 minutes actual. The bad part was we had to repeat it two more times. When we hit the coast after the first two legs (one up, one down) CAG spent about 5 minutes over the water having us check one another for holes, then off we went for legs three and four. Same story only the fire was maybe heavier, or we were getting a lot more nervous.

Around this time 'Mayday!' calls were coming from all over, along with a couple of ejection beepers. I was the most frightened I've ever been in my life. When we got to the water the second time we circled off the beach for about 10 minutes, as CAG was coordinating some of the rescue birds. We then proceeded over the beach for legs five and six. Same play, same story. This time, when we got to the north turn point the tracer fire was so intense CAG broke to the right and we started a long arcing turn to the north-east followed by a final course of south-east. He called and said, 'Screw this, let's get out of here!' He had the lead; we were way up on the speed, hugging the deck. I had not a clue as to where we were but I knew we would see a lot of water very soon.

The triple-A slowed and then stopped about half way through our exit stage right turn. I saw some karst formations coming up, over a few hills and there we were, exiting right over Haiphong harbour, 500+kt and maybe 100ft. The forward visibility was great. I remember seeing a lot of ships unloading and the biggest piles of coal I had ever seen in my life. I also saw small-arms fire coming at CAG (he was a ¼ mile in front) from the fantail of one of the freighters. I therefore chose to jettison my armed stick of six 500lb Snakeyes right across the SOB. When I went over him I saw the Chicom [Communist Chinese] flag painted on the stack. My third Snake got him directly amidships; one and two were short; four, five and six went into the water long and some docks. Big explosion. I don't think he made his scheduled departure time. CAG never saw it or at least never said anything. He jettisoned about 5 minutes later. The second wave of strikes were starting about then with the same results. We lost 7 aircraft in 45min, between both carriers, and did not find a SAM. We did get one Chinese freighter but denied the hell out of the official protest. That was the beginning of Iron Hands. They got a lot more professional after that.

AGM-45 SHRIKE

Shrike was developed from 1958 by the US Navy's Naval Ordnance Test Station (later the Naval Weapons Center or NWC) at China Lake, California, specifically to counter the new Soviet SA-2 Guideline SAM threat. The idea was simple in theory: equip Shrike with a guidance unit and seeker that would passively home on the enemy's radar emissions and knock out the Fan Song dish, thereby rendering the site's co-located SAMs blind and relatively harmless. Originally known as the ASM-N-10, Shrike was essentially a Sparrow III air-to-air missile (AAM) airframe fitted with an enlarged blast-fragmentation warhead and a somewhat smaller rocket motor, weighing in at 390lb. Development was speeded-up in response to the US Navy's first confrontation with SAMs over Cuba during the Missile Crisis in October 1962, when the Emergency Shrike Effort spawned the newly redesignated AGM-45A-1 model. A colossal 16,611 Shrikes were produced in Fiscal Years 1964–79, beginning in 1963 principally by Sperry Rand/Univac, and Texas Instruments (TI) which became the major supplier. ATM-45 training rounds were also produced for test duties, captive-carry and live-firing flight training, and ground instruction. There were a dozen foreign customers for the weapon, including Israel and the United Kingdom which have also employed it in combat.

Throughout Shrike's production run a number of improvements were made to the seeker, warhead and rocket motor. Among these, the most notable were the introduction of a white phosphorous target marker in the warhead (AGM-45A-2) to highlight where the missile had impacted, and angle gating (AGM-45A-3 et al.) to prioritize the target. Dive-Modified Shrike guidance was also fielded. The original delivery method was to 'loft' launch Shrike into a 'basket' or cone above the radar being targeted. Once the missile had peaked in altitude and had started back down, its guidance unit sensed the downward trajectory and activated the seeker, which would then steer the missile to the target dish – provided the enemy continued to transmit – by means of the forward steering fins. This worked reasonably well for mid- to maximum range volleys, employed against sites at established coordinates, or on a pre-emptive hit-or-miss basis to cover ingressing strikers. In these instances, even if Shrike failed to strike the target, its mere presence was often sufficient to oblige the enemy to shut down their radars, allowing a strike wave to pass nearby unmolested.

However, Shrike was soon found wanting by Iron Hand support teams on the prowl for radars, particularly targets of opportunity which might crop up unexpectedly. In this instance, crews would have to react at closer quarters and fire Shrike 'down the throat'. Modifications were therefore incorporated to create the Dive-Modified Shrike, by means of a plug which shorted out the 'loft logic' and allowed the missile guidance unit to activate as soon as it left the launch rail. The Dive-Modified Shrike could be used out to about 12 miles from the enemy emitter at altitude, but invariably was used at a much shorter range of 1–3 miles and, according to many crews, was consequently dangerous to employ because its use tended to result in duels with the quicker SA-2.

Shrike was composed of a number of different components that allowed it to be assembled in many different configurations. The AGM-45A used one of three blast-fragmentation warheads, each of which was interchangeable: the Mk5 Mod 0 or Mk86 Mod 0, both of which featured 149lb warheads, or the 147lb WAU-8/B. The AGM-45B similarly could be fitted with Mk5 Mod 1 or Mk8 Mod 1 149lb warheads, or the 147lb WAU-9/B. All had dual fuse arming, comprising a mechanical acceleration/deceleration arming device backed up by a 3-seconds-after-launch electrical system. The fuse would detonate the cube-filled warhead based on an electrical signal from the guidance section upon detection of target radar signals at 70 degrees relative to the missile's longitudinal axis (within which the warhead blast would be focused) as it closed to target, or by back-up impact fusing.

For propulsion, the AGM-45A employed the single-burn 22,000lb/sec Rocketdyne Mk39 motor, which accelerated the missile to approximately Mach 1.5 above launch speed during its 2.8 seconds burn time. (A second, less common motor used by the AGM-45A, the Aerojet Mk53 Mod 1, had similar performance and was also in use until the mid-1980s.) The AGM-45B introduced the dual-burn 22,300lb/sec Aerojet Mk78 motor, with an initial slower 1 second acceleration thrust supplemented by a 20-second sustaining thrust. Depending on launch altitude and delivery mode (down the throat or loft), maximum range was 25 miles.

There existed a number of launchers for Shrike. The most widespread was the US Navy-designed, Martin-built Aero 5 rail, which had originally been designed for the company's radio-controlled AGM-12 Bullpup missile. The lower profile Aero 5A followed, which the US Air Force designated as the LAU-34/A.

Scooter pilot Capt William Clark performs his ancillary duty as Landing Signals Officer (LSO) on the USS Midway. *The A-4E is carrying early AGM-45A-1 Shrikes with their unique black radomes.* (William Clark)

Several externally identical submarks followed which were lighter and which reduced costs. In this guise, virtually every US Navy tactical combat jet in production in the 1960s and 1970s was equipped to carry them, including the Navy/Marines A-4 Skyhawk, A-6 Intruder and A-7 Corsair II which employed SIDS. USAF combat jets were also wired for Shrike (using pitch and bank needles on the ADI for line-up with the target acquired by Shrike), but usage was confined to the Wild Weasels and companion killer aircraft employed in the Weasel flights, using the Weasels' specialist sniffing receivers.

For expanded ordnance carriage, beginning in February 1967 the NWC developed the Shrike Dual Launch Adaptor (DLA), resulting in what became known in May the following year as the ADU-315/A (starboard wing) and ADU-316/A (port wing) DLAs. Flight testing was performed at Naval Air Test Center Patuxent River, Maryland, between March and October 1968, clearing carriage to 550kt and Mach 0.95. It was qualified for use on the inboard stations (2 and 4) of the A-4, plus all four A-6 and all six A-7 wing stations. Leading (outboard) Shrikes were always fired first. The DLAs were also used for a short while on USAF F-105G WW-III Thuds during late 1972, flight-tested on F-4C WW-IV Phantom IIs after the Vietnam War, and by British Avro Vulcan B.2 Black Buck bombers during the Falkland Islands campaign, Operation Corporate, in 1982. Shrike was finally retired from the US active inventory in 1992.

Mark	Guidance Section	Seeker
Live combat AGM-45 rounds		
AGM-45A-1	Mk23 Mod 0	E/F-Band
AGM-45A/B-2	Mk22 Mods 0, 1 or 2	G-Band
AGM-45A/B-3	Mk24 Mods 0, 1 or 4	Broad E/F-Band angle gating
AGM-45A/B-3A	Mk24 Mods 2 or 5	Narrow E/F-Band angle gating
AGM-45A/B-3B	Mk24 Mod 3	E/F-Band angle gating
AGM-45A/B-4	Mk25 Mods 0 or 1	G-Band angle gating
AGM-45A/B-6	Mk36 Mod 1	I-Band angle gating
AGM-45A/B-7	Mk37 Mod 0	E/F-Band angle gating
AGM-45A/B-9	Mk49 Mod 0	I-Band angle gating
AGM-45A/B-9A	Mk49 Mod 1	I-Band angle gating, G-bias
AGM-45A/B-10	Mk50 Mod 0	Broad E- to I-Band angle gating

PROJECT SHOEHORN

Bill Clark continues:

> After the great SAM hunt débâcle on 12–13 August, everyone in authority decided there had to be a better way. Sanders Associates in Nashua, New Hampshire, had proposed to the Navy and Air Force active ECM [Electronic Countermeasures] in the form of the AN/ALQ-51. The Navy said yes, the Air Force no. They wanted ECM that would overpower the emitter. Called noise jamming, it requires a lot of power from a single aircraft or multiple aircraft flying together. The ALQ-51 gear was a gate stealer, i.e. it would take the pulse of radar energy and hold it for a nanosecond or two and then play with it. The emitter would either see a return in the incorrect spot in the sky, by several hundred metres, or a lot of returns where there should be only one.[7] This system allowed us to operate in single- or two-ship roles as opposed to the Air Force doctrine of maintaining a four-ship diamond while Charlie shot SAMs at you. The first kits were put in our birds in September 1965 and consisted of two antennae forward, one aft and two amidships. In the cockpit we had three lights and [a] PRF tone in our headset.

This formed the basis of Project Shoehorn, which stuffed the new Sanders AN/ALQ-51 Defensive Electronic Countermeasures (DECM) set into all US Navy combat aircraft during deeper maintenance cycles at the Naval Air Rework Facilities (NARF), beginning in April 1966. Also added was the AN/ALE-18 chaff-dispensing set, added to provide last-ditch bursts of distracting radar-painted clouds to cajole the SAMs away from their target. Generating just small errors in targeting paid huge dividends: detonating beyond 1,000ft, the SAM's warhead seldom inflicted any damage on an aircraft; at 600ft it might sustain some hits from shrapnel; at 300ft it could cause severe damage; and at 200ft it invariably totally destroyed the aircraft. The defensive equipment was later superseded by the improved AN/ALQ-100 DECM, better matched to the observed characteristics of the SA-2's Fan Song and Fire Can triple-A radars, and an AN/ALE-29 chaff-dispenser.

Complementary devices included the Applied Technology Incorporated (ATI) AN/APR-25 Vector IV Radar Homing and Warning System (RHAWS) receiver and Magnavox AN/APR-27 Launch Warning Receiver (LWR). The RHAWS determined the positions of enemy radars vectorially based on the relative direction of signals being picked up by four antenna patterns, hence its Vector IV name. The LWR provided indications of an SA-2 launch by monitoring the guidance and control frequency; when the receiver detected the characteristic shift in the power of the signal, it illuminated a bright red launch light, soon known as the 'Oh S***!' light.

Together with improved reception over Redhead – namely 360-degree coverage – these introduced a new concentric-ringed display that flashed coded strobe lines from its centre, pointing out in the direction of the radar threat being picked up. Bright, longer lines reaching out to the third ring – a so-called three-ringer – indicated that the pilot or crew was within lethal range of the SAM site. Radar PRF warbles in the headphones and flashing LWR lights added essential aural and visual cues, leaving the crew in no doubt about their next move if the SAM launch light illuminated and the PRF tone went into fever pitch: dump some chaff and take evasive action, even if the SAM was chasing somebody nearby!

Bill Clark remembers the early gear well:

The lights we had gave you a scan indication warning, including a warning of sector scan activity; basically a 360-degree versus a 20-degree sweep; also a lock-on warning; and, finally, a launch warning. The first kits were difficult to maintain and notorious for false warnings. A lot of people got very nervous initially when we first started using them, especially at night. Shrikes were also now being modified to give them a down the throat capability, i.e. low-altitude turn-and-shoot. We left in mid-November 1965 and that capability didn't get there for another five or six months. I always thought the Air Force ECM philosophy was nuts but they were not about to buy yet another Navy product.

After weeks of fruitless searches, the first successes were achieved on 17 October 1965, when four A-4Es from USS *Independence*'s CVW-7 knocked out a SAM site at Kep, north-east of Hanoi. Napalm canisters set three radar vans and one missile launcher on fire, while a further SAM cooked off and slithered through the enemy facility, aiding in the destruction of a dozen support vehicles.

SIDS

A-4 pilots bore the brunt of the US Navy's share of the Iron Hand campaign throughout the Rolling Thunder years, flying four- or eight-ship support within an Alpha Strike package with Shrikes, ZUNI rockets and Mk82 500lb bombs, and paired off against triple-A and SAM sites known to be in the target vicinity. More often than not, Shrikes would be lofted in the direction of known SAM sites pre-emptively, as part of what evolved as a raid strategy. In jets, it took only a few minutes for the so-called Yankee Air Pirate raiding force to make its mark (unless someone was brought down, in which case aircraft continued to fly suppression cover until an extraction by helicopter could be attempted, or the airman had obviously been captured or was missing).

Yet Soviet radars used by the North Vietnamese could 'see' Shrike coming off its launch rail when it was fired. This allowed them to warn their SAM operators when the missile was airborne, permitting them to revert to dummy or stand-by mode, thus denying the missile the homing signals it needed, sending it ballistic (unguided). However, while this denied Shrike a kill, it also denied the SAMs the guidance they needed, thus neutralizing them for the critical stages of an attack on the key target by the Alpha Strike package. As long as the enemy radars remained mute, they were vulnerable to attack from iron bombs and rockets – *if* they could be sighted. Ironically, this was always the biggest obstacle, given the

CAPTAIN PAUL 'HOLLY' HOLLANDSWORTH

Capt Hollandsworth USN (Ret) flew carrier attack aircraft exclusively during his 32-year career, accumulating over 6,000hr in the A-1, A-4 and A-6. Nevertheless, it was the A-4 that brought him back to the carrier unscathed after each of his 258 combat missions during two tours in Vietnam.

During the latter part of 1965, I commenced my inaugural combat tour. I was with VA-76 'Spirits', assigned to USS *Enterprise*. VA-76 conducted work-up ops from Dixie Station during December and two weeks later sailed north to Yankee Station for combat operations over North Vietnam. The A-4 was an absolute dream to fly! Since *Enterprise* was the largest carrier then in service, our Air Wing, CVW-9, was huge, with seven squadrons and three detachments, and included four A-4C squadrons of which none was Shrike-capable – they also lacked any kind of ALQ gear. However, my squadron was assigned three specially modified airplanes that had [each] been fitted with an AN/APR-23 Radar Warning Receiver (RWR). The AN/APR-23 was capable of picking up high PRF types such as Fan Song and Fire Can radar emissions. Although it couldn't distinguish between a radar's tracking or lock-on modes, it did provide us a direction and a hypothesis of the distance. As this was an add-on, the AN/APR-23 Redhead scope had been hastily fitted into the cockpit between the pilot's knees.

Redhead was good out to about 20 miles and as you got closer to the radar signal, you had to detune or turn it down. The position of an emitting radar would appear as a sort of spike on the scope and the closer

you got, the bigger the spike became. It would eventually fill the scope, so you had to turn it down at 10 miles and then again at the 5-mile mark. The concept was that the lead airplane, equipped with the AN/APR-23, would be flying at 4,000–5,000ft and would track the spike to the source while the rest of the flight followed at 8,000–10,000ft. Upon acquiring the target visually, the idea was to attempt to put iron on it in the hope of destroying it, or to at least mark the general area for the following strike element.

During this timeframe, this was the only method we had of conducting Iron Hand effectively. And we were not very successful using this system for several reasons. The first was that we had not trained with the system very much and the only bad guy radars at China Lake's Echo Range were then very primitive. The other reason was the simple fact that there were not very many SAM sites in Vietnam with which to hone our procedures during 1965–6.

We would employ ZUNI air-to-ground unguided rockets, which were

Paul 'Holly' Hollandsworth, shortly after completing the 29,000th aircraft trap on USS Bon Homme Richard's *deck, 23 May 1967. (Paul Hollandsworth)*

favoured over the cumbersome CBUs because of the drag factor. However, you had to be very accurate when employing the ZUNI, but more critical was the fact that you were drawn in a lot closer to the target due to the short range of the rocket. Nonetheless, CBUs utilizing an air-burst fuse at about 200ft were the better weapon. Ironically, the way they were packed meant that a direct hit would produce a 'doughnut' pattern of destruction, leaving an unscathed hole in the middle. You had to drop maybe three CBUs to achieve 100 per cent coverage.

It wasn't until 1967 – [we were] now assigned to CVW-21 aboard USS *Bon Homme Richard* – that VA-76 acquired a Shrike capability. There were two A-4 squadrons onboard, flying the Charlie and Echo models. Prior to this deployment, we had deployed to China Lake to train with Shrike. While there, we perfected the pull-up manoeuvre that would be necessary to loft a Shrike into the so-called 'basket'. I had departed Vietnam during July 1966 and returned in February 1967, and by this time the North Vietnamese had moved a lot more SAMs and triple-A up there. Nonetheless, this was by our doing as we had heated up the war, as we were now going deeper into the northern areas – north of Hanoi along the vital northern railroads that, among other things, connected Hanoi with Communist China. Generally, we were going into harm's way more so than we had done during the previous years.

During the February to April timeframe it was monsoon season, therefore the weather was at its worst and consequently numerous missions were scrubbed. As we got into spring and summer, three Alpha Strikes per day were flown from two of the three carriers on station. Later, we had five carriers on station, all equipped with Shrike-shooters. As such, the number of Alpha Strikes rose to as many as nine per day – and all wanted Shrike-shooters on hand. Although the carriers were re-armed about every three days, they all started to run low on everything, especially Shrikes.

Meanwhile, back in the States, an engineer in a laboratory had discovered that the ZUNI rocket when launched from an airplane produced a radar signature identical to that of Shrike. So in an effort to preserve and extend the dwindling Shrike inventories, we got pretty stingy with them. When tangling with a SAM site, we'd attempt to dupe the radar operator into at least shutting it down by lobbing a ZUNI instead. However, they soon got smart, and figured out what we were doing. As such, there were occasions when they didn't shut down and if you didn't have a Shrike to respond with, you were in a little bit of trouble! Ideally, you wanted to have both the ZUNI and a Shrike onboard. Upon executing the Shrike launch manoeuvre, if the radar had gone down, you'd launch a ZUNI, but if it was still up, you launched the Shrike.

During one Iron Hand mission up around the Hanoi area, I had a ZUNI pod on one station and a Shrike on the other. This particular Shrike just happened to be the last remaining missile from *Bon Homme Richard*'s weapons magazine. I executed the Shrike launch manoeuvre, and as the radar refused to go down, I had no choice but to launch the missile. Upon recovering aboard the carrier, I was immediately summoned by the battle group commander – an admiral – and was requested to provide a full account of the firing of 'his' last Shrike! I described the facts of the mission, including the missile's time of flight, which I remember being 86 seconds – which was about the expected time of impact. Consequently, it appeared to be a responsible shot – it wasn't wasted. During this period, we had to explain our actions every time we launched a Shrike.

There was a lot of leeway during 1967. As such, anytime you observed a SAM site, this became your primary target – no matter where you were tasked or what you were carrying. I remember one strike to the airfield at Kep, when I was leading the third division of four jets of a sixteen-plane flight, when I spotted a SAM site situated on a soccer field in a small town. You could clearly see the Star of David pattern in the dug-up field. My division rolled in on it and [we] delivered our weapons. Surprisingly, the site never came up on us – it may have been the sheer number of airplanes. Anyhow, while bombing the site we torched off a SAM that had not been elevated. Consequently, I was able to observe it as it snaked its way through the town!

During two tours, our skipper Cdr Robert B. Fuller was the only loss suffered by VA-76. However, the Air Wing did lose three pilots during each combat cruise, and all except for the skipper were due to triple-A. We had always figured that when rolling in, the change in altitude was so great that there was no way the SAMs could lock us up. Well, this idea was definitely disproved [on 14 July 1967] when a pair of SAMs launched out of the Hanoi area targeted our skipper as he was rolling in. One SAM detonated directly above him, while the second detonated beneath him. The airplane was still intact, but the engine and fuel lines were severely damaged; it looked like it had been gutted. Nonetheless, he delivered his bombs, pulled off target and ejected. He was captured and later repatriated.

prevailing weather, abundant foliage and widespread use of camouflage netting, and the rather modest Shrike warhead, which would tend to shred only the radar dish during a quick flash.

The other method of Shrike delivery – down the throat – which Bill Clark described as the 'triple dip-dive', generated a higher radar kill rate, but also cost the lives of many pilots, as it often relied on a SAM launch sighting to aid with line-up, meaning a site was active and usually targeting the Iron Hand aircraft. Several pilots recalled that using a mix of Shrike and ZUNI was particularly effective as the rocket had the same radar signature as Shrike, and even looked like it when fired singly, allowing A-4 pilots to feign attacks. If a tenacious radar remained on the air, Shrike could then be employed for self-protection. However, Joseph Pepper said: 'Shrike was slower than the SA-2 SAM. Therefore it was near suicidal to fire a Shrike at an SA-2 site that had missiles guiding on you because their missiles would get to you before your Shrike got to them.'

If the enemy reacted by turning off his emitter, Joseph Pepper remembers: 'We used to joke that at least we were wearing out the enemy's shoes, since the guy on top of the radar van was stomping very hard when he saw the aircraft go into a Dip-Angle manoeuvre. His stomp was the alert to shut down the radar.' White phosphorous markers in the Shrike warheads, which might aid visual sighting of the hard-to-spot SAM sites for follow-up attacks, were not available during the early years of Rolling Thunder combat. Overall, Shrike achieved a less than 6 per cent damage rate.

In an effort to give the A-4 community greater Shrike shooting accuracy and a more user-friendly cockpit display, the Shrike Improved Display System (SIDS) was evolved by China Lake. This retained the terrain avoidance/mapping function on the A-4's newly redesignated IP-446/APG-53A radarscope display for navigation to target, enabling the pilot to switch over to SIDS when within range of the enemy defences in order to get in position for a Shrike launch. The SIDS display essentially comprised a grid for steering instructions in elevation and azimuth, by means of physically flying the aircraft so that the target radar blip (the position of which was based on direction-finding signals furnished by Shrike) was correctly positioned within the grid for the ARM's exacting launch parameters.

SIDS was retrofitted Fleetwide to A-4E Skyhawks under Navy A-4 AFC (Airframe Change) 365, which included a hundred or so earlier surviving marks brought up to A-4L standard. As the manual stated: 'One blip (target) will be displayed on the radarscope when in the NORM (normal) mode; however, the blip may change position when a stronger signal is received from another radar emitter. An audio tone is sent to the pilot's headset when the target blip is shown so that the pilot hears and sees the target data as presented by the SIDS.'

The pilot could also select CONT (continuous) when it was felt that something might come up on the air, in which situation the 'target blips may be present on the radarscope at all times, but true target direction is not indicated until a tone is furnished to the pilot's headset'. This permitted him to perform a routine strike mission but switch over to NORM when something demanding his attention appeared on the airwaves.

In essence, used in conjunction with the Dip-Angle Shrike delivery it created more of a point-and-shoot system, making the Iron Hand tasking 'more do-able and less suicidal'.

However, US Navy pilots received little or no formal training in the Iron Hand role: it was simply considered another job, alongside other duties such as ARREC, buddy refuelling with the D-704 pod, RESCAP, or interdiction strikes with the emerging Precision-Guided Munitions (PGM) such as the AGM-62 Walleye TV-guided glide bomb. For the most part Iron Hand indoctrination simply involved listening to audio recordings of Fire Can and Fan Song in their different states of activity, learning the switchology between cruises during practice sorties over Yuma in Arizona or China Lake, where a large proportion of time was spent perfecting the delivery of special and conventional gravity weapons, and lobbing rockets. Shrike and SIDS work-up mostly consisted of reading the relevant manuals followed by a tactics briefing and hands on actual combat, usually glued to the wing of a more experienced pilot who might, or might not, have more experience working against SAM and triple-A radars. It was known as OJT: on-the-job training.

The mortifying statistics speak loudly. Between 1965 and 1968 the US Navy lost 170 Skyhawks to hostile fire, 30 of them to SAMs. An

A-4Es of VA-153 'Blue Tail Flies' flying practice Iron Hand work-up missions in July 1967 using blue, finless TGM-45 training Shrikes and ZUNI rockets. (Richard L. Ward Archives)

additional 49 were operational losses, owing to factors such as weather, mechanical failure, a mid-air collision in one instance, and what has since become known as 'controlled flight into terrain' as a result of weather, terrain and low-level flying. Six per cent of the losses were ascribed to the new doctrine of low-level flying but the concept was maintained as it was reasoned that small-arms fire could keep the plane captains busy patching up holes, but was less likely to down a jet or injure its pilot than a blast from a SAM's warhead or higher calibre triple-A. Many of these losses were due to the high operational tempo sustained during the Rolling Thunder campaign years by Skyhawk pilots, who flew 40,780 attack sorties during 1966, a monthly average of just under 3,400, accounting for 63.9 per cent of all carrier-borne attack sorties flown over Vietnam and Laos. During the second half of 1967 they were still averaging 2,570 sorties a month, representing 73.6 per cent of all attack sorties generated by the 'Tonkin Gulf Yacht Club'.[8]

The bravery and sacrifice of these young pilots in protecting their colleagues during Iron Hand work is exemplified by the actions of Lt Cdr Michael J. Estocin, who posthumously received the United States' highest award for valour in action against an enemy force: the Congressional Medal of Honor. Serving with VA-192 'Golden Dragons' aboard USS *Ticonderoga* on 20 April 1967 during an Iron Hand support mission to the thermal powerplants at Haiphong, Estocin personally led his flight against three SAM sites, knocking out all three. Despite his A-4E being hit several times by SAM blasts he remained over the target area until he had expended all his ordnance, leaving him with a mere 5 minutes fuel in his flying sieve.

As luck would have it, a KA-3 tanker was nearby and they hooked up, allowing Estocin to nurse his wounded A-4E back to USS *Ticonderoga* for a recovery. Flying back together, the KA-3 was managing to pump in almost as much fuel as Estocin's aircraft was losing, and they unplugged at a mere 3 miles from the stern of the carrier, leaving Estocin with a one-shot approach in his by now burning aircraft. He made a flawless recovery. Tragically, just six days later, during another strike against Haiphong, his jet was struck by shrapnel from a head-on SAM explosion during a close-in duel and was set spinning, trailing fire from its wing root and belly. Estocin apparently regained aileron control of his gyrating aircraft before heading for the beach. Seriously wounded and in an aircraft thoroughly trashed by the SAM's warhead, he was last seen slumped over the controls before his aircraft rolled inverted into undercast, just 3 miles from the coast, its weapons popping off the racks as electrical circuits gave in.[9]

Douglas Aircraft's El Segundo Division in California had produced 500 A-4Es before production switched to 147 of the A-4F, the definitive US Navy model for carrier-borne duties, which first saw combat with VA-23 and VA-192 onboard USS *Ticonderoga* from December 1967. However, that same month the Skyhawk's replacement, the Ling-Temco-Vought A-7A Corsair II, made its combat debut with CTF-77. Less elegant than the A-4, the Pratt & Whitney TF30-powered A-7A resembled a squatter, subsonic derivative of Vought's F-8 Crusader, hence its subsequent nickname: by comparison, the A-7 was the SLUF, standing for Short Little Ugly F***er. Nevertheless the A-7A offered comparatively fantastic range and endurance to that of the A-4 because of its turbofan engine: up to 2,600nm, or 2.86hr time-on-station over a 300nm operating radius with 500 rounds of gun ammunition and 3,000lb of external ordnance.

As part of the original VAL (Heavier than Air, Attack, Lightweight) concept initiated in 1962, A-7s were to have had the RAID system installed, a forward-sector radar-homing device to assist with Shrike launch. In the end, they were equipped with the standard Shoehorn package, and a dual radarscope offering SIDS, as pioneered by the A-4. Early production A-7s were in fact equipped with the cruder AN/ALR-15 receiver that provided forward and aft hemisphere warnings of emitters, until A-7 AFC 15 substituted the more capable Fleet-standard AN/APR-25 RHAWS and AN/APR-27 LWR. In essence, what the earlier, vanilla model A-7A Corsair II offered compared with the SIDS A-4 was longer loiter time, heavier cockpit armour, a larger (six stations, all underwing) 15,000lb payload capability, but perhaps above all else, a more roomy cockpit with fuselage space for internal avionics growth. They also featured rudimentary AN/ASN-41 Inertial Navigation System (INS) sets which furnished attitude/heading and helped to drive a roller map display, making autonomous navigation easier.[10]

VA-147 'Argonauts' introduced the A-7 Corsair II or SLUF to combat service during 1967. The type quickly supplanted the A-4 in the Fleet to become the principal Iron Hand platform. (Richard L. Ward Archives)

The first A-7A squadron to deploy to Vietnam, following conversion with the new West Coast training unit VA-122 'Flying Eagles' at NAS Lemoore, and work-ups at Yuma and China Lake, was Cdr James C. Hill's VA-147 'Argonauts', commissioned on 1 February 1967. By October the squadron had received eighteen aircraft and deployed onboard USS *Ranger* for their WESTPAC (Western Pacific combat cruise) under the evaluation code-name Coronet Stallion, flying combat missions from 3 December (local time). SAM sites located at Cam Pha, Haiphong, Hanoi, Thanh Hoa and Vinh all received attention during the course of VA-147's 1,400 combat sorties during four separate Line Periods of Action, for the loss of only one aircraft: on 22 December 1967 Lt Cdr James M. Hickerson was brought down by a SAM over Haiphong and was taken prisoner.

The squadron was joined by VA-82 'Marauders' and VA-86 'Sidewinders' on USS *America* the following spring, and then by VA-27 'Royal Maces' and VA-97 'Warhawks' on USS *Constellation* which relieved VA-147 that summer. Now combat-proven, production of the A-7 in Dallas, Texas, accelerated, and the type quickly supplanted the hard-worked A-4 in US Navy service.

Iron Hand was also finally making its mark by reducing SAM effectiveness, according to the Washington statisticians. The communists had launched a reported 194 SA-2s against US aircraft in 1965, claiming 11 aircraft, for a loss rate of over 5.6 per cent. The loss rate halved in 1966 when 31 aircraft were downed by some 1,096 SAM launches, then fell to 1.75 per cent during 1967 – a period of peak SAM activity – when 56 aircraft were downed by a whopping 3,202 reported SAM firings. It is little consolation for those aircrew downed by the soulless missiles, but there is no doubt that losses would have been much higher without the Iron Hand teams to make the enemy's shooting less effective.

During this time the Sino-Soviet-supplied North Vietnamese radar threat grew more networked and ubiquitous. There existed a mere twenty-two enemy radars in operation at the beginning of Rolling Thunder; by 1967 the number had increased twenty-fold. Triple-A gun control directions and shell fusing were gained from Fire Can and SON-4 Whiff radars, but the task of defeating those was largely left to physical suppression with gunsight-aimed cannon fire and rockets based on visual sightings such as gun muzzle flashes, owing to gradually reduced radar transmission times – a change in enemy tactics directly attributable to early Shrike launches. Previously, gun-laying radars would remain on the air for up to 10–12 minutes. Ironically, after Shrike appeared, radar transmission time was swiftly reduced to just 2–3 minutes and grew increasingly intermittent and sporadic as time went on.

Nonetheless, the enemy's triple-A arsenal had grown massively by the end of 1965 from an initial 700 to nearly 5,000 pieces, and by 1966 included new radar-directed 85mm and 100mm guns which expanded triple-A coverage from 18,000ft up to 45,000ft. By 1967 the number had risen to just over 8,000 pieces consuming some 25,000 tons of ammunition a month, their barrels fed by two rail lines from China (thus making railroads and bridges priority targets) and shipping at Haiphong. The North Vietnamese defences became ever more menacing as the interceptor force too was expanded from its fledgeling MiG-15/-17

Opposite: An 'Argonauts' A-7A over USS Ranger *on Yankee Station in the Gulf of Tonkin. The aircraft is toting AIM-9 Sidewinders, plus mostly expended ZUNI rockets. The bare inner pylons carried Shrikes, bombs and/or drop tanks – all fired or jettisoned during the mission. (Richard L. Ward Archives)*

beginnings to include supersonic MiG-21 Fishbeds, sent up in numbers for the first time on 3 September 1966 from no fewer than five air bases, all of which had remained off limits to attack by US airmen. These were netted into the P-35 Bar Lock GCI network, with each radar emitting a complex six-beam array that was hard to jam except by specialist radar-foxers carrying weighty pods.

As for the burgeoning Fan Song-equipped SAM battalions, it rapidly became apparent that they were able to derive additional target information from height-finders, with acquisiton data from P-12 Spoon Rest and lower frequency P-8/-10 Knife Rest-A/B, P-3 Dumbo and Moon Face EW emitters, which watched the skies over and approaching North Vietnam. Bearing and height information gleaned from these devices would then allow the SAM operators to set up their launchers to bring their SA-2s to bear ready for just a short, lethal burst of Fan Song activity – 30 seconds or less in many instances – to guide the SAMs, thereby denying Shrike an adequate signal except in dangerous Dip-Angle duels, thus creating a greater need for more sophisticated countermeasures to thwart the air surveillance defences to begin with.

MARINE CORPS RAVENS

US Marine Corps crews flying the twin-seat Douglas EF-10B Skynight, alias Whale (the latter a name normally reserved for the Navy's A-3), pioneered tactical radar jamming – the so-called soft kill adjunct to Iron Hand work – and proved a vital asset as the combined EW radar and SAM threat grew too fierce for the strikers' self-protection aids to handle. The EF-10B Skynights were straight-winged Korean War night-fighters adapted to the electronic monitoring mission using AN/ALR-8 and AN/APR-13 gear stripped from Martin PBM Mariner flying boats.[11] Jamming gear comprised the AN/ALT-2 carried in a pod. Setting up the receiver equipment for the mission and downloading tapes obliged the Electronic Warfare Officer (EWO, later known as an Electronic Countermeasures Officer or ECMO) to climb into the 'hell-hole' in the back of the aircraft between the engines.

In its early days, when the EF-10B was still designated F3D-2Q, the crews developed all sorts of ingenious tricks to garner intelligence on Soviet radar defences. Pre-Vietnam Cold War missions were flown by VMCJ-2 adjacent to Cuba, and by VMCJ-1 near the Sakhalin peninsula in the Sea of Okhotsk, prodding and listening to radars, enabling newcomers to learn their electronic warfare mission in a relatively hot hands on fashion. Hi-Lo mission profile tactics were also developed over Yuma, where VMCJ-3 crews would pitch themselves against US Army HAWK (Homing All-the-Way Killer) SAM batteries, invariably beating them, and devising the tactics later used in Vietnam.

To many, it was a deadly chess game; a battle of wits between the EWO and the SAM operator. Crews would start off using automatic modes with two aircraft while the opposition radars searched, then switch to manual mode when the SAM operator began shifting to target tracking, more often than not exposing their critical tracking frequencies for Elint and jamming. Analysis of the collected signals used very rudimentary technology. In one instance crews poached a spare oscilloscope from the nearby hospital storeroom and used it to play the tapes they had collected, so they could watch and note pulse repetition intervals and operating frequencies of the multifarious radars. 'We were a young and low-ranking group of pioneers in the field. In 1962 the ranking EWO was a Captain, I was a Lieutenant and our teachers were Warrant Officers,' recalled Col Joe Schvimmer USMC (Ret).

On 10 April 1965 CINCPAC ordered the deployment of a detachment (Det) of six VMCJ-1 EF-10Bs from MCAS Iwakuni, Japan, to Da Nang AB, South Vietnam, under the command of Lt Col Otis W. Corman, and in July they began flying monitoring and jamming missions in support of strikes on enemy SAM sites, the first unit to provide such close-in jamming support. By the end of the year they had helped plot fifty-six of the new SA-2 sites in North Vietnam. Intended as a stop-gap pending the arrival of the new Grumman EA-6A (the electronic combat version of the A-6A), the EF-10Bs in fact continued to operate alongside their new team-mates for many more years. 'The gear was extremely accurate and sensitive for direction-finding and, truth be told, we had to accept a degrading of accuracy in the EA-6A as the antenna was in the tail rather than in the radome, up front, as in the EF-10B,' remembers Joe Schvimmer. He recalls that the AN/APR-13 open-band direction-finding receiver was able to get a cut of two degrees. This was truly remarkable for its day.

Unusually for a jamming aircraft, which would normally have been bereft of armament, the EF-10B retained the quartet of 20mm cannon from its night-fighter days; when fired, Joe said it felt like there was 'an elephant under you hitting your seat with a hammer'. Harmonizing the cannon with the gunsight meant 'taking off from Da Nang, sometimes Chu Lai if detached there, and heading out towards Tiger Island, near Hainan, where the pilot would hose them off, see where the tracers converged and grease-mark an "X" on the windshield'. After clearing the barrels, crews flew west to support a Navy Alpha or an Air Force Rolling Thunder strike package as Cottonpicker or Pigment flights, monitoring and jamming the threats as they came on the air.

The North Vietnamese air defence network was highly integrated through land-lines, complete with EW radar and height-finders and using, as Joe Schvimmer recalls, 'a systemized zone-type hand-off. I used to report about how they would scan us from Hainan and then hand us off to Thanh Hoa or Haiphong, depending on which way we were heading. Their Bar Locks came up, then Spoon Rest acquisition radar, then they would hand over to Vinh, then Vinh Son'. A control centre in Hanoi orchestrated the enemy effort, also directing triple-A. Joe Schvimmer continues:

[There were] Fire Can all over the place. Initially they were easily suppressed, but then they got clever and would stop the rotation of the antenna so as to spotlight a new EWO who would concentrate on that guy while missing the lower-powered threat below him. The Fan Song got heavier and heavier as time went on. Initial detection was made at about 50 miles range, and then the enemy would switch to high PRF at 30 miles. When Fan Song came up you knew it. [On the headphones] it sounded *nasty*, like a rattlesnake in a cave.

Within 25 seconds there was usually a volley of SA-2s, and the AN/ALT-2's 200w jammers would reply to thwart their progress by forcing the enemy operator to revert to low PRF. The process would continue. If he fired six, he needed resupply, which left the SAM site and its radar vans vulnerable to attack.

Keeping the Skynights flying throughout the 1960s was no mean feat. NARF North Island in California maintained the old J34-WE-36 can-annular engines but their home-made nickel metal cans kept burning up. Crews went to the Military Aircraft Storage and Disposition Center boneyard at Davis-Monthan AFB, Arizona, to salvage spares, which were duly cut and rewelded to keep the engines in good order. VMCJ-1 managed to launch up to six aircraft a day, with crews flying up to three 4-hour missions apiece at peak tempo, around the clock. But the US Marine Corps eventually bade farewell to the EF-10B Skynight. As Senior Marine EWO, Joe Schvimmer flew the very last flight on 25 October 1969, when he and his pilot ferried BuNo. 124645 out of Vietnam to NAS Cubi Point in the Philippines for shipment back home to the boneyard.

The EA-6A Electric Intruder first began arriving in South-East Asia in November 1966 to supplement the EF-10Bs, Lt Col Dinnage and WO

US Marine Corps' jamming and electronic surveillance aircraft, both from VMCJ-2 'Playboys': the EF-10B Skynight (foreground), which served throughout the Rolling Thunder campaign years, and the EA-6A Electric Intruder (behind), which eventually superseded it. (Richard L. Ward Archives)

Albright flying the first combat sortie; the previous month RF-4B Photo-Phantom IIs had similarly begun replacing the RF-8As. The synthesis of Elint and photo intelligence carried out by VMCJ-1 proved invaluable. Col Joe Schvimmer said, 'It was an amazing concept. The Intel officer would brief everyone, giving us the most up-to-date sit-map in the theatre.'

The EA-6As that formed the nucleus of the VMCJ-1 electronic combat detachment from 1967 were long in development, having been initiated concurrently with the US Navy's A-1 replacement, the all-weather attack A2F-1 (later A-6A) Intruder, as the A2F-1H in 1959. Col John D. 'Halfman' Weides USMC (Ret) recalls how the Marine Corps 'fought a hard fight before Congress amid howls of protest that such an aircraft would cost too much and that the mission it was being designed to perform was impossible'.

Lt Gen Phil Shutler and Col Bob Farley were instrumental in pushing the concept and seeing it approved for funding. The testbed first flew on 26 April 1963, but the original AN/ALQ-53 receiver/surveillance system did not work well. Joe Schvimmer said, 'It was worse in reception and direction-finding than the system in the EF-10B which it was to replace, so an extensive modification of the system was made and a new system was installed called the AN/ALQ-86. This offered a vast improvement, not only in direction-finding but also in frequency coverage, able to listen to threats from the low frequency Spoon Rest EW radar all the way up to MiG Air Intercept (AI) radars.'

The ECMO used the two new side-by-side displays to monitor threats and assign jammers to them. On the right was a panoramic display, which showed up to five radar threats at a time by means of stacked cathode-ray tube (CRT) traces, or lines with peaks on them. The signals could be expanded and by moving a vertical cursor sideways on top of a given signal trace's peak it could be singled out for further scrutiny on the analysis indicator to the left, which furnished a direction-finding feather, bisected with the vertical cursor providing precise emitter bearing, plus other traces below which showed such vital information as signal pulse width in microseconds, PRF and bandwidth to help classify radar type and to match jamming output. A jammer could then be steered to block the threat, before the ECMO turned his attention to another signal, constantly repeating the process with the various signals to stay ahead of the enemy, correcting for jamming antenna drift and enemy radar activity. Hence the term 'chess game': the ECMOs had to predict enemy countermoves to ease switching about between the different signals.

In all, twenty-seven EA-6As were produced in three separate lots, providing sufficient aircraft for each of the VMCJs to be eventually assigned six aircraft each, with the balance comprising those involved in pipeline maintenance or training duties and replacements for combat losses. Noticeable differences between the EA-6A and the vanilla A-6A included a slightly elongated nose and new fin-top 'football' to accommodate the thirty antennae of the Bunker-Ramo package. Jamming equipment was all podded and carried underwing. Col John Weides recalls the stores options:

The EA-6A had seven external stores stations. Stations A and B outboard of the wing-fold were used to carry AN/ALE-32 chaff pods and, supposedly, Shrike ARMs [though ironically these were never installed during Vietnam combat]. These outer wing stations did not have the wiring to function with the jamming pods or the plumbing to serve as fuel stations. The five remaining stores stations were two on each wing and a centreline. These could carry fuel, jamming pods and, on the centreline only, an extension of the AN/ALQ-86 receiver system to work real low frequencies. The jamming systems used were primarily the AN/ALQ-31 and later the AN/ALQ-76 system that consisted of a pod with four transmitters powered by a RAT [Ram Air Turbine]. When '76 assets were scarce the aircraft used AN/ALQ-31 pods.

As was US Navy practice, the pods came in various Band numbers for different frequency ranges; for example, typically 1–2 for low frequency EW, 4 for the mid-range acquisition systems and 7 for higher frequency terminal threats. Each jammer had a steerable antenna, a feature later added to the EF-10B also, and the beam width of each frequency range was different. John Weides again:

Lower frequencies equated to a wider beam width. All the antennae in a specific pod were steered in the same direction. There was an option of having the antennae steered boresight [aircraft datum line] to a target as tracked by the navigation computer, or as determined by the ECMO. In effect, if you were good and the tactical situation permitted, you could steer a combination of twenty transmitters in three directions [all at] once. All of the frequency and bandwidth settings for each of the transmitters were manually controlled by the ECMO. Each pod thus had its own control panel located on the ECMO's right, under the canopy sill.

Frequency set-on was best accomplished by acquiring a target signal with the AN/ALQ-86 system, determining its bearing from the aircraft, steering a selected transmitter to the bearing, activating the transmitter, manually tuning the transmitter to on top of the target signal, and expanding or reducing the transmitter's bandwidth to cover the target signal's bandwidth. Once the transmitter was operating, the ECMO was blind on that frequency. It was necessary to momentarily turn off a transmitter to update the target's continued operation and bearing. Some of the transmitters had a tendency to 'drift' and you had to constantly keep checking where each one was in both frequency and bearing. It was an interesting challenge to keep up with when you were carrying three jamming pods, and you had to have your act together to handle five pods. Life was not boring in the right seat of an EA-6A!

Additional equipment to make the right-seater's job even more task-saturated included the AN/ALQ-55 communications jamming (ComJam) system, although John Weides remembers it being 'just a dumb black box so far as the crew was concerned. Just one light to tell you that a signal within its frequency range was detected, another light to tell you that it was jamming and a switch to move from Off to Stand-by to XMIT. I only used it once as a self-protective measure when we had indications that MiGs were en route to us.' Usually, ComJam calls were requested by surreptitious US Navy Elint aircraft operating in the area, to block GCI. The navigation computer that assisted with jamming steering was a manual Wind with Doppler update. Unlike its A-6A bomber stablemate, the EA-6A featured no INS. John Weides recalls how this shortcoming was overcome:

> It drifted as well, but the pilot could do a radar update off a known point (land or ship). The aircraft was also configured with both digital and analogue recorders. The digital recorder recorded the flight parameters, navigation track and direction-finding lines of bearing as indicated by the ECMO. The analogue recorder took an audio recording of the signal of interest and the ECMO's and pilot's audio comments. The read-out of both recorders allowed you to get a good recap of the mission. Paper logs were kept by the pilot [navigation track] and ECMO [intercept and jamming activity]. After a mission the recorders and crew logs were taken to the Marine Corps' unique TERPES [Tactical Electronic Reconnaissance Processing and Evaluation System] for read-out and comparison with the National and Local [squadron or detachment] radar orders of battle. Post-mission reports were prepared and submitted in accordance with instructions received from higher commands up to the national level.

Alongside the pioneering US Marine Corps jets, a veritable circus of US Navy and US Air Force soft-kill jamming and Elint aircraft were evolved to monitor the complex radar network and to provide SAM warning calls. Carrier-borne assets were extremely limited and confined to detachments of piston-powered EA-1Fs of VAW-13 'Zappers' and VAQ-33 'Knight Hawks'. Already obsolescent by the time Rolling Thunder was under way, the type remained on call in diminishing numbers until VAQ-33 Det 11 recorded its last green ink missions on the type from USS *Intrepid* in 1968. The EA-1F was superseded by the far more capable EKA-3B Skywarrior, rebuilt from the Douglas giant A-3 carrier-borne bomber, in its normal guises hitherto used solely for pathfinding, aerial refuelling and photo-reconnaissance.

The initial batch of five EKA-3Bs (starting with BuNo. 147655) was converted from the baseline A-3B configuration to the versatile Tanker, Countermeasures or Strike (TACOS) role at NARF Alameda in California in early 1967 under AFC 387-1 (to be followed by further batches), and first embarked for war duties as VAW-13 Det 61 aboard USS *Ranger*, leaving California in November 1967.[12] By the end of the following spring VAW-13 had all five of its detachments in the war zone, ushering in the beginnings of a more dedicated US Navy electronic combat force which in October 1968 duly adopted the more appropriate VAQ (tactical electronic warfare squadron) moniker, but alas just too late to make any real impact on Rolling Thunder operations. USAF Elint-gathering U-2s, Boeing RC-135s, Douglas RB-66 Destroyers and, later, Lockheed SR-71A Habu also monitored the threats, collectively creating a giant pool of intelligence on the enemy order of battle (EOB), while Lockheed EC-121 Super

Constellations were fielded to listen to Fan Song radars, and plot MiG interceptors via their AI radar and Identification Friend or Foe (IFF) transponders, so that the crew could relay 'real time' SAM launch warnings and Bandit calls to friendly pilots.[13]

However, conflicting EOB data remained a problem throughout the Vietnam War. US Air Force Intelligence officer Barry Miller, who was stationed at Korat Royal Thai Air Force Base (RTAFB) in the early 1970s, points out:

> Both the Intel personnel and the [USAF Wild Weasel] aircrews found it very frustrating to deal with the great discrepancies and inconsistencies in the SAM Order of Battle [OB] information received from various agencies. It seemed there were always problems with either the location or status of North Vietnamese SAM sites as reported from 7th Air Force, Pacific Command, SAC and the Defense Intelligence Agency. As expected, all were plotted, but in practice we went with what were the most recent combat observations of [388th TFW] aircrews, especially the Weasels, who had the greatest vested interest in the information being accurate. We never could figure out why OBs couldn't be more in synch.

'Old Crow' Joe Schvimmer, who after his extensive tours on the EF-10B and EA-6A jamming jets and the RF-4B, in which he logged a staggering 425 Rolling Thunder mission tally, was posted to 7th Air Force HQ in Saigon. There he assigned theatre electronic warfare assets for the daily mission 'frags'. He explains that the roots of part of this mismatch lay in inter-service rivalry and the different RPs they operated over: 'The Navy would turn up in their white suits at 7:30 or earlier, get briefed and then go to their office in the middle of the building and lock the door, shutting themselves in until they left at night – before the Air Force in their blue suits turned up at around 8:30 or 9:00 for their day's duty. They seemed to make a deliberate point of avoiding one another. However, although they didn't trust one another they both trusted a Marine, me, to do the allocation for each!'

It was a poignant reminder of why the Marines were doing the right thing with their integrated composite wings, aided by systems like TERPES: everybody had access to any information they needed and were cleared for, and the close proximity of the recces, jammers and strikers meant everybody knew the enemy threats and how to deal with them. However, another two decades were to pass before the services began fielding electronic combat assets in an integrated manner and pooling resources properly – mostly thanks to the Marines, who evolved the EF-10B and then the EA-6A mission which later matured into the superlative EA-6B, still at the forefront of defence suppression ops thirty years later.

IRON TADPOLES

The big A-6A Intruder attack jet was to become a formidable Iron Hand machine in its own right, systematically absorbing the latest of the newly

developed Shoehorn penetration aids throughout its production and depot-level maintenance lifespan combined with an advanced cockpit, radar and ARM capability.[14] Other than its unique canopy arrangement enclosing the stepped, side-by-side seating of the pilot and his NFO bombardier/navigator (B/N), the A-6 appeared quite conventional. That belied its revolutionary new Digital Integrated Attack and Navigation Equipment (DIANE), which combined a Litton AN/ASN-31 INS, AN/APN-153 Doppler navigation set, air data computer, Litton AN/ASQ-61 ballistics computer for automatic weapons delivery, and two radars behind the bulbous nose radome. The AN/APQ-92 radar was employed in Search Radar Terrain Clearance (SRTC) mode to provide the pilot with a forward window of the terrain ahead; in Airborne Moving Target Indicator (AMTI) mode for the B/N to track mobile ground targets, such as vehicles; and later in the Redundant Target Tracking (RTT) mode, which acted as back-up for target ranging in case the tracking radar went 'tits up'.

The tracking radar comprised the Naval Avionics AN/APQ-88 (later Norden AN/APQ-112) for ground mapping and target tracking, and which painted a sector-scan picture of the ground ahead on the B/N's Direct View Radarscope Indicator (DVRI, or radarscope), complete with a set of movable azimuth and range crosshairs, which the B/N adjusted by means

The A-6A Intruder boasted a formidable arsenal of weaponry, including Shrike missiles and thermonuclear bombs. However, the aircraft served primarily as an iron bomber. (US Navy)

of a little radar control stick on a pedestal between his knees. The next waypoint along the route, be it a coastal cove or a bend in a river, the target itself or a nearby prominent offset aimpoint (at a known range, bearing and difference in elevation to the target if the latter would not produce a strong radar return) would be called up based on co-ordinates stored in the navigation computer or entered manually, based on the pre-flight plans for the mission. The navigation system-linked crosshairs would then slide into place over the relevant ground feature (waypoint, target or offset) and their position could then be refined by the B/N to ensure precise navigation to the target and to feed radar slant-range data to the ballistics computer to give bull's-eye bombing accuracy when on the target run.

In this fashion, the DIANE bomb-nav system offered direct or offset visual or blind bombing in one of four key delivery profiles: Rocket (dive followed by pull-out), Straight Path (unaccelerated level delivery), General (dive followed by a 3–4g pull-up resulting in release, also known as 'Dive-Toss') and High Loft (Half Cuban Eight or idiot loop). Stepped into attack, the system was automated to the degree that the pilot merely had to follow the steering instructions presented on his Vertical Display Indicator (VDI), commit the system to attack by pressing and holding

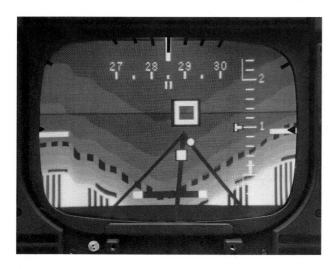

Rather than relying exclusively on traditional needles and dials, the A-6A Intruder pilot employed these graphics – his 'highway in the sky' – for navigation to target and weapons release, including Shrike delivery. (Kaiser Industries)

down the stick 'pickle' button when the in range bar appeared, and hold it down until the bombs were released automatically. Manual radar range line bombing and manual visual attack using the mils gunsight depression knob were there in reserve, of course.

But that represented only half of the magic. Instead of conventional instrumentation the pilot relied on the novel Kaiser AN/AVA-1 VDI, known as the pilot's 'highway in the sky'. This was a first-generation contact-analogue graphics display that acted as a glorified ADI, showing the terrain ahead as shades of grey-green (based on SRTC data), like a cross-sectional contour map. Sky was depicted as blue with puffy white cloud symbols, and sea as green with 'cow-plop' shapes. This was superimposed with markers for aircraft attitude (roll and pitch) and compass heading, plus command heading lines converging in perspective to a hollow square icon for steering, or pincushioned to provide a pull-up 'highway' ahead (during, say, a High Loft attack). A white dot pointed to the aircraft's velocity vector and a little solid square represented the target (all based on data from the navigation systems).

All of this meant that by skilful use of the radar and navigation systems, the B/N's box of tricks could in theory lead the pilot all the way to the target in the foulest of weather or blackest of nights, while the pilot followed his 'highway' for steering and weapons delivery without ever having to actually sight the target. To reduce danger to acceptable levels, the tracking radar generated an E-scan terrain profile of the ground ahead of the aircraft, which was displayed on a mini CRT. This, together with the SRTC-generated terrain view on the VDI and the needle-and-dial display of the AN/APN-141 radar altimeter, effective at or below 5,000ft

AGL, allowed the pilot to avoid 'rock-infested clouds', as Grumman's manuals put it, with a high degree of confidence.

All three instruments were to be scrutinized simultaneously, as none was considered entirely safe on its own, and it is important to bear in mind that DIANE did not provide hands off terrain-following autopilot flight. Instead, the pilot manually hauled the A-6 Intruder up and down and left and right of terrain obstacles by judicious use of the stick, rudder pedals and twin-J52 turbojet throttle quadrant. In many ways the Intruder was a very hands on aircraft despite its bomb-nav sophistication which, B/Ns joked, turned them into MTOs: Master Arm Turner-On'ers and Off'ers.

A total of 488 A-6As were manufactured under Fiscal Year 1959–69 contracts, first joining the Fleet in 1963. VA-75 'Sunday Punchers' aboard USS *Independence* and under the leadership of Cdr (later Adm) Leonard A. 'Swoose' Snead was the first A-6A squadron to arrive in the Gulf of Tonkin, flying its first combat missions against bridge targets on 2 July 1965. Sadly, four aircraft were lost during the squadron's inaugural WESTPAC (three very likely through premature bomb detonation, prompting a rapid switch to Douglas-designed Multiple Ejector Racks (MER) and Triple Ejector Racks (TER) originally designed for the A-4), and a fourth to triple-A fire, but they proved the type's worth. In particular, VA-75 demonstrated that solo night-time attacks were feasible in the ugliest of weather, with minimal support, thereby taking some of the heat off the A-4 Skyhawk Iron Hand support flights when dealing with more heavily defended targets. A VA-75 A-6A also executed one of the first successful SAM site kills of the Vietnam War, when on 17 October 1965 pilot Lt Cdr Cecil E. 'Pete' Garber and his B/N acted as pathfinder for four VA-72 Skyhawks that bombed out of existence an SA-2 site near Kep airfield.

Despite the early setbacks, A-6A survival rates remained among the best in the US Navy, as a result of the combination of sophisticated avionics that allowed the crew to hide in bad weather and under the cloak of night, and a higher than average pilot and B/N skill rating. Headquartered at NAS Whidbey Island, Washington (where a cadre from VAH-123 'Pros', later VA-128 'Golden Intruders', performed the West Coast Replacement Air Group training function), and NAS Oceana, Virginia (where VA-42 'Green Pawns' provided training for the Atlantic Fleet units based there), between mid-1965 and 1967 the Intruder community made seven squadron WESTPAC deployments, averaging 2,460 combat sorties annually over those two and a half years for the loss of nineteen aircraft to hostile fire, four of them to SAMs.

Unlike most other attack aircraft, which were forced to dump their ordnance if heavy evasive action was required, VA-196 'Main Battery' veteran Cdr Phil Waters proudly remembers that 'The Intruder wasn't fast or pretty, but it could still rack up a tight turn while heavily loaded, which nobody else could do back then. We soon learned that the A-6s could more or less jink together while in a loose "combat spread", pulling 3–4*g*.' ARMs were seldom employed on the Intruder before 1968. They usually left the Iron Hand missions to the lightweight but sluggish (when bombed-up) A-4s or A-7s, only occasionally carrying Shrike on single-plane night raids for self-protection, or to cover another A-6 for special interdiction missions to downtown Haiphong or Hanoi.

In Shrike mode the B/N's DVRI would act as a SIDS display, while the pilot was furnished with steering instructions on his VDI in the normal manner for loft launching at maximum range. Phil Waters remembers Lt Phil Bloomer performing just such a mission in late 1967:

He carried no bombs but a load of four Shrikes. Bloomer approached the Hanoi area from a slightly different heading and lofted the Shrikes into the Hanoi area in an attempt to take some of the heat off Cdr Morrow [and his B/N, who were conducting their target ingress in another A-6]. By approaching at low level, pulling up in a low-angle loft manoeuvre, releasing the Shrikes 2–3 seconds apart, the last at approximately 45 degrees, and then retreating the way he approached, Bloomer was attempting to distract the gunners from Morrow, achieve maximum range for the Shrikes, and do all this with a reasonable chance of survival. It was about the only tactic we could devise to remove the tremendous pressure of the Hanoi defences from the attacking aircraft.

CBU-24 anti-personnel cluster bomb units (CBU), used mainly against trucks in Laos, were also employed for flak suppression. Phil Waters said:

One version had bomblets that were delayed up to maybe 15–30 minutes, which meant that if they were scattered around a flak or

A-6A Intruders from VA-35 'Black Panthers', operating from the 'Big E', wing their way to target with Mk82 bombs. (Richard L. Ward Archives)

SAM site they would be going off like popcorn every few minutes until, hopefully, the strike group had egressed from the area. The CBU canister's dispense pattern formed a doughnut shape. For this reason they were never dropped singly, but by dropping two or more the doughnut shape could be overlapped so that there was a long oval pattern the length of which was determined by the number dropped. When dropped at night, they appeared as hundreds of tiny twinkles as each bomblet detonated, starting at a point and progressing along the flight path, forming their doughnuts.

CBUs came in many shapes and colours and US crews nicknamed some of the canisters' submunitions after fruit that they vaguely resembled in shape and size, such as guava, orange and grapefruit. The zest of these included razor-like flechettes, ball-bearings or other fragments, which proved particularly effective at holing radar dishes and suppressing triple-A batteries. The Mk20 Rockeye II, developed by NWC China Lake from 1963 and fielded five years later, comprised a 6½ft Mk7 canister containing 247 Mk118 submunitions capable of saturating an area of up to 3,333sq yd with instantaneous and time-delayed bomblets. It soon became the US Navy's mainstay CBU for area denial work, and derivatives remain in service to this day.

Washington's final approval of limited attacks on four of the five North Vietnamese MiG bases from April 1967 proved popular with US aircrews in principle, but exposed them to very intense defensive fire. The enemy had had time in which to fortify bases, extend runways and build up air defences. August 1967 was a particularly unpleasant month for losses: six US Navy aircraft were lost (including two A-6s) to 249 SAM launches, of which 51 had been volleyed on the 21st of the month against USS *Constellation*'s CVW-14 during attacks on Kep airfield and Duc Noi railway yard. A further ten US Navy aircraft were felled by triple-A fire that month. On 24–25 October Phuc Yen airfield, 11 miles north of Hanoi, was struck twice; crews encountered thirty SAMs on the first day alone.

Total US Navy losses for 1967 amounted to 133 aircraft shot down, with only one-third of the crews being rescued, the remainder having been killed or captured: a high price to pay for the reported 200 triple-A batteries and 30 SAM sites they knocked out that year. Yet the active SAM count had risen to 180 camouflaged sites. Put bluntly, the US Navy needed more anti-radar punch.

BIRTH OF THE WILD WEASELS

The shadow of an RF-101C Voodoo reconnaissance jet overflying a North Vietnamese AAA complex is visible in the jet's own recce photograph. (USAF)

Unlike the US Navy, which under peer-pressure from the US Marine Corps had quickly developed and fielded tactically deployable jamming support, the USAF went into the Vietnam War almost electronically naked and remained that way for the first year of combat. This unfortunate situation was exacerbated by the SAC-TAC split that continued to lavish critical resources on the ongoing strategic bombers and their support entourage's worldwide SIOP tasking; but also by a reluctant TAC which in the beginning saw electronic warfare penetration aids as costly and somewhat woolly in capability. Recommendations for the fitment of jamming pods (in the absence of internally installed countermeasures, such as the US Navy Sanders gear) that would not compromise range or performance had consistently fallen upon deaf ears, on cost and political grounds.

The big paradigm shift came with the first USAF loss to a North Vietnamese SAM on 24 July 1965, one day after RB-66C Elint aircraft had picked up the first evidence of operational Fan Song radars. Leopard Flight, comprising four McDonnell F-4C Phantom IIs from the 47th TFS 'Terrible Termites', were providing MiGCAP cover for a strike force of F-105s hitting the Lang Chi munitions plant 55 miles north-west of Hanoi when Leopard Two caught a full SAM blast from a salvo launch and began disintegrating as it emerged from an ugly orange-brown fireball. The crew ejected from their inverted flying wreckage. The other flight-members also received damage.[1] The stakes had changed. Two days later a McDonnell RF-101C Voodoo reconnaissance jet

was also brought down by triple-A at the offending sites while gathering photo-reconnaissance pictures. In retaliation, the following day the USAF launched a massive strike against two SAM sites and related barracks 25 miles west of Hanoi, composed of 46 F-105 Thunderchiefs or Thuds, plus twelve F-4C Phantom IIs and eight Lockheed F-104C Starfighters providing MiGCAP. With the attacking aircraft flying as low as a harrowing 50ft AGL to avoid being targeted by the SAMs, enemy small-arms fire and triple-A brought down four of the F-105s and shot-up a fifth, which began losing hydraulics. After crossing the Thai border, the aircraft gave in, pitched-up and impacted a wingman who had formated on the F-105 to assess the degree of damage. Only one man emerged from the flaming debris, and his parachute failed to open.

Of the four F-105 pilots brought down over the target, only one was rescued. To add insult to injury, post-strike reconnaissance revealed that one of the targets was actually a mock SAM installation which had probably been erected to draw jets into a shooting gallery. In a desperate bid to claim back the skies, the US Air Force undertook a series of quick-fix tactics. One of these was to keep six jets cocked ready for launch with fuel and bombs to attack any newly discovered SAM sites. However, this proved ineffective owing to the 6–8hr reaction time resulting from the need to first process and then interpret photo-reconnaissance products from RF-101Cs and RF-

Pairs of EB-66B/C/E Destroyer jamming platforms would provide coordinated noise jamming from stand-off orbits during USAF Vietnam operations. They worked on different bearings but strict timing, nulling enemy EW strobes and calling SAM launch warnings. An E model is shown here. (USAF via John T. Smith)

4Cs. Aware that they had been photographed, sites would often move to a new location well within that time, or disperse for a day or two.

Reaction time was halved when Ryan AQM-34 Remotely Piloted Vehicles (RPV) were used as bait, waking up North Vietnamese defences and allowing Air Force RB-66C Destroyer and Navy EA-3B Elint aircraft to plot the sites. This technique was first employed on 31 August, generating three fixes accurate to within 2 miles. A quartet of F-105Ds was duly dispatched to a site near Piu Tho, 40 miles north-west of Hanoi, but they failed to find any trace of enemy SAMs. While dropping a useless wooden bridge rather than dumping its bombs when fuel ran low, one of the aircraft was shot down by triple-A. Fortunately, the pilot was rescued. The Alert concept was subsequently abandoned as wasteful.

EGLIN, WRIGHT-PATTERSON AND THE PODS

It was against this grim backdrop that Gen John P. McConnell, Chief of Staff, directed Brig Gen Kenneth C. Dempster, then Director of Operational Requirements and Development, to convene a seminar and come up with some workable solutions. The meeting was held on 3 August. 'Dempster possessed locomotive clout, was able to bypass "red tape" and get programmes moving like an express train,' according to his contemporaries, chiefly by means of the Quick Reaction Capability (QRC) system. The QRC system avoided the need for excessive testing when combat needs dictated getting the equipment to the fighter wings based in Thailand and the Republic of Vietnam at the earliest opportunity.

One of the earliest tactical applications of the QRC system was to a new generation of radar-jamming devices that, unlike SAC or US Navy equipment, were self-contained in streamlined pods that could be carried on existing hardpoints and therefore strapped on as needs dictated, rather than being permanently plumbed into each and every aircraft at enormous cost. Air Force Systems Command's (AFSC) Aeronautical Systems Division (ASD) at Wright-Patterson AFB, Ohio, had for several years been working on low-drag airborne noise-jamming pods to fox radars, but the programme had foundered a little because of lack of initial interest, rather than any major technical obstacles. Under contract to the ASD, in 1961 General Electric (GE) began work on two QRC-160 magnetron-based pods (each of two subtypes, powered either by a RAT propeller on the pod, or by aircraft electrical power fed through an umbilical), thereby facilitating away-from-aircraft disassembly for maintenance and updates.

Each of the pods pumped out 150w of noise-modulated continuous-wave energy. The QRC-160-1A radiated in the S- and C-Bands (and, later, in the L-Band, in a derivative version) using mix 'n' match canisters to thwart SA-2 Fan Song-B and Fire Can radars, while the outwardly very similar QRC-160-2 was optimized for the X-Band, employing an automated jammer (with search and Set-On receivers in its tail cone to assist this process) to confuse enemy MiGs' AI radars. Flight-tested by Capt Ed White in an ASD NAA F-100F Super Sabre, initially over Ohio and from July 1962 over Electronic Sites 4 and 20 within the Armament Development Test Center's facilities at Eglin AFB, Florida, the -1A pod ably demonstrated its abilities against the triple-A and SAM radars, and also against search and height-finder radars at Crystal Springs, Mississippi.

A limited pilot-production run followed in 1963, leading to a request for GE and Hughes to build an initial 200 units. However, TAC was not prepared to fund the necessary maintenance personnel for what it saw as a purely research and development effort, while Hughes encountered production difficulties, with the result that the pods were not properly employed for another three years.[2] The early losses to SAMs resulted in a major change of heart on this matter, further propelled by Brig Gen Dempster, and the pods soon began equipping combat jets as the AN/ALQ-71 (QRC-160-1A) and AN/ALQ-72 (QRC-160-2).

The adoption of these pods resulted in changed formation work. Maj Jim Chamberlain recalled: 'The flight leader's wingman, on the far left of the formation, flew high and the element lead, on the flight leader's right wing, flew low and the element wingman flew level with the flight lead.

This was supposed to provide noise dispersion so that the flight altitude would be masked. But if one pod failed or overheated, as they were prone to do, it was recommended that the whole flight turn off their pods.' Separation was usually 1,000–1,500ft laterally and 500ft vertically, making odd-men-out easily distinguishable, so jamming had to be mutual.

ATI listening gear was also fielded from the spring of 1966 on a Fleet-wide basis, comprising the AN/APR-25 RHAWS and the WR-300-cum-AN/APR-26 LWR. This was installed on the F-4 production line at St Louis in Missouri (Group A wiring and panel slots) and at Air Materiel Area (AMA) depot bases such as Sacramento in California and Ogden in Utah (Group B actual kit installation, or complete retrofit), where it was incorporated on F-105D/Fs and F-4Cs already in service. US Air Force aircraft were sent to AMA depots every two years for major overhauls and updates on a Time Compliance Technical Order (TCTO) basis that mandated thorough overhauls, just like US Navy jets at their assigned NARFs, and these reworks offered the best opportunity to splice-in new gear under specific Technical Orders (TO). Additional work was performed in Thailand and Japan using field modification kits for the combat-assigned aircraft, to speed up the process. The first combat use of the receivers by regular US Air Force strike jets has been recorded as Friday 13 May 1966.

Brig Gen Dempster, however, had already gone one step further than getting the QRC jamming pods and warning gear for combat-bound aircraft. The August 1965 seminar set down an additional requirement for an aggressive radar 'ferret', dubbed Project Wild Weasel after the fearless little carnivore that takes on much bigger prey, which would hunt out

The original analogue RHAWS display showed threats as strobes emanating from the centre by relative bearing. Length indicated signal intensity, hence the reference to a 'three ringer' – an urgent threat. Solid lines represented the SA-2 (or other E-Band signal) and were later supplemented by dash-lined and dotted strobes to cover the G and I Bands. Compare this with the alphanumeric RWR display shown on page 144. (Applied Technology Industries)

enemy radars, especially SAM sites, knock out the Fan Song guidance radars and even mark the sites to aid companion Iron Hand aircraft in the destruction of associated launchers and missiles. It was a tall order, and the first commander to be briefed on this task – otherwise experienced and well motivated – replied with the remark 'You gotta be sh***** me!' Korean War veteran Lt Col John Kropnik expressed considerable reserve and said as much to Brig Gen Dempster. Kropnik was later removed from the programme, but YGBSM subsequently became the Wild Weasels' jocular hallmark, though it was tinged with the real fear that anyone facing combat must endure.

There would always be enough young daring pilots eager for serious adventure, but the new equipment to be installed in the aircraft required the addition of a second crewmen, a highly educated, quick-minded EWO to decipher the radar signals and coolly vector his pilot to the target, with no other control over his personal destiny. In 1965 the largest source of EWOs was men used to being stuck in the dungeon pits of SAC bombers or at the scopes in RB-66s, and on hearing of the new programme applicants rallied to the cause – transferring to fighters had enormous cachet, as veterans Stan Goldstein and Kim Pepperell reminded the author. By then, YGBSM was an in-joke and not meant to be taken literally, despite the dangers. 'Being a Weasel EWO wasn't a career, it was a combat tour.'

HUNS GO HUNTING

The aircraft selected for Project Wild Weasel was the twin-seat F-100F, known to pilots as the One Hundred, or 'Hun' for short. Legend has it that the initial work on outfitting the new Weasel was based on a meeting between ATI and NAA during which the details were scribbled on a chalkboard, signed by the representatives there in chalk and the chalkboard duly photographed on a Polaroid camera to create something akin to a binding deal. Seven low-hours Block 20 F-100Fs drawn from 27th TFW service at Cannon AFB, New Mexico, were outfitted with the AN/APR-25 RHAWS plus additional equipment in the form of the IR-133 panoramic receiver under Modification 1778, performed at NAA's Long Beach, California, facility under the guidance of Programme Manager John Paup.[3]

The new IR-133 device detected S-Band signals from Fire Can and Fan Song-B radars at long range and furnished signal characteristics to help classify the radar and its operating posture, as well as offering a direction-finding mode that provided steering cues by means of two amplitude-based spikes on the CRT trace. For example, if the threat was radiating from a two o'clock position, the right-hand spike would be bigger because of the relatively greater strength of the signals being picked up on the direction-finding antenna from the starboard side. Using these, the backseat EWO would vector the pilot until the aircraft was lined-up towards the threat, or both peaks were of equal size, so to speak.

The direction-finding display had a 180-degree ambiguity unless the crew knew for certain (from an AN/APR-25 strobe, for example) that the site was either ahead of or behind the aircraft: as the aircraft neared the

Seven F-100Fs were modified into the Wild Weasel I role by North American Aviation. (North American Aviation via Larry Davies and Mick Roth).

site, the strobe at twelve o'clock would first begin to curl, then would briefly disappear and become a six o'clock strobe as the aircraft passed over the radar. Crews could resolve this ambiguity by yawing the aircraft and observing which spike got shorter. For example, if the pilot yawed the aircraft to the right and the left spike shortened, the emitter was behind the aircraft. There was, of course, no ranging capability, so yawing was sometimes the only means of confirming whether or not the crew had overflown the site, meaning that crews could overfly a heavily camouflaged installation without knowing it and find themselves under attack.

Sighting – a tally – was accomplished purely visually whereupon the pilot would line up for a pass with rockets and 20mm cannon fire. The same methodology would be used to help line up for a Shrike volley, when F-100Fs began sporting the ARM the following year. The US Air Force textbook delivery tactic was to line up on the target in azimuth and elevation until the missile's seeker had locked on to the threat, and then pull up to loft the missile towards it, using a canned delivery angle prescribed for a given speed and altitude.

Monitoring the instruments and threat displays and referring to the complex cockpit charts took some getting used to, creating a potential nightmare workload for inexperienced aircrew during the dangerous target runs. For this reason the Weasels soon began to rely heavily on visual lining-up and aural cues, and learnt the Shrike delivery profile partly by rote, partly by instinct. True down the throat Shrike capability did not catch up with the US Air Force for several more years, so greater emphasis was placed initially on the use of standard 2.75-in Folding-Fin Aerial Rockets (FFAR) containing high explosive anti-tank/anti-personnel warheads, and the trusty 20mm cannon.

Training began at Eglin AFB on 11 October 1965 and was completed under Maj Garry Willard, the new commander who was appointed to replace the veteran Kropnik a mere ten days before the combat deployment. Additional equipment added to the sniffing suite at this juncture included the WR-300. An ATI engineer, while reviewing SA-2 Elint intercept analyses at the National Security Agency as part of an unrelated project, was intrigued by the behaviour of the SAM's guidance signal and developed the concept for the WR-300, which became the AN/APR-26 LWR. He suggested to ATI's president that a launch warning capability be added to the AN/APR-25 RHAWS in the F-100F. ATI proposed this to the USAF and received an almost immediate go-ahead. The WR-300s were delivered to Eglin AFB for installation on the F-100Fs on 14 November. There was no opportunity to flight-test the equipment!

The force deployed to Korat RTAFB on 21 November, beginning operations a week later. Thailand was the obvious choice. Although the USAF had already deployed the F-100-equipped 3rd TFW to Bien Hoa AB in South Vietnam, which might ease maintenance requirements, the 3rd TFW specialized in Close Air Support (CAS) and possessed little or no experience of the air war north of the DMZ. By contrast, two RP VI combat-seasoned wings of F-105D/Fs were operational in Thailand: the 355th TFW at Ban Takhli RTAFB and the 388th TFW at Korat RTAFB where the combat trials would be undertaken, initially under 6234th TFW (Wild Weasel Det) control. Wild Weaseling would thus commence as an F-100F/F-105D mixed affair, the F-100F acting as hunter and the companion F-105Ds serving as killers, in one of two flight mixes: an F-100F leading either three or four Thunderchiefs.

The first Weasel crew to successfully kill a SAM site was Capt Allen Lamb and his EWO Capt Jack Donovan flying as Spruce One (in F-100F 58–1226) on 22 December 1965. After Lamb had traversed four hills masking the site, Donovan picked up the tracking radar. Lamb pulled up in a hard rolling turn towards the target as they came out into the open over the valley, and spotted the SAM site nestling among trees in a village. Lamb fired two LAU-3 pods' worth of rockets, which impacted short. Instinctively switching to the four 20mm cannon in the nose, he zapped an SA-2 and hit the radar van as cannon shells walked across the site. The single-seat F-105Ds then rolled in as Lamb and Donovan pulled off target, firing their rocket loads to deliver the *coup de grâce*.

The after-action report noted 'sixteen LAU rocket pods [containing 304 rounds] and 2,900 rounds of 20mm expended, all in an area less than the size of a football field, with pattern centred on Fan Song radar van'. Mk82 bombs were used from 12 February 1966, and beginning on 18 February the F-105 Iron Hand support flights began carrying mixed loads of M117 750lb bombs and FFARs. The F-100Fs also experimented with BLU-27/B napalm canisters for target marking a few times during February, but the results were apparently very poor and the 'nape' drops were discontinued.

The concept had been proven, but problems persisted nonetheless. The use of commercial-grade coaxial cable in the wiring for the receivers presented all sorts of problems with deterioration, partly because of the humid environment and insidious corrosion, but chiefly because those installed in the tail were routed next to the engine, rapidly resulting in loss

of signal reception. Taking the tails off the aircraft for routine engine maintenance necessitated the deconnection and reconnection of wiring, which simply exacerbated the problem. Also, the F-100Fs were much less powerful than the F-105s and so required the use of a good deal of after-burner to keep pace, which in turn led to melted wiring. Ed Rasimus, who flew F-105Ds in the companion Iron Hand killer role, remembers that the obsolescent F-100 had a hard time acting as pathfinder-leader:

I arrived at Korat on 6 May 1966. At that time there were three F-100Fs on the flight line and I had no idea what they were there for. I was just out of CCTS [Combat Crew Training Squadron] and we hadn't been briefed on any aspect of Weasel ops. Neither had we been briefed on RWR gear. There was discussion during my in-brief (very brief, since the two squadrons – total of 40 pilots authorized – had lost eight airplanes and seven pilots in the previous week) of Vector gear. That was a reference to the AN/APR-25 that was being

'You haven't lived until you've been over Hanoi with everyone shooting at you.' Ed Rasimus initially flew F-105Ds in the companion Iron Hand killer role and returned to South-East Asia in 1972 with the F-4E for his second combat tour. (Ed Rasimus)

installed locally and which was in about one-quarter of the aircraft. It was classified secret and I wouldn't see one in an airplane until about three weeks and ten missions or so later. There were no pods at all. Some aircraft had cannon plugs in the main gear wheel wells labelled for QRC-160, but no one knew much about it.

On my third mission, I was scheduled as spare for a four-ship add-on which was one of two flights generated in response to a SAM site in RP II that Garry Willard had found that morning near Ha Tinh. Willard, who was dual-qualified in both the F-100F and F-105D, was leading the first flight back to kill the site. To make a long story bearable, two aircraft of the eight scheduled aborted, and I wound up flying Karl Richter's wing; he was on his fifth mission, I was on my third. It was my introduction to intense flak – wall-to-wall 37/57mm and radar-guided 85mm that even followed me into a nearby cloudbank. You've never lived till you find yourself jinking on the gauges while red and black flashes of air-bursts are all around you.

On my tenth mission, I was on my first RP VI trip – a hunter/killer (although we didn't use that terminology then, it was referred to as an Iron Hand mission), with 'Buns' Frasier leading in a '100F and three F-105Ds. The no. 2 aircraft carried a pair of Shrikes and the second element carried six CBU-24s (four on the centreline and one on each outboard) plus 450gal tanks on [the] inboards. I flew no. 4. The mission was uncomfortable from the start, since the '105s routinely cruised at 420 knots and pushed up to 540–600 knots in high-threat areas. The '100F had to work to handle 350 knots.

The refuelling was a disaster, with probe/drogue required. The F-100's probe on the wing was challenging, but most '100 drivers had lots of experience. The '105 was dual refuelling-capable and the retractable probe was so short that boundary layer airflow over the nose would move the basket away when trying to connect. Virtually no one, regardless of experience, ever felt really comfortable doing probe refuelling in a '105.

Once in the target area the '100 Weasel tended to operate at around 400 knots, and the three '105s were continually pushing in front or zooming off airspeed in the vertical to stay out of his way. His turns would bleed airspeed and his turn radius was generally smaller, so it was continual crack-the-whip. Finally, his equipment was fairly basic, so it was really difficult to get much valid electronic information. In many instances the '105D with AN/APR-25 [and] carrying Shrike had as good a picture as the Weasel, since Shrike produced real audio of radar signals and gave pitch and bank steering-bar info to the ADI.

The method described by Ed Rasimus was used as the primary steering cue for Shrike line-up on target and soon became a standard feature on all F-105 Thunderchiefs and F-4 Phantom IIs, though few non-Weasel USAF fighter crews would ever get to employ Shrike.

The Weasel Hun combat evaluation ended on 26 January 1966. However, crews remained deployed until 11 July, and continued to fly into heavily defended areas until March, by which time a second machine had been lost to triple-A and all such missions were suspended.[4] In all, three F-100Fs were lost, but the force had the honour of firing the first USAF Shrike in combat before it bowed out. On 18 April a Fire Can was located 6 miles north-west of Dong Hoi in RP 1. It was listed as a possible kill: the three escorting F-105D pilots attempted to follow the missile down for a bomb pass on the target, but the ARM disappeared into a layer of haze and the radar signal ceased at about the same time.

WILD WEASEL THUNDERCHIEFS

Replacements were already in the offing. Three follow-on programmes were being tested at Eglin AFB, all designed to give the faster F-105 self-sufficiency for Iron Hand work, under the orders of Air Force Chief of Staff Gen John P. McConnell. The sense of urgency was reflected in the timescale: some project teams, following definition, had as little as two weeks in which to mount their gear for tests! Project Wild Weasel-IA involved two F-105Ds: Maxson RHAWS and the Bendix DPN-61 were spliced into 61-0138, which provided steering cues on a modified lead-computing gunsight, while 62-4291 featured just the ATI AN/APR-25 RHAWS. Neither toted an LWR, and it was soon found that the cockpit workload was excessive. Wild Weasel-II, destined to be tested on F-105F 62-4421, was to introduce new Bendix APS-107 radar-sniffing gear in the wing-tips and an internal Navy AN/ALQ-51 DECM, following flight trials in August and September 1965 on an F-105D using wing-tip pods, but the project was terminated before the installation was completed and the jamming sets already bought from Sanders were fitted in RF-101Cs instead.

Neither WW concept was pursued and on 8 January 1966 Gen Dempster decided on Project Wild Weasel-III: the twin-seat F-105F fitted with integral fuselage equipment, already being successfully flight-tested by F-105F 62-4416.[5] This initially used precisely the same kit as that installed on the Weasel Hun (although it was soon to be expanded), with an identical crew make-up of pilot and backseat EWO, who soon came to be known as the 'Bear'. (The term may originate from a contraction of 'Backseat Ears', somebody being in the 'Bear Pit' behind the pilot, or possibly just a grumpy EWO telling his pilot what to do – which tended to be a prerequisite for survival among the Weasel cadre.)

The Thud, also known as the Lead Sled or Ultra Hog, was pushed aloft by a 23,000lb-thrust Pratt & Whitney J75-P-19W after-burning turbojet fed by inward-facing intakes at the wing roots, and employed an area-ruled Coke-bottle fuselage for minimum drag that endowed the F-105 with supersonic capability

The Weasel Thud EWO relied on these displays in the rear pit to acquire and analyse radar signals and prioritise them. Direction-finding was possible with two threats at a time, bringing the aircraft to bear on target for a Shrike launch, or gun or rocket pass. A steering marker was furnished to the pilot on his gunsight. (Applied Technology Industries via Mick Roth)

F-105D at the pre-takeoff EOR. Pilots flying the hunter/killer companion role to Weasels mostly employed 2.75-in rockets and M117 750lb bombs, which can be seen strapped on this Thud. (Larsen-Remington via Mick Roth)

down on the deck. Its only real vice was its small wing, which gave it incredible stability at low level, but at the expense of poor turning performance and a take-off roll that consumed most of the runway when heavily laden, even with water injection to boost thrust. Crews joked that if there was a runway that circled the Earth, Republic would design an aircraft that would use it! Dan Barry, who was used to the habits of the J75 engine, having previously flown the similarly powered Convair F-106 Delta Dart or Six, compared their take-off and landing performance:

The '106 and '105 cockpits were quite similar, with both having the vertical tape instruments. Take-offs were probably less than half the distance in the Six, with final approach speed being something like 172 knots in the Six and with comparable recovery fuel. The Thud varied a bit from aircraft to aircraft, but our lightest aircraft was about 199 knots. Then once you touched down, they both had a drag 'chute shear speed of something like 185 knots, which wasn't a factor in the Six as even without a 'chute you had the aero-braking of that big delta wing stopping you. The Thud was like a dart and had little aero-braking. Since everyone put the Thud 'chutes out right at the limits they were really stressed, and it was not unusual for them to fail after a number of deployments. It was not an unusual occurrence to see a Thud in the barrier.

Not surprisingly, BAK-9 arresting barriers were installed at either end of the runways as a precaution.

The F-105 was also incredibly well built, as Republic's chief designer Alexander Kartveli had intended. Astonishingly, crews expected 5–7 minutes' worth of high-speed escape flying even when the aircraft was ablaze. It just kept flying. Survivability modifications fitted after initial losses included self-sealing fuel cells by means of explosion-suppressing foam and a back-up twin-shot fire-extinguishing system, improved wheel brakes and zero-zero ejection seats. Additional modifications provided duplicate roll control via the flaps and a switch that allowed the pilot to engage a bolt to lock the tailplane if the aircraft was seriously hit, plus re-routed redundant hydraulic lines. This would sustain control in a jet with shot-up hydraulics, which otherwise would be prone to pitch-up (the cause of the tragic mid-air collision on 27 July 1965).

A pair of F-105F Thud Weasels wing their way into North Vietnam's defences, sporting just fuel and Shrike missiles. (via Jim Rotramel)

If the aircraft was hit, these modifications often gave crews enough time to head back towards Thud Ridge. Until late 1967 there were no guns located on the inhospitable upper reaches of this terrain, making it a good place to bale out and await rescue by USAF HH-3/HH-53 Super Jolly helicopter pilots and their parajumpers from the Aerospace Rescue & Recovery Squadrons (ARRS). As a result, the mountain ridge turned out to be the graveyard for over a hundred mortally wounded F-105s during the late 1960s. Later, F-105s were able to limp back to Thailand despite remarkable combat damage.

An initial twelve F-105F conversions followed the successful trials of the WW-III test-bed in early 1966, followed by further batches drawn from existing twin-seat stock over the ensuing two years (production of the F-105F had ended in 1964 at 143 machines). In July 1966 USAF HQ directed Sacramento AMA to modify an additional eighteen F-105Fs and in November 1966 a further thirty-six were added. Numbers eventually reached eighty-six aircraft when a final nineteen airframe conversions were authorized in June 1967, though the number of operational aircraft never reached those dizzy heights because of losses and the protracted conversion process, undertaken when the aircraft became due for deep maintenance at Sacramento AMA. US Air Force Europe (USAFE) F-105s were drawn into the conversion programme, most of these offering low-hours pristine airframes.

The first F-105F WW-IIIs to deploy to Thailand comprised five aircraft assigned to the 13th TFS 'Panther Pack' at Korat RTAFB (the EWOs officially being under 388th TFW Det 1 jurisdiction), which arrived on 28 May 1966. They were joined by six more at Takhli RTAFB in June, all assigned to the 354th TFS 'Fighting Bulldogs'. Combat sorties began in July. Both squadrons adopted the same Iron Hand flight mix of two F-105Fs leading two F-105Ds, split into two elements – a pattern that would endure throughout the Rolling Thunder years. CBUs were carried by both Ds and Fs, but Shrike fits varied as new models became available,

A pair of F-105Ds from Korat en route to target in 1968 with M117 750lb iron bombs, fuel tanks and AN/ALQ-87 'Beacon' mode-capable noise-jamming pods. The latter substantially reduced losses to SAMs and set the pattern for medium-high altitude ingress to target by the Korat Thud Wing. (USAF via John T. Smith)

so that by November 1966 the F-105F Weasels carried a mixed pair of Shrikes to cater for specific threats, while the supporting F-105Ds used more versatile but less discriminating broad-Band versions. Rockets were also carried, and napalm was experimented with again as a rather gruesome target marker.

Last-minute additions to the F-105F WW-III's equipment which had been responsible for its delayed service entry, but which gave it a definite edge over the F-100F, included the NAA QRC-317 Sense, Exploit and Evade SAMs (SEE-SAMs) device, which shared the antennae of the AN/APR-25 RHAWS and AN/APR-26 LWR. If the enemy SA-2 sites started switching to high PRF, indicating that a SAM launch was imminent, SEE-SAMs measured the intensity of the azimuth and vertical scan signals of the Fan Song radar and, if found to be centred within its 10-degree common sector box (as apparently required for a SA-2 launch), a warning light lit up informing the crew that *they* were under attack, not a wingman, thus focusing their attention.

Another early addition was the American Electronic Laboratories (AEL) Pointer III system, quickly superseded by ATI's similar AE-100 system which was linked to the standard IR-133 receiver. This employed four log-periodic azimuth/elevation triangular antennae screwed in around the nose-barrel of the F-105, just behind the radome, which intercepted radar signals ahead of the aircraft and deduced the enemy emitter's position within the forward cone, flashing up the target position as a green steering dot superimposed over the target on the pilot's lead-computing optical sight (gunsight). This proved to be of enormous help to pilots, and even offered 'scientific wild ass guesses' weapons delivery in Instrument Flight Rules (IFR) conditions. Thus, the EWOs could provide an initial vector based on the direction-finding strobes, and when the gunsight marker slewed into the pilot's field of view he would squint and get a tally on the site. From then on, even the EWO would be peering out of the cockpit, on the lookout for muzzle flashes or missile launch puffs, as the engagement with the enemy defences became purely visual, with crews relying mostly on aural cues for missile lock-up and to ascertain radar activity.

Other new Weasel gear to be fielded in subsequent editions of the WW-III, beginning with the second big batch of F-105F WW-III conversions authorized in July 1966 and modified at Sacramento AMA from 1 September 1966, included the ATI ER-142, which worked much like the IR-133C but expanded frequency coverage to the C-Band and offered a second scope so that the EWO could monitor both C- and S-Bands as well. Both dedicated scopes, S at left and C at right, included direction-finding display options.

Nonetheless, initial F-105F losses were extremely heavy. By mid-August 1966 only one flyable F-105F remained at Korat RTAFB from the original five, while Takhli RTAFB was left with just two shot-up hulks damaged beyond repair. Capt Kevin 'Mike' Gilroy was among the initial cadre at Takhli:

We had eight crews and six airplanes. Forty-five days later we had no airplanes, four KIA, two POWs, two WIA, one quit, one transferred to the B-66 because F-105s caused him to get airsick, two went home at eighty missions and eight months (legal to do, but not the manly thing to do), and four finished their 100 missions. We arrived at Takhli Royal Thai Air Force Base on 4 July 1966. A few days later, two crews from Korat, our sister F-105 base around 100 miles to the

Takhli's F-105D Memphis Belle II demonstrates the heavy M118 3,000lb bomb fitted with daisy-cutter fuse extenders which was particularly effective at subduing triple-A sites. The 355th TFW squadrons featured Weasel flights within each squadron and specialised in low-level ingress to target. (via Tony Cassanova)

south, came over to give us a checkout in what they knew about flying the Wild Weasel mission when people shoot back at you. The weather had turned sour though. The tough targets in the north were obscured by monsoon rain-clouds, and the only missions that were flown were easy ones in the southern part of North Vietnam. At that time there were no SAM sites in that area. It became immediately obvious that the guys from Korat, who were supposed to check us out, didn't know much more about our mission than we did; they had only been in the theatre for around a month longer than us. So, after ten days of an abortive checkout programme, the Korat crews declared to our Wing Commander that the checkout programme was complete and that we were ready to go.

Mike Gilroy and his pilot Ed Larson were shot down on their eleventh mission, one which tasked both Thailand-based F-105 wings against the rail marshalling yard on the north-east rail – the major rail link between Hanoi and southern China – on 7 August 1966. The mission exemplified the problems faced by crews in employing an ARM that was shorter-ranged and slower than the enemy's SA-2 SAMs. Mike remembers the weapons carried:

Ordnance loads consisted of two AGM-45 Shrike ARMs and two pods of 2.75-in rockets. We also had a 650gal centreline fuel tank. The Shrikes were to damage and mark the site from a distance of 7–10 miles; the SAMs had an effective range of 19 miles. Great! Then the rockets and our wingman's six 500lb bombs were to really put them out of business. The fuel tank was to give us the extra range we needed, as well as to absorb some of the flak that might come our way. I watched the signal on the scope to see if the Shrike found its target. Fifteen seconds elapsed. The signal abruptly went off the air. Bingo!

However, while waiting for the Shrike to impact, another SAM had been tracking them at their two o'clock, and the crew duly turned 30 degrees to the right to line up with the radar.

The second Shrike roared off the wing while simultaneously the yellow and red lights on my equipment lit up, accompanied by the shrill howl over the intercom that indicated that the SAM site had launched at us. Ed relayed my 'Launch!' call out over the air, followed by 'Kingfish Flight, take it down!' We lit the afterburner to get up more airspeed, put the SAM radar signal off our left wing, and dove for the ground, hoping to see the missiles and to dodge them before they got us.

Sighting it visually, Ed Larson pulled up and the SAM exploded harmlessly behind them. However, the evasion manoeuvre had bled off a lot of airspeed, leaving them vulnerable, as Mike recalls:

I heard Ed shout 'Christ!': a second missile came out of the clouds, and exploded just in front of the airplane. The airplane was rocked

SAM Fighter *on the ramp: live Shrikes and five SAM kill marks testify to its potency. The aircraft was assigned to the 354th TFS 'Fighting Bulldogs'.* (via Jim Rotramel)

hard. Seconds later, the cockpit filled with black smoke and the bitter smell of burned cordite – the gun drum which holds the 1,028 rounds of ammunition for our 20mm Gatling gun had blown up. I could see nothing but flames and the red fire warning light glaring at me through the black smoke. The plane was still rocking from side to side, but at least it hadn't exploded or gone completely out of control. I had serious trouble breathing. My oxygen mask was not sealed tightly and I was choking on the smoke. [Mike blew off the canopy to get some air.] Incongruously, I thought what a beautiful day it was. The towering cumulus clouds were as pretty and white as any I have ever seen in the States, and I saw a few patches of clear blue sky.

The Weasel kit was dead, and the left wing had a big hole in the leading edge, around 3ft in diameter. 'The top of the vertical stabilizer was gone. The nose of the aircraft was gone. Other than that, we were in great shape in our 500mph open-cockpit airplane.'[6]

As they left the target area, neither crewman knew they were flying right over the Cam Pha iron mines. These were home to one of the North Vietnamese gunnery schools equipped with several batteries of 57mm and 85mm triple-A. Three bursts of consecutively more accurate triple-A fire severed the jet's hydraulics, leaving Larson and Gilroy with no choice but to eject. Fortunately they were by now 'feet wet', and by a stroke of luck had escaped in the nick of time: their aircraft exploded just before it hit the water. A Grumman HU-16 Albatross amphibious rescue aircraft picked them up, amidst the sharks and enemy mortar fire.

Six replacement aircraft arrived in November 1966 so that each wing was brought up to five F-105F WW-IIIs, but no sooner had they arrived than the 388th TFW lost its Weasel detachment commander, Maj Robert Brinckmann, and his EWO Capt Vince Scungio. They were killed on 4 November when their aircraft (63-8273) was shot to pieces by triple-A over RP VIA. It was not a happy day.

Up to 15 July 107 Shrikes had been launched for one confirmed and thirty-eight probable hits. As noted already, the early use of Shrike had taught the North Vietnamese radar operators to stay on the air for less than 2 minutes at a time, and to make increased use of ground observers and EW acquisition radar as preliminary target collectors, their information being relayed to the radar operators via land-lines, or by radio on special occasion. Then the triple-A would open up, big-time. The figures held true throughout 1966, during which time a total of 436 Shrikes were expended. USAF Weasel crews still relied on a radiating radar for a valid Shrike shot (they were not supposed to fire missiles purely pre-emptively, the way the US Navy did), but the methods became less constrained and the emphasis had definitely shifted away from destruction and more towards suppression, to keep heads down.

Conventional bombs, the 20mm Gatling gun (offering 100 rounds a second) and the increased use of new CBUs with their 'fruit salad' contents were all effective at knocking out the mute sites, if spotted. EWO veteran Kim Pepperell, who flew Weasel combat missions from both Takhli and Korat during the course of three tours, eventually logging 203 combat missions (175 over North Vietnam), reckoned that the traditional ordnance was far more useful:

Shrike was dumb. You could do better with a peashooter. It was only fifty per cent reliable, fifty per cent accurate, and when you do the probabilities on that you realize that it takes a lot of them to hit the target. It was more the puff of smoke from the airplane that scared the radar operators! We really had to line it up with the target in an almost perfect trajectory. Homing on a threat signal gave Shrike much more credit than it deserved. You used Shrike as a marker most of the time.

The attacks were 100 per cent visual. You looked for that [SAM] ring and got to the point where you could see them, using the cockpit electronics to guide you to a visual situation. We could see quite a bit out of the aircraft, especially when the pilot rolled the aircraft on its edge. Even though I was strapped in tight in the ejection seat, I was able to see 180 degrees to the back of me too. The instructors at Nellis said you could do this and we didn't believe them. But, in combat, when being chased by a MiG, I was able to twist far enough back, adrenalin pumping, and see that little tiny silver mosquito chasing us back there. The view was pretty good for spotting SAMs and triple-A.

WEASEL COLLEGE

The USAF quickly developed a formal training syllabus dedicated to Iron Hand at Nellis AFB, near Las Vegas, Nevada. Experience of the early losses gave rise to a longer, six-week course that included both theory and flying. The Weasel College trained sixty-nine crews during 1967 (Classes WW III-7 to WW III-16), and over seventy the following year, by which time the syllabus had been expanded to include F-4 crewmen. Kim Pepperell remembers his time at Weasel College:

At the time I went through training, the course lasted approximately two months. It was approximate because the training consisted of a specific set of flights, each providing experience on a given facet of the Wild Weasel concept and tactics. Our class, however, was one of a few that were extended another month, in order to give us extra training on the use of the R-14A radar system for bombing. This was in preparation for an added mission referred to as 'Ryan's Raiders'. In my case, I heard little about that ever again, since that mission was to be flown out of Korat, and my assignment was to Takhli.

Training at Mather AFB in California [electronic warfare school], and McConnell AFB in Kansas [the principal F-105 replacement training unit base] could be considered as sort of preludes to Wild Weasel training. All the guys in the back (GIBs) were fully qualified EWOs, meaning that they had graduated from Mather AFB at some point in their careers. Actually, they could have graduated from EWO training at Keesler AFB in Mississippi, or even Boca Raton in Florida, as these were the second and first venues for the training, respectively. In the earliest years, many of the pilots, if they had no prior

Nellis Wild Weasel school near Las Vegas, Nevada, prepared pilots and EWOs for combat. Here one of its Thuds shows off its slick lines to the camera. (Frank B. Mormillo)

Hanoi Hustler, *F-105F/G 320, formerly nicknamed* Cooter, *claimed three North Vietnamese MiG kills: one with the 20mm gun, one with an AIM-9 Sidewinder, and another with its bomb rack, jettisoned in bomb-in-face fashion when the MiG was on its tail.* (Frank B. Mormillo)

experience in the Thud, were sent to McConnell for F-105 checkout (or refresher training, if they were not current in the aircraft). Later on, the F-105 checkout and recurrency training was moved to Nellis AFB.

Very early on, there was a prerequisite that the pilot had to have hundreds of hours in the F-105 before he could be accepted to Weasels. But that had to be continually revised and revisited, due to the continuing flow of crews needed for the mission. In fact, in early 1968, the school experimentally accepted the first cadre of lieutenants directly from pilot training, completely contrary to the earlier notion that the pilot needed to do many of his flight control actions almost instinctively; a trait that could only come from many hours flying the plane. The apparent success of the experiment was sufficient to cause the 'F-105 experienced' prerequisite to be eliminated.

At some point in the WW training, within the first week or so, the crews were 'married'. [Prospective pilots and EWOs would be brought together in an informal environment in the Officers' Club or around a desk and told to pair up by the end of the week.] 'There was an indescribable magic about this process,' recalled both Kim Pepperell and Gerry Knotts.[7] How the crews linked up was like magic. We were told on the first day, Monday, that we must link up as crews and stay together – you had until Friday, and you knew you had a thirty per cent chance of survival during your combat tour. But we sat around a table and it was done. Just like that. Six crews, all teamed up. The idea behind the whole marriage thing was that it divided up the roles. It was the ultimate in crew coordination. You seldom crewed up with anyone else.

The crew concept was a very significant part of the WW concept. The two men needed to be so familiar with each other that, for example, a shift in voice pattern would be immediately recognizable by the opposite crewmember. So, from the point at which they were crewed, pilot and 'Bear' flew as a crew constantly. If one got sick, the other waited until he was well to fly again. They went on R&R [Rest & Relaxation] at the same time, usually Bangkok, after ten counters. When assignments were passed out, at the end of the training at Nellis, they were as crews – to Takhli or Korat RTAFB, Thailand. In the later years of the Vietnam War, this concept began to be violated, for many reasons. I don't believe it was ever proven to be detrimental to the point of losing a mixed crew, however.

Some mixing became inevitable when crews undertook new TDYs, without their previous pilot or EWO. Ejections, which were all too common given the high loss rate among Weasels, caused spinal compression injuries that would take an airman away from operations, sometimes permanently. With regard to instructor training and pairings, as Kim Pepperell points out:

The Wild Weasel training conducted at Nellis was strictly for combat-bound crews; there was no training for instructors; and there was no full training done elsewhere. Instructors were all combat-experienced WW crewmembers. Actually, I remember being very impressed, on my own first day of training, when I learned that! And, since they were physically there to teach, that meant that they had completed their combat tours successfully, which couldn't help but add to their credibility. After my own first two tours, I can remember experiencing a certain amount of respect myself, from the crews I taught.

Once on operations, air and ground crews had considerable input over ideas for aircraft modifications, and liaised with the field representatives from the major electronic warfare kit suppliers that endured with the Wild Weasel community for decades later. One such update for the Weasels was the 'Bauman Mod', developed and implemented by maintenance technician Cpl Weldon Bauman in the field. Previously, aircraft might receive several strobes and the SEE-SAMs 'Oh sh**!' light going off simultaneously, but which site was tracking them personally? Bauman's home-made circuit board, when activated, correlated the signals being picked up by both the RHAWS and LWR. As the signal PRFs from a given site's guidance and TTR radars were synchronized, when they matched (with a known offset) it could be

EWO Kim Pepperell entitled this portrait 'Go to hell'. (Kim Pepperell)

deduced to be that particular Fan Song van. The circuitry then cleared the scope of all information except that for the launching site, allowing Weasel crews to respond appropriately and rapidly. It also provided audio alert, which crews relied upon most.

Additional avionics upgrades followed throughout the campaign years, from more formal channels. For example, under TO 1F-105F-540 the Loral-built AN/ALR-31 replaced the SEE-SAMs unit, offering improved reliability and reception via dedicated antennae built into the wing-tips.

New electronic 'chain-mail' was also being fielded for use. The GE QRC-160-8 jamming pod, designated the AN/ALQ-87 and housing four magnetron-based jammers, was introduced into combat from late 1967. Like the AN/ALQ-71 it was designed to thwart SAM radars, but yielded some additional features. The first was a sweep modulator that could introduce bursts of reinforcing noise in the Pulse-power Mode. This created automated 'blinking' jamming, which in formation use would cause the target return on the enemy radar to shift about, making individual aircraft targeting (even when using radar burn-through or track-on jam) very hard to accomplish, provided crews adhered to the already prescribed sliced-diamond formation patterns.

It also introduced the more effective Beacon Mode, which jammed the SAM's down-link positional beacon that enabled the radar operator to follow the missile and ensure it was on course and make steering corrections, thereby effectively thwarting the SAM's command guidance. Although Weasels seldom relied on jamming, because of its harmful effects on their sensitive receivers at close quarters, it was carried for self-defence purposes in case of a SAM launch. Apparently, of 495 reported SAM launches against Beacon Mode-equipped jets in late 1967 and early 1968, only three found their mark, and two of the pilots concerned were using the TTR noise-jamming mode instead of Beacon Mode when they were hit. By March 1968 the AN/ALQ-87 pod had become mandatory equipment for all strike aircraft operating over RP VI.

Embarrassed a little by the US Navy's ability to fly and fight at night in its A-6s during the winter monsoon season, the US Air Force further adapted F-105F WW-III aircraft into what became known by the crews as Ryan's Raiders, for solo night-time deep interdiction taskings, using more finely tuned R-14 radar ground-map settings. The project was initiated in March 1967 by its unofficial namesake, Gen John D. Ryan as Operation Northscape (later Commando Nail) and subsequently became inseparable from the Wild Weasels, as the aircraft could swing-role between night-time harassment interdiction and daytime anti-radar work. In the end, although highly successful in their own right, the Ryan's Raiders' bomb-nav system simply wasn't up to the job of locating anything other than highly radar-significant targets, such as railroads, bridges and other major structures. To bust SAM sites, for example, the bomb-nav system would need to be linked to the sensitive radar receivers, an accurate INS added, and the crew given accurately plotted SAM locations.

A concept called the Bistatic Aided Strike System attempted to achieve this the following year by vectoring Weasels and Ryan's Raiders on to radar targets picked up by specially modified EC-121K Rivet Top monitoring aircraft (by means of a transponder on each of four rerigged

F-105Fs, which was triggered when an enemy SAM came on the air), but it proved to be of limited success as the EC-121K kept losing track of the F-105F and the North Vietnamese quickly wised up to the concept. Col Gerry Knotts, an EWO with the 44th TFS 'Vampires', flew on one of these missions:

> The EC-121 would pick up an EW radar signal and portray what the ground operator saw on the airborne display, and then relay target position to us. If you could do that, you could see where the guy was, so we conjured up a little programme whereby if we could find him, we could knock him out. Those EW radars were the ones doing the 'heads up' for the SAM sites, so we worked with the battleship USS *New Jersey* and a couple of destroyers, using chess game callsigns. The mission was eight Wild Weasel '105s, some strikers, and over the water, right over *New Jersey*, the EC-121s got two ground targets. We 'got' the target and I called out 'Checkmate' – which means we've got it – and *New Jersey* was firing its guns; but the second time I called 'Checkmate', it was all over.

The North Vietnamese defences caught the scent of Weasels on the wind and shut down, and indeterminate damage was inflicted by the USS *New Jersey*'s guns. Though it was probably highly effective as a one-off, the programme was shelved.

Total F-105 Thunderchief losses to hostile fire over North Vietnam amounted to an unpalatable 54 in 1966 and 103 in 1967. Crews joked that none of them would achieve their 100-mission counters unscathed, as statistics demonstrated that they would be shot down by their sixtieth mission. This had a ring of truth in it for the Weasels, who were flying night-time Ryan's Raiders' missions, supporting daytime strike packages of F-105s and F-4s and also performing occasional search-and-destroy missions. Almost every mission was challenging. In theory, crews were supposed to start out with less demanding missions and work up gradually to deep strikes over the more heavily defended RP VIA, but the continual shortage of Weasels afforded them no such luxuries.

EWO Maj Francis Lee 'T.R.' Marino USAF (Ret) teamed up with Larry Matthew in 63-8320 *The Troll* (eventually a triple-MiG killer, one of them credited to a MiG flying into the F-105F's jettisoned bomb rack when flying with the name *Cooter* painted on its flank):

> [When] I got to South-East Asia the wings had figured out that the first ten missions in combat were the most dangerous for new crews. The New Guy Syndrome. So we were supposed to fly our first ten missions in increasing threat levels. That worked fine for some. For me, the first mission was a blur. It was a fairly low-threat target, and the element leader briefed us on our way to the ramp. It was short and simple. He said, 'When I go down, you go down and beat me down and when I go up, you go up and you beat me up'. And we did. As for the mission itself, I really only knew where I was twice. First when we took off and second when we landed; and I wasn't really sure about the second place at first. You see, things went a little

tumbleweed when our flight lead took a hit and had to crash-land at NKP [Nakhon Phantom AB]. The next mission was better, but then on the third mission we ended up going as no. 2 to the Hanoi area. So much for your first ten missions in relatively low-threat areas!

Weasel support tactics, described by many former F-105 crewmen as 'nobody knew what the hell to do to begin with', also varied between the two Thailand-based F-105 wings, and took over a year to evolve from the WW-III's introduction. Pilots and EWOs were being lost before anybody had got a hold on the best tactics, resulting in a continual influx of relatively inexperienced crewmen.

TROLLING

The 388th TFW at Korat RTAFB placed great reliance on the latest jamming pods for mutual flight protection, ingressing beyond the reach of triple-A at around 20,000ft, and tasked support flights of Wild Weasels from its dedicated Iron Hand and Ryan's Raiders unit, the 13th TFS (redesignated the 44th TFS on 20 October 1967), to knock out the missiles and radars in support of all 388th TFW strike activities. The chief tactic that emerged, and which was later adopted by the broader spread of Takhli RTAFB crews, was called trolling. Conjured up by 388th TFW boss Lt Col (later Maj Gen) James E. McInerney with the approval of 388th TFW Director of Operations Col 'Scrappy' Johnson and Wing boss Col Bill Chairsell, the idea was to free the Weasel flights from the main strike formations and let them move ahead into the target area as soon as they were off the tankers. This had two advantages. First, the Weasels would not have their sniffing receivers degraded by any close-quarters friendly jamming. As one retired officer put it: 'The RHAW gear was not desensitized to the pods. If the pod was turned on, the RHAW gear would go berserk, completely useless. It took some tactical decision-making right there in the flight: do we jam or do we listen?'

The second advantage was that it gave them a 35–40-mile head start, so that they arrived at the target 5–7 minutes ahead of the strike force, to locate the SAM sites electronically and visually and attack any that came on the air. This decreasingly became the case on the first pass as the North Vietnamese recognized the nature of the advance party, and sometimes sent up MiGs instead. The Weasels would then take a diving turn out of the target area and chandelle up behind the strike force, preparing to lob Shrikes in loft mode and roll in with bombs and cannon fire the moment any Fan Song radars became active – which tended to happen chiefly when the main strike waves were rolling in on the target, and were thus at their most vulnerable. Any sites foolish enough to maintain a radar lock on a strike jet were struck.

The Weasels then trolled again in another sweeping figure-of-eight as the strike force egressed the target area, giving rise to the Weasel motto: 'First In, Last Out'. Remaining more or less constantly on station in this fashion was hugely successful in keeping the enemy radar operators quiet, but it did expose the Weasels to enemy MiGs, as MiGCAP cover was with the main strike wave. The lead time was thus later reduced to provide greater MiGCAP coverage for the Weasels, while a second Weasel flight was added to the main strike wave in case those first in got hammered.

At Takhli RTAFB, by contrast, the pioneering 354th TFS detachment was expanded and parcelled out among all three 355th TFW squadrons to create additional Weasel flights within the 333rd TFS 'Redleg Lancers' and 357th TFS 'Licking Dragons'. 'We thought, and I think rightly so, that it was better to have Weasels in each squadron, so we could spread the word and have direct daily contact with the strike guys,' remembers 'T.R.' Marino. All three 355th TFW squadrons adopted low-level ingress tactics and terrain masking to maximum effect, using the pop-up manoeuvre – a climb, followed by a dive on to the target, then egress at speed with afterburner engaged – while over hostile skies. Actual Weasel tactics, however, were essentially similar to those employed by the 388th TFW. 'T.R.' describes their mission:

[We were] playing 'Here, kitty kitty' with the cat, the SAMs and guns. The trick was not to end up as cat food. Weasels were usually 'First In, Last Out', and that's not just a brass balls bar motto. There were usually four and sometimes, but not often, eight in support of a normal strike package. Weasels were always in pretty short supply. The four-ship was really two two-ship elements that worked fairly independently of each other but still provided indirect support to each other while providing direct support to the strikers. After we crossed into bad guy country, the Weasels would 'green 'em up' [select stores and engage the master arm] and start to 'push it up' [advance throttles], so as to be a few minutes ahead of the strike package. We also started our tactical split and jinking at this time.

The two elements were usually about 1–1½ miles apart and the element would be spread 3,000–6,000ft. As I remember, this changed after we started to carry ECM pods. But each mission was different depending on the threats briefed by Intel. Basically, the Weasels put a black line on the charts because we had to. But once we were engaged the 'black line' went out the window and we spent our time trying to keep our nose pointed at the threat and us between the threat and the strikers, so we could get off a Shrike as needed. Sometimes just pointing at the SAMs would be enough to get them to go down. That was nice, but it didn't always work out that way.

We stayed in the target area, maintaining this relative position to the strike flight and the threat and then followed the strikers out to cover their 'six'. But you have to understand, our mission was to cover the strikers and we positioned ourselves where we could accomplish this best, as dictated by the known threat. It was the pop-up threats that moved the night before and [which] we didn't know about that really made life interesting.

We didn't always fly escort missions. Sometimes we flew hunter/killer missions, usually two- or sometimes four-ship missions where we just went out looking for trouble. We would have an assigned area to work and anything was fair game in these free-fire areas. The formation spacing was basically the same as on the escort mission, but we were not given any specific target and went where our nose took us. Most Weasel crews had a personal target folder where we tracked areas of unusual electronic or photographic activity, and this is where we usually ended up. At night, things were different. We flew two-ship elements to the tanker but went into bad-guy country *single-ship* with specific areas to work and sometimes specific flights to support. We flew blacked out, so there was no way to fly formations of any sort. We knew where the other member of the element was supposed to be and worked using the 'big sky, little airplane' theory. When our assigned support/patrol time was up we recovered single-ship unless we regrouped on the tanker, then we would recover as an element.

HIGHLY DECORATED WEASELS

Some of the most legendary missions flown by the F-105F Weasels were undertaken in the spring of 1967 by 355th TFW crews. On 10 March 354th TFS veteran pilot Capt Merlyn Hans Dethlefsen was flying his seventy-eighth mission as Lincoln Three with EWO Capt Kevin 'Mike' Gilroy (in F-105F 63-8352), bound for the Thai Nguyen steel mill and industrial complex, one of the more lucrative targets in North Vietnam and appropriately defended. Dethlefsen and the flight leader were each paired off with a regular, bomb-toting F-105 in the customary manner, divided into two flights of two separated by about a mile in trail, coming in at 1,500ft and popping up as they approached the target to acquire the SAM sites. Lincoln One (Maj David Everson and Capt Jose David Luna in 63-8335) met a barrage of flak during their dive, which brought the aircraft down as they loosed off a Shrike. This missed its target, but the two managed to eject successfully.

In the frenzy of triple-A fire and with his headphones concussing with SAM signals and ejection bleepers, the leader's wingman was forced to break off his attack, his own aircraft peppered with 200 holes from gunfire and shrapnel. This left just Dethlefsen and Gilroy, plus Lincoln Four (Maj Kenneth Bell), to knock out the threats. As Capt Gilroy had already located a SAM site at about 2 miles out on their first pass, they elected to go in again – something crews seldom did as the triple-A had already been warmed-up and would find its mark, and on this occasion it was so heavy that it presented few openings. As they lined up for a weapons pass, two MiG-21s began closing on them. Dethlefsen loosed off his first Shrike against the radar, then broke hard right, down through the flak, to evade the MiGs' AA-2 Atoll heat-seeking AAMs and cannon fire about to greet them from the rear quarters. The MiGs elected not to enter the flak barrage.

As he lined up for a third pass against the SAM sites, another two MiGs appeared, and this time Dethlefsen broke hard left, back down into the triple-A again. Standard procedure was to jettison stores and hug the treetops in an afterburner-assisted escape manoeuvre, but Dethlefsen kept his ordnance despite receiving 57mm shrapnel in the left wing-tip and

aircraft belly and hearing over the radio that the main strike wave had already done its job and was outbound. The favourable weather and working hydraulics convinced him to continue his attack. A second SAM site came up on the air with a three-ringer on the RHAWS, dead ahead of them. It shut down soon after the remaining Shrike was fired and impacted, so Dethlefsen and Gilroy turned their attention once again to the first site, which duly received a stick of CBUs smack on top, followed by a spray of 20mm cannon fire. Remarkably, Maj Bell was still on their wing, despite his F-105D having taken hits in its ailerons, which limited it to turns to the right.

Both made the tanker outbound from the target, returning to Takhli RTAFB where their aircraft were patched up again by the Rapid Aircraft Maintenance men, and the crews rested. Capt Dethlefsen was decorated with the Medal of Honor for his tenacity, while Capt Gilroy received the Air Force Cross. A lesser crew might have gone home after seeing their flight lead go down, or jettisoned their weapons when the MiGs appeared, or even hidden behind the radar shield of Thud Ridge. Dethlefsen, however, made a good situation out of an appalling one: the three men had braved five passes amid ninety triple-A pieces in damaged jets to set the SAM sites ablaze. As for the MiGs, they also did not go unscathed.

Weasel F-105s taxi back to their revetments, showing their stalky undercarriage when lightly loaded. Compare this stance with some of the heavy ARM configurations flown, see page 137. (Frank B. Mormillo)

That same day, 355th TFW F-105D pilot Capt Max C. Brestel downed a pair of MiG-17s to become the first twin MiG-killer of the war.

The second famed Weasel Medal of Honor and Air Force Cross mission occurred six weeks later. On 19 April 357th TFS crew Maj Leo K. Thorsness and his EWO Capt Harold E. Johnson, short of only a few mission counters to bring their tour to an end, launched as Carbine One (F-105F 63-8301), one of four aircraft bound for the Xuan Mai army barracks and storage supply area 30 miles south-west of Hanoi, on the edge of the rice-paddied Red River Delta. Thorsness directed Carbine Three and Carbine Four to hook in from north of the target while he and his wingman came up from the south, to cause confusion among the enemy gunners. A Shrike was fired against a strong signal at 7 miles out, resulting in the radar being silenced. A second site was located visually and Thorsness dived at it steeply, depositing CBUs dead on top before pulling out amidst heavy triple-A fire. Egressing at treetop level, it was clear that Carbine Two (63-8341), flown by Tom Madison and EWO Tom Sterling, had been hit in its engine by triple-A fire. The subsequent rescue beeper sounding through everyone's headphones on Guard frequency indicated that they had ejected.

Undaunted, Thorsness and Johnson fired their final Shrike at a third site and remained in the area, circling Madison's and Sterling's descending parachutes, to provide covering fire pending the arrival of rescue forces. Carbine Three and Carbine Four, low on fuel and with inoperative afterburners, had already exited the target area after tangling with MiGs, which now turned on Thorsness and Johnson as they radioed co-ordinates to Crown, the rescue control aircraft. Johnson spotted a MiG off their left wing. Uncertain whether it was about to shoot his wingmen, Thorsness dropped down 1,000ft and got behind the MiG, hosing 20mm cannon shells at it at ½ mile and 550kt, and closing rapidly for a second burst. Fortunately, the shells missed – had the jet disintegrated the debris would have been unavoidable and would have crippled the F-105 – but the cannon fire had the desired effect of making the enemy run.

Meanwhile Johnson, all the time rubber-necking on the lookout for missiles and fighters, noted another pair of MiGs closing on their rear quarters. The crew disengaged and sped towards the nearest tanker, topped up and headed back into the fray again, in time to provide cover for the A-1s, which would fly in ahead of a rescue helicopter to suppress small-arms fire at the pick-up point. Three MiGs were spotted initially, one of them haplessly drifting into Thorsness's gunsight at 700yd range for a good shoot, resulting in pieces falling off the MiG. A further four MiGs were spotted closing in on their rear. With six angry MiGs after them, Thorsness and Johnson had no choice but to engage the afterburner and race away through the mountain passes to shake them off. However, when the MiGs turned on the A-1s, in desperation Thorsness bore in again to act as MiG-magnet, despite being 'Winchester' (out of ammunition), and instructed the A-1s to keep turning hard so as to keep out of the enemy fighters' gunsights.

Relief arrived just in time in the form of another flight of F-105s, these claiming four more probables before the evening. However, the intense enemy triple-A fire and MiG presence meant the rescue was called off,

Madison and Sterling eventually being captured. Also, one A-1 had been downed. One of the F-105 pilots had also lost sight of his flight and was down to about 800lb of fuel, so Thorsness cajoled a tanker north in time to top it up. Terribly low on fuel himself, Thorsness headed for the nearest base, Udorn, and with 70 miles to go pulled the throttles back to idle, gliding back down with empty on the fuel gauges as the runway loomed into view! Sadly, Maj Thorsness and Capt Johnson never made it to the end of their tour. On 30 April (in F-105F 62-4447), on their ninety-second mission, they became entangled with MiGs over RP V and were downed. They ejected and were taken prisoner, surviving captivity.

Trolling pioneer Lt Col James McInerney and his EWO Capt Fred Shannon each received the Air Force Cross for their SAM-busting support during attacks on the Paul Doumer Bridge on 11 August 1967; McInerney's flight knocked out six SAM sites and damaged two others. Part of the success of the strike lay in some of the attackers using M118 3,000lb bombs fitted with daisy-cutter fuse extenders. The sheer explosive power of these bombs sent out shock waves that knocked out gunners' eardrums or set them ringing for up to ½ mile around the target, considerably reducing the effectiveness of the triple-A. Kim Pepperell remembers using M118s on some missions and remarked that 'it took the strength of both crewmen pulling back on both sticks to avoid hitting the ground during a dive if such a bomb became hung on the wing'.

Mustering together Weasel flights proved problematic on many occasions, owing to the high loss rate among the units and turnover of

Eglin's test force in Florida trialled much of the new countermeasures and Weasel gear, including the QRC-335-cum-AN/ALQ-101 noise/deception jammer, shown on this Armament Division F-4D. The aircraft is also equipped with Bendix AN/APS-107 receivers, which were intended to enable it to undertake Wild Weasel tasks. However, technical problems in matching the system with the Phantom II meant it was never utilised in that role. (Westinghouse)

surviving crews. 'First In, Last Out' meant hanging about in hostile airspace for up to 3hr on RESCAPs if anyone was brought down, which happened all too often. Weasel strength sometimes dipped to as few as five crews and aircraft between the two bases, and at any one time seldom exceeded more than fifteen aircraft, including those grounded for repairs. The long and bloody Rolling Thunder confrontation with North Vietnam's air defences in 1967 was extremely costly. A total of 1,322 Shrikes were expended that year, but losses now amounted to twenty-six Wild Weasel aircraft and forty-two crewmen shot down.[8] Perversely, this danger element cultivated a new pride. Aided by their specialized training, the Weasels had become an institution; and while the US Navy continued to use the term Iron Hand for defence suppression activity, in US Air Force circles it had become Weaseling.

Altogether, by early 1968 American Iron Hand crews had racked-up eighty-nine North Vietnamese SAM sites destroyed with another sixty-eight damaged, most of these knocked into submission by the Weasels. However, in common with the US Navy the Weasels yearned for greater anti-radar punch, to mitigate the very heavy loss rate.

T H R E E

ENTER THE STANDARD ARM

At the end of March 1968, as US ground troops were thwarting the Viet Cong Tet Offensive – so named because it had been initiated on the Chinese Lunar New Year on 30 January – in South Vietnam, and US Marines were repelling a siege by North Vietnamese regulars at Khe Sanh near the DMZ, President Johnson ordered a halt to bombing north of the 20th Parallel, in an effort to induce North Vietnam's leaders to return to the Paris peace table. While Hanoi agreed to begin discussions, it continued to pour over 20,000 troops across the border into South Vietnam every month. As a result, the United States doubled its air operations south of the 20th Parallel, concentrating on troop bivouac areas and supplies crossing the DMZ.

Following several months of discussions in Paris, and in deference to new domestic protests, on 31 October President Johnson ordered a complete cessation of the Rolling Thunder campaign. Predictably, the enemy steadily expanded their infiltration routes through neutral Laos, attacking the country in the Plaine des Jarres to establish staging areas and supply depots there, and further afield in Cambodia. US aircrews sent in to interdict these targets knew it as the Barrel Roll area of operations. From here, supplies and troops were trucked or bicycled south through the Laotian panhandle – known to aviators as the Steel Tiger operating area – and thence into South Vietnam, to cause serious mischief.

Laos thus dominated the air war in Vietnam from November 1968, in a fresh series of campaigns formally initiated under the Commando Hunt banner, designed to stem the tide. Sensors that detected trucks' ignition systems or ground vibration, and even 'people-sniffers', were systematically seeded along known infiltration routes under the Igloo White effort, the signals from which were processed by a big mainframe computer and its staff at Nakhon Phanom in Thailand, after being intercepted by ground-based and airborne sentinels. US Navy and Air Force strikes were then launched, around the clock, in an attempt to strike trucks, ammunition caches and troop staging areas along these supply routes. Coordination of these strikes (to ensure some accuracy while preserving deconfliction) was provided via Lockheed EC-130 Airborne Command and Control Center (ABCCC) Hercules, and by Forward Air Controllers (FAC) patrolling the target areas on the lookout for the obvious. To the aircrews, it became known as the Trails War: a relentless campaign against nondescript targets hidden amid sheer limestone outcrops shrouded by a jungle canopy, presenting hazardous flying conditions by night.

Yet enemy defences were far from unsophisticated. At four key bottle-necks in the mountainous karst leading from Laos into South Vietnam (Barthelemy and Ban Karai in the south, and the Mu Gia and Nape passes further north) the North Vietnamese rapidly began to field triple-A, brought in piece by piece and reassembled on hillsides and rocky crags. In addition, in the absence of air attacks within the main SAM belts around Thanh Hoa, Hanoi and Haiphong from late 1968, they were at liberty to begin spreading out their SAM coverage to encompass this border region, steadily placing US aircraft at greater risk. By November 1969 the established concentration of defences around Vinh had been extended to the Nape Pass, and by early January the following year a SAM site in Dong Hoi was covering Ban Karai. Triple-A 85mm and 100mm guns were also fielded, which were able to reach high-altitude bombers from locations where SAMs could not be easily sited.

Vietnam air operations became a frustrating melting-pot of men and *matériel*, handled by sensor-sowers, bombers and specially rigged gunships. US Air Force crews flew their mandatory tours of combat, US Navy crews their WESTPAC combat cruises, operating with the enthusiasm and camaraderie borne of flying fast jets to bind them together in what many were beginning to see as a mere testing ground for new equipment, such as smart bombs and targeting sensors, in an otherwise never-ending endeavour. However, much was in the offing to enable air power to protect its own.

STARM A-6 INTRUDERS

Helping to monitor the radar threats and kill them if necessary was a new breed of ARM, two years in the making, which arrived at the tail-end of the Rolling Thunder bombing campaign over downtown North Vietnam. Although Shrike was effective at keeping heads down, it had several fundamental limitations. First, its seeker offered only limited reception capabilities, resulting in a variety of alternative seeker heads to cater for different needs. Moreover, it had to be fired precisely at the target. Thus, if an aircraft was carrying a 'round peg' version and needed to slam it into a 'square hole' radar, or if it was fired off-axis from the emitter, it would not do the trick, even if it was otherwise functional.

Secondly, Shrike was range-limited, invariably obliging crews to enter the SAM-radar envelope they were attacking, placing them in great peril. Its top speed was such that, given the short time enemy TTRs remained on the air for a missile launch, it often proved incapable of reaching the dish and thereby denying guidance to the enemy before the quicker SAM had attempted to do its deed. Allied to this, Shrike was reliant on the enemy radar remaining on the air; once the radar had reverted to stand-by or dummy load, Shrike lost all sense of direction and went ballistic. Finally, in the early days there was no means of assessing Shrike's effectiveness reliably or of tracking where the ARM had struck. Hunter/killer F-105D pilot Ed Rasimus sums the situation up:

Back in '66, the big issue with the Weasels was Shrike hit validation. We yearned for a flare in the tail (as was used on the AGM-12B Bullpup control-guided air-to-surface missile) for tracking after firing. We were directed, when tactically possible, to roll a wingman back behind the firing aircraft who was to accelerate and attempt to follow the missile visually to see where it went. This proved virtually impossible and impacts usually couldn't be seen due to the small warhead.

These shortcomings created South-East Asia Operational Requirement 52, resulting in Project 304A: the comparatively massive, 1,370lb, longer-range AGM-78 Standard ARM, based on a marriage between the US Navy's shipborne General Dynamics RIM-66 Standard SAM and a passive anti-radiation seeker. To US Navy crews it was often referred to simply as STARM. Development was rapid, with a start-up lot of 224 contracted by Naval Air Systems Command (NASC) to General Dynamics' Pomona Division in fiscal year 1967, resulting in initial batches reaching the Fleet and USAF F-105F Wild Weasels as early as February 1968.

Several Mod 0 subvariants entered service swiftly that year. The original AGM-78A-1 repackaged the Dash 3A Shrike guidance section with a movable seeker in the new missile, effectively creating a 40-mile range

Standard ARM AGM-78 general arrangement. (US Navy)

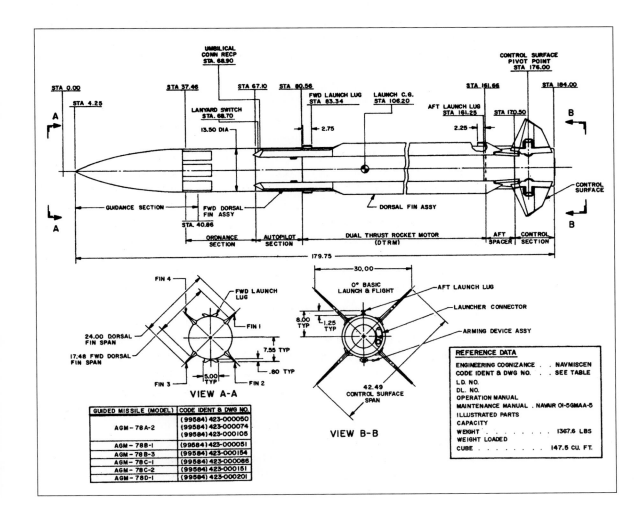

Shrike with a 215lb warhead, 'four times the size but not much better'.[1] This was quickly superseded by the AGM-78A-2, offering a crucial Bomb Damage Assessment (BDA) capability and a red phosphorous target marker, allowing the associated SAM site to be readily identified and mopped up with bombs or rockets. This offered more serious prospects. .

Concurrent with Standard ARM development, in the autumn of 1966 the Chief of Naval Operations settled upon the A-6 Intruder as the platform for the new missile, and work began in some haste at Grumman Calverton the following year on modifying ten A-6As drawn from Fleet service. The first example, BuNo. 149957, was handed back to the US Navy on 22 August 1967.[2] Modifications included the Bendix AN/APS-107A (or later B model) to provide a general picture of threat status and bearing by means of directional strobes and the ATI ER-142, which furnished signals analysis and direction-finding for ARM launch.[3] Other new equipment included a target range and bearing computer, BDA unit and missile control assembly. To make room for the new black boxes, the A-6A's DIANE was stripped of its ballistics computer and tracking radar, thereby removing the aircraft's all-weather bombing capability. In fact, the modified aircraft shared so little in common with the basic A-6A that NAVAIR 13100 was issued by the NASC office in October 1967, directing that the type be redesignated A-6B Mod 0.

The A-6B Mod 0 weapons load was always symmetric and typically comprised two STARMs on the inboard pylons, attached via hefty LAU-77 rails, with the outboard pylons given over to either Shrikes or bombs. The crew used the radar-receiving apparatus to pick up and head towards (but not necessarily straight at) a desirable radar target and achieve a lock-up with an AGM-78A STARM. Confirming seeker lock-up on the chosen emitter was accomplished by the B/N pressing the correlate button, to gate the threat to be attacked. So long as the missile's choice corresponded with that highlighted in the receiver display, all was ready. With the switches set, the crew were free to lob the STARM and stay in orbit out of range of the enemy SAMs. The missile would zoom to altitude after launch and then descend on to the chosen Fan Song or Fire Can radar.

First to get to grips with the new equipment at Yankee Station was VA-75 on USS *Kitty Hawk*, which launched its first STARM in anger on 6 March 1968, with VA-85 'Black Falcons' on USS *America* and VA-196 on the USS *Constellation* getting into the action close on VA-75's heels. Early attacks were conservative and involved few launches, as VA-196 veteran B/N Philip H. Waters points out:

After my first cruise with VA-196 in 1967, several of us 'experienced' aircrews attended a Standard ARM school in NAS Oceana to learn the A-6B system prior to our 1968 deployment. Only those crews trained in the system would fly the 'Bs, usually covering a bombing strike up north. The original intent was for the A-6B to provide long-range, possibly 30-mile, coverage of the strike group without itself being placed in jeopardy. In reality, things did not work out that way. The North Vietnamese gunners had long since realized the danger in operating their fire-control radars for anything but the briefest amount of time.

Opposite above: A-6B Mod 0s flown by VA-75 'Sunday Punchers' were some of the first Navy jets to employ AGM-78 Standard ARM in anger. The new radar-receiving 'diamonds' are located atop the radome near the in-flight refuelling probe, and on the lower portion of the intake lips. (US Navy)

Opposite below: The Mod 0 cockpit, in this instance BuNo. 149957. Note the new radar warning displays at centre and right, the displays and controls for the ER-142 (located near the right-hand warning indicator) and the console. Crews could programme the AGM-78 to turn to any heading after launch – even 180 degrees to the rear! (Grumman History Center)

The high cost of the ARM prohibited its use unless a kill was pretty much assured. Therefore, the long range of the ARM, and its consequent long flight-time, proved of little use, and the A-6Bs were not utilized much differently from the Shrike A-7s. We were acutely aware of the fact that both our performance and the performance of the Standard ARM were being monitored quite closely, and were hesitant to use them in any way that might cause embarrassment. A bombing halt of the northernmost area of North Vietnam had been declared. This pretty much ended the large Alpha strikes that had characterized a large part of our 1967 cruise. We therefore used the A-6Bs to cover smaller strikes into southern North Vietnam, and single A-6 raids at night.

The audio sound associated with the Fire Can and Fan Song fire-control radars was usually present when near or over the beach. However, only the L-Band guidance radar was a positive indicator that an SA-2 was on its way in your direction. The North Vietnamese would sometimes 'play the L-Band' at a strike group, which originally had quite an unnerving effect on your performance, especially in determining where your bombs might fall. When we caught on to the fact that L-Band [sound] did not necessarily mean an SA-2 had been launched, we became less acrobatic while maintaining our vigilance.[4] I also believe the North Vietnamese gunners soon learnt that the lone Navy aircraft lurking behind an A-6 bomber or flying a racetrack pattern just off the beach while other jets conducted ARREC was not to be trifled with, as the threat radars would consistently shut down as soon as we pointed in their direction. This, of course, provided some respite for the bombers, but deprived us of any opportunity to try out the ARM as we dearly wanted to.

I can recall only one firing of an ARM on our cruise. Lt Gary Koch and Lt (jg) Dick Little were flying shotgun for one or more A-6s working on the nightly truck traffic when an SA-2 was suddenly launched in their general direction, either directly at their A-6B or at one of the other aircraft. As Gary later told the story he simply lowered the nose and launched the ARM right down the throat of the SAM site. The missiles passed each other in mid-flight, with the ARM arriving first. Upon ARM detonation the SAM immediately went out of control, confirming the kill of the guidance radar. As exhilarating as this was, the same results would probably have been achieved with a Shrike, at much lower cost.

However, STARM was far less fussy than Shrike and crews could dial in a heading to target before launching the missile anywhere up to 180 degrees off-axis. Phil Waters said:

The Standard ARM had several different launch modes depending on launch circumstances, which made it more flexible than Shrike. It could be programmed to turn to a certain bearing after launch and then seek to acquire the target. The B/N had absolutely no control of the ARM after launch, but if it had been locked on to a radar that subsequently shut down, it would continue to guide to the last known location of the radar, which might not ensure a hit, but was an improvement over Shrike which would then have gone its own way.

Stan Walker, another VA-196 1968 A-6B combat veteran, added: 'We generally flew cover at about 22,000ft. Occasionally the North Vietnamese would send a stream of conventional anti-aircraft fire up to our altitude, just to distract us. It is very likely they did that when they considered firing an SA-2 at one of the lower aircraft.' Lt Cdr Bud White noted that the North Vietnamese appeared to know their carrier launch-cycles. Radars would shut down when they knew the A-6Bs were up, and would be turned on again once the cycle had ended. Double cycles were introduced on occasion, 'and when the radars came up on schedule, we had plenty of targets'.

Immediately after Ramjet (the US Navy call used to signify a STARM launch), crews would enter the evaluation phase of their attack, and monitor missile and radar site simultaneously for BDA purposes. This was made possible by a radar pulse repeater housed in the dorsal fin of the STARM, and an allied receiver display set in the cockpit. The repeater retransmitted the target's signals being picked up by the seeker as a coded homing echo at the same PRF. If the radar shut down in response to the missile during flight, a pre-set no-homing signal was sent out instead. In essence, this allowed the B/N to track the target on his radar receivers while monitoring the missile's progress on the BDA repeater display.

One of four target damage assessments could thus be deduced when the signal from the missile ceased, which would happen the moment it had impacted something. First was the best case, or a Hit Indicator, resulting from the homing signal and radar transmission ceasing simultaneously. Obviously, a miss would be scored if the missile went dead but the radar was still active. But two other BDA judgements could also be made. If only a no-homing signal was received throughout Ramjet flight, it could be assumed that the STARM never successfully tracked the victim radar and had just gone ballistic and flown into the ground somewhere (no acquisition). If the STARM switched from a homing to a no-homing repeater signal, then it was not tracking the target just before impact (loss of acquisition), and so it was debatable whether or not the missile had smashed the dish, or was a possible.

Whereas Shrike launches invariably produced unknown results, with a replaceable trashed dish often being the best case, crews were expected to report the BDA results from each and every STARM launch in consider-able detail, especially in the early days, as a direct hit from its bigger warhead meant that the enemy would most likely have to replace the whole Fan Song trailer wagon.

However, there were losses. The desire of A-6B Iron Hand aviators to press home their attacks while on escort duties within reach of the Vinh SAM arrays soon created a plucky game in which timing became crucial. Two A-6B Mod 0s were lost in August 1968. The first went down during an otherwise routine sortie, unattributed to hostile fire. The second (BuNo. 151561) from USS *America*'s VA-85 'Black Falcons', was lost on the 29th of the month. Lt (jg) R.R. Duncan and Lt (jg) A.R. Ashall were flying night-time support in Buckeye 521 over the city of Vinh Son in RP III.

The last tragic radio crackle to be heard from them was that they were under attack from at least three SAMs – the missiles were invariably fired in twos or threes. The sites at Vinh and Vinh Son were known to be operated by some particularly wily North Vietnamese operators, who obviously employed deadly timing. An intensive RESCAP operation was initiated, but to no avail. It was later reported that two A-7 pilots a few miles away saw two SAMs detonate high in the night sky, followed by an explosion on the ground which they believed to be the third SAM. In all likelihood it was the A-6B, and the crew were subsequently listed as MIA.

By March 1969 the follow-on AGM-78B Mod 1 STARM had been introduced. This awesome weapon used a digital interface with the aircraft and employed a brand-new Broad Band Maxson seeker, offering sensitivity in the E–G and I Bands, to render it effective against some surveillance and GCI radars as well as Fan Song. It also featured a memory circuit, so that it would continue to fly to the emitter's previously known location even if the operator shut down his radar. The definitive AGM-78A-4 Mod 0 model also offered this capability, though it lacked BDA, having been based on updated early missile stocks.

The fielding of this more versatile STARM saw the A-6B Mod 0's radar-receiving kit further modified under AFC 193, after which time they were referred to as Mod 0-Update A-6Bs. No further losses were incurred until October 1971, when an A-6B Mod 0-Update was lost to unknown causes – often the case for solo, night-time attackers – leaving an inventory of only seven of these valuable aircraft. However, numbers were made good by two additional A-6B subvariants, designed to employ the AGM-78B Mod 1 STARM from the outset, which propped up Fleet numbers.

A-6B PAT/ARM

First on the scene was the A-6B Passive Angle Tracking, Anti-Radiation Missile (PAT/ARM), which was a rather different breed. With the introduction of the Mod 1 STARM's broad signal reception capabilities coupled to the weapon's movable seeker, John Hopkins' APL in Maryland suggested a modification which would use two or more directions of arrival of signals from an emitter acquired by the missile to triangulate its position and compute an 'in range' firing cue. There would be no additional receiver equipment installed in the aircraft beyond its normal Shoehorn package, just a couple of black boxes to help DIANE compute target position and the B/N to determine STARM status, seeker look angle and to conduct BDA. PAT/ARM was subsequently installed in three A-6As (BuNos 155628–155630), the first of which was test-flown by Al Quinby and A.J. Beck on 28 August 1968, and all three were accepted by the US Navy by 13 June 1969. Externally, they were indistinguishable from the FY 1967 A-6As from which they had been adapted.

The employment of PAT/ARM was straightforward. On picking up a signal, the STARM seeker would slew in the direction of the radar and the crew would obtain a preliminary lock-up and note the prospective target's bearing; by turning the aircraft towards it and obtaining a final lock-up, a second azimuth was obtained, thus permitting the system to triangulate

the enemy emitter's location. The onboard Shoehorn gear assisted this process, principally by means of determining approximate enemy radar bearing and status. Lock-up could be achieved off-axis from the target, and the missile even fired in that manner, to maximize surprise.

STARM could thus be launched at any time after the aircraft had come within optimum firing range, which varied with its relative look angle and aircraft altitude. With target position computed, DIANE would provide target steering information on the pilot's VDI and the B/N's radarscope, and this could be used to dial in a heading for STARM, to provide steering for a Shrike delivery, or for a bomb pass if the target could be sighted on radar or visually.

The A-6B PAT/ARM's inaugural cruise was in 1969, when two embarked with VA-85 aboard USS *Constellation*. There was little for them to hit given the lull in activity, but operational techniques were refined. The aircraft's peculiar alternating landward/seaward orbits over the beach while on the prowl for radar prey, coupled with its own search radar beaming away, were sufficient to warn any cautious SAM radar operator of impending destruction. As a result, no aircraft were lost while directly

A freshly reworked PAT/ARM A-6B Intruder at Grumman's Long Island plant, complete with inert Standard ARM missile for pre-acceptance flight trials. The aircraft relied on the AGM-78B's passive receiver to derive target position and a firing solution. (Grumman History Center)

supported by the A-6B PAT/ARM aircraft, but no SAM sites were destroyed either. It was the typical A-6B 'Mexican stand-off'.

The A-6B PAT/ARM made its second combat cruise with Cdr F.M. Backman's VA-165 'Boomers', assigned to CVW-9 on USS *America*, flying five Line Periods of Action at Yankee Station during 1970, beginning in late May. The squadron's activities that year paint a representative picture of CTF-77 Iron Hand operations during the bombing halt, when attention shifted to the Trails War. The weather played a key role, keeping the enemy in their revetments and underground, while the paucity of radar-significant targets (compared with industrialized Hanoi and Haiphong) made navigation and target acquisition extremely challenging. However, this deployment made greater use of the A-6B PAT/ARM in ancillary roles.

Command of VA-165's two A-6B PAT/ARM aircraft (one had been made available to the unit at NAS Whidbey Island, prior to embarkation) passed to Cdr R.A. Zick on 9 June 1970, operating in company with three standard A-6As (used mostly for buddy refuelling operations) and eight of the experimental A-6C Trails, Roads Interdiction Multisensor (TRIM) cupola-equipped aircraft, which were making their combat debut as the world's first fast jets equipped with optronic sensors for night vision.[5]

Operations were almost exclusively in the Steel Tiger area, interdicting enemy supply convoys. The squadron's nineteen aircrews flew the noon–midnight cycle, with daytime sorties comprising mostly Commando Nail interdiction missions if the weather was bad; if the weather was

A VA-165 'Boomers' PAT/ARM A-6B is readied for a combat outing, including Mk82 general purpose iron bombs and an AGM-78B Standard ARM. The latter features a big protective cover over the radome. The cover was removed before flight and several former Iron Hand pilots and B/Ns kept them as souvenirs. (US Navy)

good, they were directed by FACs to targets such as truck parks, storage areas and river fords.

Night-time missions comprised Commando Bolt and ARREC sorties, which were more free-ranging and made use of the A-6C's AMTI and TRIM capabilities. Igloo White sensors sown along the Trail to monitor enemy traffic were monitored by the Headshed Task Force ALFA agency, which the A-6C crews would query once in flight. Suspected direction of travel and times were then supplied (via a KY-28 secure radio), assisting the B/Ns in providing a timely rendezvous with the target. They would then employ the A-6C's AMTI capability and Black Crow truck ignition-detecting sensors to help deposit a string of bombs on the suspected enemy vehicles. However, secondary explosions (fuel tanks or munitions erupting in fireballs) were the only sure means by which crews knew that they had hit something worthwhile. Obviously, Low Light Level Television (LLLTV) and Forward-looking Infrared (FLIR) helped a great deal. Truck lights, if active, would shine like beacons in the cockpit display; and crews could pick up their own aircraft carrier from a range of 50 miles! But darkened, camouflaged SAM and triple-A sites were not visible using these first-generation electro-optics.

The A-6C TRIM carried FLIR and LLLTV sensors (linked to Black Crow truck ignition receivers) in the ventral cupola, and the standard Intruder Radar-Bomb-Nav DIANE system for night interdiction along the Ho Chi Minh Trail. These pioneering devices paved the way for today's electro-optic DEAD (Destruction of Enemy Air Defences) aids such as LANTIRN. (Grumman History Center)

The first Line Period of Action (26 May to 15 June) involved the customary work-up, though it was rather more dramatic than usual when A-6s silenced two 37mm triple-A sites with bombs, along the Route 912 complex in the Ban Karai Pass area. Crews bombed the source of the tracers. The A-6Bs flew 24 Iron Hand missions, operating as a pair on separate racetrack orbits in support of RVAH-12 Speartips NAA RA-5C Vigilante Blue Tree reconnaissance missions in the manner established by VA-85, as the 'Vigis' were considered the most likely to wake up SAM sites and draw their fire.

The Vigilante would use its canoe load of framing and panoramic cameras, an Infrared Linescan and a Sideways-Looking Radar (SLR) to monitor North Vietnamese activity, but also to map critically important well-used aimpoints and OAPs (Offset Aimpoints) in the Steel Tiger operating area. Among its recce products were forward-oblique camera snapshots and SLR footage, which, duly processed and printed, A-6 B/Ns would carry with them on missions. These prints could be pulled out of their knee-pockets and compared with the imagery on the dual-mode Indicator, Azimuth, Range Multisensor (IARM) cockpit display or DVRI radar display, to help with general navigation and in locating critical aimpoints and OAPs. Enemy radars were locked-up on nine occasions using A-6B PAT/ARM aircraft during these missions, but 'no missile firings have been initiated due in most cases to the short duration of the threat signals. In one case the missile was determined to be unreliable,' Cdr Zick concluded in his report.

Operations were somewhat thwarted by the discovery of wing cracks on the Intruders, resulting in a Fleetwide grounding order on day two of the Second Line Period (29 June to 3 August), pending inspection under Interim Airframe Bulletin 106.[6] One A-6C (BuNo. 155660) was grounded immediately, while on 3 July the remainder of the force was restricted to 3g manoeuvres, 420kt and no dive-bombing runs. Unrestricted flight was resumed three days later. Yet the weather presented the biggest obstacle. 'The effects of the south-west monsoon prevailed during the majority of the time, with heavy broken and overcast conditions. The bottoms were low, usually 2,000–4,000ft, with tops generally around 8,000–10,000ft and much intermittent thunderstorm activity,' noted Cdr Zick.

Given the poor weather, the RA-5Cs spent a great deal of time on deck. Accordingly, A-6Bs were launched on five occasions to make up for the Blue Tree shortfall, using the KD-2 camera linked to their DVRI for radarscope photography. Similar mapping was conducted during some thirty-nine sorties when A-6Bs dropped bombs on standard visual or radar-assisted deliveries. Unlike the A-6B Mod 0/0-Update subvariant, the PAT/ARM modifications did not degrade DIANE's all-up Straight Path Full System bombing capabilities.

In their primary role, a mere nine A-6B Iron Hand sorties were flown during the Second and Third Line Periods, mostly during daylight hours. The VA-165 report for 1970 said: 'Triple-A defensive reactions were quite light. Most of this can be attributed to the weather conditions and subsequent low level of enemy activity. Approximately 4 per cent of total day sorties, and 13 per cent of night sorties reported triple-A reactions . . . for an overall reaction rate of approximately 8 per cent. The highest-threat area was unquestionably along Route 912 in the Ban Karai area, in which the majority of night missions were flown.' Despite this, a third A-6B PAT/ARM joined VA-165 during this Line Period.

Frustratingly, enemy radar activity remained negligible. Cdr Zick recorded that 'there were no SAM reactions to Blue Tree sorties. Occasional PAT/ARM lock-ups have been obtained on signals considered to be threat radars, but never of sufficient strength or duration to warrant firing a missile.' This meant that the A-6Bs were habitually returning to USS *America* with two STARMs and their heavy launch rails, weighing 3,200lb. It was considered a safety issue right from the beginning of the cruise, as crews were having to dump dangerously large quantities of fuel during recovery to meet allowable trap weights, thus precluding a diversion in the event of an emergency on deck. Even a go-around in the busy CTF-77 landing pattern might have caused their J52 engines to die of thirst, while they awaited a new landing slot on the ball.

By the end of the Third Line Period, Cdr Zick had obtained authorization for the A-6Bs to be modified under AFC 244. This beefed up the rear empennage and added the EA-6A tailhook truss assembly, increased gross trap weight to 36,000lb and, critically, doubled recovery fuel to just under 5,000lb. Otherwise, at these heavier landing weights, A-6Bs risked serious structural damage and the possibility of losing a tailhook, with the attendant problems of deceleration precluding a 'bolter', so that the crew found themselves flopping off the bow into the sea, or worse. Such risks reflected the scarcity of the Standard ARM.

The strength of the south-west monsoon during the first part of Line Period Four (25 August to 17 September) meant that the A-6s were virtually the only aircraft routinely flying. This pattern was repeated every year. Enemy anti-aircraft activity remained light, though US Air Force Intelligence agreed with VA-165 crews, who remarked that only muzzle flashes were being seen. This was worrying. The enemy were using fewer tracer rounds, which had previously helped aircrews to pinpoint their location. USAF RF-4C crews had been reporting the same phenomenon. Most, if not all, of the anti-aircraft fire was unguided.

Nine Iron Hand sorties were flown out of a total of 59 A-6B sorties during that Line Period. According to the VA-165 report for 1970: 'Enemy reaction was limited to one Fan Song lock-up of about 25 seconds duration. Other signals were received for short intervals, usually when the A-6B was headed seaward. Those signals, which were nearly always intercepted through the missile, disappeared when the aircraft turned to achieve a final lock-up. There were no missiles fired.' One A-6B (BuNo. 155628) was in check most of this time and did not fly a single Iron Hand mission, and was transferred back to NAS Whidbey Island on 10 September for crew familiarization duties with VA-52 'Knight Riders'. Most of the A-6B crews were meanwhile acquainted with the A-6C's systems, and flew TRIM missions.

The Fifth and final Line Period of the cruise (14 October to 7 November) began with appalling weather. Two typhoons and a Siberian cold front forced CTF-77 south for several days. The final week brightened up, and crews located nine suspect 100mm triple-A sites in Laos, in Sandbox Alpha around Mu Gia, and Sandbox Bravo at Ban Karai, while the A-6Bs'

STARMs indicated that the North Vietnamese had moved at least one SA-2 battalion towards the Ban Karai Pass. SAM and triple-A defences had been increased to harass ongoing B-52 Arc Light bombing sorties. Four Iron Hand threat-monitoring sorties were completed, out of 73 A-6B missions launched. These, as usual, were in support of RA-5C reconnaissance sorties.

The A-6B crews also took part in an Alpha Strike during early November. According to the VA-165 report for 1970: 'Two A-6Bs were employed to support this strike in their capacity as Iron Hand aircraft and, in addition, carried [Mk82] bombs to contribute to the attack. Inbound to the target, one signal was detected by the AGM-78B, but its validity could not be verified by either missile steering or PAT/ARM and it was held for no more than 15 seconds.' It was the same old routine that had endured since the halt of bombing over North Vietnam two years earlier: endless patrols while the strikers bombed suspected truck parks, supply staging areas, crossing-points and convoys.

VA-165 dropped 7,308,788lb of ordnance during the 1970 cruise: huge tonnages for each truck hit. Crews in-theatre joked that they had probably created an anomaly in the Earth's magnetic field! However, to their credit, Cdr Zick noted that 'the A-6B/PAT [sic] aircraft have successfully sustained their previous success, in that no aircraft supported by an A-6B has been attacked by enemy SAMs or radar-directed triple-A during its mission'. In truth, there wasn't a great deal to hit. The Hanoi–Haiphong enemy SAM sanctuary remained largely out of bounds.

At the close of the 1970 cruise, which took USS *America* to Sydney and Rio de Janeiro, the two remaining A-6B PAT/ARMs were cross-decked to VA-52, to complete its complement NAS.[7] Five A-6Cs were similarly prepared for transfer to VA-145 'Swordsmen'. Cross-decking procedures sometimes meant dropping the aircraft off at NAS Cubi Point for more thorough maintenance prior to their new squadron assignment. At this time A-6Bs were subject to a 26-week, or twice-yearly, thorough check. Reworking of the wings was carried out at NAS Cubi Point under IAFC 254 at the same time, and modifications to the tail truss completed. Corrosion in the wing-fold plugs (connecting the AN/APR-25 wing-tip antennae and pre-amps to the heart of the aircraft) was noted. Without such attention, loss of signal reception may have resulted. Some of the reworks had become necessary as a result of 'crunches' when towed or taxiing aircraft hit one anothers' control surfaces. Eight such incidents had been reported during VA-165's time at sea.

The A-6B PAT/ARM's third combat cruise, with VA-52, offered the first real opportunities to launch STARM from the aircraft. The tactics remained the same: long, figure-of-eight Iron Hand patrol patterns along the North Vietnam–Laos border, waiting for radar activity. In the spring of 1971 a VA-52 crew lobbed a STARM against a site that came up, only to subsequently realize that the North Vietnamese panhandle was a mere 30 miles wide at that point, and that the STARM was in danger of vaulting cross-country and careering into friendly ships in the Gulf of Tonkin! The story goes that everyone in South-East Asia heard a voice with a strong southern accent issue the following transmission over Guard frequency: 'All you ships in the Gulf of Tonkin, shut down your radars!'

No damage was caused to either side but the incident inevitably led to further restrictions on the use of STARM.

The squadron's most successful SAM-bust involved all of CVW-9 in a Protective Reaction mission that spring. It was launched against a North Vietnamese missile maintenance and assembly facility in the jungle that had proved to be the major depot for the seemingly random, mobile SA-2 batteries along the border. Lt Cdr Daryl Keff led the raid. A-7s conducted Iron Hand operations with Shrike, accompanied by a pair of A-6s lobbing iron bombs at the assembly sites, quickly followed by a second wave of A-6s which scattered the contents of twenty-eight CBUs. The facility was demolished.

MOD 1 AND P-8 INTRUDERS

The third A-6B subtype, also designed to operate specifically with the AGM-78B, entered service during 1970 as part of the great experiment. To Grumman and IBM, who created this variant around the then revolutionary 4 Pi digital computer, it was known as the Target Identification and Acquisition System (TIAS). To the flyers it was another A-6B model with different switches, and was widely known as the Mod 1 A-6B. Its protracted development had also begun in 1966 and the first example (BuNo. 151820) made its maiden flight on 1 October 1968 in the hands of contractor crew C.H. Brown and R. McDonnell. It was followed by five more conversions from FY 1965 A-6A stock, all of which were reaccepted by the US Navy between 30 April and 1 August 1970.[8]

The Intruder Mod 1 A-6B's radome sported this multiplex of carefully aligned radar-receiving 'buttons' associated with the AN/APS-118 TIAS system, which was the crux of its radar-locating capability for semi-automatic AGM-78B STARM launch. (Ben Knowles via Mick Roth)

The Mod 1 A-6B was readily distinguishable by virtue of the eighteen radar-receiving buttons associated with the AN/APS-118 amplitude-based detection system, standing proud on the nose radome and tail empennage at different look angles, providing near all-round coverage. These allowed the system to locate an emitter's position based on the declination, azimuth and relative strength of the signals being picked up, with aircraft pitch and roll factored into the calculation.

With this package working properly (each antenna had to be calibrated precisely), it was possible to provide extremely accurate threat information within the short periods of time that the enemy stayed on the air, as well as permitting more discriminating target lock-ups in a dense electromagnetic environment. As a novelty, the threats were

A Mod 1 TIAS Intruder from VA-34 'Blue Blasters', awaiting rework and gutted of its J52 turbojets. (Author's Collection)

presented on the radarscope as digital symbols, not as strobes or blips, and it offered two modes: Immediate Threat and Operator Enters Targets (OET). The former was essentially automatic, while the latter permitted the B/N to select a chosen radar operating frequency and PRF to ferret out a specific radar type before handing it over to STARM for attack.

The bulk of Mod 1 A-6Bs were retained for test duties during the early years rather than deployed to WESTPAC, fine-tuning STARM in concert with General Dynamics at Lindbergh Field, San Diego, and the US Navy's Point Mugu test facility further along the road in southern California. From these locations they could operate over such venues as China Lake's Echo Range, determining the ability of STARM to lock-up against both ground and simulated sea defences.

Echo Range boasted ships fashioned from sand, like giant sandcastles, bristling with simulated Soviet naval radars. With its focus of attention over North Vietnam and the Trails War in Laos, it had become all too easy to forget that the US Navy was actually a saltwater service, with the primary job of maintaining dominance over the Soviet Navy and holding down a nuclear strike role as part of the United States' SIOP. Mod 1 A-6Bs thus spent most of their time operating with the Sixth Fleet in the Atlantic and Mediterranean, and made their debut cruise between October 1971 and October 1972 with VA-34 'Blue Blasters' onboard USS *John F. Kennedy*.

A fourth A-6B subvariant, known to the author solely by the acronym PASES, was to have formed the basis of a production run encompassing fifty-four new A-6Bs (BuNos 154046–154099), but the programme was cancelled and the aircraft never built.

Amid this turmoil, development of the AGM-78 missile continued with the new C model, produced by General Dynamics' Pomona Division primarily for the USAF as part of a programme to provide an active inventory of some 470 Broad-Band AGM-78 missiles by November 1971. An initial batch of 135 AGM-78Cs was funded in fiscal year 1969 and it stayed in production in further lots through fiscal year 1972 (when it was supplanted by the D series). The chief differences introduced by the AGM-78C were reduced production costs and increased reliability, a full-Band radome and a white phosphorous target marker. A limited number of AGM-78Cs were made available to the US Navy. Shrike production continued unabated in much larger numbers, as ten of them could be bought for the going rate of a solitary STARM. Training with the newer weapon remained theoretical and was largely based on reading the manuals and receiving briefings from other crews who had actually employed it during trials or combat.

Of far greater potential impact to the Fleet was the Intruder's new P-8 DIANE computer programme, which would be operational by the time bombing of North Vietnam was resumed in earnest in early 1972. Its chief advance over the P-7 series was the introduction of an optional stand-off automatic Shrike delivery mode. Target information was first derived from a new Shrike Ranging Mode, or based on set co-ordinates known beforehand and fed into the system. DIANE was then stepped into attack at least 20 (and never closer than 5) miles from the suspect enemy radar site. Once within Shrike's firing parameters, the pilot would be given an 'in range' cue and would follow the VDI 'highway in the sky' graphics for an automatic loft launch towards the target for maximum aerodynamic and ballistic reach. The Intruder crew could then break off and leave the missile to its own devices.

The Shrike Ranging Mode employed the ARM's seeker to pick up targets at distances of up to 40 miles. With this mode selected, the moment the ARM acquired a target, steering information was presented to the pilot on his VDI. He then flew the A-6A so that the steering symbol was centred, then pressed his stick commit button to the first detent to input a single-point azimuth reading. Thereafter the pilot commenced a long, slow turn away from the enemy emitter in either direction (continued until the aircraft was at a relative bearing of between 20–30 degrees), holding the aircraft steady until the in range cue started flashing. This instructed the pilot that the aircraft had flown far enough to permit a second azimuth reading to be taken, which he duly did by turning back towards the target, centring the square steering symbol in the VDI once more, and pressing the stick commit button again. DIANE used the two azimuth readings to triangulate the enemy emitter's position, which it also displayed on the radarscope.

However, because of Shrike's limitations and the demands of strike planning, the system was rarely employed in combat. Intruder Crews preferred to rely on the A-6Bs and their STARMs for stand-off missileering while the A-6A/Cs bored in with bombs, leaving short-range Shrike-shooting to A-4s and A-7s employing both loft-launched and dip-angle deliveries.

Concurrently, Fleet aircraft were in the process of being updated with the US Navy's latest RWR, the Itek/ATI AN/ALR-45 and allied Magnavox AN/ALR-50 LWR, which were fielded from 1970 primarily in response to new Soviet sea-going threats. The new RWR sensed pulsed threats in the E–J Bands, using hybrid microcircuits incorporating digital logic and analogue clock drivers, which allowed it to be reprogrammed on ship using just a screwdriver. It was a great advance.

WILD WEASEL THUDS GET MORE PUNCH

The USAF bought into the Standard ARM right from the beginning, equipping its F-105F Wild Weasel IIIs at Korat and Takhli RTAFBs with the weapon in the spring of 1968. F-105Fs 62-4414 Ridge Runner and 62-4434 at the Armament Development Test Center, Eglin AFB, undertook the initial and follow-on trials. A start-up batch of sixteen Wild Weasel IIIs received the necessary wiring and new LAU-78/80 launch rails to carry the weapon, and twelve of them were distributed between the Thailand-based F-105 wings, with the first examples going to Takhli's 357th TFS. Crew training continued to be hosted at Nellis AFB but, unlike with Shrike, crews did not expend a single round during training. 'We had some advantage with Shrike over Standard in that we could fire one in training. They were about $7,000 at the time, as opposed to about $200,000 for the Standard ARMs. In fact, the latter were so expensive we had to fill out a long form during flight debriefing if we had "expended" one on the mission,' recalls Kim Pepperell.

US Air Force Standard-related tactics were very different from those of the US Navy, and were revised to take advantage of the new missile, based on earlier trolling tactics. Rather than standing back in an orbit on their ingress route from Thailand and lobbing the missiles from maximum range (where they might home in on friendly radars before crossing the border), the escorting Weasels carried a mix of ARMs, working as two flights: the first with Shrikes a minute ahead of the attack package (instead of the 6–7 minutes originally employed with the trolling method), and the second with Standards in the second tier. Kim Pepperell said: 'The Standard ARM was equipped with its own electronics, which gave the Bear an aural indication when the missile had acquired the signal. Based on azimuth he saw on the RHAWS, the Bear could then dial in a heading of up to 180 degrees, for the AGM-78A to turn to, once it left the rails and cleared the aircraft.'

In theory, they would shoot the Standard ARMs at any threats coming on the air first (using the launch callsign Ramjet or Cannon), beyond the SAMs' reach; this had the added advantage of reducing aircraft weight and thereby increasing agility. Meanwhile the advance party, which would have awoken the enemy and relayed threat information, closed on the emitters, able to deliver the *coup de grâce* with Shrikes and iron or cluster bombs to take out the remaining launch rails and missiles, running in with the typical F-105 tactic of transonic speed or faster with afterburner engaged, getting in and out as quickly as possible. The main attack waves' passes would invariably be performed in a single run, with all the strikers

Wild Weasels Standard ARM.

in and out in less than 60 seconds if they had met their scheduled times over target. Ever vigilant on the target periphery while the bomb debris settled, the Weasels remained ready to bore in again to provide covering fire, adhering to their praiseworthy motto 'First In, Last Out'.

ARM carriage was different also. To extend their zig-zag over-the-target loiter time (Weasel crews never used the same attack heading more than once), F-105Fs would sometimes take off with an asymmetric stores load, with a Standard ARM on one wing and a fuel tank on the other. Col Daniel Barry recalls the procedure associated with such a load:

> We usually dealt with the AGM-78 asymmetrical problem by burning fuel down in the opposing drop tank until we could zero out the aileron trim. We then burned from other tanks. Of course, if you fired the missile you then got the sudden heavy wing feeling, but you were ready for it and there was enough aileron to control it. It was not as bad as rolling in to drop a pair of 2,000lb bombs, one on each station, and having one hang as you were trying to make a high-g pullout! I never experienced this but it did happen on occasion.

In practice, however, they would have to wait a further four years to really put the new tactics to the test, and the above description is chiefly based on Linebacker combat ops in 1972, when the USAF unleashed AGM-78s in quantity. By contrast, initial results with the new missile were something of an oddity, because of the limited capability of the early AGM-78 A-1, and only eight were fired by USAF Weasels that year. This privilege fell to a flight of Takhli's 357th TFS jets, callsign Barracuda, on 10 May, in what turned out to be a one-off demonstration of their new firepower that year. There were several Fan Song radars transmitting that day as the flight crossed into North Vietnam. Apparently the first three missiles failed completely, one tumbling into the jungle, another barrel-rolling madly until it broke up, while the third decided to go AWOL beyond the line of sight (the US Air Force did not possess STARM BDA capability at this juncture). Things then got more interesting. Barracuda Three, lead aircraft in the second element and flown by Maj W. Kerzon and his EWO Lt Col Scottie McIntire, lobbed its second Standard ARM and blew a Fan Song radar to pieces. Of the ensuing volley of four missiles from the wingmen, all apparently hit their intended targets, resulting in two additional probables.

Overall, some twenty-six strikes were launched against SAM sites dotted south of the 19th Parallel around Dong Hoi, Bai Duc Tanh and in the DMZ during May, increasing to thirty-eight in June and peaking at eighty-two in August. However, a shortage of AGM-78 launchers (which tended to be dumped) obliged crews to rely greatly on Shrike and CBUs. After that time crews were restricted to ops around North Vietnam's borders except on rare, special occasions. This gave the enemy a respite in which they reconstructed their defences.

Another F-105F modification to see only brief service during 1968, despite aggressive encounters with MiGs earlier in the year, was the Combat Martin. Distinguishable by virtue of their large dorsal antennae, thirteen aircraft were modified with Hallicrafters QRC-128 VHF jammers in the rear cockpit, which ousted the rear crewman's position. The new black boxes became known as 'Colonel Computer', and the idea was that an inbound strike formation could jam communications between GCI and enemy MiGs without obliging relatively vulnerable EB-66s (which carried similar devices) to amble close to the target area. Combat Martin aircraft were distributed to both F-105 wings in Thailand, but apparently did not see much service, most being flown as single-seat strike machines just like the F-105Ds. The one and only Combat Martin aircraft to be lost (63-8337) went down over RP I on 15 April 1968, Col David Winn ejecting successfully.[9]

Of the F-105F specials, the surviving six Ryan's Raiders had all reverted to pure Weasel tasks by mid-summer 1968, with numbers subsequently bolstered by ten remodified Combat Martin aircraft over the ensuing eighteen months (another was noted at McConnell AFB in 1971), all of which received the latest WW-III TCTOs. Numbers had to be increased not just because of losses but also because 1968 saw the Weasels being committed to the Korean Peninsula, the beginnings of an ongoing rotational TDY assignment that combined Alert with a Weasel theatre-indoctrination school for combat-bound crews, further stretching often limited resources. The *Pueblo* Incident – the seizing of the intelligence-gathering ship USS *Pueblo* on 23 January by North Korean gunboats – allied to the crossing of the DMZ into Seoul by a squad of North Korean commandos intent on assassinating the South Korean President actually kick-started the process, when a detachment of 12th TFS 'Bald Eagles' F-105Fs was sent from Kadena AB on the Japanese island of Okinawa to Kwangju AB in South Korea as part of Operation Combat Fox.

Combat-seasoned Weasel aviators were needed for both Alert duties and for the new school in South Korea, causing some personnel problems at Takhli and Korat by threatening to split up some crews mid-tour; by vocation the two-man crews stuck together from their training days right until the bitter end of their combat tour, whenever possible. The assignment was not especially popular either. EWO 'T.R.' Marino of the 333rd TFS was one of those affected:

One day my 'nose gunner' came up to me and said we had a problem. It seemed that since I was the junior Wild Weasel Bear in South-East Asia (in rank, not experience), I was going to go to Korea to train new Wild Weasel crews that had just finished Wild Weasel school at Nellis and were in Korea for three months en route to South-East Asia. I would be training them in the latest South-East Asia tactics. Needless to say, I was not exactly thrilled. I was going to be rushed to finish my 100 missions (this was good) so I could get there asap (this was not good). The powers that be were going to crew me with another, less senior pilot and send us to Korea as a crew. My nose gunner wanted to know what I thought about the idea. I said I thought it was pure B/S and didn't want us to be split as a crew and what were they going to do with him? I said again that I really didn't like the whole idea. He said good and said he would see what he could do.

Well, what he could do was not exactly great. It was decreed that I was going to Korea – end of discussion. I would go with another pilot; or, if my pilot wanted to go and spend three months in Korea on the way home, we could finish our missions together and go to Korea together. But I was going (low rank doesn't have its privileges). So my pilot decided that instead of splitting us up we would finish together and he would go to 'K' with me. It made me feel good that he really didn't want us to split. Well, we finished our 100 at Takhli and off we went to 'K'. To say that we dug our heels [in] on the way there would be a masterpiece of understatement.

Once in 'K', things were as bad as we had expected: cold, dirty, bad food, bad rooms – and great flying. There had to be something good about it! We were on a kind of Wild Weasel Alert but really spent most of our time flying with the new South-East Asia-bound crews, trying to teach them what we had been doing a few weeks before. We flew against the Army and Republic of Korea missile defences and went to the range. We also gave Allied missile defences a look at what it was like to try to work against Wild Weasels. We had some exchange briefings where we told the Army guys what we were, how we operated and how we could operate against them if we were on other side. We also played some 'cat and mouse' with some of the North Korean SAM sites for intel-gathering purposes. Any number of funny and not so funny incidents happened. Anway, after all was said and done, I finally got back home on Christmas Eve 1968. Unfortunately, never to fly that monster from Republic again.

MORE WILD WEASEL III MODS

New digital interface equipment was rapidly fielded during 1969, con-current with the AGM-78B Standard ARM's introduction on the F-105F Thunderchief, and the first two Mod 1-capable F-105Fs were completed at Sacramento AMA in January. F-105F WW-III RHAWS were upgraded to the AN/APR-36 and -37 systems, and the ER-142 was replaced by a new ATI AN/APR-35 analysis receiver to make the most of the AGM-78B's greater receiving spectrum, expanding frequency coverage by adding X-Band reception. The AN/APR-35 had both panoramic and analysis receivers, the former to display the overall signal environment and the latter to allow the EWO to expand a given signal on a separate scope (which could also be used for a homing display, by means of the now traditional direction/finding amplitude-based spikes for lining up with the target), as back-up to the steering dot on the pilot's lead-computing gunsight.

To free up a wing pylon for occasional operations over downtown Hanoi, where at least one noise jammer per aircraft was mandatory equip-ment, the F-105F WW-III also received the Westinghouse QRC-380/ALQ-105 noise- and repeater deception-jamming device (faired into the fuselage flanks), along with QRC-373/ALT-34 noise jammers in the nose. The fit essentially comprised a split multiple-Band AN/ALQ-101 system developed under the Seed Sesame project, this being an improved version of the pilot-production examples originally tested in 1968 in underwing podded form. Using a Travelling Wave Tube (TWT) for rapid frequency agility in jamming, the early trials QRC-335 devices, which were capable of conducting SA-2 fuse-jamming (known as fuse-popping, to trigger the missiles' warheads prematurely and beyond their lethal range), proved a little too eager and started singing to each other in response to their jamming, forcing crews to turn them off. The fully-fledged QRC-335/ALQ-101 pods dropped the fuse-jamming feature but provided excellent noise/deception-jamming against TTRs and downlink SA-2 beacons, thus lending the Weasel crews new-found autonomy.

The AN/ALQ-105 upgrade formed the second part of the F-105F WW-III Mod 1 kit, carried out under Class V Mod 2079 during depot-level maintenance. A third component was the provision for Standard ARM BDA, performed under yet another TCTO update, ultimately creating a force of sixty-three aircraft (including training and test aircraft). Coincidentally, whether or not the F-105Fs had yet been fully modified, the aircraft designation was changed. A letter dated 3 October 1969 from USAF Chief of Staff Gen John D. Ryan decreed that, for the purposes of more efficient Weasel documentation, the Wild Weasel III would thenceforth be redesignated F-105G to distinguish it from regular F-105Fs. Moreover, future Weasel aircraft, when eventually put into production, would also employ the Golf suffix.[10]

However, losses continued to take their toll during 1969, mostly to enemy gunfire over the Steel Tiger operating area, which had become the Weasels' primary operating area. F-105F 62-4435 Roman Knight went down over Laos on 14 May, and one of Capt Dethlefsen's former aircraft, 63-8352, crash-landed at Udorn after receiving hits from triple-A on 8 December. Most of these B-52 support missions were physically taxing in the extreme. No strike package in and out in a minute or two, with some interesting trade along the flight legs – just endless trolling around the threat areas in support of the BUFFs (*Big Ugly Fat F***ers*), as the B-52s were known, as they laboriously 'dipped a toe' into Laos or North Vietnam and dropped their capacious loads, then ambled out again, in separate waves, an hour or more apart. Multiple B-52 cell attacks, concentrating firepower in shorter bursts, had been abandoned owing to the presence of the enemy's high-reaching 85mm and 100mm triple-A pieces, which would be up and firing in time to become a serious threat to those bombers in the rear cells. This meant that the Weasels' work became boring, which made it all the more dangerous.

NEW GUNS AT KORAT

The single-seat F-105D had performed equally valiantly, but its days were numbered as it was progressively retired from the war zone. Under the 388th TFW at Korat RTAFB, the 469th TFS 'Fighting Bulls' ceased F-105 operations in November 1968 (having accumulated 40,000 combat hours in the F-105 by 30 October), to be followed by the 34th TFS 'Rams' which flew its last F-105 mission on 9 May 1969. Both converted to F-4E Phantom IIs, resplendent with new sharks' mouths painted on their noses.

Col Hillding's almost factory-fresh F-4Es boasted more-powerful GE J79-17 engines than their F-4 predecessors and would burn fuel more quickly than an F-105D killer companion to keep pace with the Weasels at

the F-105Gs' preferred lower altitudes. But they also featured a new transistor-based jack of all trades Westinghouse AN/APQ-120 multimode radar, and retained the AN/ASQ-91 Weapons Release Computer System (WRCS) pioneered by the Ubon-based 8th TFW's CAP-cum-Interdiction F-4Ds during 1967, which offered an uncanned Dive Toss radar-aided visual bombing mode. The backseater would lock the radar on to the ground ahead of the aircraft while the pilot manoeuvred to put his lead-computing gunsight pipper (a small ranging circle centred by an aiming dot) on target. The pilot then pressed the joystick pickle button, to input radar slant-range to target into the WRCS. As long as he kept the button pressed, weapons release would follow automatically during the swoop over the target, to deposit the bombs smack on top of it. The backseater – at this juncture a rated pilot waiting to gain a slot up front – would act as oral bomb tone or verbal radar altimeter, as back-up. This was something that was always done, for insurance purposes.

With the radar or WRCS out, the pilot had to revert to manual, Direct attack and release the weapons at a strictly prescribed altitude and airspeed for the chosen dive angle, having first set up the manual depression in the gunsight. The bombs would leave the racks the moment the pickle button was pressed. Many of the more seasoned pilots actually preferred this method. Ed Rasimus, who returned to Thailand to fly the F-4E at Korat RTAFB, recalls:

> Dive Toss is somewhat of a misnomer. It still required 'going down the chute', but it provided an accurate range to target at 'freeze'

The F-4E entered the war zone in late 1967, introducing the first Phantom II with a stable, integral 20mm gun. This model superseded the F-105D as companion to the Weasels in the hunter/killer mission, using primarily CBUs and its Gatling gun to pound the enemy defences. (Frank B. Mormillo) (pressing the pickle button with the pipper on the desired point of impact). That then allowed the computer to analyse dive angle, drift, true airspeed, g-load and then release the bomb(s) at a point in the flight path that would result in a hit. You still needed to enter a dive to put the target under the pipper and then (as the cliché goes) 'fly your ass over the target'. The bombs were released somewhere during the pull-out. This is in contrast to manual dive-bomb which requires that you pre-compute a mil depression based on weapons ballistics and anticipated delivery conditions. Then you must accurately establish dive angle, indicated airspeed at release, altitude AGL at release, unaccelerated g condition and (most difficult) wind offset. The method I described allowed for some flexibility in dive angle, but the airspeed, g-load and drift all had to be handled. Fortunately with CBUs, the accuracy doesn't have to be perfect.

The problem with Dive Toss was that the pickle button must be held from the point the pipper is on the target through the release of the weapons. That meant that a pre-set switch decision was required to set the number of munitions to be delivered. Then, the radar WRCS had to be recycled – the switch moved out of Dive Toss and back to reset for another delivery. Clearly, in a high-threat 'Dr Pepper' situation (SAMs at ten, two and four o'clock), it was better to be 'heads out' than to be fiddling with switches changing from one to two to four CBUs and recycling. In Direct I could just pickle multiple times before starting the pull-out to release more weapons as desired. But, Dive Toss didn't really toss very far; and it was possible to be inside a release solution (as determined by the computer) when things got hot and heavy and you really got into your work.

The F-4E's supreme advantage over the F-105D was that it could switch to air-to-air work at the drop of a hat, to provide mutual protection against enemy MiGs, using its arsenal of AIM-7E Sparrow semi-active radar-homing and AIM-9B/E Sidewinder heat-seeker AAMs plus the Vulcan M61A-1 20mm cannon. This might mean dumping bombs, but it was preferable to anyone getting shot down by a MiG. They could always come back to the target later.

By December 1970 Takhli RTAFB was reduced to 'caretaker' status with the final disbandment of the 355th TFW HQ. The wing had flown its last F-105 mission on 7 October: Dino Flight, led by Col Waymond C. Nutt, which brought the wing's final Vietnam combat sortie tally up to 101,304, in which crews had logged 263,650hr, dropped some 202,596 tons of ordnance on 12,675 targets

PACAF Thud Weasel assets were consolidated under the 6010th WWS during the Trails War period. Operating from Korat, they became the 17th WWS in December 1971, and often flew in the asymmetric configuration demonstrated by the aircraft here, with centreline tank, outboard wing Shrikes or jamming pods, and inboard wing Standard ARM counterbalanced by a drop tank. During earlier years, when flown by Vern Harris and Kim Pepperell, tail '301 carried the name Jinkin' Josie. *USAF Pacific Air Forces documents cite the combat firing of 2,263 Shrikes and eight Standard ARMs between March 1965 and October 1968.* (Don Logan via Jim Rotramel)

and downed 22 MiGs into the bargain, not counting damaged probables and aircraft blown to pieces on enemy airfields. The few remaining Weasel F-105Fs and their crews had already been consolidated at Korat RTAFB to become the 6010th WWS on 1 November, combining with 12th TFS Det 1 from Kadena AB, which had had six aircraft and their crews on TDY at Korat RTAFB since 25 September 1970.

The new squadron remained the only Wild Weasel unit in the war zone, amid a diminishing US presence in general. President Nixon's Vietnamization policy was under way. This meant turning over light attack aircraft and fighters, helicopters and some gunships and transports to the Republic of Vietnam Air Force, which was supposed thereafter to be responsible for some 70 per cent of all theatre air combat operations. The presence of American ground troops and aircraft was thus progressively reduced. For example, at peak strength in early 1968, the US Air Force boasted some 737 aircraft and 54,434 personnel in-theatre; by the close of 1971 this had dwindled to 277 fighters and strike aircraft flown, maintained and backed up by half that number of people.

SON TAY AND PROTECTIVE REACTION

While the 6010th WWS's duties mostly comprised providing support for B-52s and other high-value assets pounding the Trail or eavesdropping on North Vietnamese defences, undoubtedly the unit's greatest claim to fame was its participation in the Son Tay Prison raid, known as Operation Kingpin. This was a bold attempt by a Joint Task Force of USAF and Army Special Forces headed by Brig Gen LeRoy J. Manor to liberate between seventy and eighty POW airmen held captive 30 miles from Hanoi, using two MC-130 Combat Talons special operations transports and six CH/HH-53 helicopters, aided by A-1Es (modified with QRC-128 GCI ComJam gear), and the omnipresent Weasels which provided SAM suppression. In addition, one HH-3E would be deliberately crash-landed within the compound to deposit the extraction troops.

The 400-mile range raid was launched on the night of 20/21 November 1970 after receipt of the Red Rocket go-code, while the 7th AF and CTF-77 put up a diversionary raid around Haiphong involving 116 sorties from eight bases, working up enemy radars on the coast into a rabid froth. 'It became obvious that the North Vietnamese' total concern was directed eastward. Our raiding force, coming from the west, in effect, had a free ride,' noted Gen Manor. Everything went like clockwork, with one important exception: for reasons unknown, probably flooding of Son Tay, the North Vietnamese had previously relocated all the POWs to another location known as Camp Faith, 15 miles to the east.

Remarkably, there were no American casualties despite fierce SAM opposition as the five F-105Gs closed towards the pick-up area. Between fourteen and sixteen SAMs were fired at the Firebirds, one of them exploding over Firebird Three, covering the aircraft with acid propellant. The F-105G descended on fire, appearing to be a loss, but its pilot was merely extinguishing the unpleasant coating in a duck-and-dive manoeuvre. The crew pressed on with their mission.

Less lucky was Firebird Five, 62-4436, when a SAM's shrapnel blast took out its flight controls and fuel system. Boeing KC-135A Stratotankers moved their orbit closer to Laos to prop up the stricken aircraft's reserves in anticipation of a boom-ride all the way to Homeplate, but frustratingly the wounded F-105G's engine flamed-out just prior to refuelling contact. Maj Don Kilgus and his EWO Capt C. Ted Lowry baled out over a mountainous area and spent several hours on the ground until Apple Four and Apple Five, helicopters from the Son Tay raid, located their position, picked them up and whisked them back to Thailand.

The whole operation was a case of brilliant planning and execution, but flawed intelligence, despite repeated reconnaissance data collected by 'Giant Plate' SR-71A Blackbirds and unmanned Buffalo Hunter Ryan RPVs. To the internees in the north, however, it was a welcome reminder that they were not forgotten, and the subsequent publicity focused attention on the prisoners' plight in captivity. Apparently this had improved a little since the death of North Vietnam's figurehead Ho Chi Minh in the previous year.

North Vietnam's infuriated response to its own heavy losses during the raid was renewed aggressive fire against marauding US photo-reconnaissance and Signals Intelligence (Sigint) jets, which had remained active over the northern RPs since the bombing halt two years previously, but which had enjoyed a tacit arrangement of sorts whereby they were allowed to photograph and listen to the north mostly unimpeded provided they flew 'alone, unarmed, and unafraid', as the saying went.

What were known as Protective Reaction strikes – piecemeal retaliatory strikes – had actually begun in earnest on 28 January 1970, after an RF-4C and its escort drew three SAMs. Later that day, five more SAMs were launched against another reconnaissance jet, and its F-105G Iron Hand support flight responded with a Shrike launch (the only launch in three months) and strafing of the SA-2 launchers, resulting in several secondary explosions. However, Seabird Two was shot down, probably by triple-A (believed to be F-105G 63-8239 flown by Maj John Sexton and Maj Jim Jones, who ejected successfully).

Once located and attacked, the North Vietnamese generally shut up shop and shifted the whole site – radar vans, missiles and launchers – to a new location. This could be accomplished in something like 2–3hr, requiring the EOB to be constantly updated. For example, on 1 February 1970 site VN-374 was photographed near Ban Karai. The following day F-4 crews observed the SA-2s and rolled in with CBUs, resulting in a freshly launched SAM losing guidance and tumbling back to ground from 1,500ft shortly after the F-4s' CBUs sprinkled their deadly cargoes. On day three a follow-up reconnaissance mission revealed that the site had been cleared out, lock, stock and barrel.

However, much like the lauded bomb shortage of late 1966–7, there apparently existed an ARM shortage in 1969–70 which forced many Iron Handers to rely exclusively on cannon fire or rockets. 'Twenty mike-mike' could do considerable harm to a volatile rocket perched on its launcher, but the hit rate for cannon fire is notoriously low and superficial damage to radars would soon be patched up. 'We'd go and do an "armed recce" instead, flying on limited bullets,' recalled EWOs Kim Pepperell

and Gerry Knotts. US Navy crews relied on firing ZUNI rockets during this period.

Further losses in 1970 claimed another USAF Wild Weasel in addition to the 28 January and December Son Tay downings, yet by luck again the crew were reported to have ejected and been rescued by ARRS teams. The Wild Weasel in question was F-105F 63-8281, which went down on 21 February, hit by triple-A fire over Laos. The aircraft crashed at Nakhon Phanom at night, Maj Tom Halley making a spectacular sideways ejection. Making a 'nylon letdown' over Laos was definitely to be avoided, as crews would receive worse treatment there than was meted out by the North Vietnamese, and so pilots would nurse their damaged aircraft back across the Thai border whenever practicable.

The only other reported combat loss of a Weasel aviator during the Trails and Protective Reaction period occurred a year later, when F-105G 63-8326 was brought down by a SAM on 10 December 1971, while supporting B-52s near the North Vietnam border. Although their RHAWS told them something was awry, heavy cloud cover prevented the crew from sighting the enemy SA-2 in time, and it vaulted up through the cloud-tops and struck the aircraft. Both crewmen ejected from the burning F-105G, Maj R.E. Belli being picked up the following day. Sadly, his EWO, Standard ARM pioneer Lt Col Scott W. McIntire, was never found.

Entirely unrelated to this, nine days previously the 6010th WWS's numerical designator was renumbered 17th WWS. Apparently a visiting hard hat general did not take kindly to the SAC-style four-digit number and ordered it changed.

The year 1971 was far from quiet and witnessed a series of Protective Reaction strikes: Louisville Slugger, in February, which accounted for the destruction of five radars and fifteen missile transporters around Ban Karai; Fracture Cross Alpha on 21–2 March; the 7–8 November bombing of MiG bases at Dong Hoi, Vinh and Quan Lang; and Operation Proud Deep Alpha, which saw the US Air Force and US Navy launch some 1,025 sorties on 26–30 December, losing three aircraft, the Iron Hand teams replying with 51 Shrike and 10 Standard ARMs to even the score, destroying 5 Fan Song and 4 Fire Can radars, one GCI radar plus two additional acquisition radars.

GCI and other EW emitters had increasingly become targets, some of them lucky shots. F-105 Bear Kim Pepperell remembers heading away from a target one day and hearing an audio lock-up signal come from his AGM-78. He then dialled in the full 180-degree off-axis Standard ARM capability, and fired it. 'It appeared to work properly; the signal went off the air at about the time I had calculated it should!' The 17th WWS stayed in-theatre, on call, for a further three years – much of it in arduous combat.

WILD WEASEL IV DEBUT

With a huge production run that peaked at seventy-two aircraft a month, it was inevitable that the F-4 would filter into the Wild Weasel role in one guise or another: two men in the tub as standard crew and wedded to a team concept gave it that extra edge. However, rather than draw on its latest mainstay variant, the F-4E, the USAF elected to recycle earlier airframes into the programme. Development of the first such machine, a Shrike-only platform based on the now obsolescent valve radar, manual gunsight F-4C, had been initiated in 1966 when the F-4C was still red-hot.

The original 'Wild Weasel IV' concept called for the aircraft to be equipped with standard AN/APR-25 and -26 receivers and a Weasel pod (containing the IR-133, strike camera, mission recorder and an air-conditioning unit), the latter attached to the port aft Sparrow AAM well, so that flightline aircraft could be switched between defence suppression and other tasks. As things transpired, it proved to be a nearly insurmountable technical challenge, owing to problems with the F-4C's wiring and the electronics' close proximity to the engines, which caused problems with vibration.

The F-4Cs received the AN/APR-25 and -26 and IR-133 nose, tail and intake trunking direction-finding receivers and associated wiring, but it soon became apparent that the pod idea was a bust, as problems persisted. TAC finally agreed to give up one Sparrow well indefinitely, and the Weasel equipment (now comprising the ER-142 receiver, strike camera and recorder contained in a semi-permanent internal fairing) was installed in the port forward Sparrow well. Further problems persisted with the electronics, supposedly because of ground potential, until coaxial cable and some other refinements were introduced.

The problems took well over eighteen months to solve, but once done a total of thirty-six F-4Cs drawn from production Blocks 16–24 were adapted to the new WWIV-C configuration at Ogden AMA beginning in August 1968, with preliminary deliveries going to the Wild Weasel school at Nellis AFB for crew training.[11] All pilots had to possess a minimum of 500hr on the F-4 (most candidates had logged double that number, plus a previous combat tour in South-East Asia), while EWO training on the new systems was furnished by specially modified NAA T-39F Sabreliners that bristled with the same receiver kit, before getting to grips with the F-4C.

The first batch of crews qualified to operate the new aircraft graduated during October 1968, the majority being posted to Japan to join one of two wings: either the 347th TFW at Yokota AB, just outside Tokyo, which operated three squadrons (35th TFS 'First to Fight', 36th TFS 'Flying Fiends' and 80th TFS 'Headhunters'), or the 375th TFW at Misawa AB further north (67th TFS 'Fighting Cocks', 356th TFS 'Green Demons' and 391st TFS 'Bold Tigers'). The 375th TFW received its first two F-4C WW-IVs (63-7433 and 63-7474) on 31 March 1969, while the 347th TFW received its first pair (63-7423 and 64-0757) just over two weeks later on 16 April.[12]

Initially, because of the mix of Weasel and non-Weasel aircraft, much of the original squadrons' make-up comprised the typical F-4 two-man crew set-up, but that began to change as dedicated navigators entered the programme. Before long, an increasing number of F-4 backseaters would come from specialist navigator training to become Weapons Systems Operators (WSOs, or Wizzos), skilled in radar interpretation, navigation, communications and operating the self-protection devices.

Qualifying for the 'pit' of the F-4C WW-IV was restricted to already-qualified or experienced EWOs who underwent additional Weasel training

at Nellis AFB, just like that for the F-105 Bears, most of them coming from the F-105F, EB/RB-66 or B-52. Initial EWO reactions were mixed. To many, the F-4C WW-IV was just the same as the F-105 Weasel but one generation back, because its ongoing electrical anomalies meant that it always seemed to be technically inferior to the latest F-105 Weasel configuration; others praised the 'easier ride'.

The F-4's huge shock absorbers, designed for aircraft carrier landings, meant that, according to 'T.R.' Marino, 'no matter how hard the pilot landed, it felt like a soft landing. In an F-105 the same kind of landing might jar your teeth and drop the aircraft [BAK] hook! Others felt that while backseat forward visibility was ostensibly better the elbow room was the same because they were so tightly strapped in (essential for safe ejection) – and the real advantage of the F-105 was top speed when "stuck on the ground". We routinely went through the Mach on the ground in an F-105.'

'T.R.' Marino recalled:

When I first got to Japan in April 1969, the squadrons were set up as at Takhli. That is, the Weasels were divided up into one flight in each squadron. However, we only had a few aircraft in each squadron as they were still coming onboard, and the WW-IV programme was just getting started in PACAF. In fact I was the first non-pilot backseater

Early F-4C Wild Weasel IV aircraft were assigned to the 66th WWS at Nellis, Nevada, and distributed between the three F-4C Phantom II squadrons of the 347th TFW at Yokota, Japan. (USAF)

in the 36th TFS. But as I was also the only backseater in the squadron with a combat tour, and as a Weasel to boot, things worked themselves out pretty fast.

Unfortunately there was no electronic training range available for our use in the area. Our missions at Yokota normally consisted of standard intercept, air-to-air or air-to-ground gunnery missions with maybe a mock attack on a GCI site. The TDY schedule was gruelling and we spent a lot of time in Korea at Osan AB. Even in 'K' the missions were similar to [those in] Japan. However, we also spent a lot of time on nuke alert, air defence alert, conventional alert, 'Night Owl' alert – the operative word here being *alert*. We used to joke that we were jacks of all trades and masters of none.

Lt Col William C. McLeod II (USAF Ret, then a Captain), who arrived at Yokota AB in July 1969 and attended Weasel school at Nellis AFB later that year (as part of the new experimental 414th Fighter Weapons School, which combined air-to-air combat with Weaseling), echoed Marino's sentiments:

The primary mission was SIOP (nuclear deterrence), and the wing was responsible for maintaining one full F-4 squadron deployed to Korea (with several aircraft on nuclear alert) at all times. The 347th deployed to Osan while the wing at Misawa deployed to Kunsan. In addition to our normal deployments, every time there was a load-out exercise, an evaluation, or the North Koreans did something that got our attention, the other squadrons would immediately deploy to Korea. As a result, we spent a lot of time in Korea, where we would practise nuclear and conventional deliveries and intercepts, but rarely get any realistic Weasel training.

Mission-ready checks were single-ship nuclear-delivery missions, and as soon as the initial check was passed the crew studied for and certified on a real-world nuclear target. After completing that, you were qualified to spend time on alert with a B-61 [thermonuclear bomb] strapped to the belly of the jet and a real mission folder and authenticators stuck into each cockpit. When not on Alert we flew a lot of range missions as we needed to maintain our weapons qualifications.

Lots of interesting missions occurred while the crews were deployed to Korea. Before I arrived the 36th TFS had been involved in the EC-121 shoot-down and numerous BARCAP missions to protect other EC-121s, including at least one which came very close to an engagement with a North Korean MiG.[13] I managed one combat support mission. A bunch of us were eating lunch in the Osan O'Club one day when the Base Recall siren went off. We all jumped into some trucks and made for the squadron. When we arrived, we found the Squadron Commander standing in front of the entry doors. He grabbed my EWO Capt Ray Penley and I and told me to get my gear and get the aircraft in a certain shelter airborne immediately. He told my EWO to get one of the maps being prepared in Mission Planning and to be in the aircraft before I took off.

When I got to the aircraft I found a weapons load crew down-loading a centreline gun with training ammo so they could load one up with HEI [High-Explosive Incendiary]. As I was sorting this out the Assistant Ops Officer drove up and told me I was no. 2 in a two-ship, to forget the gun and get started, and call the tower for Scramble instructions as soon as I did. He didn't leave any doubt in my mind that I was to get airborne NOW, but he didn't tell me why. I cranked the jet while the load crew hustled to get the gun uploaded, which they managed in record time.

The Scramble instructions took us to Kangnung on the east coast, just south of the 5th AF Buffer Zone. Further instructions directed us to co-ordinates that plotted off the North Korean coast well north of the [Korean] DMZ. When we got there we found a US Navy ship, probably a destroyer escort, surrounded by several North Korean patrol boats/MTBs.

We 'Capped' them for so long that I was beginning to think that I was going to have to divert to Japan, because I wouldn't have enough fuel to get back to South Korea. At the last minute the Squadron Commander showed up with the rest of the squadron and relieved us, and we were able to just get home without running out of gas. At some point I guess the North Koreans gave up. The ship had to be an intelligence collector of some type.

WEASEL CONSOLIDATION

McLeod said:

Piecemealing the F-4C Weasels out among the multiple squadrons in both wings did not work out very well, because with only one or two Weasel aircraft and just a few crews in each squadron the Weasel crews rarely managed to fly the Weasel aircraft. We would be on Alert when the aircraft were flying and they would be on Alert or in maintenance when we were flying. Eventually, 5th AF mandated a change and by July 1970 all the Weasel assets (including those at Misawa) were transferred into the 80th TFS at Yokota. The wings' missions stayed the same, as did the deployment requirement, but at least we were now flying the Weasel aircraft. This proved to be a good deal for the 80th TFS and its new commander, Lt Col David Oakes, because it consolidated much of 5th AF's experienced F-4 crews in that one squadron and we had a great flying club for about a year.

In the fall of 1970, without any notice at all, we were informed that both 5th AF wings were going to reorganize and move out of Japan. The plan called for three F-4 squadrons to activate in Korea (the 35th TFS and 80th TFS at Kunsan and the 36th TFS at Osan) and two more, including one Weasel squadron, to activate at Kadena (the 44th TFS and 67th TFS). The plan specified when each squadron would activate, deactivate, move, etc. However, it did not take into account a number of real-world factors and as a result things didn't always take place when the plan said they would.

One key factor that caused problems initially was the personnel rules concerning which crewmembers would return to CONUS [Continental United States] after the reorganization. Under the plan almost all the Weasel crews fit the criteria for returning to the States, which would have left 5th AF with a Weasel squadron without Weasel crews! As a result, none of the Weasel crews returned to the States. PACAF involuntarily extended [the tours of] all those who fit the criteria to return and we all moved to Kadena with the aircraft.

Not long after the plan was announced, the 80th TFS deployed to Kunsan to cover the requirement for a deployed squadron and the nuke alert at that base. We eventually returned to Yokota, where we were told that the 80th TFS was going to deactivate. Since we were not due to move to Kadena for about another month, the powers that be solved the problem by issuing an order that transferred all the 80th TFS crews to the 35th TFS – only on paper, however. We continued to wear 80th TFS patches, go to work at the 80th TFS Ops Building which still said 80th TFS on the front, and fly 80th TFS aircraft. On 11 March 1971 we cranked up the aircraft and flew them to Kadena, my flight logging 3hr en route. Our Squadron Commander was waiting for us and as far as I know we activated the 67th TFS upon arrival. A lot of new guys from CONUS were there also and for a while the squadron had a lot of non-Weasel crews. Eventually they were split off and formed the 44th TFS.

The 67th TFS was another great flying club for about a year. We flew lots of low-levels, dropped a lot of bombs on Ie Shima Range, went cross-country on the weekends. A few of us spent some time on TDY to Taegu AB in Korea, and we also sat air defence alert at Kadena for a while. One 67th TFS crew intercepted a Soviet May Ilyushin Il-38 [Sigint aircraft] after scrambling off the Alert pad. Another 67th TFS flight was scrambled against an unknown blip that turned out to be a kite that a Soviet trawler had put up to lift a very long antenna.

Further rotations and deployments were made to Korea before the crews received their call to arms.[14]

The third F-4C WW-IV unit to equip, beginning on 26 November 1969 (when its first two deliveries, 63-7443 and 64-0741, arrived), was the 81st TFS 'Panthers', based at Hahn in West Germany, where it developed its Weasel crews and tactics as part of USAFE's 17th AF. The unit was deployed to Zweibrucken AB in June 1971 and transferred there officially during July, before ultimately settling down fifteen months later under 52nd TFW control at Spangdahlem AB, with a notional fourteen aircraft flown exclusively by paired-off pilot-ACs and EWOs. The 81st TFS was the first ever Weasel unit to be stationed in Europe, though it faced the same training challenge as PACAF crews: the absence of a dedicated electronic warfare range to practise against. A hefty proportion of their day-to-day training embraced air-to-air and air-to-ground combat proficiency, aerial refuelling and the seemingly never-ending SIOP Victor Alert tasking, though Weaseling did get a look-in: most targets comprised friendly SAM, GCI and EW sites, with a favourite being the be-domed complex at Spadeadam in Northumberland, England, which offered a multiplex of signals to decipher.

F O U R

LINEBACKERS

T he beginning of 1972 signalled a major turn of events in
Vietnam, as the North prepared for an all-out invasion of the
South, masterminded by Gen Vo Nguyen Giap who had defeated
the French at Dien Bien Phu nearly twenty years earlier. To the
FACs and reconnaissance crews flying over the DMZ it was clear that
something had been afoot since January, as air defences rapidly intensified.
Apart from the usual 23mm, 37mm and 57mm triple-A pieces peppering
the sky with dirty, dangerous smudges there were new 85mm and 100mm
guns, plus an expanding SAM presence. This was something new and
worrying. Da Nang AB's FAC commander Gabriel A. Kardong noted that
'On the 17th [February] I narrowly evaded a SAM-2 while flying at
1,200ft in the DMZ. That day, eighty-one SA-2s were fired in the DMZ
area and downed three F-4 aircraft.'[1] This was just a taster. In the early
morning darkness of Good Friday, 30 March, 40,000 North Vietnamese
troops, plus armour, began grinding their way across the DMZ, in what
became known as the Easter Offensive.

   The United States' response was swift, fielding air power both to thwart
the enemy invasion and to bring pressure to bear on North Vietnam for a
peace settlement. For the first time, virtually every target – bar foreign

*As a matter of some urgency,
Weasel Thunderchiefs of the 561st
TFS 'Black Knights' based at
McConnell AFB, Kansas, were
redeployed to South-East Asia
under Operation Constant Guard
in April 1972. (via Jim Rotramel)*

shipping in port in Haiphong and the enemy inner sanctuary around Hanoi – was up for grabs, but with the focus on bridges, rail lines and depots, petroleum, oil, and lubricants (POL) stores and industrial facilities. The offensive started on 6 April as Operation Freedom Train and became Linebacker from 8 May. However, North Vietnam had had three years in which to reconstruct its domestic air defences, and these had grown into a formidable network encompassing all of the country, with virtually blanket SAM and triple-A coverage comprising over 300 potential SAM sites and 1,500 triple-A pieces netted to almost 200 radar stations. There was nowhere to hide.

Defence suppression was a top priority and to ease the burden on the 17th WWS at Korat RTAFB, Operation Constant Guard I ordered the deployment of the 561st TFS 'Black Knights' and their F-105Gs from McConnell AFB. The squadron's Intel Officer, Capt Barry Miller, recalls:

The squadron had been closely following the increased SAM activity, with the resulting Wild Weasel involvement for several weeks, and had even been tasked to send over additional crews to augment the 17th WWS in advance, comprising volunteers. There was a general feeling it was only a matter of time until the whole squadron was required to help out [in] the rapidly escalating war in South-East Asia.

We were briefing the crews almost daily about the many SAM engagements, shootdowns and ARM expenditures, so the 561st TFS members were becoming very familiar with the situation, and recognized there would be demand for Wild Weasel assets. So it came as no surprise when the alert recall/deployment notification came on 6 April. There was a high level of excitement and activity as the unit responded rapidly, launching its first F-105Gs within 48 hours. Its quick response was due in part to the low-level preparations that had already been accomplished in anticipation of such a deployment order. Twelve aircraft were deployed to become Det 1, and they were flying combat missions within a week.

Det 1 departed McConnell AFB on 7 April and arrived in Thailand by the 12th, bringing in-theatre Weasel assets up to twenty-eight jets. Crews were thrust into combat immediately, those making the actual deployment being given a two-day theatre familiarization, flying near the DMZ in support of the CAS strikers and numerous US Army and Air Force gunships pounding the enemy armour, their short reprieve a means to adjust to the climate and jet lag. Additional aircraft deployed included EB-66s from Shaw AFB, South Carolina; and thirty-six F-4Es from the 4th TFW at Seymour-Johnson AFB, North Carolina, comprising crews from the 334th TFS 'Eagles' and 336th TFS 'Rocketeers', which deployed to Ubon RTAFB from 8 April, to become part of the 8th TFW's 'smart' bombing interdictor force, acting as Laser-Guided Bomb (LGB) companions to the wing's Precision Avionics Vectoring Equipment (Pave) Knife target laser-designating aircraft, among other duties.

The follow-on operation, Constant Guard II, deployed F-4Es from the 58th TFS 'Gorillas' at Eglin AFB, and the 308th TFS 'Emerald Knights' at Homestead AFB, Florida, to Udorn RTAFB, to expand the air superiority

561st TFS crew majors Roy Brenner (pilot) and Norm Maier (EWO) just after their excursion into North Vietnam. (Barry Miller)

establishment from 28 April. Meanwhile the 49th TFW's entire complement of F-4Ds were sent from Holloman AFB, New Mexico, to Takhli RTAFB (rapidly reactivated from caretaker status) beginning on 6 May under Constant Guard III, to provide the hard-pressed US Army ground forces with CAS, bringing the in-theatre US Air Force F-4 force (split between Korat, Da Nang, Takhli, Ubon and Udorn) to just over 344 aircraft by mid-May.

LINEBACKER CHAFF BOMBERS

Linebacker interdiction strikes typically embraced four F-105Gs providing Iron Hand, followed by a mutually protective ensemble of more than three dozen F-4D/Es: eight MiGCAP jets to keep the enemy fighters at arm's length, and four flights of four F-4 strikers supported by a further eight F-4 strike escorts, flown as outriggers with the bomber stream. In addition, at the apex of each strike package, about 20 minutes in advance, were eight to twelve F-4Es from the Ubon-based Wolfpack or their TDY-ing cousins from Seymour-Johnson AFB, which laid a chaff carpet that would prevent the main strike formation from being tracked by radar for SAM attack. Pioneered during the Second World War under the code-name Window, chaff comprised aluminium strips cut to suitable quarter wavelength dipole lengths to match the enemy radars, so that each apparently innocuous strip would appear as a target, and collectively they would swamp the enemy radar displays. Somewhat surprisingly, Linebacker represented the first wholesale use of this countermeasure during the Vietnam conflict.[2]

However, the chaff corridors pointed like an arrow to the droppers themselves, and Chaff Lead would invariably comprise one of the most experienced crews in the wing, because at the head of the package it was they who would determine whether or not (owing to weather, such as

cloud cover) the strike proceeded against the primary target, or would switch to an alternative target. The widespread use of electro-optic Pave PGM or smart bomb systems during the Linebacker campaign made this all the more crucial.

Dispensing chaff carried by F-4D/Es cruising at 24,000ft, line abreast, with a 2,000ft wing-tip separation straight-and-level, the MB Associates AN/ALE-2 underwing pods pumped out their cargoes at 20-second intervals so that each chaff flight created a corridor measuring approximately 2 miles wide by using pre-planned dispense Initial Point and switches off points. The process would be repeated at specifically timed 'turn on/turn off' co-ordinates. MJU-1/B chaff bombs were also dropped, comprising an M129E2 leaflet dispenser filled with RR-68/AL chaff packets and fitted with a mechanical timer fuse.

In the opening stages of the campaign it was not uncommon for chaff-laying crews to draw up to forty SAM launches, but strict TOTs, onboard jamming and skilful EB-66 support created near-misses of 400yd, at worst. AN/ALE-38 dispensers were also employed later in 1972, each housing 300lb of chaff. Instead of fluttering away from dispensers as packets that would subsequently blossom, the AN/ALE-38 would cut and dispense chaff from six exit tubes in its rear that could be ejected continuously or in batches, at ten different rates of output.[3] The dispensing rate and cut length were set during pre-flight work on the pod. Eight F-4s working together in line abreast could lay down a chaff corridor some 5 miles wide and 105 miles long, usually sufficient to cover the complete ingress and egress routes over North Vietnam. The chaff was cut and dispensed primarily to defeat triple-A radars and Bar Lock GCI frequencies as well as Fan Song – i.e., those actually used for vectoring MiGs or guiding SAMs and triple-A, leaving EW radar-jamming to the dedicated support jammers.

No aircraft were shot down by SAMs when protected by the chaff corridors, but the chaff-layers themselves became more vulnerable to MiG attack, as they were out in the open, flying strict formation patterns. Enemy interceptor pilots were briefed to go after the green jets (not the Navy MiGCAP grey jets) precisely for this reason, and several crews were shot down by hit-and-run MiGs during the spring and summer. One such chaff crew got their revenge: Capt Fred A. Sheffler and Capt Mark 'Gunner' A. Massen were hit by an AA-2 Atoll AAM in early August and baled out over the Gulf of Tonkin. A week later, on the 16th, they returned as Date Four in the second chaff flight during a mission to the north-east railroad, and evened the score by bagging a MiG-21 Fishbed with a Sparrow III semi-active radar-homing AAM, while their leader was still warming up his missiles!

The early encounters rapidly led to revised tactics whereby the chaff-layers operated as two or four flights of four aircraft about 3 miles apart, in echelon. The second flight acted as MiGCAP for the lead flight, while a strike escort flight provided them with protection and flew point for the bomber stream.

Thus the package expanded, eventually comprising an almost 3:1 ratio of MiGCAP protectors and Weasels to strikers, not counting stand-off jammers and command and control aircraft. As long as the strike element was smart (in both senses of the word), the bombs worked as advertised and everyone met their TOTs, the tactics paid off handsomely.

For the Weasels, snaking around ahead of the main wave on the search for radar prey, the biggest problem was the short time the enemy radars stayed on the air, thereby denying them guidance for their ARMs. Fan Song TTRs often transmitted in brief bursts of only 10–12 seconds' duration, usually just after launching a SAM. The use of decoy sites, and switching between live radars after any ARMs had been fired, meant that Shrikes would be drawn off target by two or more simultaneous signals, resulting in many wasted shots as the missiles became confused and ran out of steam. This forced the crews to press home their attacks closer to the emitters, employing Dive-Modified Shrikes within the SAM sites' lethal radius.

F-105G Iron Hand losses in the first half of the year were commensurately heavy, reflecting the crews' hazardous professional lifestyle: four jets were downed by hostile fire and a further three were written-off or went missing. Some of these losses occurred before Freedom Train/Linebacker got under way. In addition to 17th WWS F-105F 63-8329 flown by Capt Richard J. Mallon and Capt Robert J. Panek Sr which disappeared on a theatre familiarization flight over the Laos/North Vietnamese border on 28 January, two of the squadron's all-up F-105Gs were lost in February: 63-8284 was written off on the 2nd, and 63-8333, callsign Junior, on the 17th, hit by a SAM over RP I. Heading 'feet wet', Capt James Cutter and

Capt Kenneth Fraser were forced to bale out near the beach and were captured and interned.

Linebacker merely upped the ante. On 15 April F-105G 63-8342, callsign Suntan, crewed by Capt Alan P. Mateja and Capt Orvin C. Jones Jr was hit by a missile while attacking a SAM support site. They apparently ejected but were not heard from again. The 17th WWS suffered another two combat losses, both of which occurred under less than usual circumstances. The first was F-105G 62-4424, flown by Maj William Talley and Maj James Padgett (both part of the advance party of volunteers who arrived at Korat RTAFB before the 561st TFS Det 1 deployment proper) with an Icebag callsign, were downed by a MiG-21's AA-2 Atoll AAMs on 11 May after being lured into an apparent trap by a radiating Fan Song. Both banged out to become POWs. Some have questioned whether it was a trap or just a lucky shot by a marauding MiG, but anecdotal evidence suggests the North Vietnamese knew what they were doing. Barrage firings of SAMs – six on this occasion – were typical as strike flights egressed the target area, and the missiles successfully diverted the Weasels' attention while the MiGs attacked from their rear. Yet any F-105 crew was foolish to tangle with MiGs – its advantage lay with its huge acceleration and top speed down on the deck.

The 17th WWS lost F-105G 62-4443 under very similar circumstances on 29 July, but with a happier ending. Maj T.J. Coady and Maj H.F. Murphy got into a scrap with a MiG over RP IV while attacking a SAM site, and were apparently hit by a projectile of some sort. They successfully made it out to sea before ejecting, and were picked up by friendlies. The report at the time, based on post-flight debriefings, suggested that the crew flew into a wingman's jettisoned drop tank or rack, but other eyewitness accounts indicate that it was another form of own goal: the pilot had just released an ARM and it is possible that this missile impacted the aircraft's wing during the ensuing split-S defensive break against the MiG. At 480–600kt, even a gentle tap could cause critical damage.

A further loss during this time was 561st TFS F-105G 63-8347, on 17 May. The crew aborted their mission but the aircraft blew a tyre and caught fire on landing with a full weapons load. Both men jumped out without injuries before the flames totally engulfed the machine. Tragically, one of its Shrikes cooked off 'and sprayed its deadly fragmentation cubes, causing many casualties (and some deaths) among the base firemen and others gathered around the aircraft'.[4]

Nonetheless, the combination of Weasels, chaff and onboard self-protection systems minimized losses. For example, during a May strike against the Ham Rung or 'Dragon's Jaw' bridge, the North Vietnamese launched 160 SAMs at the strike package without achieving a single hit.

NAVY WHALES

The US Navy's contribution to Linebacker persisted in the Alpha Strike concept, although targeting was considerably less confined than it had been during the Rolling Thunder era. Launches typically comprised a mix of F-4B/J Phantom II or F-8 Crusader MiGCAP/TARCAP, plus A-4F,

A-7C/E and A-6A strikers supported by Iron Hand ARM-shooters and whatever jamming assets were available.

Although by now the oldest aircraft in the Fleet, the EKA-3B Skywarrior provided essential electronic combat support when bombing over North Vietnam was resumed. The aircraft had originally entered service in the reworked TACOS configuration in late 1967, but Linebacker represented its first true combat introduction. The aircraft were easily distinguished by electronic gear in the form of a small pod atop the fin, blisters flanking the fuselage and a large blade antenna under the nose, comprising the receivers and barrage- or spot-jamming arrays. There was also a variety of receiver equipment, working across the spectrum.

All the specialized equipment increased the empty weight of this already heavy aircraft by 2 tons, up to a whopping 44,900lb, leaving a sporting margin of only 5,000lb of fuel at landing. Take-off was even more dramatic, especially from older ships such as USS *Shangri-La*, whose short deck demanded maximum catapult pressure to get the aircraft safely off its bow. Intel Officer Barry Miller: 'I was told nothing was launched for several minutes prior to an A-3 launch, so as to allow maximum steam build-up for the very heavy "cat" shot. It was personally unnerving to watch the skin "ripple" along the side of the KA-3 as I watched it during the "cat", knowing I was about to depart by KA-3!'

Typical crew composition was three men: the pilot, an NFO to manage navigation, COMJAM and the refuelling hose and pumps (maximum give-away was 21,500lb, and a second NFO who worked with the receivers

Douglas EKA-3B Whales show off their jamming wares. The aircraft shared a common ancestry with the USAF's EB-66 Destroyer but did not feature ejection seats like its land-locked counterpart. (Frank B. Mormillo)

A TIAS A-4F from VA-55 'Warhorses' on USS Hancock *in September 1972 displays its lethal Iron Hand cocktail of Mk20 Rockeyes and Shrikes.* (Barry Miller)

and ALT-27 radar jammers. Unlike the US Air Force equivalent, the EB-66, the EKA-3B did not feature ejection seats. Former EB-66 and F-105 crewman Stan Goldstein remembers it well: 'They had to lower the entrance door and slide down. They took off [from] the carrier with the pilot's canopy a little open because the only way out was to climb out. Not to say that we did not have problems with the EB-66 control stick stowing on take-off, a hairy instance, or having an upper canopy hatch blow off on take-off.'

VAQ-130 'Zappers', based at NAS Alameda, California, where the Skywarrior force was concentrated, provided *ab initio* training as part of the Fleet Readiness Maintenance Training Program (FRAMP), three-ship detachments for seagoing operations via its own unit and the co-located all-up operational VAQ-135 'Black Ravens', and conducted various evaluation exercises and trials. It also furnished NFOs for VQ-1 'World Watchers' and VQ-2 'Batmen', who employed EA-3Bs along with turboprop-powered Lockheed EP-3B Bat Racks and the EP-3E Airborne Reconnaissance Integrated Electronic System (ARIES). These eavesdroppers conducted Elint on enemy ground and shipborne radars around the world, flying principally from land bases such as Da Nang AB, NAS Cubi Point or Atsugi AB, and would provide SAM calls using the callsign Deep Sea: typically 'Deep Sea on Guard. SAM . . . SAM . . . vicinity of [location]. Deep Sea out.'[5]

Cdr F.L. Bottenberg's VAQ-130 was the US Navy's biggest electronic combat squadron, with twenty-two EKA-3Bs and KA-3s counted among its ranks during the opening months of 1972. Yet by far the greatest tranche of VAQ-130's aircraft were at sea, riding the waves, monitoring enemy emitters with their receiver gear and jamming them as necessary. In response to the spring invasion, VAQ-130 Det 1 was already on station when the proverbial s*** hit the fan. Dets 2 and 3 left on 10 April and 5 June to board USS *Midway* and USS *Oriskany* respectively, for gruelling eleven-month deployments. It was hard work flying from tiny aircraft carriers in such a monster of a jet, and VAQ-130 crews averaged 410.4 flight hours during the year.

EKA-3B duties were varied, in line with their official role of TACOS. Their hoses and drogues replenished A-6 and A-7 strikers, as well as BARCAP F-4s and F-8s, and their noise jammers helped suppress North Vietnamese air defences in Stand-Off Jamming (SOJ) mode, feet wet and out of range of the SA-2s, in practice mostly working against Fan Song radars with ALT-27 in Band 7. In addition, their AN/ALQ-92 COMJAM system featured a limited Band 2 jamming facility against Spoon Rest EW radar, partially degrading this system which could be used as an acquisition system for the SA-2. Grumman EA-6B Prowler ECMOs, who arrived in the war at the end of spring with their 'Four-Holers' (A-6s stretched to accommodate a pilot and three ECMOs, working with the more advanced Eaton AIL AN/ALQ-99 Tactical Jamming System), reckoned that at least two of those jammers were needed to foil Spoon Rest radars. Surveillance of 'merchant shipping' (Soviet listening ships) was also performed.

These tasks were carried out independently because of electromagnetic radiation hazards to JP5 kerosene during refuelling, involving separate tracks and thus many more sorties. Tanking was always in demand for the thirsty carrier-borne jets. Typically, SOJ meant flying an orbit out of reach of the SAMs at 20,000ft, with the EKA-3B's jammers aligned so that it, the air wing it was supporting and the target were all more or less on the same line. 'If we were doing our job properly, SAMs launched at the Air Wing flew through it without detonating and we could see them streaking toward us. We were beyond the SAM radar's tracking range, but the missiles would fly beyond us and detonate high above. It was quite exciting to see that happen.'[6] Like the US Air Force EB-66s, the EKA-3Bs bought valuable time for the attackers.

Helping relieve the immediate tension in the war zone was VAQ-135, led by Cdr Robert S. Jackson. Dets 1 and 5 (three EKA-3Bs apiece) had deployed onboard USS *Kitty Hawk* and USS *Hancock* on 17 and 11 February respectively. They were originally destined for the customary gradual combat familiarization at Dixie Station, but the spring invasion generated some impromptu adjustments. Det 1, for example, was hurried out of NAS Cubi Point on 2 April, three days ahead of schedule, with only 6hr notice. The two detachments supplemented and then replaced the hard-pressed Det 3, which was already onboard USS *Coral Sea*, and which remained off the coast of North Vietnam with CTF-77 until 3 May.

During the course of several 51- to 56-day Line Periods, the nine EKA-3Bs provided jamming cover and refuelling for over sixty Alpha Strikes, including Marine Corps A-6 Intruders from CVW-15 during the mining of the approaches to Haiphong harbour with AWT-1 and other magnetic/acoustic devices – a long-overdue operation, code-named Pocket Money, initiated on the eve of 9 May. Det 5 deployed two of its aircraft onboard USS *Constellation* to accompany the Pocket Money Alpha Strikes. The EKA-3B Skywarriors also participated in the breaking of the North Vietnamese Army's sieges of An Loc and Quang Tri during June, returning to NAS Alameda in October and November.

Operations had increased to four aircraft carriers in the Gulf of Tonkin when bombing resumed, with an additional pair steaming towards Dixie Station and Yankee Station. Reducing fuel consumption from the aircraft carriers' reserves and extending the EKA-3Bs' endurance was made possible by using US Air Force bases in South Vietnam. For example, VAQ-135 Det 3 recovered and launched sorties, alternately, between USS *Coral Sea* and Da Nang AB, while Det 5 performed much the same routine between USS *Hancock* and Da Nang AB or Bien Hoa AB. In the tanker role, a typical combat detachment averaged a weekly offload of 13,070gal.

When airborne, EKA-3B crews were expected to support whoever was assigned to them. Electronic warfare missions were briefed by radio, so that, for example, Det 5 found itself working with jets from USS *Saratoga*, USS *Oriskany* or USS *America* during its 1972 tenure with the Tonkin Gulf Yacht Club, working double cycles like the other Skywarrior detachments. To give some idea of the tempo, the combat-deployed detachments averaged 174 sorties a month, one-third of them by night, and that includes time in port and TRANSPAC'ing. Not bad for a three-aircraft establishment![7] No EKA-3Bs were lost to enemy fire in 1972 – for the fourth year running – nor any to operational causes.

ELECTRONIC INTRUDERS

US Marine Corps' EA-6As, affectionately nicknamed Sky Pigs, were also redeployed to bolster jamming coverage, fragged by CTF-77 instead of the USAF's 7th AF HQ in Saigon, as had been the case up until the previous year. Col John 'Halfman' Weides:

In April 1972, the EA-6As of VMCJ-1 were the first Marine Corps aircraft to re-deploy in support of Linebacker operations. While the VMCJ-1 birds established an operating base at NAS Cubi Point, a VMCJ-2 detachment under Maj Fred Ogline was diverted from a scheduled carrier deployment in the Med and TRANSPAC'ed to Cubi Point. During the April to December 1972 period, a combined Marine Corps unit of VMCJ-1 and VMCJ-2 [Carrier Task Group 77-6], first under the command of Maj John D. Carlton and later under Maj [later Asst CMC] Jack Dailey, proved to be a vital if not key part of the Linebacker operations.

The unit maintained over a 98 per cent on-station support record and had only two supported aircraft lost to enemy action while supporting hundreds of aircraft. A typical day of operations consisted of an 0300hr wake-up, followed by briefing, and three aircraft made a pre-dawn take-off from NAS Cubi Point scheduled to arrive at Da Nang shortly after dawn. After landing, a hot pit and crew switch was made. A VMGR-152 Sumos KC-130F was assigned to the unit,

and took off prior to the EA-6As with spare black boxes and ground maintenance personnel. Two EA-6As then took off for one of three pre-designated operating areas off the coast of NVN.

After checking in with Red Crown using the secure KY-28 for changes to the frag or mission adjustments, the two EA-6As switched to a strike radio frequency, checked-in with and monitored the inbound strike aircraft, and established a moving racetrack orbit to best support both the ingress and egress of the strike aircraft to the target. The EA-6As remained on station until feet wet by all strike aircraft and then either returned to Da Nang for a crew change or tanked off Navy A-3s; or, if a long pump was needed, off the organic KC-130 which flew north off the coast to 'just short' of the DMZ. Sometimes, when time was critical, 'just short' became 'a little long'. After landing at Da Nang, another hot pit, maintenance scramble, and crew change was made for an afternoon on station by the morning flyover crew who had grabbed a few hours' sleep, something to eat, and checked the latest Intel for new Flat Face, Fire Can, and Fan Song info.

The afternoon sortie was similar to the morning's go. Again, the aircraft hot pitted and changed crews and all three aircraft took off for NAS Cubi Point. Arrival at Cubi was usually about 2000hr, with a TACAN IFR approach through the duty thunderstorm to a GCA final. The morning's flyover and afternoon sortie crew RON'ed

EA-6As were used to considerable effect through the Linebacker campaign, coming under US Navy Task Force 77 control. (Richard L. Ward Archives)

[rendezvoused] at the sumptuous Navy VQ-1 quarters and partook of libations at the Red Dog Saloon. The returning crew had the next day 'off' to perform the inevitable test flights, paperwork and mission planning. The three-day cycle worked well. Most of us never had to buy a drink when the carriers came into port. We ran this NAS Cubi Point-based operation because the security of Da Nang was in doubt, so the '800 pound Gorillas' didn't want to let us play in that sand box overnight.

The EA-6As, in common with the EKA-3Bs, focused on Fan Song radars, but also paid attention to the North Vietnamese panoply of radar-directed triple-A, pressing home their jamming at closer quarters, if required. Col John Weides said:

> For Linebacker ops we carried two ALE-32 chaff pods, three jammer pods (or twelve transmitters), and two 300gal fuel tanks. Frequency coverage was for the surface-to-air threats such as Flat Face, Fire Can, Fan Song, Fire Wheel and air-to-air threats in I Band. Remarkably few EA-6As were lost – just three in fact. Capt Dave Leet and Capt John M. Christensen were a combat loss in April in the initial few sorties supporting Linebacker. We don't know exactly why they went down but assume that a SAM got them as they were returning from station off Hanoi in the early morning darkness. Another was lost when Hal 'Weird' Baker and Fred 'Killer' Killerbrew ejected due to fire (bleed air duct failure) in the vicinity of Cubi Point. 'Killer' was over fifty at the time and is the oldest one I know of to make a 'nylon letdown' from an EA-6A.

To add to its bite, CTF-77 was also hastily re-equipped with all-Pacific Fleet A-6Bs, which were kept extremely busy throughout the year. The remainder of the squadrons' aircraft, which flew to their home bases at either NAS Oceana or NAS Whidbey Island at the close of the cruise, stopped off at various locations for sundry training exercises and a beer or two – US Navy ships remained dry. However, the A-6Bs were always held at NAS Cubi Point, to be picked up by another Intruder Atkron en route to the battle zone.

Maintenance parties detached from the ships were responsible for bringing the aircraft back up to full mission-capable status, and redecorating the machines in their typically flamboyant squadron logos. Pride tended to ensure that the latter received equal priority with full mission-capable status. Typically, six of the more experienced B/Ns, along with three pilots, would be nominated for training on the use of the Standard ARM and the specific displays and controls pertinent to the A-6B subvariant they would be flying. It was very much pure theory followed by hands on training in combat.

Undoubtedly the most successful were the six A-6B crews assigned to the US Marine Corps all-weather attack squadron VMA(AW)-224 'Bengals', flying A-6s from the USS *Coral Sea* that spring under the leadership of the CAG, Cdr Roger Sheets, and his B/N Col Charlie 'Vulture' Carr: the Pocket Money strikers. They also made two extremely daring 100ft AGL ingresses against Bai Thuong airfield in April and May, popping up for their bomb runs on the base as the skies swirled with MiGs in the process of dumping fuel tanks – *over* their heads! Cdr Sheets and Col Carr even contributed to a MiG-17 kill, by drawing it away from the attacking elements so that an F-4 could get on the MiG's tail and bag it. Enthusiastically press-ganged into service from their home base at MCAS Cherry Point, North Carolina, as part of the growing commitment to deploy the hitherto largely land-locked US Marine Corps squadrons aboard carriers, Cdr Sheets and Col Carr knew little of the mission until they picked up their initial three aircraft and were briefed on STARM at NAS Cubi Point by General Dynamics' field representative Ed Duvall. Col Carr: 'We trained in an A-6B hanging a practice missile, on a carrier pier in Cubi Point. We would sit in the cockpit, sweating out hangovers big time while the rep would simulate Fire Can and Fan Song emitters by walking around with a dummy emitter, and we manipulated the switches. Great fun.'

Within two months they were in action and by the end of June had notched up ninety-five A-6B combat sorties, firing forty-seven STARMs against North Vietnamese radar sites, mostly against the dense SA-2 cluster in the Hanoi–Haiphong conurbation. Col Carr flew one of the Iron Hand strikes and recalls that the weapon 'just came off its rails, heading for the sky'. It was exhilarating to watch but the threats would light up the displays well before the strike force was feet dry, so that the A-6Bs were sometimes Winchester by the time they had crossed the beach. The squadron was launching with four STARMs on each A-6B!

CTF-77 had about forty-eight of the new AGM-78C model, and VMA(AW)-224 got through them all in two to three weeks of fierce fighting. Col Carr also recollects that the ones they were employing caught the North Vietnamese defences by surprise, following the USAF suspension of Standard ARM activity, which they were not subject to. Conservative estimates suggest that the squadron single-handedly decommissioned no fewer than eighteen Fan Song radars. Col Carr said:

The birds had a [BDA] hit indicator in the system which seemed to go off usually 45–48 seconds after Ramjet or launch of missile call. This may have explained the spectacular results. I do know that when going after SAM sites, we always tried to bomb them after Shrike or Standard ARM went in, so as not to have any surprises. This was especially true when supporting B-52 raids. All in all, the squadron got a great reputation for knocking down SA-2 sites. We did not dispute the matter. We did go after SAM sites utilizing the ALR-45 and its direction-finding capabilities. In a four-ship we would go towards a known site at about 100ft, and around 15 miles pop up, let him take a look, and we would note his direction, do that at least one more time until we had a three-ringer, pop up offsetting the direction, see the site and roll in on it. However, this was not always successful.

The Shrike-launching job was seen as drawing valuable bomb rack space away from the A-6s' weapons load, and close-in mopping up of the SAM and triple-A sites was mostly handled by the A-7s of VA-22 'Fighting

Redcocks' from USS *Coral Sea*, using Shrikes and Rockeyes, while the A-6As pressed home their bombing.

No matter how important their role was, Col Carr considered the A-6Bs' mission somewhat benign, standing off and lobbing the big missiles. However, several Marines became expert at the stand-off missileering job and began to specialize in just that. Among the squadron, Col Carr remembers pilot Roger Milton and B/N Tommy Gamble as being particularly proficient at knocking out radars. A division of labour ensued.

The seven US Navy A-6 squadrons that saw action that year similarly operated a hotchpotch of four to six KA-6D tankers, seven to ten A-6As, many equipped with the P-8 DIANE software and new ATI AN/ALR-45 RHAWS and Magnavox AN/ALR-50 LWR, and (with the sole exception of VA-35, which had A-6C TRIM aircraft modified with an additional laser gun for LGB drops) two to four A-6Bs with Mod 1 STARM capability for at least part of their cruise, picked up when available during in-ports in the Philippines, or cross-decked at Yankee Station if no in-port maintenance was due. As was customary, these aircraft worked primarily in support of US Navy Alpha Strikes, while also providing protection and back-up Electronic Support Measures (ESM) during RA-5C reconnaissance missions.

As a gauge of the increased activity, the pre-Linebacker cruises seldom witnessed the A-6B complements launching more than a handful of STARMs, if any. For example, the two A-6Bs assigned to VA-196 fired only four during Protective Reaction strikes in 1971, and VA-165 fired none the previous year. This increased massively as the heart of the enemy defences was woken up and engaged with fewer restrictions, including increased use of the bigger, more expensive ARMs in pre-emptive mode, which had not been possible earlier.

Despite a shortage of AGM-78s during the summer, which obliged A-6 crews to launch with four Shrikes instead of the usual two STARM plus two Shrike or bombs combination, VA-75 aboard USS *Saratoga* shot twenty-four AGM-78s during the Linebacker series of operations. However, one Mod 0-Update A-6B was lost in July when relying on just Shrikes – the fourth of this type to be lost in four years of combat operations, reducing that particular force to just six machines.

Overall, A-6 losses were relatively light given the ferocity of the enemy defences, and the massive operational tempo: between May and September 1972 the US Navy launched a colossal 4,000 combat sorties a month, comprising 60 per cent of the total US effort at this time. No A-6 Intruders were hit by MiGs, and only one US Navy Intruder was destroyed by SAMs: this was a VA-165 A-6A, mortally wounded by one of two missiles fired at it over Vinh airfield. The crew were pathfinding as part of a forty-aircraft Alpha package, but became distracted by an ailing DIANE bomb-nav system on the strike run, and never saw the missiles approaching. The B/N ejected successfully and was picked up.

VMA(AW)-224 may also have lost an A-6A to a SAM. Major Clyde Smith and his B/N 1/Lt Scott Ketchie were downed flying Bengal 505 (BuNo. 155652) on 9 April, while bombing an enemy convoy on Route 9 near Tchepone, Laos. F-105Gs were sent in twice and took out the SAMs with Shrikes, but the triple-A fire was too intense for a helicopter to attempt an extraction, especially with a MiG base nearby. Maj Smith sat it out and was rescued four days later by an HH-53, but only after the perennially concerned Captain Bill Harris, skipper of USS *Coral Sea*, asked why it was taking so long for the Air Force to commit defence suppression assets to provide covering fire to bring out his boys. Told they were already overstretched, Harris called the captain on USS *Constellation*, and between them they launched a 78-aircraft strike which pulverized the triple-A in the area during a 5hr non-stop bombardment, allowing the Air Force helicopter and its A-1 escorts to get in and out with only minor hits from small-arms fire. The only casualty was an HH-53 door gunner, hit in the knee, who bravely kept his fists on his minigun to squirt the tree-lines with suppressive fire.

Every loss to a SAM had to be catalogued and accounted for. EA-6A ECMO John Weides recalls that 'I had to go with the skipper and explain to the Commander of CTF-77 why one of his aircraft got "bagged". [The] simple explanation was that he turned north when the frag had him going south, and overflew an SA-2 site. He accepted the explanation and the coffee tasted better all of a sudden. Not as acid.'

OPTICAL SAMS

As well as the increased density of defences, the North Vietnamese had fielded some new SA-2F Mod 5 SAMs during the previous eighteen months, adding to the diversity of threats. The related Fan Song-F featured a Moving Target Indicator (MTI) capability, which allowed it to distinguish the fast-moving jets from bursts of distracting chaff during the brief time it was transmitting to engage aircraft. It also featured optical tracking, allowing the SA-2 to be launched without radar guidance in good weather. According to Lt Col Barry Miller, 'Two operators sat inside the small, box-like cabin atop the Fan Song-F radar, using optics to track the target and feed target data to the guidance system in the van'. The North Vietnamese operators employed crude but often lethal measures such as using wax crayon marks to show how big an American jet should appear in the sights at optimum range, while shouting orders to those turning the wheels to bring the SAM to bear on its gears. As VAQ-132 'Scorpions' skipper Cdr E.F. Rollins Jr noted in his 4 September to 8 October Anchor-to-Anchor report: 'It appears that the SA-2 missile sites are relying more and more on techniques of optical guidance than tracking signals. Engagement might be accomplished through initial target data provided by a co-located Spoon Rest or another type of EW radar such as Knife Rest or Flat Face. Fan Song radar target tracking might consist of short bursts to provide occasional range data.'

The use of optical tracking to guide SAMs had been noted by the US Air Force as early as April, at the very beginning of the campaign. Even without optical tracking, if the target could be ranged by EW radar and the missile brought to bear and fired, the Fan Song would then pop up on the air for just long enough to guide the missile during the closing stages of its intercept, or the launchers would rely on the SAM's proximity fusing inflicting some damage. Such innovations in this ferocious battle forced

Fan Song-F. Optical target tracking was possible via the little cabin atop the radar 'trough' installation. (via Barry Miller)

crews down to terrain-skimming heights. This was true of night-time ops too and the North Vietnamese were clearly using optical tracking devices by night when moonlight was available; they also were habitually more aggressive with their SAMs under the cloak of darkness.

Crews from VA-35 'Black Panthers' were flying night ARREC missions into RP VIB between Haiphong and Cam Pha, operating in the 1300–0100hr shift, when they encountered some particularly tenacious missiles, as skipper Cdr V.G. Donnelly recorded:

> This was the first time since VA-42 training hops that the majority of the crews had flown low-level night missions. Much good information was brought back to the squadron by crews that had been into the Hanoi–Haiphong area through the back door (north of Haiphong) and had used the Karst ridges as a shield against SA-2 sites. When SA-2s were fired at our crews, many never-before-used tactics were developed and unpublished characteristics of SA-2s were observed. An example was an SA-2 tracking one of our crews down to 200ft.

However, a further eight A-6As were brought down by triple-A during the year – always the bane of crews attempting to locate targets visually beneath the cloud bottoms (as low as 3,000ft), which placed them in the sights of manually aimed triple-A. Cdr Donnelly and Lt Cdr K.R. Buell were shot down during their third Line Period of Action (in BuNo. 157028) on 17 September, while attacking the north-east railroad. They were listed as MIA. The squadron would exact its revenge under the leadership of Cdr M.D. Beach later in the year, when they attacked SAM complexes around Haiphong with cluster bombs with devastating precision, using more discreet Delta flights of three aircraft at a time.[8]

DAMBUSTERS AND DRAGONS DODGE THE SAMS

The by now expanding Corsair II attack force was also flexing its newfound muscles in the Iron Hand role, utilizing the latest A-7C and A-7E models which featured a new Navigation and Weapons Delivery System (NAV/WDS) comprising a 4-Pi IBM TC-2 bombing computer, Litton AN/ASN-90 INS, CDC film-based moving map and an advanced GEC Avionics Head-Up Display (HUD). This offered Continuously Computed Impact Point (CCIP) visual bombing as well as Shrike capability, which would become its forte. The latest A-7's computers held the ballistics characteristics of up to a hundred different types of weapon and recomputed the impact point in the HUD twenty-five times a second. Its employment was very simple. The pilot selected weapons and lined up on the target, wings level, for either a dive or laydown attack pass. With the HUD's bomb fall-line lined up with the target, he then pickled the bombs the moment the continuously computed release marker on the fall-line 'rose' to intersect it. Pilots talked of 8 mils Circular Error Probability bombing accuracy with the system, which meant that CBUs or iron bombs released at, say, 8,000ft AGL would impact within 65ft of the target. It was a superb daylight or moonlight bombing system. The new IBM computer allowed for considerable flexibility during the attack pass, making some degree of jinking possible without degrading weapons accuracy.

First assigned to VA-146 'Blue Diamonds' (whose skipper, Cdr Jesse R. Emerson III, became the first Fleet pilot to fly the A-7E on 8 October 1969), after two years of bombing nondescript targets along the Ho Chi

A line-up of pristine A-7Es from VA-146 'Blue Diamonds'. The squadron was assigned to USS Constellation *during 1972.* (Richard L. Ward Archives)

Minh Trail, the A-7E and its A-7C cousin were thrust into a full-scale confrontation with the enemy's SAM and triple-A sites for the first time during Linebacker operations.[9]

The Corsair II thus became the principal Shrike-shooter in the Fleet, using its standard AN/APR-25 receivers to get good azimuth data on threats, and attacking them by means of the SIDS radar display mode which would derive target bearing from Shrike's seeker in the customary manner. The A-7 had the ability to launch with Aero 1D drop tanks on the inboard pylons, Shrikes on the intermediate pylons, and four or six Rockeye IIs or an extra pair of Shrikes on the outboard pylons, allowing for different frequency coverage. Also, it normally carried at least one AIM-9D/G Sidewinder AAM on one of the fuselage flank rails and featured an internal M61A-1 Vulcan 20mm cannon for self-protection and strafing. On top of these features, it also had the facility to use smart TV-guided bombs such as the Walleye, its ground-mapping radarscope tripling as an optical display for weapon aiming as well as SIDS.

The A-7 was an outstanding all-rounder and was rapidly earning pride of place as the mainstay light attack aircraft of the US Navy, replacing the

The A-7 SLUF could carry a wide range of ordnance, including AGM-45 Shrikes and AGM-62 Walleyes, as exhibited by this training example from NAS Lemoore, California. Much of this was made possible by the new HUD and multifunction radar display. (Richard L. Ward Archives)

venerable A-4. In all, nineteen SLUF attack squadrons saw action during 1972, ten of them operating A-7Es. The activities of VA-192 and sibling squadron VA-195 'Dambusters', deployed from NAS Lemoore onboard USS *Kitty Hawk*, provide some insight into what a typical pair of A-7E squadrons got up to, and some of the problems the units encountered.

No sooner were they in the western Pacific than VA-195 ominously lost squadron boss Cdr D.L. Hall (in BuNo. 158655/NH-400) on 6 March. He crashed 15nm astern of the ship during night operations in waters off the Philippines. A search effort failed to locate him, and command passed to Cdr Mace C. Gilfrey, who flew the first combat mission of the first Line Period three days later. Both squadrons were plagued by persistent engine problems which twice grounded their aircraft after two A-7Es from Cdr R.L. Kiehl's VA-192 were lost due to this cause. Lt Fred M. Knee ejected (from BuNo. 157529) on 19 March over the Gulf of Tonkin, and on the 23rd of the month Lt Dennis S. Pike's aircraft (BuNo. 157520) conked out over Laos. He ejected 60 miles south-west of Da Nang, but sadly became listed as MIA when search and rescue attempts failed to find him.

The problems with the engines were potentially grave as, alongside the A-6Bs, the A-7s were to become the principal Shrike-shooters during Linebacker operations. *All* of USS *Kitty Hawk*'s A-7Es were armed with a Shrike, usually on the outboard starboard pylon, regardless of their individual assignment, and losing this protective component posed a serious threat. However, they were soon up and running again. VA-195 boss Cdr Gilfrey was shot down on 6 April (in BuNo. 157590/NH-415), the day that bombing of North Vietnam was resumed in earnest. Eleven SAMs were fired at his strike group north of Dong Hoi. He pointed his burning aircraft feet wet, ejected over the coast and was rescued 4 miles out to sea. The knowledge, however, that Lt R.G. Pearson had wiped out a SAM site near Tchepone on 15 March helped to even up the statistics, and an Alpha Strike on 7 April against SAM sites near Quang Khe proved successful, despite the strike waves confronting seventeen SAM launches and fierce triple-A fire.

A popular leader, Gilfrey quickly got back in the saddle, and reached his 1,000 A-7 hours milestone on 28 April. By the end of the year he had set the highest blackboard score in the squadron: 205 combat missions, 40 Alpha Strikes and 231 traps on deck. Command of VA-192 passed to Cdr R.C. Taylor Jr on 8 May, and it was all go: between February and November they accrued 8,100 flight hours, amassing 3,799 arrested landings of which over 27 per cent were at night.

The second Line Period, when USS *Kitty Hawk* had been called out of port to counter the North Vietnamese Easter Offensive, kept its strike crews flying for fifty-one consecutive days, during which the A-7E pilots each logged an average 90hr combat time. Flying into RP VIB was especially hazardous. During an Alpha Strike against Haiphong on 16 April (led by the CAG, Cdr Hardisty, in his F-4), the strike package encountered no fewer than forty SAM launches. VA-195's Lt Charlie Brewer (in NH-413) was hit by a missile. 'He loses virtually all hydraulic systems, but makes a successful emergency landing at Da Nang,' his skipper wrote at the time. Lt Pianetta (in NH-401) caught some shrapnel from a SAM, but made it back to the carrier without further incident.

The squadron continued to strike the usual array of North Vietnamese Army and POL stores, industrial targets and bridges that the US Navy and US Air Force were tasked against, Lt Michael Ruth scoring a famous direct hit on the Hai Duong bridge on 10 May, the event recorded for posterity by the strike camera in another VA-195 A-7E. They also demolished a SAM repair facility north-west of Thanh Hoa three days later. Missiles snaked about after being hit on the ground. These actions helped put the A-7 on the map, securing its continued viability for another nineteen years.

However, the cost was huge. Cdr Gilfrey's aircraft was one of fourteen Corsair IIs that succumbed to SAMs that year, VA-192 XO Cdr D.D. Owens being similarly obliged to exit his aircraft after it took shrapnel hits from an SA-2 on 17 June. A further twenty A-7s were lost to triple-A fire during 1972, though in its favour no aircraft was lost to a MiG and a reassuringly large number of pilots ejected successfully and were picked up.

Whereas the A-6Bs invariably stood back at altitude with AGM-78s primed, the do-it-all A-7s proved excellent at 'mixing it up' in the Iron Hand role. It comes as no surprise that USS *Saratoga*'s VA-37 'Bulls' and VA-105 'Gunslingers', working with the A-6s of VA-75, accounted for a hefty percentage of the 256 Shrikes fired by CVW-2 that year; while USS *Kitty Hawk*'s VA-192 and VA-195, in company with fellow CVW-11 A-6 squadron VA-52, accounted for a whopping 334 Shrike launches. Many were 'shot from the hip' pre-emptively, using the US Navy's by now customary raid strategy, which had the desired effect of shutting down enemy radars while the primary strike tasking of the mission was under way, but a good number were lobbed down the throat at close quarters.

The SLUF's sole limitation compared to the US Air Force Shrike-shooters was its non-afterburning engine. The A-7E pilots would roll in on the target, check the Shrike was within its Dip Angle firing limits on the SIDS, and fire it. But if there was a much faster SAM heading in the opposite direction, some observers reckoned it was close to a fifty-fifty chance who won. One such casualty was Cdr James W. Hall, who was flying Iron Hand from USS *America* on 29 October. Over the target area in Nghe An province, Hall radioed 'Two SAMs, lifting at twelve o'clock'. That was the last anyone heard from him. The first SAM whooshed by his wingman, but Hall's jet (BuNo. 156762) plummeted after the second SAM struck him. His remains were returned to the United States twenty-seven years later.[10]

Aboard USS *Hancock* were the last three A-4 squadrons to see Fleet service. Some eight aircraft from VA-55 'Warhorses' were fitted with the unique China Lake-designed, TI-built AN/APS-117 TIAS receiver package which manifested itself as a large lump under the nose of the aircraft. This provided forward coverage and worked much like the standard SIDS, but was self-reliant for acquiring radars, allowing the pilot to monitor multiple threats, filter any out and attack them with Shrike. The nimble A-4 could pack four Shrikes under its wings.

Throughout their WESTPAC, VA-55 helped to keep heads down while sister squadrons VA-212 'Rampant Raiders' and VA-164 'Ghost Riders' pounded their targets, some of the sorties involving the novel use of TA-4F twin-seaters with the backseater (invariably a maintenance officer) lugging a lightweight laser gun for buddy bombing. It was the US Navy A-4s' combat swansong. Thereafter the jets were employed exclusively for fast jet training and dissimilar air combat, emulating MiGs, their seagoing job having been taken over by the A-7.

BLACK SAM

Iron Hand played a crucial role in keeping friendly losses to a minimum. The raw statistics of the missile duels between SAM sites and ARM-shooters are staggering, yet they hide the true nature of Iron Hand as a means of keeping the enemy Integrated Air Defence System (IADS) shut down or in harmless stand-by mode, on the basis that 'the cat likes fish but rarely wishes to wet its paws'. For example, between 1 April and 30 September 1972 the F-105G Weasels launched 678 Shrike and 230 Standard ARMs, knocking out 3 confirmed dishes and gaining 96 possible hits. Yet over 300 ARMs were launched simply to prevent the enemy from coming on the air. 'In some cases, Fan Song transmitters had fallen silent while guiding SAMs toward a target. Saltwater planes that used these same missiles reported similar results: 1,425 launches, 254 of them pre-emptive, resulted in 33 confirmed and 38 possible hits, plus 521 instances when an enemy radar shut down abruptly.'[11]

US Navy Intruders undertook myriad tasks during 1972, including Iron Hand, mining and bombing. Three A-6As from VA-145 'Swordsmen' trialled the AN/AVQ-10 Pave Knife for LGB delivery. The pod coupled LLLTV with a laser for target marking. (Ford Aerospace)

Mid-June saw particularly heavy strikes against the North Vietnamese air defences, when the daily Linebacker sortie rate reached 300. 'It was estimated that seventy-six SA-2 missile launchers were destroyed on 19 June and another forty-six accounted for on the 21st.'[12] Without this barrage of ARMs the enemy would have exacted a heavy toll of US jets. SAMs were in plentiful supply and radar damage only moderate, given the ease with which they could be repaired – which they were. However, while the North Vietnamese air defence system may have possessed nine lives, it was running out of them in fast order.

Constantly patching up their IADS, the North Vietnamese appeared to have added several new Sino-Soviet pieces of hardware beginning in the summer of 1972. One particular enigma was the sighting in July and August, by US Navy, Marine Corps and Air Force aircrews, of an altogether new SAM, as F-4E pilot Ed Rasimus remembers:

> We had some firings of what we called a 'fat black rocket' – the des-cription says it all. The missile was fat versus 'telephone pole' and black versus [SA-2] Guideline white. Guidance was apparently digital or pulse since its flight movements were jerky (sort of like an 'all or nothing' command input). Some thought it might have been a Chinese variant of an SA-4 [the kerosene-fuelled, ramjet-sustained Ganef, which had been operational in Eastern Europe since 1965 for Strategic Home Defence], but rumours among aircrews are often not very well grounded in reality.

As already noted, the North Vietnamese were also increasingly employing EW radars to derive target bearing, range and altitude for a SAM volley. The long-established P-15 Flat Face EW radar could be used as an acquisition system for the SA-3 Goa, and Ed Rasimus said 'they were on the threat EOB at several times during Linebacker, but never showed'. One site was apparently later established around the Hue/Khe Sanh area, and F-105G EWO Sam Peacock insisted he confronted an SA-3, though apparently nobody at the time believed him.[13] Barry Miller recalls:

> The infamous Black SAM caused all sorts of headaches for Intel folks (like myself) and aircrews alike. It was first reported in early summer [1972], when crews described it as being 'fatter', having a 'different' flight profile/response to target manoeuvres, little plume, and of course much darker/black in colour. Since these observations were from experienced Wild Weasel aircrews who'd seen many SA-2 Guideline missiles in flight, they were taken very seriously. There was a determined and exhaustive effort to establish if in fact our crews were indeed facing a new SAM. The SA-4 (or some Chinese-produced version) became the primary suspect.
>
> An extremely extensive special debriefing was required of those aircrews who felt they'd encountered a Black SAM, with a long list of questions asked and a detailed report filed. Both were considered a major hassle to accomplish, sometimes requiring follow-up debriefing sessions – much to the irritation of all concerned. There was even one case where small warhead fragments suspected as being from a Black SAM were recovered from an F-105G which had experienced a near-

The SA-3 Goa was first encountered by Israeli air crews during the War of Attrition, but some American crews believed they confronted it over North Vietnam during the summer of 1972. (Barry Miller)

miss from one in late summer/early fall. To my knowledge, the warhead results were inconclusive.

As the amount of data gleaned from aircrew debriefs, Elint and aerial recce mounted, the intelligence community could not find sufficient evidence that the Black SAM was the SA-4 or even some other heretofore unknown system. Recce photos failed to reveal any of the usual SA-4 equipment (Pat Hand radars, twin-rail tracked launchers, or SA-4 missiles/storage canisters), no Elint was received from Pat Hand radars, aircrew descriptions of the missiles didn't match the unique configuration of the SA-4, and no spectacular breakaway/separation of strap-on boosters was observed.

The final assessment was [that] the Black SAM was nothing more than a darkly painted standard SA-2, which somehow appeared different to aircrews, and possibly was being guided in a slightly different manner. Some of the aircrews did not fully accept this; nevertheless, reports of encountering it soon began to fade. It was indeed a short but intriguing saga.

Further problems were encountered with the F-105G and Standard ARM match, which did not always behave as briefed when volleyed from the aircraft during the summer. Ed Rasimus recalls the problems:

The Standard wasn't really held in high regard by most folks at the time. The '105 would generally try to get a return and programme the blivet for launch as early as possible in the mission. Usually he'd fire by the time we got in sight of the 'Red'. The missile profile was almost dangerous. It fired forward and then went vertical in front of the flight, climbing out of sight. A minute or two later it would be plunging straight down and on several occasions passed right through the flight.

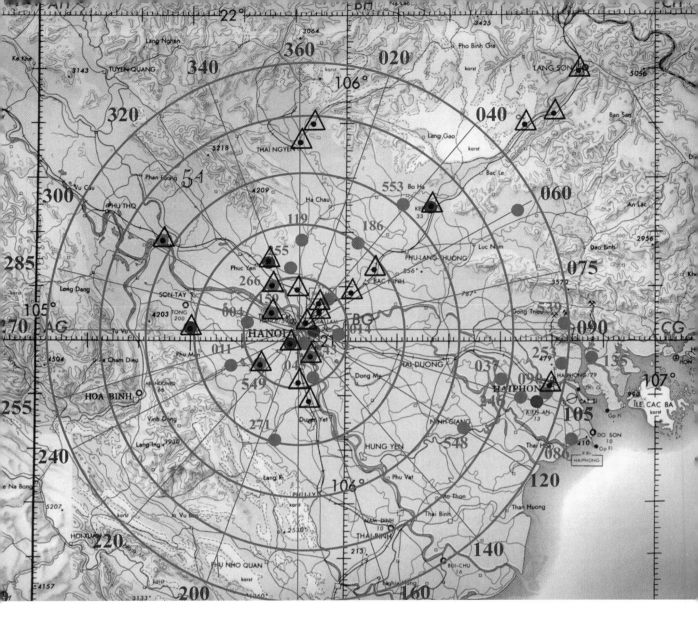

The 'bull's-eye' used for combat ops over North Vietnam, laid out like a dartboard around Hanoi, with small circular blobs denoting enemy SAM sites active during Linebacker II, all featuring triple-digit identification numbers. The triangles represent B-52 and Tac-Air targets, many of them MiG bases. (Al Palmer)

Apparently some 30 per cent of launches that spring were mechanical failures. Either the rocket motor failed to ignite, the guidance system went haywire or the warhead exploded prematurely only several seconds after launch. Anecdotal evidence from Ed Rasimus suggests the big ARMs were 'getting "beat up" while being shipped to theatre by ship, and that the problem was solved by loading the missiles on to a C-141 as soon as they came off the production line and flying them directly to Korat, to minimize the "moving and shaking", resulting in a much more reliable missile'. Barry Miller recollects:

Due to some serious operational problems with the AGM-78 Standard ARM, it was temporarily withdrawn from service in the late summer. Apparently some missiles had seriously misguided, and I was told even pitched back into the formations behind the Weasels. Crews of the F-105Gs and the strike flights both distrusted the missiles. A special team from General Dynamics' Pomona Division and Eglin AFB were dispatched to Korat to try and correct the problems. After several months, the missiles were cleared to return to combat service.

During the downtime, the North Vietnamese radar operators (both Fan Song and Bar Lock) apparently figured out [that] the Weasels were not employing the AGM-78, and hence became more bold in keeping their signals up when the Weasels were out of Shrike range or off-axis. So when the AGM-78 again was an option, several F-105Gs were loaded up in a heavyweight configuration with two AGM-78s each (as well as the normal two AGM-45s) to surprise the enemy. The Bar Lock EW radar/GCI radars were to be particular targets for this change. There was some success in taking out some unsuspecting Bar Locks with this tactic.

Before the end of the year, however, the North Vietnamese would pull further tricks out of their sleeves.

HUNTER/KILLER OPS

With the invasion of South Vietnam successfully repelled, US air power assumed ARREC missions, primarily working the lower RPs of North Vietnam, including the southern area in the panhandle known as Happy Valley. However, things were far from quiet, and considerable success was achieved as Korat-based F-105Gs and F-4Es began undertaking joint hunter/killer missions, these composed of aircraft from the 34th TFS. Ed Rasimus wound up as part of these teams, despite his preference for air-to-air taskings:

I arrived at Korat (again) in July. Because of my previous F-105 tour, I got qualified quickly (despite having only about 35 hours in the F-4 and no time at all in the F-4E). By the end of July, a visiting General from 7th AF declared that the Linebacker missions (those to RP VI) were so critical that only 'dedicated crews' should be scheduled for them – less-experienced folks would fly the Laos, Cambodia, South Vietnam missions while the dedicated crews would fly exclusively to the high-threat area. My Ops Officer called me in and asked what my preference would be for dedicated Linebacker ops – the two missions we flew from Korat were air-superiority escort and hunter/killer. I said I liked escort and chasing MiGs. He then asked me what my second choice was – so I became a hunter/killer specialist!

The hunter/killer concept, unique to Korat, called for two ARM-toting F-105Gs to be teamed with two F-4Es lugging four CBUs and three AIM-7E-2 AAMs to protect the Iron Hand flight from any marauding MiGs. The smoke from an ARM impact on the radar would serve as a marker to highlight the enemy missile launchers for a CBU pass. If the site was not radiating sufficiently long for an ARM launch – as was often the case in the spring and summer, owing to the enemy making increased use of optical tracking – the F-4Es would be vectored to the target co-ordinates for their bomb runs. The heavy weapons loads necessitated two Air-to-Air Refuelling (AAR) plugs en route to the target. The F-4Es apparently operated at the same height as the F-105Gs. Ed Rasimus:

> Typically the 'Gs had to take off with the centreline tank empty to stay below max gross take-off weight. We then hit a PRE-pre-strike tanker to top off the Weasel, then met the full strike package on the main tanker cells for a full load and extension to 20 degrees North latitude and drop off to the target. We would blow the F-4E centreline tank when empty and usually retained the outboard tanks except when going overland all the way to the north-east railroad targets. The Weasel would blow the centreline occasionally and usually retained the inboard '450s. We had no problem lasting as long as mission requirements dictated and usually bingo'd about the same time as the Weasels.

The wealth of experience in these flights made them highly effective. On 29 September Condor flight noted two SAMs being launched at them from site VN-159. Condor One and Condor Two lined up on the site and lobbed four Shrikes against the two Fan Song, while the F-4Es kept the MiGs at bay by bombing Phuc Yen airfield with CBUs, resulting in one MiG-19 being blown to pieces, two MiG-21s burning and a further four MiG-21s damaged.

Another well-known hunter/killer mission was flown on 6 October, over the heart of North Vietnam's air defences. In the air were three Iron Hand flights: Condor, Goose and Cardinal. Condor shot Standard ARMs against site VN-159 for a possible and site VN-142 for a confirmed kill, and then volleyed a pair of Shrikes at site VN-159 pre-emptively, to keep them quiet, while later turning on site VN-243 with a further two Shrikes which struck the target. The F-4Es rolled in on site VN-263 with CBU-52s and CBU-58s, probably causing serious damage. Goose F-105Gs came under attack from two SAMs shot at their tail, missing by about a mile. Turning on the sites, they lobbed Shrikes at sites VN-159 and VN-005 with no apparent results, but their accompanying F-4Es dropped eight CBUs on sites VN-243 and VN-142, completely obliterating both SAM complexes, numerous fires and secondary explosions being observed, including a SAM cooking off at site VN-142.

Finally, Cardinal F-4Es each dropped a pair of CBU-52s and CBU-58s on sites VN-159 and VN-005, with one SAM seen to torch off at the latter site.[14] The net result was two radar sites knocked out and their accompanying SAM launchers and missiles completely trashed, with another possible radar kill and three SAM sites seriously damaged. It had been a good day's hunting.

The chief limitation of hunter/killer operations was that they were essentially limited to daytime, VFR weather. The thick undercast prevalent over North Vietnam from 3,000–8,000ft during the late autumn precluded the concept being used as routine, and the F-105G crews shortly after were obliged to revert to pure Weaseling in support of the strike packages bereft of the F-4s' armoury of CBUs and AAMs, for the remainder of the Linebacker campaign. In addition, two F-105Gs were downed by SAMs in September. On the 16th, Capt Thomas Zorn and 1/Lt Michael Turose (in 63-8360, callsign Condor) were struck by a missile during an ARREC over RP VI while engaging a Fan Song. The aircraft crashed at sea. Neither crewman ejected. On the 29th, Lt Col James O'Neil and Capt Michael Bosiljevac (in 63-8302, callsign Crow) went down over RP VIA during another duel with a Fan Song. O'Neil was captured and Bosiljevac was listed as MIA. The cause was apparently avoidable. Repetitive, uncoordinated SAM alerts and radio chatter from all and sundry were choking the radio channels so that neither crew was able to receive a critical launch warning from their wingman. The Weasels relied on radio announcements based on mutually supportive visual sightings, as the receivers in the cockpit became so saturated with signals in heavily defended areas.

Ops were restricted to south of the 20th Parallel on 22 October 1972, as the North Vietnamese regime seemed to be ready to resume serious peace talks. However, strikes and sensor-seeding operations continued virtually unabated in the military regions in South Vietnam, Cambodia (a new playground for the bombers since 1971) and Laos. As the talks faltered, the need for further dedicated defence suppression assets became more pressing as it became clear that round two, Linebacker II, was in prospect: a wholesale winter offensive against North Vietnam, which would see the full fury of waves of US Air Force B-52 bombers sent to attack the inner industrial sanctuaries of Hanoi and Haiphong.

This brief but fierce campaign, known to the B-52 Stratofortress crews as the Eleven Day War, was initiated by President Nixon on 18 December, five days after the North Vietnamese delegation walked out of the stop-go peace talks. It represented the United States' last shot, forcing an agreement of sorts in January 1973 that would result in the desired 'Peace with Honour', allowing the withdrawal of US forces from the conflict.

Linebacker II represented the first time in the Vietnam War that gradualism was ditched in favour of an all-out, no holds barred, round-the-clock air campaign directed at the heart of the North Vietnamese regime, with commensurately decisive results. Targets included rail yards, power plants, communications facilities, POL stores and ammunition supply dumps, but also – and arguably more significant – the principal North Vietnamese Air Force fighter bases and SAM sites. The target list numbered thirty-four strategic objectives, over 60 per cent of which were situated within a 25-mile radius of Hanoi.

By necessity, Linebacker II involved massive jamming and the fielding of all available radar-killing assets. Two new players thus entered the defence suppression combat arena over RP VI for the first time: the USAF's F-4C Wild Weasel IV and the US Navy's AN/ALQ-99-equipped EA-6B Prowler – and just in time. With only a month or so in which to rebuild its IADS while peace discussions were under way, North Vietnam managed to draw on some fresh technology from the Soviet Union and China, the most serious of which appeared to be modified or new triple-A fire-control radar systems capable of providing ranging information to SAM battalions.

'DON'S DIRTY DOZEN & CREW CHIEFS'

In mid-September six F-4C WW-IVs and nine crews from Lt Col Donald J. Parkhurst's 67th TFS, on a TDY to Kunsan AB, were ordered to return to Kadena AB and prepare to deploy to Korat RTAFB.[15] F-4 Weasel pilot and Squadron Mobility Officer Capt William C. McLeod II recalls: 'We redeployed some of the crews and a few aircraft back to Kadena, and once there spent the next few days putting the load plans together, and packing up the gear. We also made a simple modification to the aircraft. Maj Don Lavigne designed a simple mod to install three switches in the rear cockpit which would allow the EWO to turn off some of the system logic and thus allow him to look at more of the signals that were out there.'

Lt Col Parkhurst and Maj Belles determined which aircrews and aircraft would be going. The aircraft flew down on 23 September, with the maintenance package and spare crews following on a C-141A. Everyone who deployed was highly experienced: the pilots all possessed a previous combat tour and over 1,000hr in the F-4. Pilots Capt John Bremer and Capt Dick Myers (a four-star general and chairman of the Joint Chiefs of Staff at the time of writing) were both Fighter Weapons School graduates. The EWOs were exceptional as well. For example, Capt Al Palmer had flown aboard all three models of the EB-66 during 1967–8. Maj Don Lavigne had a previous F-105 Weasel tour and had been an instructor at the EWO school. Bill McLeod remembers him with considerable respect:

Don was about eight to ten years older than I, a man of few words, an electronic warfare expert, and the bravest man I have flown with. He must have had ice water in his veins. By the time Linebacker II started, we had flown quite a few missions together and I knew that the 'old major' in my 'pit' knew as much about the North Vietnamese air defense system as they did. In addition, the hotter the action got the cooler he got. He was clearly up there to shut as much of their system down as possible, and risks did not concern him at all. He clearly wanted to be where the action was and did everything he could to see that we were.

Bill McLeod also speaks highly of the ground crews involved. The USAF had long since replaced all of the in-theatre war-weary F-4Cs with F-4D/Es, so the Wild Weasel IV, with its old manual 'iron sight' and lack of WRCS ballistics computer, was something of an anomaly in late 1972 in the war zone:

Our maintenance personnel were superb, and were directly responsible for the high sortie rate we managed throughout the deployment. Our old, beat-up F-4Cs were the oldest F-4s in-theatre and the fact that we flew them at a sortie rate of almost 1.0 was unbelievable. I beat the hell out of '423 during Linebacker II, pulling scab patches off the wings almost every night I flew it, and my Crew Chief just kept putting it back together until finally an inspection team caught up with it and grounded it, sending it back to Kadena for repair. Our maintenance guys worked wonders, and the fact that

Opposite above: Bill McLeod and his EWO Don Lavigne crewed Jail Bait *during Linebacker II operations.* (Al Palmer)

Opposite below: F-4C 63-7423 Jail Bait, *radome open and receiving radar maintenance between combat sorties. It is loaded with live Shrikes.* (via Jim Rotramel)

they did helped ensure that we never lost an aircraft. When the chips were down, our jets kept flying no matter how bad we abused them. To the best of my knowledge, we never had a serious mechanical problem in the target area; also, both Maintenance Non-Delivery and air aborts for aircraft problems were rare as well. To do that well with old F-4Cs was unheard of.

When we got to Korat, we were given a room in the 17th WWS Ops to operate from and used their Ops Counter and Duty Officer. Our missions were posted on their mission board and we used their building as our home, but we operated as an independent squadron. Aircraft configuration for all early missions was two outboard fuel tanks, an AGM-45 Shrike (either -3, -3A or -3B) on an LAU-34 launcher mounted on each inboard station, an ECM pod in the starboard front Sparrow well, two AIM-7E [or E-2] missiles, plus chaff in the speed brakes. A centreline fuel tank, which was jettisoned as soon as it was empty, was added for Linebacker II missions.

As soon as we completed theatre indoctrination, we started flying B-52 escort missions in the lower Route Packs (RP I–III) and over MR I. [The] first mission was flown on 25 September by Tom Floyd and Al Palmer. Initial missions were flown as wingman with an F-105G as lead. We didn't do this [for] very long because the F-105Gs operated at lower altitudes than the F-4 was optimized for and we ran out of gas. We then flew a few missions as a separate element with an F-105G two-ship as lead (we were usually about 5,000ft higher than the Thud element) before we began to operate independently.

Operating in the lower RPs was no big thing as most of us had been there many times before. These areas were relatively low threat at this point in time in 1972, but all B-52 missions in these areas still required Weasel escort. We flew almost exclusively in the lower RPs

EWO Al Palmer and his pilot Tom Floyd flew the first ever F-4C Wild Weasel IV mission during September 1972. Their aircraft was later nicknamed Brain Damage. Al Palmer was later a Navy NFO on Tomcats and currently is director of the Naval Air Museum in San Diego. (Al Palmer)

and MR 1 for about a month, which gave us time to get our act together, modify the F-105 tactics to fit our airplane, get our maintenance guys well motivated, and bond into a close-knit unit. We flew missions both day and night and determined that operating single-ship with altitude separation in the target area at night was far preferable to trying to stay in formation. We also determined that we could provide adequate coverage by remaining in orbits at key points and thus did not copy the tactic used by some of the F-105G crews of flying a parallel course to the B-52s, and as far as I know, no one had a SAM shot at them during this period. Many of these missions lasted 3–4hr and covered more than one B-52 mission.

In November the B-52s were sent against targets near Vinh in RP II. This raised the stakes, as Vinh was defended by a known SA-2 site. A B-52 was hit on one of the missions [on 22 November, sustaining a near hit by an SA-2] but made it back to Thailand before the crew baled out. Also, on the night of 16 November (Zulu date) an F-105G was shot down by a SAM during one of these missions. [The aircraft was 63-8359, flown by Capt K. Thaete and Maj N. Maier, callsign Bobbin 05. They baled out and hid in long grass until an HH-53 and supporting A-7D Sandys, the USAF's latest version of the Corsair II, in this instance led by Capt Colin A. Clarke, eventually extracted them the next day.]

Following the shootdown, three 67th TFS Weasels (it had been a mixed 561st/67th flight) teamed up with an Owl Flight and attempted to work their way to the shootdown location. Weather prevented that, however, and two 67th TFS Weasels ended up 'Capping' the crew (from over water) for several hours. We logged 8½hr, but much of it was boring, orbiting just far enough feet wet to keep from being shot down and listening to SA-2 and Fire Can operators use us for 'training' all night.

It was during November 1972 that the 67th TFS Weasel aircraft acquired some very flamboyant markings: 'DDD & C/Cs' was painted on the variramps, standing for 'Don's Dirty Dozen & Crew Chiefs'. Individual artwork also flourished on the noses, all with a story behind them. EWO Capt Al Palmer's aircraft was christened Brain Damage, 'for an accident in which I was seriously injured in a hit and run bicycle accident in early November. Ironically, I was hit by a drunk driver on the flightline after a night combat mission over North Vietnam! When I returned from hospitalization in Okinawa, I discovered that my Crew Chief had painted the name on the nose for my arrival.' Squirrely Bird, the Det Commander's aircraft, got its *nom de guerre* 'because Don kept writing it up as feeling "squirrely" in flight, much to the dismay of the maintenance troops who couldn't figure out why'. Bill McLeod's Jail Bait originated with his EWO Don Lavigne: 'Don clearly intended for us to go into harm's way, and therefore messing with this "female" [i.e. the aircraft] had the potential for getting us both into a lot of trouble. A slightly different version would be that he viewed this aircraft as a ticket to jail, i.e. the "Hanoi Hilton".'

Bill McLeod resumes his account of the Det's activities:

When Linebacker II kicked off on 18 December the 67th was not fragged to participate, [because] 7th AF had a requirement that a Weasel aircraft had to be able to carry two ECM pods in order to fly missions into the northern RPs. We were only wired to carry one, consequently we were left out of the frag. Col Parkhurst compared the number of F-105G lines fragged with the number of F-105Gs that would be available and knew that they would not be able to 'cover' all their lines. He then put several of our crews into crew rest and told Capt Larry Miller (the 67th TFS Maintenance Officer) to have all our aircraft loaded and ready to go. At the appropriate time our crews gathered at the 17th WWS Ops Building, and not too long after we arrived we were told we were going.

Night One of Linebacker II tasked Hammer Flight (four F-4C Weasels) on harassment and killing orbits to the western side of Hanoi. They flew to the north-west of the city as a flight and then split up, with at least nine overlapping enemy SAM sites to keep suppressed while the B-52 cells passed over the F-4Cs' orbit points. The North Vietnamese completely lost signal discipline that night, maintaining transmission for up to 30 seconds at a time – Bill McLeod said 'it was just like flying on the Nellis electronic warfare range' – and were seriously hurt as a result. However, it was hardly a free-for-all: solid undercast at 8,000ft, a sky full of aircraft, SAMs, triple-A, and raining bombs and debris all presented serious in-flight hazards, so crews relied principally on the 'big sky, little airplane' theory for deconfliction.

F-4C Hammer 01 (Bob Belles and Pat Kelly) operated near the split-up point amid an incessant SAM barrage, firing one Shrike at site VN-266 and then executing a 180-degree turn away from the site so as to keep it interested and transmitting long enough for the ARM to successfully guide to the dish – the typical luring tactic, but one which required considerable nerve on the part of Belles and Kelly given the Day One scenario. Maintaining a heading towards the site would invariably make the North Vietnamese shut down their radars, but it was another tactic that could be employed once ARMs had been expended, though at obvious risk to the Weasels.

Hammer 01's remaining Shrike was launched against a second site, resulting in a shutdown. Despite being Winchester, the crew then kept up their cat and mouse game with the enemy radars, flying to and fro from active emitters to keep the enemy's transmissions sporadic, while the B-52s plied their canned tracks outbound from the target. Hammer 02 (John Bremer and Hal Bergmann) was working slightly further west, then north and launched their first ARM when they came under attack from four SAMs under the control of a radar at site VN-119. The ARM either impacted the guidance radar or it was shut down, as the SAMs lost control. The result was repeated not long after against another site when two SAMs looped over and impacted the ground the moment the crew volleyed their second ARM.

Adding to Hammer Flight's success, Hammer 03 (Tom Floyd and Al Palmer) knocked out a Fan Song at site VN-255, adjacent to Phuc Yen airfield, which was attempting to guide three SAMs towards a B-52 cell.

They also obliged another to shut down with their second missile, repeating the other crews' actions. Both Shrike launches were made amid fierce triple-A opposition, which demanded especially cool nerves during the tricky target line up; heavy evasive manoeuvring could only be conducted immediately *after* ARM launch, because of Shrike's strict firing parameters.

Hammer 04 held a lower-altitude hunter position owing to electrical cooling problems which obliged pilot Bob Tidwell to maintain the jet's engines at 95 per cent or less throttle, while his EWO Dennis Haney guided him in for their two Shrike shoots. The first occurred while the crew came under attack from two different triple-A pieces at their one and ten o'clock positions, one of which nearly caught the aircraft's right wing. The enemy radar at site VN-159 stayed active long enough for the Shrike to impact, going off the air abruptly, indicating a valid hit. The second Shrike was fired against an intermittently transmitting radar, resulting in another possible but unconfirmed kill. Hammer Flight's successful night's work comprised radars at four sites shut down (three of them knocked out), and an additional five sites suppressed into silence or only sporadic transmissions.

The North Vietnamese relearned rapidly, however, and subsequently did not have many signals up. They clearly had their radar systems hooked together and apparently used a surveillance radar or a gun-laying radar to provide the picture for their entire system. Some of their missiles were launched without guidance, others were launched with only the guidance active (Fan Song TTR not operating) and were clearly being guided off another radar's picture. A few missiles were launched with a full-up Fan Song system – primarily on Night One, but occasionally on other nights as well. A member of the F-4C WW-IV crews said:

Our standard mission scenario for most Linebacker II missions was to brief as a flight (bare bones in most cases, we all knew how to do it), take off and refuel as a flight, then split up as we headed inbound and proceed to individual orbit areas on the western side of Hanoi (when the B-52 target was Hanoi) from which we could engage any radars that came up. We usually arrived in the orbit areas just in advance of the B-52s and normally were fragged to operate at 18,000ft. We operated without lights (kept the triple-A from shooting at us as much) and stayed until our gas ran out or the B-52s were clear of the target area. Then we returned to the post-strike tanker single-ship, refuelled, and returned to Korat by ourselves.

Each of us had our own procedures for doing this. In my case I not only blacked out the aircraft, but my cockpit as well. I had all the switches set well before I entered the target area and once there my attention was one hundred per cent outside the aircraft. I taped over all the warning and other lights in the front cockpit so that they would not 'blind' or distract me if they illuminated, and hooked the map light up in a way that would allow me to use it to dimly illuminate the Attitude Indicator if it didn't fall off during the manoeuvres. Any navigation I did was done visually, and when I used a map (not often) I read it by moonlight.

One of the results of flying single-ship is that most of us didn't have much of an idea about what the other guys did once we split up. Therefore it was difficult, if not impossible, to get a complete picture of what went on during these missions. Night Three was rough: six B-52s were shot down. [That night, 20 December, Tom Floyd and Al Palmer were attacked by a MiG-21 while proceeding into the target area.] The North Vietnamese vectored the MiG-21 into a classic head-on pass, above with a slight offset, followed by a stern conversion to employ an AA-2. Tom picked the MiG up visually, outmanoeuvred it, and ended up behind it. He fired an AIM-7, but it did not guide.

The author was privileged to hear a harrowing cockpit tape made during this encounter by Al Palmer and the heavy breathing is self-explanatory: a lot of g was pulled, and a lot of frustration shouted out about the unreliability of the Sparrow III missiles. What is overwhelmingly obvious from the tape is the constant crescendo of whistling warbles, signifying enemy radar activity at fever pitch. To the EWOs, each and every warble had a specific meaning. Unlike the F-105 Weasels or occasional killer F-4Es, they had no M61A-1 20mm cannon with which to ground-strafe or take pot-shots at MiGs – just Sparrows and limited-capability Shrikes.

Bill McLeod reckons his toughest combat outing was a night hunter/killer mission on Night Four, flying as Suntan 01, on a mission designed to address the B-52 losses.

On Night Four, 7th AF fragged a night hunter/killer mission against the Hanoi air defence system during the B-52 strike. The mission was made up of five F-4Cs and five F-4Es with CBUs. Don and I planned and briefed the mission, and we were lucky that all of us survived. We had flown on Night Three and after we returned I hit the sack because we were scheduled to lead the 67th TFS flight on Night Four. Someone showed up at my room late on the morning of Day Four and told me I was needed at the squadron (this was early, as I normally slept until early afternoon during Linebacker II).

When I arrived at the squadron, Maj Belles filled me in on the frag change to add the night hunter/killer mission and told me to go over to Intel and find my EWO. When I got there, Don already had the night's targets plotted (all in the Hanoi area) and had pretty well analysed the mission. We discussed it for a few minutes and decided on a plan – which differed from the way the mission had been fragged. The frag called for five two-ship flights (one F-4C and one F-4E), but there wasn't enough room in the target area to operate five flights. We divided the aircraft up into two three-ship flights (one F-4C and two F-4Es), one two-ship flight (one F-4C and one F-4E) and two single F-4Cs. We assigned one three-ship to the Bac Mai complex (south of city centre) and the other to an area north-west of the city – probably between Viet Tri and Thai Nguyen. Both of these flights were backed up by a single F-4C operating in an orbit 10 miles or so to the rear. The two-ship was assigned to another SAM complex which, if I remember correctly, was somewhere along Thud

Ridge. We also determined that we would be unable to adequately protect the F-4Es without carrying Dive-Modified Shrikes on three of our aircraft.

We then went back to the squadron and hooked up with Maj Belles who took us to brief Col John T. Chain, the 388th TFW Director of Operations [Jack Chain later went on to become a four-star general, and CINCSAC]. We briefed him on what we intended to do and he approved our plan. After he had done so, Don spoke up and told him that we couldn't properly protect the F-4Es without Dive-Modified Shrikes and Col Chain approved their use.

I briefed the five F-4C crews before the mass briefing and then we all went to the large briefing room where someone provided an overview of the entire mission. All of us then went to a briefing room at the squadron that was providing the F-4Es, where I briefed the crews how we had rearranged the frag, gave them an overview of the mission, briefed them on their areas of responsibility, matched the F-4E crews up with the F-4C crews who were leading and told them to break up into individual flights and work out their own procedures and tactics.

I took the two crews who would be going with me and briefed for operations against the Bac Mai complex. I would be in an orbit just to the west of the complex, with an F-4E in an orbit just to the north and the other orbiting just to the south. Whenever one of the sites in the complex launched, they were to roll in and drop CBUs on it. I would roll in also and point my nose at the complex, so I could fire a Shrike down the throat if one of the sites fired at one of the F-4Es.

We were the first flight off the tanker and everything went according to plan until we had crossed into North Vietnam – the first flight in. Both F-4Es were flying formation on me and I had my strip lights on to allow them to stay with me. Then Red Crown called and told us that they had a MiG-21 in front of us, several thousand feet high and coming head-on – and then told us there are no friendly aircraft in front of us, meaning shoot the guy head-on. It was the same scenario that Tom Floyd had been faced with the night before, except I had two F-4Es in formation and my lights on. I immediately told the two F-4Es to break off and proceed to their orbits, while Don locked the MiG-21 up on the radar.

The offset was just starting to develop, so I needed to manoeuvre slightly to engage him, but when I looked outside to make sure my wingmen were gone, one of them was still hanging on. So I turned out my lights in the hope he would get the hint, but he still tried to fly formation on me in the moonlight. At this point I decided that the biggest threat was a mid-air with my wingman, so I turned slightly into the MiG to take away his offset, lowered the nose, and blew through directly under him. The three of us then pressed on to our briefed orbits.

The first B-52s came into range of the SAMs about a minute or so after we reached our orbits and the sites to the north and east of us opened up, firing some seventy missiles in the next ten minutes. Two B-52s were hit, one going down into the city while the other made a

sweeping right turn while streaming flames, but still flying. Unfortunately the turn took him south over Thanh Hoa and a site there shot him down. Then the Bac Mai complex fired a couple of SAMs and my F-4Es rolled in with their CBUs. I rolled in to protect them, only to have one of the sites fire at me. The missile lifted off in my windscreen at very close range. I had just enough time to slam the stick and rudder pedals into the front right corner and move the aircraft before the missile went past my left side and exploded in my rear-view mirror. The missile was obviously being guided off another radar's picture because no Fan Song TTRs were up in the complex, but the guidance light on the AN/APR-25 was illuminated. Not long after this occurred, both F-4Es called Winchester and left the target area for home.

Once the F-4Es left, Don told me that *one* site on the east side of Hanoi was responsible for the hits on *both* B-52s (despite the fact that numerous sites were firing missiles) and that the site in question had an India-Band radar co-located with it. My immediate thought was that the North Vietnamese had slipped an SA-3 into the theatre, but Don didn't think that was what it was. It was apparent to both of us, however, that under the plan that we had put together, no one was operating against this site, so it was up to us to do something about it. The site was several miles further to the east, however, and was separated from us by several B-52 Target Boxes. I asked Don if he could get us there without getting us blown away by a bomb from a B-52. He told me that he could, so we headed east and we ended up in an orbit between the site and the B-52 ingress and egress routes, on the east side of Hanoi.

We stayed in a figure-of-eight orbit at about 18,000ft at this location until the last B-52 had cleared the threat ring to the east. This put us several miles further east than we had planned to be so it took longer for the last B-52 to clear to the east. At the same time the B-52s had cleared everyone else's areas of responsibility, and since all of us were running out of gas, everyone on the west side of the city was going home. The EC-121 called us about a minute before the last B-52 was clear and told us that we were the last aircraft remaining in the target area, and made it plain that they thought that we should get out of there. As soon as I answered the EC-121, Red Crown came up on Guard and announced 'SAM, SAM, SAM!', which was followed by Don's calm voice from the rear cockpit saying 'We're the target'.

The APR-25/-26 lit up with a classic full-system launch with a strobe that went clear to the edge of the scope and part way back to the centre, the launch audio started screaming and two SAMs lifted off at our eleven o'clock. I kicked my left rudder to put the strobe and missiles at twelve o'clock and fired both Shrikes at the guy, then rolled into an inverted slice and pulled the aircraft toward the ground with at least 4–5g. As soon as the nose was well down, I rolled out part of the bank and reacquired the two SAMs over the canopy rail. Just as the SAMs reached the point where I expected them to start back down toward us, and as I was preparing to use all the energy

I had just acquired to pull up and over them, Don said 'He's down' (meaning that the site had shut down because of our Shrikes) and then calmly gave me instructions on how to get out of the manoeuvre we were in without hitting the ground or heading the wrong way.

We spit out the bottom on a westerly heading, very close to supersonic, and blew across the city while using our excess energy to pop back up to our fragged altitude. The North Vietnamese brought up various Fire Cans to check our progress and shot at us with several batteries of 85mm AAA. They were very careful, however, and would shut down the Fire Cans as soon as we started to point our nose at them, so they clearly knew that they were dealing with a Weasel. I could also see the muzzle flashes of the 85mm guns, so as soon as I saw a battery fire I would move the aircraft to a different place in the sky and then watch as the place we had just vacated exploded with ten or twelve bursts.

By the time we got across the city we were really low on gas and Don gave me a vector to the post-strike tanker track. When we got to the track there were seven KC-135As in trail formation flying an orbit, with F-4 flights everywhere. We came into this head-on from above and the lead tanker assigned us to Tanker 6. I did a humungous barrel roll around and down through the formation and popped up just behind No. 6. When I contacted him he told me that he had a flight of four F-4Es on and the F-4E flight leader (who was running a very professional, by the book flight and was clearly very experienced) asked me to hang back while his No. 4 took a couple thousand pounds of additional fuel. I told him I didn't have the gas to do that and slid right into the middle of his formation, and into close formation with the guy on the boom.

I do not know who these guys were, but it certainly must have gotten their attention when this old F-4C, that was alone and very late getting out, and which didn't have anything left hanging on it except an ECM pod and some AIM-7s, came sliding in there while announcing that he didn't have enough gas left to make it back across the river! On the way back to Korat after refuelling Don went Cold Mike and wrote a message about the use of the India-Band radar, which he sent immediately after we landed.

T-8209 AND GUN DISH

What EWO Don Lavigne had witnessed on Night Four was the T-8209 TTR. These had been noted by USAF Combat Apple Elint aircraft earlier in the year, and their positions had been mapped by EB-66 crewmen from August onwards, but their exact role had remained unclear until now. As Cdr E.F. Rollins, skipper of EA-6B-equipped VAQ-132, noted in his 8–27 December Line Period of Action report: 'It is apparent that the North Vietnamese are now employing T-8209 as a range-finding radar, complementing the Fan Song TWS (Track-While-Scan) under heavy jamming conditions. The T-8209 is an I-Band signal that probably radiates from a People's Republic of China-developed triple-A fire-control radar.

The EA-6B Four Holer entered combat service in 1972, flying standard models with VAQ-132 'Scorpions' and VAQ-131 'Lancers'. The expanded capability or Excap version followed in 1973. (US Navy)

Elint and photographs tend to confirm the co-location of Fan Song/T-8209 at several SA-2 sites in the Hanoi area.'

The Vietnamese were using the range data to bring their SAMs to bear, and then using track-on-jam azimuth information available from Fan Song working in a passive mode, to obtain a straight point-to-point firing solution by lining up the missile's beacon with the jamming strobe, and relying on the salvoed missiles' proximity fuses to inflict damage.

Tactics were thus immediately revised to counter the new threats, as the heavy-duty US jammers – the EA-6B Prowlers and EB-66 Destroyers working with the B-52s' own Smart Noise Onboard Equipment (SNOE) to provide overlapping jamming – were incapable of adequately blocking the new signals. The only effective counters to this threat were US Marine Corps EA-6A jammers, seven of which were usually airborne each night out of Da Nang AB, concentrating on the triple-A fire-control radars using their receiving gear, jamming pods and chaff dispensers.

I-Band radar was also successfully foxed by Ubon-based F-4s dispensing chaff from high altitude in blanket fashion, and thickening chaff at the vulnerable B-52s' post-target turnpoints (PTT) by means of dumping more M129 chaff packets, which created a vertical column to add to the blanket. (Noise-jamming had been least effective at the PTTs because the turn focused the B-52s' SNOE away from the enemy radars, permitting Fan Song to distinguish the bombers' radar reflections and then track them.)

The third measure was AGM-45A-6 and AGM-78C ARMs tuned to the new threat – and further examples of these were supplied to Korat's Weasels in an emergency airlift operation because stocks of the AGM-78C, shot in volume by the F-105Gs, had dwindled to just fifteen missiles by Night Four!

Several of Korat's twenty-three remaining F-105Gs were also fitted with outboard wing ADU-315/A (starboard) and -316/A (port) DLAs, raising Shrike carriage to two under each wing in addition to the Standard ARM

Above: 17th WWS F-105G Snaggletooth, *awaiting its next combat sortie. The ADU-315 Dual-Shrike Launcher Adaptor (DLA) doubled AGM-45 carriage on the outboard pylons, but proved a heavy load. Vibration problems were also encountered by the high-speed Weasel Thuds. According to HQ Pacific Air Forces documents, some 1,032 Shrikes and 286 Standard ARMs were expended in combat by the USAF between April 1972 and January 1973. (via Jim Rotramel)*

Left: A close-up of the Shrike DLA, originally developed by the US Navy, featuring a pair of ATM-45 training rounds on an F-105G at George AFB, California. (Barry Miller)

load. These had originally been fitted earlier in 1972 so that the F-105Gs could carry a Shrike and a special Elint pod, and 17th WWS planner Maj 'Lucky' Ekmann (who had laid down much of the electronic support tactics well in advance of the December campaign) suggested they employ the device to double Shrike carriage. However, problems with considerable drag and vibration at the high speeds F-105 drivers were accustomed to flying at soon put a halt to that concept.

While the Shrike DLA was qualified for an impressive 550kt max on US Navy jets like the A-4 and A-7, nobody had really tested them on the F-105, which shortly after reverted to the two Shrikes, one Standard ARM and two fuel tanks configuration, or two Shrikes, two Standard ARM and a centreline fuel tank. Dan Barry, an F-105 Weasel pilot with the 561st TFS, recalls the effect of the latter configuration:

[It] was such a heavy load we had to light load fuel to avoid overstressing the aircraft. This meant they set up a tanker en route to the Udorn jettison area. If you couldn't take fuel for whatever reason, it would require jettisoning those pricey munitions and squeaking into Udorn. I only remember doing this once, and although I'm sure some others must have done it, it wasn't practised for very long. I remember we did it out of Korat. What I really remember was coming down Thud Ridge feeling like a 1,000lb gorilla!

The ferocious sabre-toothed jaws were a hallmark of the 17th WWS. The protrusions are associated with the KA-71 combat camera and Wild Weasel III kit. (Barry Miller)

Daytime F-105G/F-4E hunter/killer missions also were resumed, gaining one of their biggest successes on 29 December, including the destruction of the vicious combined SAM site VN-549 (in south-west Hanoi) that had been responsible for downing or damaging at least five B-52s. As the site was not radiating for long enough for the F-105Gs to launch ARMs accurately, and the F-4Es were unable to acquire the targets through the heavy cloud cover, Condor One and Condor Two, the F-105G flight lead and his wingman, dived down through the triple-A to 4,000ft, firing a Shrike right at the site in an unguided manner simply to mark it. The F-4E crews saw where the ARM exploded and deposited their CBUs on top, resulting in the radar van, three SAMs on launchers and three more in storage containers being destroyed. Altogether that day the F-105Gs fired one AGM-78 and thirteen Shrikes, while the 34th TFS F-4Es deposited twenty-four CBUs, completely flattening SAM sites VN-159, VN-266 and VN-549.

The North Vietnamese had also fielded at least two of the new Soviet self-propelled ZSU-23/4 four-cannon Shilka anti-aircraft pieces. These married a colossal rate of fire with an onboard J-Band Gun Dish fire-control radar. Although some crews doubt that they were there, the presence of Gun Dish was noted in Cdr Rollins' reports alongside his observations about the new T-8209 TTR.

The terrain-hugging F-111A crewmen of the 474th TFW were some of the first to confront and survive encounters with this new weapon. Two squadrons of the 474th TFW had been dispatched from Nellis AFB to Takhli RTAFB beginning in late September under Constant Guard V, and were busy attacking SAM sites (claiming site VN-004 as 50 per cent knocked out) as well as enemy airfields in support of Linebacker II, by means of the by then perfected low-level night radar interdiction technique. Lee Dodd's memory was of a 'solid wall of tracers when they got a lock-on. We had no defences against this weapon. If the Soviets were to load it with non-tracer ammunition no one would know they were getting hosed until the airplane disintegrated.'

Having locked on, the ZSU-23/4's turret would be brought to bear and its quartet of cannon would pump away for up to 5 seconds at a time, about the duration of its lock on low-flying aircraft. To the flyers, that seemed like an interminable length of time. F-4E AC Ed Rasimus recalled that 'high-output 23mm weapons were certainly encountered in both the Phuc Yen and 'downtown' lake areas. The guns were particularly impressive at twilight, when they quite literally resembled a fire hose being sprayed through the air. I don't know what the tracer to ball ratio was, but they looked like a stream of fire.'

Bill McLeod picks up the story from the 67th TFS perspective again:

Starting on Night Five, the B-52 targets were moved out of the immediate 'downtown' area for a couple of days. One of these missions (Night Six) went well north of the city and resulted in at least two of our F-4C crews (including Don and I) flying orbits in the Chinese Buffer Zone. On this particular mission a Fire Can was being used to gather the radar picture for the North Vietnamese. The

A pair of Weasels bound for North Vietnam on the wing of a fuel-replenishing KC-135 tanker. (Barry Miller via Jim Rotramel)

operator was very careful and would shut down whenever anyone pointed their nose in his direction. Don and I played with this guy for quite a while and were eventually able to get a missile above him and turn away before he came up again. He didn't know we had fired a missile and there is a reasonable chance that we killed him, because he went down at missile impact. If we didn't hit him we sure scared him, because he never came back up again. [Other Weasels operating within the Buffer Zone fired at Fire Can radars that night, one missile apparently going astray across the border.]

After the short Christmas break the B-52s were back over Hanoi at night again, and the 67th TFS continued to fly Weasel missions until Linebacker II ended. While Linebacker II was going on at night, the 67th TFS was also flying B-52 escort missions in the lower RPs during the day. Once Linebacker II ended, the squadron continued to escort missions into RPs I–IV until the meetings in Paris produced some results and the North Vietnamese agreed to a cease-fire. We stood down from combat on 28 January and flew a few training missions in Thailand, then flew combat missions again between 3 and 13 February (all appear to have been over Laos), then flew a couple more training missions before re-deploying to Kadena. The last training mission in Thailand was flown as a three-ship on 15 February 1973. The absolute last mission (at least the last listed in the Mission Log) was a functional check flight flown by Dick Myers and Don Triplett on 16 February. The 67th TFS aircraft redeployed on the morning of 18 February 1973, and the maintenance personnel and equipment departed later the same day aboard a C-141.

In all, the 67th TFS had flown some 460 combat sorties, without loss, the Weasel crewmen all earning two Distinguished Flying Crosses or a Silver Star and Distinguished Flying Cross for their involvement during Linebacker II, which has remained a little-known aspect of the air war owing to them flying mostly at night and solo. The F-105G squadrons suffered no losses during Linebacker II either, despite the crews flying dangerous parallel tracks to the B-52s with heavy ARM loads throughout the campaign.

Up to 1,242 SA-2s had been fired against the B-52s and their protective support, for the loss of 15 bombers, a kill rate of as little as 1.2 per cent. There's no doubt in the B-52 crewmen's minds that without the Weasels and electronic support aircraft, losses would have been in the order of half a magnitude higher. Altogether, during 1972, the enemy had expended a staggering estimated 4,244 SAMs (representing a tad under 49 per cent of the all SAM launches sighted during the Vietnam conflict), for the loss of forty-nine US aircraft. Nevertheless, many many more were hit by triple-A. US Air Force F/RF-4 losses as a whole over North Vietnam alone totalled fifty-six that year. Along with the other losses already described, it was a very high price to pay to get North Vietnamese forces out of South Vietnam and their leaders back to the conference table in earnest.

North Vietnam signed the Peace Agreement after talks resumed early in 1973, with formal signatures being put to paper on 28 January. Air operations over Vietnam had ceased the previous day, and all US aircraft

F-105G 63-265, nicknamed Northbound, *was assigned to Maj 'Lucky' Eckman, who completed 200 combat sorties over North Vietnam and was responsible for much of the Iron Hand mission planning for Linebacker II. He also expounded the use of heavyweight ARM loads.* (via Jim Rotramel)

and related personnel pulled out of South Vietnam within sixty days. Operations over Laos ceased on 17 April, and those over Cambodia ended on 15 August, when, in accordance with a Congressional edict, all US combat operations in South-East Asia ceased altogether. American POWs held captive in the North were repatriated under Operation Homecoming.

However, an air presence in Thailand was maintained at Udorn and Korat RTAFBs, including a contingent of F-4D/Es assigned to the 432nd TRW, and F-105Gs and F-111As pooled under new 347th TFW control at Korat, in order to send a clear message: We might be back in force again. But that was not to be, and attention shifted to the Soviet might in Central Europe and the Middle East. Overall Weasel losses throughout the Vietnam conflict now stood at forty-eight, forty-six of which were F-105s.

POST-WAR PROCESSORS AND PODS

Inevitably, much new hardware was in development during the closing stages of the Vietnam War, designed to counter some of the new threats detected during Linebacker II operations. These included the SA-3 SAM's Flat Face acquisition radar, the novel and unexpected T-8209, now code-named Teamwork, and the worrisome J-Band Gun Dish fire-control radar. The new threats would challenge low-flying aircraft attempting to evade the clutches of the strategic defence SA-2 SAMs in any future conflicts, and between them formed the prospective new enemy IADS in Eastern Europe and North Korea, alongside other threats such as the SA-4. The US Navy also had an additional agenda, based on radars it had been monitoring on Soviet shipping in the North Atlantic and Mediterranean, resounding to fanciful NATO code-names such as Head Light, Drum Tilt, Hawk Screech, Muff Cobb and Pop Group, among others.

The principal innovations embraced digital RWRs, offering broader reception capabilities and quicker response. The US Navy's AN/ALR-45 RWR and allied AN/ALR-50 LWR were rendered more widely available,

The PRC Teamwork I-Band AAA radar was outwardly similar to Fire Can and caused much mischief during the Linebacker II campaign, acting as a surrogate target acquisition system for the SA-2. (via Barry Miller)

and updated, while the follow-on AN/ALR-67 all-in-one RWR effort with ATI proceeded apace. This new package added a small digital computer that ran software routines dedicated to analysing pulse characteristics much more quickly, thus allowing the system to be reprogrammed with fresh threat data on the flightline. It was initially designed for the EA-6B (which, ironically, never got it), to replace its hard-wired AN/ ALR-42 'traffic cop receiver', yet started to find its way into most other US Navy carrier aircraft by the end of the 1970s, A-7Es receiving a cheap but cheerful derivative which added some of the system's components to create their similarly capable AN/ALR-45F and AN/APR-43 receivers.

DECM was also revisited. The ubiquitous Navy Sanders track-breaker AN/ALQ-100 was updated to multiple-Band AN/ALQ-126 standard, while the Goodyear AN/ALE-29 became the standard US Navy chaff dispenser, based on the 'round hole' dispensing system.

Dedicated Iron Hand aircraft were the first in the queue for the modifications, with Mod 0-Update A-6Bs receiving Indianapolis Avionics Center AN/ALR-55 and -57 receiving sets (under AFC 285 and AVC 1296/1297), which updated the ageing Bendix AN/APS-107 and ATI ER-142, with the latter expanded to display I-Band signals.

The by now perfected pimple-radomed Mod 1 TIAS A-6Bs became the most valuable asset, seeing service with VA-35 in early 1973. Cdr Gerald H. Hesse's maintenance troops brought three aircraft up to full operational status before passing them back to the depot where they were held on a contingency basis and returned to the Mediterranean Fleet's VA-34, onboard USS *John F. Kennedy*, with the Sixth Fleet late in the year. The switch reflected the shift of focus from South-East Asia to the Middle East. VA-34 retained the aircraft for the remainder of their operational lives in the TIAS configuration, but managed to write-off BuNo. 152616 during a training accident.[16]

In a major modernization, all 14 surviving A-6Bs along with 226 other Intruders were reconfigured as A-6Es during the mid-1970s. This rework programme, known as Conversion In Lieu of Procurement (CILOP), was carried out concurrently with production of new A-6Es by Grumman, extending the operational career of the Intruder in US Navy service by a further twenty years. DIANE was ousted by a solid-state IBM AN/ASQ-133 general-purpose computer, and a single Norden AN/APQ-148 radar replaced the cumbersome twin search-and-track radar arrangement used previously. Reliability rocketed.

The first delivery of a factory-fresh A-6E took place on 17 September 1971. An initial lot was allocated to Intruder training squadron VA-42, followed by VA-85 which became the first operational A-6 squadron to get to grips with the A-6E, logging its first training sortie on 15 December 1971. The first CILOP examples became available in May 1973 and were issued to VA-35.

AGM-45 Shrike capability was retained on all A-6Es, though STARM was limited to just a select twelve Intruders fitted with the Indianapolis Naval Avionics Facility's home-grown AN/AWG-21 weapon control system, development of which was initiated in the summer of 1973 under the direction of Fred Macreno Jr. It became available for flight testing within a record nine months, by using mostly off-the-shelf electronic modules, and was fitted to the aircraft at NARF Norfolk, Virginia, under AFC 409.

The AN/AWG-21 monitored emissions from land and shipborne radars, analysed the signals and prioritized them based on both the stored threat and activity files in its computer, and displayed up to three of them at a time. It worked in several modes, chief of which were Automatic and OET for hand-off to the missile. It also worked in identification mode. The B/N would move a switch to shift the marker strobe clockwise or counter-clockwise over a desired threat strobe flashed up on the Instantaneous Frequency Measurement display, which was a back-up AN/ALR-45 dartboard installed for this task, thereby telling the system to analyse that and treat it as a priority target. Any of these threats could be correlated with the AN/ALR-45 RWR and the missile's seeker if desired and, once ready, the Standard ARM could be fired in the normal manner.

AN/AWG-21-capable Intruders were distributed according to need over the ensuing decade, but were known to have served with VA-34 'Blue Blasters', VA-115 'Arabs' (later 'Eagles'), VA-145 'Swordsmen' and VA-176 'Thunderbolts'. They were never employed in anger, and STARM was even-tually withdrawn from the US Navy's active inventory thirteen years later in 1986, when cracks in the propellant sections caused the entire missile stock to be grounded. However, the Pacific Missile Test Center at NAS Point Mugu conjured up a 10ft long STARM pod based on the AGM-78D weapon seeker married to a tube. This pod permitted AN/AWG-21 A-6Es from VA-145 to continue using the Standard ARM missile as a pure ESM device. A new ARM was already in service at this point.[17]

By the same token, the 1970s saw the USAF add a Dalmo-Victor DSA-20 processor to its standard F-4 AN/APR-25/-26 RHAWS and -36/-37 and LWR systems to create the field-programmable AN/ALR-46 RWR, capable of listening to selected enemy radar pulses in the C–J Bands.[18] First introduced to the Thailand-based F-4D/E squadrons from March 1973, these provided an altogether new presentation using alphanumeric icons. In place of the coded strobe lines, the ostensibly similar little green cockpit dartboard displays would flash up numbers corresponding to the terminal threats, such as 2 for a SAM-2, A for triple-A and a little aircraft symbol to denote an enemy fighter tracking them. Flashing icons surrounded by a diamond denoted they were posing an immediate missile threat.

Warning lamps and audio were retained, as most crews considered the latter the principal means of being alerted to danger, especially as audio gave some clue of radar activity before a tracking radar had obtained a lock. Although the noise was potentially distracting during a bomb run, crews turned down the volume on their headphones at their peril.

The RWRs were in turn linked to the new-generation Westinghouse AN/ALQ-119 ECM pod under a programme originally known as Compass Matrix. The marriage offered 'power management', whereby the receivers' processors furnished the pods with precise set-on threat information and prioritized them so that all available jamming power could be focused on the emitters posing the greatest imminent danger, using one of a number of automated jamming modes. The processors would then determine how the enemy radar was behaving and issue new instructions, all in nanoseconds.

The new pod itself was an enlarged version of the TWT-based QRC-335/ALQ-101 noise/deception-jamming device that had seen combat use from 1968, with added deception-jamming and frequency coverage capability added via a ventral cupola housing new modules. As well as traditional lower frequency mainlobe-blanking and command downlink Beacon noise-jamming, it offered deception-jamming techniques almost identical to those of the US Navy's internal AN/ALQ-126 system and its precursor the AN/ALQ-101 pod, for use against higher frequency TTRs which were already tracking the aircraft.

The theory was simple, though the engineering behind it was extremely complex indeed. The Repeater Mode deception-jamming systems transmitted carbon-copy waveforms precisely matching the incoming threat signals, but increased in power. The enemy radar's automatic gain receivers invariably would then lock on to the jammer's clearer signals instead of the echoes from the aircraft's skin, and the battle would begin, and be won, lost or end in a draw in a matter of seconds.

Using the range gate pull-off method, a time delay in transmission of the fake echoes was employed to deceive the radar into believing the aircraft was further away than it really was, thereby creating incorrect lead-firing angles for command-guided SAMs and triple-A. These small differences were often sufficient to create significant targeting errors, because missiles relied on command guidance and were unable to make sudden, dramatic last-second changes in course.

Inverse conical scan jamming could be used against radars that scanned a small sector of sky using a beam describing a cone-shape, such as Gun Dish. Having acquired the target by means of a bigger search scanning routine, co-located acquisition radar or manual slewing, the dish would constantly realign the axis of its conical scan in the direction of the strongest radar return, thus maintaining lock on the aircraft. The jammer's carbon-copy waveforms were thus amplitude-modulated out

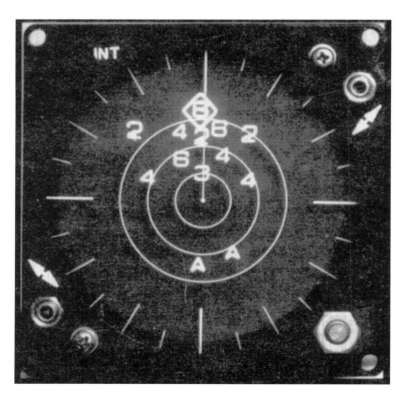

Alphanumeric Radar Warning Receiver displays, such as the AN/ALR-46 system shown here, began supplanting the old strobe-based systems from 1973. The 2 represents an SA-2 Fan Song, A denotes triple-A and 4 marks an SA-4 SAM system by bearing. Those further out present the greatest danger (the equivalent of the old 'three-ringer'), with the greatest perceived threat – here an SA-6 dead ahead – surrounded by a diamond. Such highlighting could be used to select targets for hand-off to anti-radiation missiles. Aural cues given over headphones were considered by most crews to be equally, if not more, valuable for adequate SAM warning. (Applied Technology Industries)

of phase with the true echoes, creating the impression that the aircraft was in another part of the dish's scan, thereby prompting the dish to move its axis there, slightly away from the aircraft. The time phase would be gradually increased until the radar was off the mark. A sudden drop in jamming power output would often cause such a radar to hiccup and break lock altogether, obliging it to reinitiate its broader search pattern all over again.

Velocity gate pull-off techniques similarly mimicked pulse-Doppler frequency changes in enemy fighters' track-while-scan radar carrier waves that normally allowed its processor to determine target velocity or closing speed. With the jamming abruptly terminated, the radar became confused for want of signals, and broke lock.

Transponder mode deception-jamming was also introduced. This was more complex and used predictive techniques. One former USAF EWO said it started 'to work its magic in anticipation that a pulse will arrive at a specified time, and matching the appropriate parameters', being switched on by the EWO or WSO when aural tones suggested certain SAM radar activity. A prerequisite of this mode was that the characteristics of enemy radars (operating frequencies, PRF, transmission times, etc.) were known well in advance and programmed into the pods based on constantly updated Elint data garnered by electronic snoopers and catalogued by organizations such as the Joint-Service Electronic Warfare Center (JEWC) at San Antonio, Texas, for various contingency operations. Pods could thus be programmed for specific theatres of operation or special missions against known threats. By generating errors in range, bearing and speed predictively, enemy radar operators would constantly have to intervene, and reinitiate search routines all over again. Transponder-jamming thus bought critical seconds of immunity during potentially perilous phases of attack.

Used against the terminal threats in the process of guiding SAMs and pointing triple-A guns, or fighters attempting to gain a lock for an AAM launch, jamming caused sufficient confusion to send missiles off on a wild goose chase and for guns to decorate empty portions of the sky with shrapnel. Moreover, the new processors gave the fighter and attack aircraft crews greater autonomy. There was no longer any need for mutually protective jamming formations among strike packages. The RWRs, working in concert with the jamming gear, would automatically select the best mode for use against the threat in hand based on known threat characteristics programmed into its library, so that the crew could simply switch the devices upon receipt of a threat and shift their focus of attention to navigation, and setting up their sensors and weapons for the target pass, making evasive manoeuvres as necessary, trusting all would work as advertised.

Chaff could be activated automatically as well, but in this instance most crews preferred to stab the appropriate button manually when missiles were in pursuit. In the dense electromagnetic environment of Europe, in particular, false radar indications remained a problem, and nobody wanted the chaff-dumping procedure going insane all by itself. Instances of jets dumping all their chaff in 30 seconds or so happened during training, when crews neglected to watch switch positions.

POST-WAR WEASELS

Beginning in 1973, digital AN/ALR-46 RWR upgrades were installed in the F-105G WW-III and F-4C WW-IV, much of this work being carried out at Crestview, Florida, while structural upgrades were completed 'in the field'. However, in common with F-4s for overseas customers, Group A mods introduced wiring harnesses and structural modifications to facilitate new gear, while only Group B modifications fitted the actual sensors and displays, as and when available, resulting in a hotch-potch capability pending complete updating. Many crews reckoned no two aircraft were alike, battle damage scabs notwithstanding.

The F-105G also received an updated ATI AN/APR-35A, while the Shrike-only F-4C was reconfigured with the AN/ALR-53 in place of its Vietnam-era ER-142 at Ogden AMA, to permit the EWO to better scrutinize waveforms and line up for a Shrike pass.

Some Bears did not like the new RWR icons, citing anomalies in signal reception in terms of bearing and intensity compared to the old coded strobes, but as a fleetwide upgrade it helped improve pilot situational awareness considerably among the non-Weasels.

The miscellaneous updates were completed by 1975, by which time the Wild Weasels' training school had moved from Nellis AFB to George AFB, near Victorville, in the Californian Mojave Desert – focal point and home of the Wild Weasels for the next sixteen years. The 35th TFW at George AFB boasted three Weasel squadrons: the 561st TFS 'Black Knights', relocated from McConnell AFB in July 1973; the 562nd TFS 'Weasels', effectively relocated from Korat RTAFB (where it had served as the 17th WWS until 15 November 1974), along with the 563rd TFS 'Aces', reactivated on 31 July 1975. The first two, under Vietnam veterans Lt Col Yates and Lt Col Perry respectively, commanded some forty-four remaining F-105Gs and their crews, with the 563rd TFS providing training for both Thunderheads and the F-4C WW-IV establishment, using a mix of aircraft.

The shift of the nucleus of Weasel activities from Kansas to California was based on the emerging pre-eminence of the F-4 as Weasel aircraft, and George AFB had been operating for several years as an RTU base within ready flying range of Caliente and Nellis's impressive Tonopah Range simulators, obliging F-105G crews to conduct regular training from Nevada, as their nearby Smokey Hill Range near Topeka offered only one small emitter. The US Navy's Californian China Lake Range also offered a realistic means of testing emerging weapons and tactics. 'Electronic warfare ranges for training on a regular basis, along with the natural tendency to group like aircraft/mission/crews together, was the main consideration for the relocation. However, it is worth noting that there were occasions when the Weasels would fly to Eglin AFB for tests or exercises against the formidable array of SAM simulators on Santa Rosa Island,' remembers Barry Miller.

Obviously, the F-4 Weasels got the better deal, but the F-105G establishment – flying the last Thunderchiefs in the active inventory – benefited from the pooling of Weasel know-how, and this consolidation kept them from premature retirement. The jets were beefed-up to extend their service lives, as many were already reaching or surpassing the 4,000hr mark. Crew Chief Marvin P. 'Mad Max' Maxson recalled that Dynaelectron Corporation worked on the digital upgrades and airframes at George: 'A lot of the guys that were retiring from active duty were going to work for them. Uniform one day, then the next day instant DynaCorp.' It was a thankfully calm period for the crews. The F-105Gs made only two overseas deployments during their tenure at George, the 561st TFS for a 'Reforger' (Return of Forces to Germany) exercise during 1976, and the 562nd TFS to Karup AB, Denmark, just over a year later.

The F-4C WW-IVs were later reformed under the 39th TFS 'Cobras', providing training for crews destined for postings to the 67th TFS at Kadena AB, or the 81st TFS at Spangdahlem AB, each retaining some fourteen or fifteen Weasel aircraft. PACAF and USAFE numbers were bolstered by vanilla F-4Cs for theatre familiarization and other basic training tasks, and by the F-4Ds of their fellow squadrons which could serve in the companion killer role and which were beginning to make use of the newly perfected second-generation smart munitions. Among these were the launch-and-leave TV-guided AGM-65A/B Maverick, Pave Spike laser designators and allied Paveway LGBs, navigation extras such as the ARN-92 Long Range Radio Navigation (LORAN) Towel Rack and most of the weapons formerly exclusive to select F-4D/E Phantom IIs which possessed a WRCS and dual-mode radar tube to double as optical display.[19]

For the F-4C Weasels, there was one last shot. In April 1975, as the North Vietnamese were grinding their way south on their third, this time

In the event of drogue 'chute failure on landing, a Thud pilot employed both wheel brakes and aerobraking. This ensured a safe if somewhat stinky recovery – and required a tyre change! This shot was taken at George AFB, home of the Wild Weasels from 1975. (Frank B. Mormillo)

unimpeded, campaign, President Gerald Ford ordered the evacuation of all US citizens under Operation Frequent Wind. Nine 67th TFS F-4C WW-IVs were deployed from Kadena AB to Korat RTAFB between 20 April and 7 May to provide defence suppression support for the evacuation of US personnel from Saigon.[20]

Once at Korat the Weasel crews were 'married' up with crews from the (then) F-4D squadron, the 34th TFS, at Korat to form two-ship hunter/killer packages, the F-4C WWs with two AGM-45s and two external tanks, the F-4D with two external tanks and four CBUs on the centreline. The crews worked out their tactics and then were put on stand-by. All came in each morning for a situation brief, then after the brief they were released to go to the O'Club, sit around the pool, or whatever on stand-by, in case they were needed.

The missions were launched on April 29th, and covered the evacuation of Saigon throughout the day. The airspace over Saigon was divided up into several areas of responsibility, with two hunter/killer teams assigned to each area so there would be continuous coverage (one team in the area and the other on the tanker, with swaps as necessary). Special Rules of Engagement sent directly from the JCS to the Weasels restricted the teams to operating within 20 miles of the Tan Son Nhut TACAN and restricted them from engaging unless fired on. If fired upon, they could return fire. Other fighters held at various holding points, but only the hunter/killer teams were allowed to rove in their areas of responsibility and the other fighters remained at their holding points throughout the day.

Miller Flight [its F-4C WW-IV lead component crewed by Capt Jack R. 'Jay' Suggs and Capt John Dewey] launched, refuelled, and worked in their area of responsibility which was north-east of Saigon, in the vicinity of Bien Hoa. They alternated between the area and their tanker throughout the day, logging over 5 hours with four periods on station in their orbit area. While in their area, they received electronic indications that a Fan Song was situated just outside their area; however, they could never obtain a visual on the site.

During their fourth period on station, the F-4D wingman told Miller Lead that he was receiving AAA fire and suggested he start moving his aircraft around a bit more. Shortly thereafter, Jay Suggs spotted the muzzle flashes of the battery that was shooting at them. He advised Cricket (the controlling ABCCC) of a defensive reaction and then attempted to describe the target to the F-4D (with the CBUs). When the F-4D pilot could not readily acquire the AAA site, Capt Suggs fired an unguided Shrike (no target radar present) at the target, barely missing it. The F-4D then attacked the gun battery with cluster bombs, knocking out one of the guns and getting a good secondary explosion from within the battery area.

Miller Flight's action represented the last ARM expended by USAF fighters during the Vietnam conflict, and apparently put a stop to the AAA fire from the NVA Army that was rolling toward Saigon.

F I V E

ADVANCED WILD WEASELS

n its guise as both hunter/killer and air supremacy jet, the F-4 helped the United States achieve air dominance during the Vietnam War and was much coveted by overseas air arms. Among its chief foreign Military Sales (FMS) clients was Israel's Tsvah Hagana Le Israeli/ Cheyl Ha'Avir (Israeli Defence Force/Air Force, or IDF/AF), which, like the United States, had been wrestling with Sino-Soviet radar-guided air defences for several years. During the pre-emptive Six-Day War of May 1967 Israel achieved air dominance with French-built jets in record time, but at the cost of one-third of its Air Force to enemy SAMs and triple-A. Ironically, the conflict led to an arms embargo by France, making the acquisition of replacement aircraft all the more difficult.

Impressed by the F-4's do-it-all performance in Vietnam, Israel turned to the United States instead and a deal was signed for an initial fifty Phantom II jets, plus a number of Skyhawks. In exchange, Israel furnished the United States with some remarkable intelligence, for a number of Egyptian Fan Song batteries had been overrun during fighting in the Sinai, permitting detailed scrutiny of this system and its associated SA-2B Mod 1 missiles. An unfortunate incident involving Israeli jets strafing the Mediterranean-based US Navy intelligence-gathering ship that year was swept under the carpet.

In another scoop, two years later in December 1969, Israeli commandos raided an EW radar site near Ras Gharib, and helicoptered out vital parts from a P-12 Spoon Rest EW radar, the long-range eyes of the SA-2. Further Soviet-built air defence assets that were captured (or seized, following defection) included several MiGs. The intelligence – and the hardware itself – was put to good use by the United States on its Red Hat and Have Donut/Have Drill air-to-air programmes, though mostly by the US Navy as the US Air Force was still firmly stuck in the SIOP groove and more interested in aircraft it could not obtain, such as the MiG-25 Foxbat Mach 2.8-capable interceptor, deemed to be the principal adversary to its SAC bomber fleet. Nonetheless, the ties with Israel thus grew even stronger and paved the way for the supply of up-to-date defence suppression hardware from the United States to strap on to the newly delivered fighters, as the US Air Force began to realize the potential of the new relationship.

KURNASS

At 1730hr on Friday 5 September 1969 the first four F-4Es thundered into Israel. It took only a month before the jets were in action, knocking out Egyptian SA-2 batteries at Abu Suweir. Initially equipping Shmuel Hetz's 201 'Ahat' Squadron at Hatzor, and then Avihu Ben-Nun's 69 'Ha'patishim' (The Hammers) Squadron at Ramat David, it was the F-4E's bomb load that amazed the Israelis, and they quickly nicknamed it the Kurnass, or Sledgehammer.[1]

What was significant about this period was the new threats being encountered by the IDF/AF, well ahead of anything confronted by the US. This so-called War of Attrition gradually escalated from piecemeal interdiction strikes and 'supersonic booming' of Cairo and Damascus to coordinated interdiction and defence suppression work known as the Prikha (Blossom), or the rolling missile campaign, in response to the Egyptians moving a line of anti-aircraft defences steadily closer to the Suez Canal. The first missions were launched against SAM and triple-A batteries in February 1970 using eight F-4Es at a time, each toting M117 750lb bombs, to hit SA-2 sites at Dahshur and Helwan. Over the ensuing months these missions graduated to include targets further south along the Red Sea coast, generating a series of deadly duels between the IDF/AF and Egyptian SA-2 SAM and flak batteries. Three F-4Es were brought down in one week alone, two on 30 June during a strike against three sites at Rubeiki, and a third on 5 July.[2]

QRC-335A/ALQ-101 ECM pods were introduced from US stocks, and at 1215hr on Saturday 18 July a reprisal raid was launched by both F-4E squadrons against five Egyptian SA-2 batteries, some 31 miles west of the Suez. It turned into an horrific exchange as salvoes of unexpected SA-3 SAMs were launched which could not be outmanoeuvred, one of them exploding near 201 Squadron boss Shmuel Hetz's aircraft. He went down

In the blur of its J79 turbojets in afterburner, an F-4E begins its take-off roll. (Author)

with his crippled aircraft during an attempted 600kt diving egress, although his navigator Menaheim Eini ejected to be taken prisoner. Either the ECM was not working properly or the Egyptians were employing new frequencies, possibly Soviet War Reserve Modes (WARMS) unknown to the United States and Israel. Thus Israeli losses to Arab defences began to escalate and there were more to come. (Hetz's aircraft was one of two F-4Es downed that day.)

STRAIGHT FLUSH AND GAINFUL

Soviet pilots known to be flying Egyptian Air Force MiG-21s were on 'alert' at Cairo, Beni-Suef, Kom Awshim, El Mansura and Kotmiya, and scrambled on 18 April 1970 to engage Israeli F-4Es, which were ordered to return home, for fear of diplomatic repercussions. Deep bombing into Egypt ended that day for the same reason. However, strikes against the radar sites along the Suez continued. A week later A-4Hs were forced back by the marauding Soviets, one being damaged in a tail-chase by the MiGs.

On 30 July the inevitable clash occurred. The operation had been planned by IDF/AF chief Moti Hod in a bid to regain air superiority, so that Israel would no longer be intimidated by the Soviets. Two F-4Es were tasked to hit the Sohana radar station near the Suez Canal, cover being provided by four Dassault-Breguet Mirage IIIs which provided MiGCAP, with another four in trail, and another four F-4Es behind them, all of which pressed on provocatively into Egyptian airspace while the two radar strikers returned home, job done. Within 20 minutes eight MiG-21s were scrambled from Beni-Suef, followed by a dozen from Kom Awshim, and then another four from Kotmiya. The ensuing clash between the Mirage IIIs, F-4Es and MiG-21s resulted in five MiG-21s being downed before the Soviet pilots fled, humiliated.

Plans for the bombing of the Suez SAM defences were extended and on 3 August F-4Es were dispatched to strike an SA-3 battery that had been relocated near Isma'iliya. However, the strike went horribly wrong when one of the F-4Es was hacked down by an altogether new SAM – the Soviets had ferried in this new weapon and set it up solely to exact some revenge.[3]

The new weapon, later given the NATO code-name SA-6 Gainful, was a completely new breed of threat: fitted in threes on modified caterpillar-tracked PT-76 armoured personnel carrier chassis for battlefield mobility, it was effective down to around 150ft, and guided to its target using an equally mobile caterpillar-tracked Straight Flush radar. This twin-radar array did not merely track targets in the G and H Bands and send command guidance signals to the SAM in the I Band, it also *illuminated* the target with J-Band Continuous-Wave (CW) energy during the terminal phase of intercept, which the missile homed in on using Semi-Active Radar-Homing (SARH) techniques. This feature, coupled with the SA-6's diminutive size and its unlimited mobility (including an amphibious capability, for river crossing), made it a particularly worrisome foe. It was effective out to about 15 miles, intercepting targets using a (post-thruster-separation) ramjet engine that accelerated the weapon to three

The SA-6 Gainful was guided to target using target illumination furnished by the Straight Flush radar, shown here. Radar array and missiles, carried in threes, were fitted to the same class of amphibious tracked vehicles, turning the SA-6 into a highly mobile weapon. (via Barry Miller)

times the speed of sound. Impact or proximity fusing detonated its 176lb warhead.

A typical Egyptian air defence unit comprised three SA-6 vehicles, plus radar and loading vehicles (the missiles being resupplied by truck), meaning that aircraft could confront up to nine of these deadly weapons without much prior warning. In response to the early losses to this SAM, twelve replacement F-4Es were supplied to Israel in 1971 under Operation Peace Patch (not counting further Peace Echo deliveries). More significantly, AGM-45 Shrike ARMs were made available at this time.

IDF/AF crews first began testing Shrike on 18 September 1971, but not against the new Soviet radars – the War of Attrition had ended in a cease-fire on 7 August 1970, three days after their initial encounter with the new SA-6, leaving the aircrews with a sense of considerable unease about the Arab defences. These now provided integrated overlapping IADS coverage via SA-2, SA-3 and the new SA-6 missiles, along with examples of the deadly ZSU-23/4-P Shilka. Worst of all, nobody in the United States or Israel yet understood the implications of the SA-6's SARH homing, even though such techniques were employed by US Army HAWK SAM batteries. It was still believed that the SA-6 was primarily command-guided and could be defeated by the use of suitably tuned Beacon mode noise-jamming to thwart command guidance, or Fan Song TTR mainlobe-jamming from the ECM pods.

At 1400hr on Saturday 6 October 1973 Israel, celebrating the festival of Yom Kippur (the Day of Atonement), was caught completely off guard by a simultaneous Egyptian and Syrian air and ground offensive code-named Operation Badr. The first four days were mostly a disaster for the IDF/AF. The Suez Canal area was blanket-covered by the new SAMs. Six F-4Es were lost on the first day of counter-air strike operations (7 October), and a seventh landed at Ramat David on fire, taking it out of the war. Rear-facing KB18 strike camera footage noted up to four SAMs simultaneously chasing one F-4E crew lucky to evade the onslaught and return home safely.

Day Two witnessed IDF/AF aircraft repeatedly attacking Egyptian SAM belts along the Suez, at terrible cost. Skyhawk CAS losses were partic-ularly high. To the east, heavy rain clouds over the Golan Heights pre-vented attacks against Syrian SAMs and airfields, as planned, and many strike missions merely degenerated into air-to-air encounters as aircrews were forced to dump their bombs shortly after take-off, so as to engage enemy aircraft entering Israeli airspace. In the late morning of Day Three, Operation Dugman was launched, comprising fifteen F-4Es, to hit Syrian SAM batteries. However, the mobile SA-6s and ZSU-23/4s had dispersed or were staying radar-silent beneath camouflage netting. During a second attack pass, in an effort to identify them, one F-4E was brought down – the first of six destroyed that day during the ensuing mêlée. Only three SAM sites were knocked out, and five damaged, of the thirty-one targets in the operation.

Any plans to conduct further wholesale attacks against the enemy SAM batteries were binned, and on Day Four sixteen F-4Es were instead dispatched to bomb the Syrian Air Force headquarters in Damascus, *after* a challenging morning strike against airfields in the Egyptian Nile Delta. The building was heavily damaged, but two aircraft in the first wave were hit by triple-A, one limping back to Ramat David; the second wave turned back and then rerouted to hit a Syrian armoured division that was on the point of breaking through Israeli ground forces. These actions were typical of the first four days of the counter-offensive.

The major reprieve came on Day Five when, to the IDF/AF aircrews' delight, the SAMs ceased soaring skyward – the Egyptians and Syrians had all but run out of missiles. This left them wide open to attack pending Soviet resupply, and over the next six days the IDF/AF took advantage of the situation, helping to repel enemy ground forces, knock out artillery batteries, strike airfields and trash radar stations.

This interesting image shows the Dome of the Rock in Jerusalem photographed by an Israeli Phantom II, the shadow of which falls over its companion's port wing. (McDonnell Douglas via John J. Harty)

However, with a depleted force and replacement Soviet equipment beginning to arrive, the IDF/AF feared they might be defeated in Round Two. In response, the United States intervened with its own emergency resupply effort, bringing in fresh armour, aircraft and ordnance. The urgency of Operational Nickel Grass (a name poached from the saying, 'Throw a nickel on the grass, save a fighter pilot's a**') was apparent to F-4E delivery crews as they entered Israeli airspace. Replacement aircraft were taken from USAF inventory stocks at Seymour-Johnson AFB and flown to the hot-spot beginning on 13 October.

The pipeline for deliveries was through Lajes Field in the Azores. As jets landed from the United States, they were met by fuel trucks and the crews who were to fly them on to Israel. The crews swapped info on the jets' status at the bottom of the ladder, and as soon as they were topped-up with fuel the new crews climbed in and launched. As they neared Israel's coast they were met by armed IDF/AF fighters and escorted to their destination, which may or may not have been where they were flight-planned for – all part of Israel's deception/war plan. The USAF delivery crews were directed to flow through TAB-V shelters where they shut down the jets. Even as they were unstrapping and climbing out of the jets, the fuel tanks were being dropped, the 20mm training rounds were being cycled out for warloads, fuel was being pumped, and jammers were loading MERs and TERs with bombs already attached. They were met by the IDF/AF crews at the bottom of the ladders for a quick brief on the jet, and then watched as the Israelis climbed in, taxied out, took off, turned out of traffic, rolled in on Egyptian positions and dropped their bombs. They were that close.[4]

A total of thirty-six replacement F-4Es were ferried from American stocks at Seymour-Johnson AFB, North Carolina, along with supplies of Shrikes by C-5 and C-141 cargo lifters (comprising 50 AGM-45-3As, 135 -4s and 115 -6s), plus Hughes Missiles' new AGM-65A Maverick AGM. The newly transferred F-4Es featured dual-mode radar/electro-optical cockpit displays and were wired for Maverick, which they were only just in the process of introducing to service. The pilot would roll in on a target using his gunsight pipper wherever possible, and Maverick's television seeker – boresighted with the aircraft's nose or velocity vector – would present a magnified image of what lay ahead on the dual-mode display. The WSO or backseater could then trim the desired image lock-on point *under* the seeker crosshairs on the display by means of a sidestick control, confirm lock-up on the target, and the missile would be fired at a range of 1½–2nm

Trials launch of a AGM-65A Maverick TV-guided missile. The weapon entered service in 1972 and was supplied to Israel the following year. (Hughes Missiles)

Close-up of the Maverick missile on a LAU-88 triple-launcher. By the late 1970s the AGM-65A had been superseded by the scene magnification B model (inboard rail), while trials were under way with an imaging infra-red D version (bottom rail). The Maverick formed part of the Advanced Wild Weasel F-4G arsenal. (Hughes Missiles)

from the target, shooting off its Teflon-coated launch rail (at which point the radarscope went blank) to deliver a rocket-assisted 125lb warhead in a launch-and-leave manner.

In the clear Middle East skies Maverick offered a staggering 87 per cent hit rate, taking out parked aircraft, armour and radars alike. Once fired, aircrews could immediately undertake evasive action, unlike a traditional bomb run which would have them hanging over the target, although preliminary target alignment took considerable initial concentration and coordinated front and backseat action, just as with a Shrike delivery – the supreme advantage of having a two-man crew. Anecdotal evidence suggests that Maverick's accuracy actually surpassed desire, as Stan Goldstein recalls: 'The Israelis were not entirely happy with the Mavericks as they were *too* good. Maverick tended to destroy the tanks and they wanted them to repair and use. I don't know if this story is valid. The anecdotal fix to this problem was to shoot at the shadow of the tank and hope to disable it and not destroy it.'[5]

By comparison, Shrike performance remained poor, and of the forty-three F-4Es and a staggering fifty-three A-4s felled or written off during the conflict the majority had succumbed to ZSU-23/4-P fire or SA-6 SAMs, which they were largely unable to counter except by brute overkill. In daylight the ZSU-23/4 was particularly nasty as there were no tracers to highlight the hosing of supersonic projectiles, and gunners could employ optical gun turret-cueing in radar blind fashion. The SA-6's Straight Flush CW illumination system was similarly invisible, as F-4E and A-4 RHAWS were looking for pulsed guidance signals only, not the CW illumination. Onboard jamming systems were unable to respond either as, even with the necessary Set-On frequency information, it would have been ineffective against the illumination or paint.

Many otherwise extremely competent IDF/AF fighter crews were brought down by the SA-6. The only known effective counter was chaff, hastily placed behind airbrake doors, and dumped in a one-shot method when the rubbernecking aircrew spotted a SAM launch, to offer an alternate radar paint for the SAM's SARH seeker to home in on. Coupled with good SAM breaking, this finally did the trick.

Much information about how to manoeuvre against the strategic SA-2, and the SA-3 in particular, came from former USAF pilot and Vietnam F-4E veteran Joel Aronoff, who was flying F-4Es from Ramat David shortly after hostilities broke out. He was evading more than twelve SAMs on some missions (his wingmen counted sixty on one occasion!) and still getting his bombs on target. He passed on his knowledge to an eager audience once his strike talents had been spotted. His apparently bizarre tactic became known as wagon-wheeling, hence his high 'SAM magnet' rate.

Instead of going in and out quickly, Aronoff circled the defences at the edge of their effective range but outside their guaranteed kill reach at low altitudes, outmanoeuvred SAMs individually, and bored in for the bomb run only when he reckoned that the launchers had been depleted of missiles. Wagon-wheeling resulted in many bombs on target and in the space of a few days the IDF/AF effectively subdued the Egyptian air bases in the Nile Delta – operations which had previously cost them up to three F-4Es shot down per mission, with little net result.

However, when pressing in closer towards enemy ground forces near the Suez Canal and Golan Heights, a further threat to the IDF/AF came from shoulder-launched man-portable air defence systems (MANPADS) such as the SA-7 Grail, first encountered by the USAF the previous year. These fired a heat-seeking missile that locked on to the exhaust plumes of aircraft engines. Although most effective against slow-movers such as C-130 transports or helicopters, fast-movers pulling up from Dive Toss and dive releases at lower altitudes were vulnerable to hits in their hot jetpipes, especially if the afterburner was engaged to maintain airspeed during egress, as was customary to ensure safe clearance from the ground – and their exploding ordnance.

With the arrival of the new US-supplied equipment, tactics were again quickly revised. F-4Es were dispatched to knock out specific defences with Shrikes and iron bombs; impromptu helicopter-borne jammers, hastily matched to the new threats, hovered near the enemy lines at low level and artillery was brought forward to hammer enemy SAM installations – probably the most effective anti-SAM technique of the whole war, as mere puffs of artillery explosions in the vicinity of an SA-6 shut it down. Before long the IDF/AF reassumed air superiority against the Arabs' Soviet-supplied missiles and fighters.

The day was won by this decisive reaction to the sudden and un-expected, coupled with the United States' diplomatically daring emergency resupply effort – which had brought East and West closer to nuclear Armageddon than at any time since the Cuban Missile Crisis. The frantic pace of operations continued until 21 October, Day Sixteen of the Yom Kippur War. By then, Israeli ground forces had finally outflanked the Egyptians in the Sinai and had driven the Syrians back into a defensive position on the Mount Hermon line. The United Nations then called for a cease-fire on the 22nd, and all hostilities finally halted two days later, allowing everyone to count the cost.

To their credit, the IDF/AF maintained air superiority over Israel throughout the conflict, creating two new ace pilots and many with several kills each. Veteran Yiftah Spector added five MiG-21s to the nine he had already felled during his Mirage IIICJ days. Overall, Israeli aircrews enjoyed an air-to-air kill ratio of 18.4:1, far in excess of American results in Vietnam. Of the seventy Egyptian and thirty-one Syrian theatre SAM batteries noted at the war's outset, forty-three Egyptian and eight Syrian sites – half of them (mostly Egyptian sites) dotted along the Suez Canal between El Qantara and Suez – had been pounded into submission. However, over 140 of the 1,300 SAMs launched, most within the first few days, had claimed a kill: a totally unacceptable situation. Judging by the worldwide media's knee-jerk reaction to the new Soviet weaponry, air power had become an expensive pariah.

YOM KIPPUR CONCUSSION

There were many knock-on consequences as a result of the lessons learned vicariously through the bitter Israeli experience that autumn. The United States' power-projection remained firmly rooted in air power. While triple-A was a perennial problem, the most immediate objective was to find new ways to counter the SA-6 Straight Flush radar and the abundant heat-seeking MANPADS systems. SA-6 CW sensing alongside C- and D-Band direction-finding associated with SA-3 and SA-4 command guidance links was added to fighter-bombers' AN/ALR-46 RWRs under the Compass Sail/Compass Clockwise initiatives; and the Compass Matrix RWR/jamming pod 'power management' marriage was revisited under Compass Tie to provide more precise Set-On jamming prompting for the new threats. The LWR subsystem of the RWR also was able to display un-correlated missile guidance signals by quadrant, giving crews a better idea of threat bearing when opposed by unestablished systems, if any other new ones emerged by means of a U-for-Unknown.

Adding to this new capability, by late 1976 Westinghouse's Project 669A AN/ALQ-131 modular noise/deception-jamming pod had been developed. This new equipment was flightline reprogrammable using a briefcase-sized device and could cope with over forty waveforms simultaneously, giving it the facility to use pre-emptive Transponder mode jamming, along with traditional repeater-deception and noise-jamming modes. The AN/ALQ-131 is still regarded as the best ECM pod in the US Air Force inventory, and was built in two principal configurations: a three-band deep pod used by F-4s, and a two-band shallow pod employed by F-111s. (A giant five-band, RAT-powered version was also tested but not built, its size overcoming its advantages. Two or more F-4s would have to be airborne within each strike package, toting only these devices, fuel bags and AAMs for self-protection.)

Concurrent US Air Force RWR developments included the ATI AN/ALR-69 which in 1978 began equipping the US Air Force's F-4 fledgeling replacements, the General Dynamics F-16 Fighting Falcon and the Fairchild-Republic A-10A Thunderbolt II tank-buster, as a follow-on to the AN/ALR-46.[6] Onboard chaff dispensers also arrived from mid-1974 onwards, standardized around the Tracor AN/ALE-40 Square Shooter, fitted to the rear of the F-4s' inner wing pylons. Typically, four such dispensers were fitted to the F-4s for Alert or combat assignments, providing up to sixty chaff cartridges per aircraft. The same devices, known to the crews as ice-cube trays because of their appearance, later found their way into the rear empennage of the new F-16 and the A-10A wing-tips. A burst from these devices would provide a distracting target cloud to draw SA-6s and ZSU-23/4 cannon fire away from the aircraft for critical seconds during pop-up manoeuvres over the target.

Countering the infrared guidance of MANPADS and enemy MiGs' AAMs was possible thanks to a special downwards tilting AN/ALE-40 module, which could house up to fifteen fierce-burning pop-out MJU-10 flare pyrotechnics to lure away heat-seeking weapons. The introduction of these was timely, for a new range of Soviet radar- and optically cued SAMs which employed terminal infrared guidance made their debut at the November 1975 Moscow Parade, reaching front-line Soviet Army armoured units in East Germany shortly thereafter. The first was the short-range SA-8 Gecko, mounted in fours on six-wheeled amphibious armoured cars and toting G/H-Band surveillance and J-Band tracking using Land Roll radar based on the Soviet Navy's Pop Group system. At the same parade

The SA-8B Gecko SAM fitted to amphibious vehicles relied on radar for target acquisition and tracking, but on heat-seeking for terminal intercept. (Barry Miller)

the Soviets wheeled out the short-range SA-9 Gaskin, which mounted four modified SA-7 MANPADS missiles on a BRDM-2A amphibious scout car.

By the end of the 1970s a typical Soviet field army would boast three SA-2 and nine SA-4 batteries at the rear, five SA-6 batteries positioned in tiers 2–3 miles apart, with gaggles of ZSU-23/4s, SA-8s and SA-9s at the sharp end, moving with the tank formations. If NATO aircrews had to confront a Soviet thrust through the Fulda Gap – a prospective scenario for a Warsaw Pact invasion of Western Europe, where multiple threats would be encountered over an area the size of several football pitches at a time – they would have their work cut out just to survive this assault, let alone hit the enemy armour.

The US Navy's response was similar, directed by its electronic warfare office, PME-107; EA-6B AN/ALQ-99 jamming coverage was expanded as part of the EA-6B's Improved Capability (ICAP) and ICAP-II programmes. Two ECMOs in each EA-6B could now cope with up to ten transmitters at a time. In addition, the capabilities of the US Navy's Fleetwide AN/ALQ-126 deception-jammer were expanded with finer power management (under the -(V)4 initiative) and SA-6 Straight Flush CW target illumination radar track-breaking added. Some strike and jamming jets also received the AN/ALQ-162 dedicated track-breaker. The Fleet also experimented with special pods and built-in devices to counter infrared-homing weapons, but soon settled on flare cartridges as a cheaper and more reliable method for protecting its A-6Es and A-7Es, based on the US Navy's then-standard round hole dispensers which had been dumping bursts of chaff as a last-ditch defence since Vietnam.[7]

European air arms also began investing in US-designed RWRs and jamming pods cleared for FMS, equipping their fighters with the devices for the first time ever. Until then, only the United Kingdom's V-bombers had any sort of radar-countermeasures, and its fast-jet tactical fleet, like the remainder of NATO's forces, remained entirely unprotected.[8]

The most far-reaching consequence, however, of the Israeli combat experience during the Yom Kippur War was massively increased funding of parallel, interdependent electronic combat programmes in the US, resulting in several billion-dollar efforts. As the Israelis were essentially operating US state-of-the-art equipment, the argument that 'If it happened to them, it could happen to us' became the catchphrase in the Pentagon, and the people involved used every lever they could to get electronic warfare updates. Three programmes already in existence but suffering lacklustre funding were given urgent new priority status. The US Navy's AGM-88 High-Speed ARM (HARM) was one, designed to replace both Shrike and STARM. The second initiative was the USAF's Pave Strike effort which embraced, among other things, a brand-new dedicated support jamming aircraft to replace the obsolescent EB-66s, already being turned into scrap without a successor in sight.

Based upon forty-two converted swing-wing F-111A airframes, the EF-111A Raven offered penetration capability (essential for the ongoing SIOP) with a highly automated, built-in AN/ALQ-99E version of the EA-6B's jamming pods tucked into its former weapons bay, operated by a right-seat EWO. Its pilot would be an 'old head' well-versed in both flying the F-111 and using the navigation-only remnants of the Aardvark's bomb-nav system, the displays and controls of which were relocated in the centre of the instrumentation for easy reach by either crewman, while the EWO played with his new jamming controls. The latter dominated the right-hand side of the cockpit and were based on later EA-6B ICAP switchology and displays.

ADVANCED WILD WEASEL

Equal prominence within Pave Strike was afforded to the third top-drawer element: the F-4G Advanced Wild Weasel, designed to replace the war-weary F-105G WW-III and limited-capability F-4C WW-IV, which, by the close of hostilities in South-East Asia, had dwindled to a combined force of eighty obsolescent aircraft. In order to get the Advanced Wild Weasel into service as quickly as possible it would rely initially on the Shrike and Standard ARMs and the Maverick AGM, absorbing the new HARM as soon as was practicable.

In fact, a series of efforts had been under way since July 1967 to give USAF's F-4s a Standard ARM capability.[9] This initially involved two trials F-4Ds (65-657 and 65-660) which acted as system engineering testbeds under the Wild Weasel IV-B programme, matching the missile with Bendix AN/APS-107 and ATI ER-142 receivers, as used aboard US Navy Mod 0/0-Update A-6Bs. However, only the former subsequently became a standard feature on F-4Ds, progressively updated to AN/APS-107E standard by the end of the 1970s, but never used in a Weasel role. The two F-4D testbeds' chief contribution to the Advanced Wild Weasel effort was in helping to aerodynamically match the Standard ARM and new-generation receivers with the F-4.

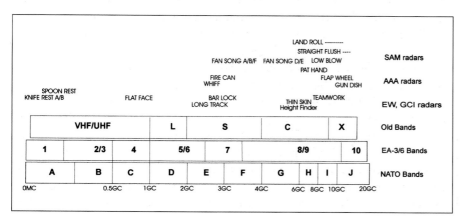

Old and new radar bands, with c. 1968–73 US Navy jamming bands included. References to both old and new bandings are made throughout the book, and this chart is offered for easy comparison with Soviet-originated radar threats of the era. (Author)

Two F-4D APR-38 testbeds explored the Advanced Wild Weasel configuration while the equipment was being perfected for the definitive Phantom II-Weasel F-4G. This is one of the testbeds. (Dennis R. Jenkins)

By 1973 production of the Standard ARM had progressed to the AGM-78D model. This was further refined into the ultimate D-2 model with greater digital reliability, active optical fusing and a 223lb blast-fragmentation warhead. It remained in production until August 1976, giving the US a net inventory of some 700 missiles, backed up by inert blue TGM training versions for captive practice lock-ups.

Marrying the big Standard ARM to the F-4 met with little success in the early years, until McDonnell Douglas and IBM teamed up to create the AN/APR-38 Radar Attack and Warning System (RAWS) to receive, analyse and sift through the threats and hand them off to the weapon. At last, a respectable replacement for the venerable F-105G seemed to be in the making. With four 9in synchronized arrays of radar-receiving interferometers and super-heterodynes on each side of the jet to sift through the radio frequency portion of the electromagnetic spectrum to analyse threat type and status, plus direction-finders built into the nose barrel and vertical tail of the aircraft – fifty-two antennae in all – the package gave 360-degree coverage and could provide a cut in the pie of less than 2 degrees on any radar threat.

Using phased interferometry to sense the different azimuth and declination readings to the emitters as the aircraft plied its course, the system could triangulate each emitter's position and identify its status and type, thus creating the first Wild Weasel to provide a truly automated target-ranging capability. Early test results demonstrated this, allowing for a 2nm error at 50nm range to target, which would diminish as the aircraft closed range, ultimately attaining accuracy to approximately 6ft at duel ranges. Two F-4Ds (66-7635 and 66-7647) were involved in the new programme, both of which received trials versions of the AN/APR-38 and allied Homing And Warning Computer (HAWC) between May and December 1974, for preliminary flight-test work.[10]

F-105F EWO Vietnam veteran Maj Gerald 'Jerry' Stiles was involved in the HAWC programme in the Pentagon, and describes the early trials:[11]

Management of the overall task was assigned to McDonnell Douglas who served as the prime equipment integrator. Under them on sub-contracts were IBM and Texas Instruments, who built the complex receiver equipment and the brains of the configuration, the HAWC; Loral, who built the state-of-the-art displays and controls; and General Electric, who modified the existing lead-computing gunsight. The programme manager for this effort was located in the ASD at Wright-Patterson AFB, Ohio, the real focus point for all these undertakings. The programme manager when I initially joined was Col Bob Hayden, who stayed with the project for approximately one year and was followed by Col Ross Rogers, who essentially completed the effort. A flight-test organization for the Advanced Wild Weasel programme was established at Edwards AFB, California. Lt Col Frank O'Donnell was the test project officer and performed a super job in this role.

The programme seemed to go from one crisis to another. The big effort under way was to conduct, essentially, a smoke test on the newly developed configuration. It was called a smoke test because, for all practical purposes, in order to conform with a DoD-mandated schedule, we had to initially test-fly the configuration by a certain date. Our goal was thus to cram the equipment into the F-4D, get it airborne, and hope that nothing caught fire – no smoke. We did and it didn't, so we called the test successful and declared the milestone was met! Fortunately, a more orderly progression of events followed which proved that it was possible to mate the AN/APR-38 with the F-4D.

Problems, however, emerged with the display units and power supply for the black boxes and one subcontractor nearly pulled out before more money was made available for them to complete their task. A second issue arose with the HAWC, a 32K memory system, as Jerry Stiles recalls:

[The HAWC became] filled to the brim with ones and zeros and couldn't digest any more. But we still had more software to add, and now we couldn't do so without a larger computer – one with 64K words, the final capacity. Thus, by late 1973, early 1974, the pro-gramme faced several severe obstacles. We had a power supply that didn't work, a computer deficient in memory and, as might be expected, costs which were escalating. We had a non-performing product, an obliterated schedule and lots of costs – the programme was in trouble. Fortunately for the Advanced Wild Weasel project, the germ of electronic warfare again budded for us, this time in a Middle East war version. The Israelis and Egyptians were having a go at it, but the Egyptians were playing rough with some new SAMs, something we hadn't seen exported from the Soviet Union before. It is well known that their newly acquired SA-6 batteries, along with some of their other radar-directed threats really put a serious hurt on the Sons of Abraham.

The result for us was that increased impetus was gained for a new Weasel – if it could happen to them, it could happen to us. Thus, as can often happen, a far-off war saved our skins. The big bosses in charge of the monies decided that the Weasel was a must regardless of cost and schedules (we helped them reach this decision) and thus the programme was restructured to take care of the deficiencies and newly found threats.

It was concurrent with this new salvation that I came up with the idea: as long as we were going to spend time and money, why not put the advanced equipment in a newer airframe, namely the F-4E? The F-4D was certainly capable, but it hadn't been produced for some time, had seen a lot of combat service in South-East Asia and had a few other problems.[12] One of these was that the F-4D lacked adequate internal space in which to put the Weasel gear – within reason, that is. One of the space problems that had been a plague to the F-4D was that some of the black boxes had had to be tucked away into an almost inaccessible dead space between the engines. Needless to say, this hot-spot required that we air-condition the sensitive electrical equipment, so special ducting had to be created, again through almost inaccessible territory.

The lack of space was a real problem. Imagine what it would have been like in the field without the availability of the special factory jigs that would have been used to emplace the equipment! Thus, at my suggestion, we began to investigate the possibility of adapting the F-4E into the Weasel configuration. One aspect immediately became evident: we would have to remove the 20mm gun in order to accommodate the AN/APR-38A. We had studied the problem in depth and there was no other viable solution. The sensitive Weasel antennae had to be mounted in an assembly on or near the nose of the aircraft. No other place would do. Some suggested the wing-tips, but vibrations there caused inaccuracies in the system. Some suggested under the fuselage area, but this limited signal reception to below the aircraft.

We looked into placing the antennae configuration in a bump below the gun lip, but the instantaneous vibrations from firing the gun were in the order of $100g$. We even looked into placing the antennae complex above the nose radome, but this caused problems for the pilot in seeing ahead. We had to either remove the gun or remove the radar (and place the Weasel antennae behind this radome), but no one wanted to do the latter – it would limit the Weasel to visual conditions only. The gun had to go.

The programme schedule now proceeded at a more leisurely pace. The F-4D test-flying continued, patched up as it was with a deficient power supply and limited computer memory, and more was learned about the system. The emphasis for fast movement was lacking because the real effort awaited equipment yet to be perfected. Why push hard when we might have to do it all over again?

We had to come up with an official designation for the new Weasel. The differences between the Advanced Wild Weasel version and the vanilla F-4E version were just too great to continue to use the same designation to be reasonably efficient. So, a new designation was sought. My recommendation, which was not adopted, was to call the new Weasel the F-4W, in recognition of its role. The powers that be, however, rejected this idea in preference to the F-4G designation; the F-4W designation would be too high on the alphabet and, besides, the F-4G designation was more coincident with the designation of the F-105G Weasel Thud. I stuck to my guns for a short while, however, especially when my research showed that the US Navy already had a modification [entirely unrelated] which they called the F-4G. Although this US Navy designation was now defunct, I half-jokingly suggested that some day, some giant computer with a long memory would try to land the Wild Weasel on an aircraft carrier.

The F-4D testbeds were gutted of their gear and resumed other duties, while McDonnell Douglas began the lengthy task of converting the first F-4E-based airframe, 69-7254, to the Advanced Wild Weasel configuration, drawing on the newly perfected, pre-production black box technology that was only just emerging from the subcontractors, under the guidance of such skilled engineer-managers as John J. 'Mr Maintenance' Harty and J.C. Coefield.

The F-4G made its maiden flight on 6 December 1975 for preliminary aerodynamic trials, subsequently absorbing the full AN/APR-38 repertoire, and was joined by two additional examples: 69-7263, adapted

F-4E 69-7254 served as the premier all-up F-4G Advanced Wild Weasel prototype, flying in December 1975. It was later brought up to full production standard. (Brian C. Rogers)

to verify production-related TCTOs 1F-4E-600, which created the structural 'sex change' from 'E to 'G and added the basic wiring, and 1F-4G-501, which installed the Weasel gear; and 69-7290, which was converted at Ogden Air Logistics Center (ALC) in Utah under McDonnell Douglas supervision, acting as the kit proof aircraft to validate the complex Class V modification procedures at OOALC. The trio then moved on to perform Initial and Follow-on Operational Test & Evaluation work, mostly conducted at Nellis AFB.

IOT&E was completed on 1 January 1977, and initial operational-standard conversions funded. A further 113 F-4Es were nominated for conversion to F-4G configuration, all drawn from F-4E production Blocks 42–45, based on their fatigue index.[13]

'DOWN IN THE WEEDS'

Initial F-4G deliveries all went to the 35th TFW at George AFB, a huge, high-desert operational and training centre for the F-4 that qualified both US Air Force and FMS F-4E customers on the big supersonic brute. The first F-4G (69-0239) was crewed by 35th TFW boss Col Dudley J. Foster and Linebacker Weasel veteran EWO Capt Dennis B. Haney, and arrived on 28 April 1978, four days after the aircraft were completed and signed for at Ogden ALC. Deliveries continued at around three aircraft per

The F-105Gs served out their final years, 1980–3, with the Georgia ANG. The 116th TFW resurrected the 'snaggletooth' jaws and introduced wraparound camouflage, not dissimilar to that first used by the Ryan's Raiders. (Lindsay T. Peacock)

month, initially equipping Lt Col James H. Martin's 39th TFTS 'Cobras', which achieved Initial Operational Capability (IOC) on 1 April 1979.[14]

The new steeds quickly ousted the 35th TFW's veteran Vietnam Wild Weasel jets. On their official retirement in July 1980, George AFB held on to F-105G 62-4416 for gate guardian duties, while Maj Jim Boyd and Capt Gary Crystal flew F-105G 63-8320 *Hanoi Hustler* to the Air Force Museum at Dayton, Ohio. Many of the F-105G WW-IIIs passed to the 128th TFS, Georgia Air National Guard (ANG) at Dobbins AFB, which maintained the Weasel mission until flying the type's last sortie on 25 May 1983, when Maj Duff Green flew 63-8299, callsign Peach 91, to NAS Patuxent River. Age had caught up with the F-105Gs, and many others sadly ended their days as Battle Damage Repair hulks.

The F-4C WW-IVs, including USAFE examples, passed to the Indiana ANG beginning in November 1978, and were distributed between its two fighter squadrons located at Hulman Field (113th TFS 'Racers') and Fort Wayne Municipal Airport (163rd TFS 'Marksmen'). They did not fly as Weasels, and after their eventual retirement between May 1986 and October 1987 four were acquired by Flight Systems Inc at Mojave Airport, California, for contract flight-test duties, flying for several more years.

The F-4G represented a quantum leap in capability over its predecessors, and took some getting used to. The initial training programmes were somewhat unstructured, as former F-105F WW-III and F-4C WW-IV EWO Francis 'T.R.' Marino recalls:

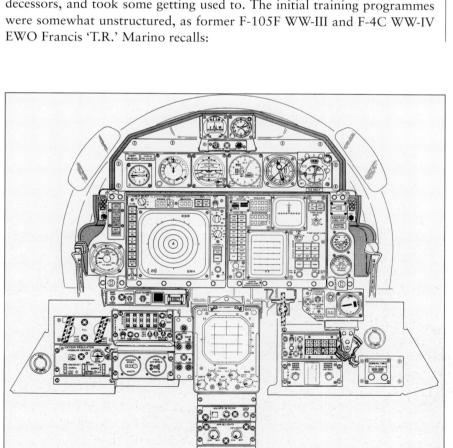

The F-4G rear main panel featured panoramic, homing and detail display indicators showing the threats in alphanumeric form on the concentric rings, and providing amplitude-based steering spikes and other threat data. The system would search for priority threats at selectable ranges of 10, 25, 50, 100 or 200 miles and could be handed-off to an ARM at the flick of a switch. (USAF)

First, my own training. It falls into the 'blind leading the blind' category. As I remember, I think there were eight or ten crews in my class. I was in the initial cadre of the 'G so we had no real books or well-developed training aids or real instructors. Our instructors were the first test crews and the tech reps from the manufacturers, and our texts were, in many cases, their tech notes or draft tech manuals. Added to this, we didn't have too many birds; they were still being delivered as we were training. Some of us, myself included (I had just come from a tour with the Air Force Inspector General's staff), had to get recurrent in the F-4 first. Since we were all fairly high-time F-4 guys (I had over 1,000hr in the 'C, 'D, 'E and slatted 'E), we sort of ran the recurrency and 'G checkout programme as one.

I will say that the training was probably as thorough as it could be. But our 'instructors' were learning right along with us. On top of this, the systems were still not in their final operational configuration and we just kept the training going and developed the basic training syllabus as we went along. As I said, there were no real Air Force-certified instructors because *we* were them, or would be as soon as we checked each other out as the first F-4G instructors. This really complicated things because we had to get a lot of the things we did in training cleared through TAC HQ (sometimes after the fact). If you think it sounds complicated, you should have been in the classroom on the flightline or on some of the training missions.

Our first 'faze' of training covered the new integrated RAWS system inside and out, switch by switch (and many of the switches had two or three functions, depending on the mode you were in), and the electronic theory and principles that made the system work the way it did. Then after the 'book' learning, it was out to the range for a couple of sorties to see how the system actually worked in the air. You tried to use all the switches and learn how to use each and every function. This was a real impossibility. You see, one of the engineers had figured out that with all of the switches, lights, bells and whistles – remember, many had two or three functions and many were integrated with the front seat systems; and then you have to add the many different types of ordnance we could carry – there were approximately *one million* switch combinations/functions!

I think the next phase was more of the same, but the missions were a little more tactical and integrated the various types of weapons and tactics in a little more realistic scenarios. The last part of the basic course was the tactics section. This consisted of realistic missions and tactics flown to the Tonopah Ranges. Well, as realistic as we could make them. However, this was not the end of our training as we had to just keep going and check ourselves out as the first 'real' TAC F-4G instructors. Basically, we intensified both the academic aspects and the flying to a level required for an instructor rating. As we were all previous instructors at one level or another, we knew what we wanted from an instructor and could get pretty hard on one another. Basically, we rotated practice class presentations and missions. That is, one day you were the 'student' and the next you were the 'instructor'. In actuality, the student was the instructor checking out the 'instructor in training'. We did this until all of us had completed/performed to what we thought was an acceptable level to be a real instructor with real students.

Of course, once again TAC HQ kept a very close watch on us and our progress to ensure we came up to their standard. Well, we all made it through the training and then set up the training and operational squadrons.

After we had checked ourselves out as 'no kidding real F-4G instructors' we were ready for the first class of real students. Now remember that here again these 'students' were very experienced F-4 types. We were not equipped or expected to be a normal F-4 RTU. We didn't have the time needed or the inclination to teach these guys how to fly and fight in the basic F-4. They were expected to be experts at that level when they got to George to be trained as Weasels. Our job was to teach our students to fight in the F-4G and the systems and tactics unique to the 'G and the Weasel mission. The syllabus expanded from what we were taught and eventually was divided into three levels. That is, normal operational line aircrew, instructor and fighter weapons instructor.

Obviously not everyone was selected for instructor or fighter weapons instructor training. Each level got more detailed in the academic areas and demanding in the flight programme requirements. For example, I remember one mission where my pilot and I were 'students' and were being 'instructed' by the student/candidate fighter weapons instructor crew. It was a two-ship, low-level, combat tactics mission – probably the most demanding mission we flew. The student/candidate crew was required to catch any mistakes that the student crew (my pilot and I) made during any phase of the mission, ground or airborne. We were capable of many mistakes, believe me. Well, we briefed the mission and flew as lead.

During the low-level tactical manoeuvring portions of the mission we descended lower and lower as the candidate crew got further and further out of position. I'm flying the formation and my pilot is missing the rocks. To make a long story short, we busted the candidate crew for getting out of position and allowing us to descend too low for safety, and not calling us back up or warning us. So you can see, a lot was expected of the crews at all levels of training. These guys re-flew the mission and did fine and completed the course. But they said they got a little better understanding of their job as instructors from the mission: so far and no further. However, I have to say that we did get some of the best pilots and Bears in the Air Force into the Weasel programme and that made the instructors' job somewhat easier.

All instructors were required to be qualified in all flying phases of the syllabus. However, we usually concentrated more on a couple of areas. As I remember, I concentrated on the tactics and weapons areas in both the flying and academic areas. Later on, I was commander of the Training Development Team (TDT) and didn't teach academics, only the flying phases. The TDT was responsible for the development and constant upgrading of the syllabus as the systems changed. This was easier for us as we had the test people and engineers at George and had easy access to them. Most of the time the syllabus was upgraded and ready for use before the systems were upgraded.

It's funny, I remember telling my students as they moved from the basic equipment and weapons phases to the more advanced combat oriented portions of the syllabus: 'We have just spent a lot of time learning all of the different switches and functions. Now I am going to try to help you find the best way to employ the fewest switches in the fastest manner to get the most out of the aircraft systems both offensively and defensively while pulling 6g, being shot at and trying to tell the other guy in the airplane what the hell you did, are doing and will do in ten words or less. We are going to talk about crew coordination in a Weasel combat environment. If you haven't got crew coordination don't get in the bird.'

I really think that was probably the hardest thing about the Weasel mission. There was so much going on and both guys had to know what the other guy was doing, and you had to trust the other guy completely. If crew coordination broke down, you were a statistic waiting to be counted.

Take, for example, a communications-out, low-level ingress with a four-ship. The Weasels could really get 'down in the weeds' in formation if they had to, because the Bear flew the formation and the pilot flew the plane and missed the rocks. What the hell does that mean? First, you were com-out – no radio chatter. All turns were signalled with wing flashes [rocking wings within visual sight] and changes in heading. The backseaters watched (flew) the formation by telling the pilot when to turn, how far to turn, when to roll out and what to do to get back into position if out. The pilot concentrated on the rocks ahead and missed them. The pilot would peek at the formation if he could and the Bear would peek ahead at the rocks if he could, but mostly it was as I have described. However, at the same time you were both monitoring your onboard systems, checking your radar and most importantly, checking six. You didn't stop doing all the other things you had to do to fight the F-4. You added the Weasel stuff *on to everything else*!

I remember briefing students or pilots I had never flown with: 'You fly the plane and miss the rocks. I'll fly the formation and keep us in position. If I mess up and we get out of position, I'll fix it. If you mess up and hit the rocks, you can't fix it and I'm gonna be really pissed – and you don't want me pissed.' But God was it a *kick*! I could probably go on for hours about the training. It was the absolute best that student crews got anywhere in the Air Force. It was the most, minimum 110 per cent, we could give the students. On average, the instructors spent about 12hr a day in the squadron preparing briefings and mission scenarios, dry-running academic presentations to other instructors and flying with the students. Nobody wanted to go *anywhere* without Weasels in support.

Much emphasis was placed on learning to survive while neutralizing enemy defences, as had been highlighted by the post-Vietnam Harvest

Corona analysis: what came out of Vietnam was the clear message that Iron Hand was a rather self-absorbed method of dealing with enemy defences. Radar dishes could be repaired or replaced. But Weaseling was sound doctrine. If by just flying in the enemy's locale the enemy shut up shop, then that was just as good provided the strike force went in, hit the target and came out all in one piece – something akin to what the US Navy had been doing for many years, but at enormous cost in men and *matériel*.

The US Air Force's Vietnam-era trolling tactic thus became much more sophisticated, taking advantage of the ranging techniques available to the F-4G. Experienced Bears taught junior EWOs how and just when to break off, and when to reinitiate attack. It might be mock, but the flying was real. Takhli's old pilots and Bears, many of whom did early tours on the F-4G, had an edge in that respect: they had developed terrain-masking attack techniques (all the rage after Vietnam) to avoid the new omnipresent Soviet SAM threats in East Germany and the other prospective war scenario, North Korea. This used new tactics such as porpoising, with aircraft alternatively popping up in ranging arcs for a look and cut while the other stayed under cover; and using different headings, and frequent changes of them, to confuse the radar operators.

Such tactics were only possible with the AN/APR-38, which effectively uncanned the whole Weasel concept, combined with a veritable panoply of weaponry: Shrike, Standard ARM, Maverick and CBUs. Rockets were no longer employed. If there were a million switch options, there also seemed to be a million ways of keeping radar operators subdued.

Concurrent with the formation of the three F-4G squadrons within the 35th TFW at George AFB – the 561st, 562nd TFTS (ex-39th TFTS) and 563rd TFS – whose ownership passed to the 37th TFW on 31 March 1981, two overseas units were equipped with one F-4G squadron each. USAFE's 81st TFS at Spangdahlem AB received its first F-4G (69-0273) on 28 March 1979, flown in by squadron commander Lt Col 'Duke' Green and EWO Capt Mike Freeman. The squadron reached its complement of twenty-four F-4Gs when their last new arrival flew in on 3 November the following year. Linebacker II Weasel veteran Lt Col Bill McLeod remembers arriving at Spangdahlem AB in May 1981:

The 562nd TFS were the last active duty unit to fly the F-105G Thunderchief, and bowed out finally during an official ceremony at George AFB in July 1980. During their final months they wore these large sharks' mouths. (Frank B. Mormillo)

Spangdahlem's 81st TFS 'Panthers' received their first F-4Gs in the spring of 1979. This aircraft was photographed taxiing back to its TAB-V shelter, still dragging its tail 'chute. These were normally dropped after the aircraft came to a stop, and were collected by the base's 'cotton pickers'. (Lindsay T. Peacock)

Our primary mission was to train for the annual NATO Tac-Eval [Tactical Evaluation] and for the USAFE ORI [Operational Readiness Inspection] that occurred every other year. The squadron spent one month each half year using the gunnery range at Zaragoza AB in Spain. We also deployed to RAF Alconbury for a month in 1982 to use the RAF electronic warfare range [at Spadeadam] and to Karup AB in 1981 and 1982 to fly in the annual exercise hosted by the Royal Danish Air Force. (If the 81st deployed to those bases in '83 and '84 I didn't go with them.) While at Spangdahlem we primarily flew low-level training missions, practised with the AGM-65 and played with the Belgian and German HAWK batteries in the 2nd Allied Tactical Air Force area. When the weather was bad we would occasionally fly a high-altitude sortie along the inter-German border and look at the East German SAM radars on our Weasel gear. We also participated in several Luftwaffe exercises and sent several crews to the Tactical Leadership Program.

It was great flying and a great assignment, except that we lost two aircraft and four crewmembers during the three years I was there. Both EWOs that were killed had been crewed with me at one time during their careers, so it was a hell of a loss. One of the crashes also took the life of the squadron commander, Lt Col Jerry Lynn.[15]

While at Spangdahlem I flew one memorable mission on the Spadeadam Range. The range did not have a minimum altitude except over the buildings in the admin complex. On the day in question I led a flight in at very low level, popped up to 500ft at the last minute to pass over the buildings, then immediately pushed over to get back into the weeds. An RAF unit was having a parade in the field beyond the buildings and I gave them a real buzz job. The RAF station commander wasn't impressed and summarily kicked me off the range. A couple of years later an RAF wing commander told me that my flight had really put on a good show!

Maj Jerry Stiles, who had flown F-4C WW-IVs against the Spadeadam electronic warfare complex, explained that despite its varied signals, 'it was disadvantageous in that each and every one of those emitted from the same small piece of real estate, much unlike the real world. After about your second or third time on the range, you knew exactly where the radars were and the challenge of finding the target diminished rapidly. In the real world, one would hardly expect the foe to concentrate his radar systems at one spot and then put a big white radome on them!' Crews later had access to the new NATO Polygone Range on the German border, which featured MUTES (Multiple Threat Emitter Stimulator) and other more realistic threat simulators. It became operational during the mid-1980s and offered Serene Bite electronic combat evaluation and training, previously only available at Nellis AFB and Eglin AFB.

Last to form and new to the F-4G mission was PACAF's 90th TFS 'Pair o' Dice', based at Clark AB in the Philippines, which began to equip with twelve F-4Gs after the squadron's first two aircraft (69-0275 and 69-0279) arrived from Ogden ALC in August 1979. The F-4Gs flew alongside the squadron's vanilla F-4Es as a mixed hunter/killer squadron. The last F-4G delivery from Ogden ALC in the first series (69-7268) was accepted in the summer of 1981, after which time Air Force Logistics Command began refurbishing earlier examples; each and every F-4G was recycled through depot-level maintenance every fifty-four months.

By this time the Vietnam camouflage scheme had changed to a lower-visibility wraparound version, which extended the upper tan and two-tone greens to the underside, more in keeping with the aircraft's low-level role. Beginning in 1983, the tan was replaced by Gunship Gray to produce the so-called European One finish, lending the aircraft a very sinister appearance. The new paint jobs were not merely cosmetic. Ridding the aircraft of high-visibility white tail codes, numbers and copious maintenance stencil instructions was helping to lower their infrared as well as their visual signature by measurable amounts.

In December 1983 the 52nd TFW underwent a restructuring akin to the 90th TFS set-up: the F-4Gs were redistributed throughout the 52nd TFW's component squadrons, flying in three parallel F-4E/G hunter/killer units: the 23rd TFS 'Fighting Hawks', 81st TFS 'Panthers' and 480th TFS 'Warhawks'. This effectively trebled Wild Weasel assets in Europe.

It was PACAF's 90th TFS which came the closest to first firing ARMs in anger from the F-4G. On 26 August 1981 an SR-71A operating from Kadena AB over the North Korean periphery came under attack from a

newly established SA-2 site at Choc Ta Rie. It missed the SR-71A by 2 miles and for defensive purposes a further four sorties were conducted with support from the 90th TFS, which flew near the DMZ carrying ARMs. The North Koreans did not rise to the bait and instead ceased hostile activity.

GREEN FLAG

Supplementing the EF-111A Raven and F-4G Advanced Wild Weasel from the mid-1980s was the newly developed EC-130H Compass Call communications snooper and jammer – a mission known as buzzing. The project began in 1977 as Compass Widget when the Big Safari office at Wright-Patterson AFB contacted Lockheed and Sanders and asked them to develop a Command, Control and Communications Countermeasures (C3/CM)-disrupting aircraft. Using powerful onboard exciters and amplifiers, this would principally use bursts of heavy noise-jamming to clog up communications airwaves, but could also undertake communications snooping and nuisance jamming (such as playing heavy metal music to taunt enemy radio operators). Distinguished by their new Raven-style ghost grey paintwork and conspicuous 'soccer net' YAGI-type antennae under the wings and atop the rear fuselage, two prototypes were flying by 1980, by which time it had evolved into an integrated system code-named Rivet Fire, using new state-of-the-art computers.

Programme authorization for the conversion of sixteen airframes followed swiftly and the project was renamed once again, this time as Compass Call. Most of the initial deliveries from E-Systems at Greenville, Texas went to the 41st ECS 'Scorpions', 355th TFW, at Davis-Monthan AFB, which provided training alongside its operational cadre, and subsequently five aircraft to the 43rd ECS 'Bats', 66th ECW, at Sembach AB, West Germany.[16] On 1 July 1985 the 42nd ECS 'NATO Ravens' EF-111As at RAF Upper Heyford became part of the 66th ECW so that USAFE could develop a 'unified strategy to coordinate electronic combat assets'. Along with the F-4G-equipped 52nd TFW at Spangdahlem AB, it placed all USAFE electronic combat assets under 17th AF control. This allowed them to exercise as a cohesive force more easily within the NATO framework, and the electronic ensemble first worked together on Exercise Distant Hammer '85, held in Italy and sponsored by 5th ATAF. It turned out to be good preparation.

More sweeping measures had already been instigated by Eglin AFB's TAWC commander Gen Tom Swalm, who in 1982 began the regular all-airborne electronic combat exercise Green Flag. This was run as an adjunct to the already successful Red Flag war-games at Nellis AFB, which had pitched fighter pilots and support aircraft in realistic war-games on a regular basis since 1976, helping them to hone their combat flying and survival skills. The new Green Flag initiative combined three combat support tasks: electronic warfare, C3/CM and Suppression of Enemy Air Defences (SEAD), the latter a term in use in NATO since 1977 and which subsequently became synonymous with Vietnam-era Iron Hand and Weaseling.

US Navy/Marine Corps EA-6Bs operated alongside F-4Gs, EF-111As and EC-130Hs in a frenzied electronic battle lasting six weeks. Flying as the Blue force, they encountered a Soviet-styled Red force IADS run by the 554th Range Group. Over time the IADS grew to include Raytheon devices capable of jamming communications and IFF gear, a full panoply of real and counterfeit Soviet air defence radars, the MSQ-T13 SA-6 Straight Flush simulator, US Army HAWK and Roland SAMs, and GCI systems vectoring opposing F-5E and F-16 Aggressor interceptors, with Smokey SAM firework launches thrown in for good measure. Jostling into jamming positions, the EC-130Hs dealt with communications and data-links, the EF-111As and EA-6Bs with acquisition and TTR radars, while the F-4Gs worked the SAM sites, backing off and calling up a jamming carpet if they bit off more than they could chew. It was more good preparation.

Real-time 'as it happens' Elint also gained ground. The Litton-Amecon AN/ALQ-125 Tactical Electromagnetic Reconnaissance (TEREC) system, developed from 1971 under Project Pave Onyx and field-trialled by USAFE from 1975 aboard RF-4Cs of the 38th TRS at Zweibrucken AB, was fabricated for retrofit to twenty-three selected RF-4Cs. Most of these aircraft were subsequently deployed to the 38th TRS and to the 15th TRS 'Cotton Pickers', which operated an intelligence-gathering detachment at Osan AB. The force achieved IOC by 1982.

TEREC was a peacetime wonder that never saw combat use, yet was capable of sniffing out ten preplanned radar types during a sortie, allowing the RF-4C backseater both to tape the Elint for post-mission analysis and to transmit, in real time, urgent threat data to ground-based TEREC Remote Terminal (TRT) and Portable Exploitation Processor (T-PEP) wagons, to derive EOB maps. The resultant data could then be used in mission planning by the Weasels. Although highly effective, TEREC was phased out of service only eight years later, when Elint garnered by SAC Boeing RC-135 Rivet Joint RF-spectrum electromagnetic vacuum cleaners became available to theatre mission planners.

HARM DEBUT

Probably the single most important peacetime advance came from the US Navy in the guise of the AGM-88A HARM: a huge leap over both Shrike and STARM. Work began at NWC China Lake as early as 1969, with test-flying beginning in 1975. However, the project had to overcome numerous technical obstacles throughout the next decade before it was ready for service. One of these was called multipath; when working against higher-frequency threats the super-sensitive seeker could not easily distinguish between signals emanating from the prospective target and those reflected from some point on the ground. Changes to the missile's logic cured the problem and it was eventually cleared for production in September 1981, as test shots began to achieve a 75 per cent success rate.

HARM's first operational deployment was aboard the A-7E, which was fitted with the TI AN/AWG-25 HARM control system, comprising the CP-1269/AWG-25 Command Launch Computer (CLC) and the C-10035/

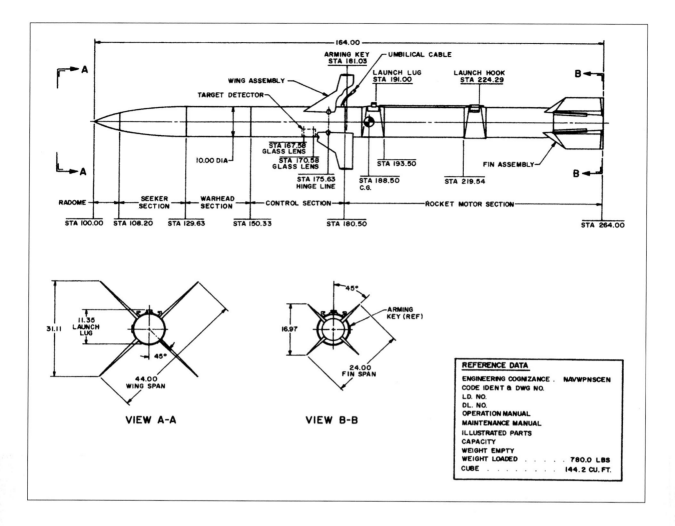

HARM AGM-88 general arrangement. (US Navy)

AWG-25 Control Indicator (CI), which held a regularly updated threat library of known radar threats, each with its own HARM identification number. These were used to programme the HARM ready for firing. The weapon offered several semi-automatic firing modes, with a target steering option presented on the APQ-126 radarscope (very similar to the Vietnam era SIDS grid) and the AN/AVQ-7(V) HUD, when the switches had been set up for a launch.

For strategic strike purposes HARM was volleyed in Pre-Brief (PB) mode on a pre-emptive basis, chasing pre-programmed primary, secondary and even tertiary targets' HARM numbers, based on the mission flight brief. The corresponding threat type and class code numbers (unrelated to the RWR iconography) would be entered via thumbwheels into the CI panel before aircraft take-off. Alternatively, the sensitive missile seeker itself would acquire a threat in the Target of Opportunity (TOO) mode while in flight at medium to long range and highlight it on the RWR, giving the pilot the option to attack with a good chance of a kill if the appropriate CI code was entered into the panel. (This required a little in-flight juggling, but such reversionary codes for possible new threats were briefed before launch wherever possible.)

Finally, the Self-Protect (SP) mode could be chosen for more reactive shooting, based on completely unexpected threats picked up at close quarters by the RWR rather than the missile; and the system could even switch over from TOO to SP automatically using the Pullback feature, when the ECM system detected any such pop-up threats. The pilot pressed the control stick firing trigger to the first detente to acknowledge the pullback, and lined up on the new threat for launch. (Alternatively, he would select Override so that the weapon remained ready for firing in the TOO mode.)

These modes gave significantly greater target discrimination combined with greater shooting flexibility, as well as massive speed and range advantages compared with Shrike. Equally significant, HARM supplemented the AN/ALR-45F's capabilities by acting as sentinel well beyond the range of the unaided RWR. When the A-7E saw action with the missile, it became common practice for pilots to fire all but one of their HARMs, so as to maintain superior warning of enemy radar threats, with that final round available for use if they came under attack during egress from the target area.

The A-7E executed its first live launch with the weapon on 5 October 1981, conducted out of the PMTC against the mock vessel *Savage*. VA-146 was tasked with introducing the weapon to the Fleet during 1983, but the honour of the first successful launch went to Lt Cdr John Parker from VA-83 'Rampagers', while on a HARM training detachment to NWC China Lake, on 24 January 1985.

A-7E SLUFs inaugurated HARM in combat during Operation Attain Document activities in spring 1986. (Frank B. Mormillo)

AGM-88 HARM

INTRODUCTION

The AGM-88 High-speed ARM was developed with the US Navy as project leader in direct response to its experience with Shrike and the Standard ARM in South-East Asia. Shrike was far too limited in capability and resulted in deadly duels between SAMs and shooters, STARM was too expensive and cumbersome, and both missiles proved grossly unreliable. HARM thus had to combine a number of advanced features: supersonic speed (and quickly once off the launch rail), flexible targeting and delivery methods (a 'big footprint'), reliability, a realistic warhead size to knock out radars definitively, and ease of maintenance and use to boot. That was certainly a tall order, and it took eighteen years to mature into a fully capable weapon.

At its inception in 1969 the missile measured some 13ft 8in in a purpose-built airframe weighing 800lb with its guidance and propellant gizzards. It was powered by a Thiokol dual-thrust virtually smoke-free solid-propellant motor, offering a range of up to 80 miles and a speed of up to 760mph. Entering production in 1983 under contract to Texas Instruments, the new AGM-88A HARM achieved IOC with the US Navy in 1985, and with the US Air Force in 1987. Companion Captive Air Training Missile (CATM-88) rounds used for flight training and featuring an inert warhead and motor, along with ballast-filled Dummy Air Training Missile (DATM-88) rounds were made available in advance of AGM-88As as a method of training both air and ground crews on the new weapon, illustrating the well thought-out nature of the entire programme. The relatively peaceful nature of US military operations in the years since Vietnam meant a protracted but no-rush philosophy in its development.

EARLY BLOCKS AND SUBMARKS

AGM-88A. The first operationally deployed live weapon or All-Up Round (AUR) was the **Block I** Alpha, fitted with a WAU-7 146lb blast-fragmentation warhead containing 25,000 pre-formed steel fragments. Its seeker was pre-tuned at depot-level maintenance and thus shipborne or air base armouries held a number of different pre-tuned examples, to counter likely contingencies, much like its predecessors. The Block I was the version used in the Gulf of Sidra in the spring of 1986, when HARM made its combat debut, and thus was used mostly in a pre-emptive mode. The **Block II** version that quickly followed shared the same warhead, but incorporated a vital new Electronically Erasable/Programmable, Read-Only Memory (EEP-ROM) seeker allowing threats to be updated at short notice at the intermediate level or air base shop maintenance.

AGM-88B. This superseded the A-model on the production lines by 1987 and featured the Block II EEP-ROM seeker from the outset, along with some computer hardware differences that permitted it soon to incorporate **Block III** software improvements, allowing for superior PB mode targeting, based on the latest EOB furnished by theatre intelligence. It was also more compatible with in-flight programming, or flexing. The Block III was the Gulf War Desert Storm workhorse, used by all three US Services, though especially by the US Air Force F-4Gs stationed at Sheikh Isa, Bahrain, which provided the lion's share of sophisticated HARM targeting. Unfortunately, changes to Block III software required powering-up the missile to accomplish the update, and because of concerns about providing electrical power to a live weapon below deck the US Navy elected to retain AGM-88B Block II capability from its aircraft carriers during that conflict.

MODUS OPERANDI

Operating modes varied according to the shooter's capabilities. The US Navy built HARM based around three key modes of use: Pre-Brief (PB), Target of Opportunity (TOO) and Self-Protect (SP), with Pull Back from TOO to SP as an option. PB was selected for use on a pre-emptive basis, against pre-planned targets which were made known to HARM prior to launch; TOO against targets picked up by HARM itself and verified as valid prior to launch; and SP, as its name implied, against unexpected, pop-up threats usually identifed by the launch aircraft's ECM equipment.

Crews originally used a HARM radar display akin to the Vietnam SIDS system, based on initial vectors from the AN/ALR-45 or -67 RWRs. The steering 'blob' became a discernible dot on the radarscope in HARM shooting mode, and launch steering cues (providing pull-up and in-range indications) were also furnished on the HUDs, where they were of far more practicable use. However, with HARM pilots could exercise considerably greater freedom: compared to Shrike, HARM's preferred +/– 12-degree launch 'fan angle' almost increased the desirable envelope by an order of magnitude. The best-case launch mode, known as Equations of Motion (EOM) and using 'Range Known' derived from the F-4G's AN/APR-47 system, was employed exclusively by the US Air Force 'Advanced Wild Weasel'.

HARM was first deployed with the A-7E Iron Hand Shrike-shooter (which retained its AGM-45 capability), quickly followed by the new McDonnell Douglas F/A-18 Hornet (which became exclusively HARM), and both employed them in combat for the first time during Operation El Dorado Canyon. Next in line, and unquestionably the most potent US Navy platform because of its later ability to flex between targets, was the EA-6B. Block 82 (and up) EA-6Bs were furnished with HARM capability, the first EA-6B-HARM trials launch being conducted by P-35 (BuNo. 158805) in May 1985, with the first Fleet launch being conducted by VAQ-131 'Lancers' on 5 August 1986. This squadron made the first sea cruise with the missile in the summer of 1987 onboard USS *Ranger*, resulting in the VAQs receiving a change of designation from Electronic Warfare to Electronic Attack.

The A-6 also was qualified to use the weapon on its Systems Weapons Improvement Program (SWIP) A-6Es as these became available to the Fleet. VA-75 was the first to demonstrate this capability on 14 June 1988, when skipper Cdr John T. Meister and B/N Lt Cdr Richard D. Jaskot scored a direct hit on a target ship during exercises.

Lofting was still the preferred method for maximum reach, and was conducted in one of two ways: 'aircraft pull-up', whereby the pilot yanked back on the stick with weapons release following automatically when the in-range and optimum pull-up angle had been achieved; and 'HARM pull-up', which entailed release in level flight once in range and aligned with the target in azimuth, after which time HARM zoomed up in an autonomous loft trajectory towards the target. Weapons carriage was based on the later-generation Shrike LAU-118 launch rail, allowing for up to four HARMs on US Navy jets, though trap weights typically limited carriage to two on the F/A-18 and three on the A-7E. The EA-6B and A-6E SWIP would typically carry only one or two missiles, the other stations being given over to jamming pods or other strike weapons respectively.

HARM arrived just a little too late for US Navy action over Lebanon, when the Mediterranean Fleet was called into action on a one-off Protective Reaction strike. This mission, described by some as a débâcle, effectively ended the daytime Alpha Strike concept in use since Vietnam. The mission was conducted on 4 December 1983 by Rear Admiral Jerry O. Tuttle's Carrier Group Two cruising in the east Mediterranean at Bagel Station. Repeated SAM firings by Syrian and Druse militia against reconnaissance Grumman F-14A Tomcats threatened the aerial peacekeeping role being performed by the Group, so the aircraft carriers USS *John F. Kennedy* and USS *Independence* were authorized to launch a counter-attack against SAM and artillery positions located at Falouga and Hammana, some 10 miles north of the highway linking Beirut and Damascus, and at Jabal al Knaisse and Mghite, 19 miles east of Beirut. A total of sixteen A-6Es led by USS *John F. Kennedy*'s CAG and VA-85 'Black Falcons' boss Cdr J.J. Mazbach, flying alongside VA-176 Thunderbolts and carrying Mk82 Snakeye bombs, were accompanied by twelve A-7Es from USS *Independence*'s CAG Cdr Edward K. Andrews's VA-15 'Valions' and VA-87 'Golden Warriors', employing Rockeye CBUs.

The launch-cycle began at 0545hr, with the Alpha Strike package arriving over their targets just after daybreak at around 0800hr at 20,000ft. Although the strikes were in themselves successful, two aircraft succumbed to enemy IR-guided SAMs. First down were Lt Mark A. Lange and his B/N Robert A. Goodman (in A-6E BuNo. 152915/AC-556), struck by an SA-7

while rolling in on an SA-9 SAM battery at Hammana. Only Goodman survived, and was captured. In a bid to provide SAR cover, Cdr Andrews (in A-7E BuNo. 160738/AE-300) repeatedly struck Syrian Druse gun positions until his aircraft was hit in the tail by another missile. He ejected and was picked up by an SH-3H Sea King SAR party, his aircraft continuing to fly on until it crashed into a villa in the town of Zuk Mkayel.

The losses prompted a rapid rethink of US Navy tactics. No longer would aircraft fly into potentially hostile airspace in broad daylight at medium altitude without SEAD support and the new HARM. What was especially ironic about the Lebanon operation was that night-time vision was already available to the aircrews, allowing them to use the cloak of darkness and more discreet ingress tactics. A-6Es had been fitted with the Hughes heads down AN/AAS-33 Target Recognition and Attack Multisensor (TRAM) turret (a mere nose pimple compared to the huge Vietnam-era TRIM pallet), which presented a FLIR image to the B/N and revised terrain cues on the pilot's VDI. TRAM could be slaved to the radar or vice versa for precision targeting, and a laser was employed for delivery of Paveway LGBs or to compute target slant-range for accurate dumb bomb release.

The single-seat A-7E was fitted with a FLIR sensor mounted in an underwing AN/AAR-49 pod, which projected its eerie green view of the outside world directly on to the pilot's modified IP-946B/AVQ-7 HUD combining glass. It turned night into day, as did TRAM, and so both Fleet strikers could conduct moderately safe low-level target ingress and accurate weapons delivery in the blackest of nights.[17]

A NEW BUZZ IN THE FLEET

In February 1981 the US Navy began introducing the McDonnell Douglas F/A-18A Hornet into Fleet service. Within no time they had a new

F/A-18A Hornets from VA-25 'Fist of the Fleet' and VFA-113 'Stingers' were assigned to CVW-14 aboard USS Constellation *for the Hornet's debut cruise, touring the Western Pacific and Indian Ocean between February and August 1985. (McDonnell Douglas)*

'winner' which, despite weight growth for naval use, still offered a thrust-to-weight ratio in excess of unity, permitting acceleration in a climb; but it was destined to be short-legged, with only a 400nm combat radius because of fuel consumption, and thus was very dependent on AAR tanking requirements. Additional A-6 airframes were subsequently converted for dedicated KA-6D tanking duties, to make room for the new striker and to ensure its thirsty F404-GE-400 engines were slaked. No fewer than 410 F/A-18A/Bs were built through 1987, before production switched to the improved F/A-18C/D model, with improved avionics and F404 enhanced performance engines offering greater performance and somewhat reduced fuel consumption.

The first Hornet squadron to form was VFA-125 'Rough Riders' at NAS Lemoore, which provided training for both the first cadres of Navy and Marine Corps pilots concurrent with Navy Bureau of Inspection and Survey duties, using pilot-production examples of the F/A-18A/B.[18] The first Atlantic Fleet Readiness Squadron, VFA-106 'Gladiators', began forming at NAS Cecil Field, Florida, during April 1984, and in February the following year West Coast squadrons VFA-25 'Fist of the Fleet' and VFA-113 'Stingers' made the type's first extended seagoing cruise with CVW-14 onboard USS *Constellation* in the Indian Ocean.

HARM capability was featured as standard on the F/A-18 (Shrike never was an option), and based around the CP-1001/AWG CLC. This offered the same modes as in the A-7E, but in conjunction with its cleaner Digital Display Indicator multifuction displays and a comprehensive set of instructions on its AN/AVQ-28 HUD. Like the US Air Force's contemporary all-digital 'teenager' fighters, it also offered Hands-On-Throttle-And-Stick (HOTAS) weapons selection and cueing in a heads-up environment, making shooting much easier. The AN/ALR-67(V) was interfaced with HARM via the countermeasures computer, which showed a priority target on the RWR and on the HUD, surrounded by a square symbol.

The left throttle-grip button allowed sequencing of prospective targets in TOO and SP modes, and handing-off of the target to the HARM using a button on the right throttle (both in the pilot's left hand). The pilot would then line up for attack and once within range press the firing trigger on the control column to initiate the HARM launch sequence. For PB, Aircraft Pull-up or HARM Pull-up delivery methods were available, using commensurate azimuth steering line and pitch cues furnished on the HUD, along with an in-range indicator, target designator symbol and command heading diamond, release cue and distance to target.

Launch sequence was activated when the pilot pressed the weapons button on the control stick again, and weapons firing ensued *automatically* when the system adjudged that optimum firing parameters had been met. It made light work of an otherwise complicated job. This was all the more essential because of the inexorable switch to night-time strike tactics, which made visual sighting of enemy SAMs extremely difficult. As with the A-7E, the trade-off was massively increased ARM firing range (thus avoiding deadly duels) while also allowing pilots to better dodge triple-A fire and spot SAM launches, which were more obvious at night.

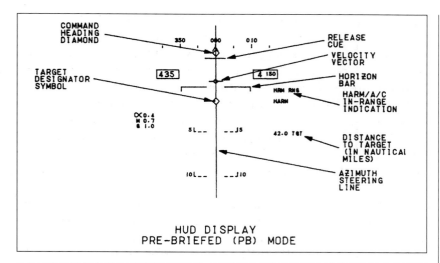

HUD DISPLAY
PRE-BRIEFED (PB) MODE

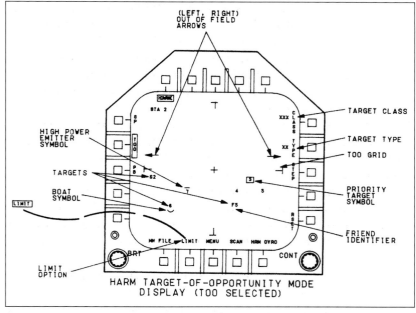

HARM TARGET-OF-OPPORTUNITY MODE
DISPLAY (TOO SELECTED)

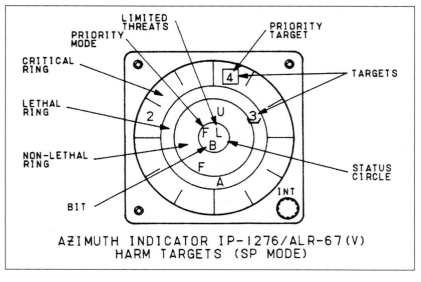

AZIMUTH INDICATOR IP-1276/ALR-67(V)
HARM TARGETS (SP MODE)

F/A-18 Hornet heads-up, multifunction and RWR displays are all active during HARM operations, but for representative purposes the symbology associated with Pre-Brief (PB) mode is shown on the HUD; Target of Opportunity (TOO) mode on the MFD; and Self-Protect (SP) mode on the AN/ALR-67 RWR. These displays relate to operational software used between around 1986 and 1991. (US Navy)

VFA-22 'Fighting Redcocks' was the first West Coast F/A-18 squadron to demonstrate HARM properly. During exercises in 1985 the unit achieved a direct hit against a simulated target using an AGM-88 built up (from its storage crates) in a ship's magazine. The timing was extremely fortunate.

PRAIRIE FIRE AND EL DORADO CANYON

In the spring of 1986 President Ronald Reagan authorized Carrier Task Force 60 in the Mediterranean to undertake Operation Attain Document, the third phase of reclaiming international waters cut off by Libyan leader Col Muammar al-Qadaffi, who had declared a 'line of death' across the Gulf of Sidra out to Parallel 32.5 some years previously. Qadaffi held particularly pernicious anti-American sentiments and the West had grown tired of his threats, his support of international terrorism and acts of atrocity via his henchmen. The killing of an unarmed policewoman in St James's Square, London, during an otherwise peaceful protest and the supply of Czech plastic explosives to the IRA focused the United Kingdom's resolve, and this was capped, from the United States' stand-point, by the savage killing of an elderly disabled American tourist on the cruise ship *Achille Lauro* and by a hand-grenade attack at Rome Airport, which stretched tolerance beyond breaking-point. These actions led to gradually escalating payback by the US Sixth Fleet.

However, Libya's air defences were considerable. In addition to ZSU-23/4s and Swedish 40mm L/70 cannon for local point defence along the coast, there existed three regional defence sectors – Tripoli, Benghazi and Tobruk – each with headquarters, French Crotale SAM units, two SA-2, two or three SA-3 and two to four SA-6/8 SAM brigades, plus several radar companies. A further threat to US Navy aircraft came from the three

The SA-5 Gammon was a strategic SAM, much like the SA-2 but further-reaching. American tactical jets first confronted it at Sirte, Libya, in 1986. (Barry Miller)

new brigades of S-200 Angara (NATO code-name SA-5 Gammon) SAMs, with a key site located at Sirte. This long-range, high-altitude strategic weapon with a reach of up to 135 miles or 100,000ft had begun supplementing the SA-2 and SA-3 in domestic Soviet ZA-PVO service from around 1964 when it was initially code-named Griffon. The weapon was huge, measuring some 54ft long, and each was ferried individually on an articulated ZIL trailer pulled by a transporter, which fed the fixed launchers at the assigned site.

Guidance was slightly different from the rest of the Soviet strategic SAM panoply. After the SA-5 battery had received standard EW reports from Big Back and Side Net surveillance and height-finder radars in the customary manner, the operators relied on the SAM battalion's Square Pair radar to bring the missile to bear in the correct block of airspace and compute an intercept trajectory. Command-guided on launch, it accelerated to Mach 3.5 and then switched over to onboard *active* radar for terminal guidance once it had dumped its boosters and was nearing the target, to deliver a 132lb HE warhead.[19] The SA-5 was the principal adversary of SAC's SR-71A and U-2R reconnaissance fleet flying along the Soviet and North Korean periphery, and its key siting at Sirte was clearly intended to enforce Qadaffi's so-called 'line of death' and 'sea of blood'.

Mediterranean Task Force 60 numbered three aircraft carriers: USS *Coral Sea*, USS *Saratoga* and, just reporting on station, USS *America*. On the afternoon of 24 March 1986 USS *Saratoga*'s CVW-17 was exercising freedom of navigation rights in the Gulf of Sidra in support of the Aegis-class cruiser USS *Ticonderoga*. At 1452hr Z, Libyan radar locked up two F-14A Tomcats from VF-102 'Diamondbacks' which had just repelled a brace of marauding Libyan MiG-25s, and within moments two SA-5s were salvoed in their direction. The F-14A pilots dived for the surface in sharp evasive manoeuvres as briefed, breaking lock with the SAMs which splashed harmlessly into the sea. Admiral Frank B. Kelso II, Commander Sixth Fleet, onboard his flagship USS *Coronado*, authorized Battle Force Zulu to make immediate preparations to execute Operation Prairie Fire. This was effectively initiated by another pair of F-14As, which flew provocatively at the Sirte shore radar, drawing two SA-5 firings, then an SA-2, then a third SA-5, all thwarted by jamming from EA-6Bs, the earlier firings having given away the jamming frequencies the EA-6B ECMOs needed.

The Libyans responded as predicted, launching several combat vessels in a backlash reply to the ineffectiveness of their top-league MiG-25 interceptors and SA-5s that day. At just after 2100hr Z, an E-2C sighted the first Libyan Navy vessel heading for Mediterranean Task Force 60, the 260-ton French-built La Combattante IIG-class ship *Waheed*, equipped with Italian-built Ottomat ASMs.

Four A-6Es of VA-34 were launched from USS *America* to attack the *Waheed*, mortally wounding it with direct hits from the Fleet's new AGM-84 Harpoon ASM (marking its combat debut), plus Mk20 Rockeye CBUs which between them reduced the vessel to a shattered burning hulk. The same night several A-6Es from USS *Saratoga*'s VA-85 attacked and seriously damaged a 780-ton Nanuchka II-class corvette with Rockeyes, sinking another, the *Ean Mara*, the following day with Harpoon at a range

An A-6E Intruder brandishes a SEAD load of two AGM-88 HARM missiles and ten Mk82 500lb iron bombs. (Northrop-Grumman)

of 9 miles after A-6Es from VA-55 had stopped it dead in the water with two Rockeye hits.

The nuisance SA-5 site at Sirte did not escape unscathed either. It had become active again just before 2200hr Z, locking on to US Navy jets. Finally cleared to attack the site, four A-7Es of VA-83 launched from USS *Saratoga* and closed in for the kill. The first pair, led by Cdr Brodsky, came in at high altitude to divert the Libyans' attention before breaking off, while a second pair bored in below 500ft and launched two AGM-88A HARMs when the site became active – HARM's first ever combat use. One HARM missed, but the other successfully demolished a radar antenna, putting the SA-5 site out of action for some four hours. Early the next morning, when the Sirte radar again became active, more HARMs were fired at it by A-7Es from USS *Saratoga*, putting the site out of action for the remainder of the operation.

The A-7Es suffered no damage, despite drawing several SAM launches, mostly SA-2s, from both Sirte and Benghazi. Throughout the entire operation US air power suffered no casualties during 1,546 sorties, 375 of them south of the 'line of death', where Mediterranean Task Force 60 operated with impunity for over three days. Moreover, the action had introduced the F/A-18A and HARM to combat.[20]

Round Two code-named Operation El Dorado Canyon, was executed in response to the West Berlin *La Belle* disco terrorist bombing on 5 April 1986, which killed a US serviceman. There was evidence of Libyan complicity in the terrorist action and the Reagan administration decided, as laid down under Article 51 of the Charter of the United Nations, to exercise its inherent right of self-defence, and hit key terrorist resources in the Tripoli and Benghazi defence sectors. Daytime unsupported aerial attack, based on experience over Lebanon three years earlier, was ruled out in favour of the employment of night sensors to aid with bomb delivery, using low-level ingress followed by a pop-up attack over target.

In the early morning hours of 15 April six A-6Es from USS *America*'s VA-34 hit Benghazi's Al Jumahiriya barracks with Mk82 Snakeyes while eight A-6Es from USS *Coral Sea*'s VA-55 bombed Benina airfield, using a mix of Mk82SEs (Snakeyes) and Mk20 Rockeye-based APAM (Anti-Personnel, Anti-Munition) cluster bombs. TRAM was used to assist with navigation and target line-up, and the bombs struck their targets with aplomb. Pave Tack F-111Fs from USAFE's 48th TFW were also involved in the strike, tasked to attack Tripoli airport, the Al-Aziziyah barracks and Qadaffi's 'tent', plus the Murat Sidi Bilal terrorist training facility. The F-111Fs met with mixed success owing to down systems as a result of their inordinately long transit from Suffolk, England (which required four AAR plugs on the way out, and two on the home legs), forcing several aircraft to abort.

F-111F callsign Karma 51 dropped its bombs 1½ miles from the intended aimpoint in the Bin Ghashir neighbourhood of Tripoli, damaging the French Embassy and several other embassy buildings (though some of this 'collateral' damage came from SAM boosters). Another F-111F, callsign Karma 52, was the sixth in trail over Tripoli, and was hit by triple-A or MANPADS. Capt Fernando Ribas-Dominicci and his WSO Capt Paul Lorence flew out to sea before ejecting, but sadly their escape capsule apparently hit the water before its parachutes had deployed properly. Overall, the US Air Force contingent claimed six Ilyushin Il-76 Candid transports damaged or destroyed (plus secondary explosions) and damage to the barracks, along with the destruction of administration buildings and small training vessels at the terrorist school.

SEAD support was highly effective and shut down the Libyan radar networks at both Benghazi and Tripoli. It was furnished by a mixed 'non-lethal' contingent of 42nd ECS EF-111A Ravens, using several stand-off orbit points, and ICAP-I EA-6Bs from Battle Force Zulu's VAQ-135 'Black Ravens' and VMAQ-2 'Playboys' Det Y. The shooting element, comprising six F/A-18As from USS *Coral Sea*'s VFA-132 'Privateers' and VMFA-323 'Death Rattlers', plus six A-7Es from USS *America*'s VA-46 'Clansmen' and VA-72 'Blue Hawks', relied on pre-emptive launch tactics and shot off twelve Shrikes and thirty-six Pre-Briefed HARMs against the SA-2, SA-3, SA-6, SA-8 and Crotale missile/radar systems. Any SAM firings from the surviving launchers were reported as being unguided, while the notorious SA-5 battery at Sirte, hit twice in March, only came up as the attack waves egressed, and fired no missiles. The US Navy had regained its spurs with night-time targeting devices and HARM.

Redundant Shrike rocket motors were fitted to GBU-16/B 1,000 Paveways to create the AGM-123A Skipper II laser-guided missile, shown here being fired from an A-6E Intruder. The weapon was first successfully used by VA-95 'Green Lizards' in April 1988 during Operation Praying Mantis on a protective reaction strike against Iranian Navy gunboats posing a threat in the Straits of Hormuz. (Emerson Electric)

F-4G PUP

The US Air Force's F-4G, although probably the most capable HARM-shooter ever devised, was virtually the last to receive the new ARM, which replaced the Standard ARM under Phase One of its Performance Update Program (PUP), given the go-ahead on 15 October 1982, with IOC achieved at George AFB by the spring of 1987.[21] This modification resulted in the AN/APR-38, the heart of the F-4G, receiving the new designation AN/APR-47 RAWS (under TO 1F-4G-529).

Tested in earnest by TAWC Det 5 at George AFB from March 1985, PUP essentially added a new Sperry CP-1674 Weasel Attack Signal Processor (WASP) and increased computer memory to 250K to increase threat signal processing rates five-fold. The concurrent Lear-Siegler AN/ARN-101 Digital Modular Avionics System (DMAS, nicknamed the Arnie Mod and installed under TO 1F-4G-504) replaced aged F-4 analogue systems such as the Litton LN-12 with a new digital INS and new ballistics computer, uncanning all its attack modes, introducing CCIP attack capability and providing significantly better interoperability with the new generation of smart bombs.

Unrelated to these upgrades, the F-4E/G fleet was provided with smokeless J79-GE-17F engine modifications, making them less visible to triple-A gunners and enemy fighters.

Alongside these enhancements, the F-4G force was bolstered by eighteen fresh conversions from FY 1969 F-4E stock at Ogden ALC, while the whole Weasel establishment underwent something of a shake-up.[22] Apart from the new paint job of semi-gloss medium-altitude Hill Gray II monochrome hues, beginning in July 1987 the 52nd TFW's companion hybrid analogue-digital Arnie Mod F-4Es were redistributed among the 37th TFW's three Weasel squadrons for training and hipshot Shrike and Maverick missile hunter/killer work; while the 52nd TFW in turn replaced them with new Block 30 F-16C/Ds for companion slapshot hunter/killer taskings, able to employ the more capable HARM missile. Former EWO Capt Mike Pietrucha explains:

> The F-4E could carry Shrikes, and would be put into position and directed to fire by the F-4G, called a hipshot. The F-16C, with the Aircraft/Launcher Interface Computer [ALIC], could carry and shoot HARMs using directions from the F-4G, called a slapshot. The ALIC was originally designed to allow the F-4E to carry the HARM, and it was intended to be used with a data-link, so that the F-4G could hand off precise radar parameters. The data-link never made it into service in the F-4E, and by the time the ALIC was ready, most of the F-4Es were gone.

Slapshot HARM firing mode entailed the F-16 pilot using PB HARMs against a known threat at a known location, furnished over radio by the F-4G hunter which guided it into optimum firing position. In-flight flexing of targets (adjusting the priority threat assigned to HARM on a reactive basis) was available only to the F-4G, which could employ HARM in the EOM Range Known mode for a maximum kill probability. Flying abreast

of the targets in an arcing ascent or descent manoeuvre, the RAWS could derive a precise cut for HARM-shooting, including off-axis launch. The upgraded RAWS antenna were over ten times more sensitive than any fighter-deployed RWR at the time, as Mike Pietrucha explains:

> The AN/APR-47 system could display up to thirty radars at once on the PPI [Plan Position Indicator] in the rear cockpit, and once a threat was detected, the AN/APR-47 would download all the necessary data on the primary target (threat type, frequency, PRF, pulse repetition interval or PRI, location, etc.) to the HARM. In addition to the primary target data, the AN/APR-47 would also download data on additional threats in the vicinity of the primary radar. Once the missile was fired, if the threat radar stopped radiating or was destroyed by another HARM, the missile would flex to another radar target.

Weasels would very often work their way in behind a radar target, for greater surprise. Down the throat Maverick and Shrike capability was retained, but these missiles quickly fell out of favour as preferred weapons because of their limited range, while HARM proved so good that the cumbersome Standard ARM was declared obsolete, and training with the missile finally ended during 1987. As a consequence, surplus Standard ARMs were made available for export to Israel and South Korea, which were able to employ them on Block 60 (and up) models of the F-4E, using a special hybrid analogue-digital interface tied in with the standard RWRs. Each country received some 300 rounds, Israel's comprising supplementary stocks, making good expenditure of what they called the Purple Fist over the Syrian Beka'a during combat in the early and mid-1980s. Indigenous modifications tailored the seeker to domestic needs.

Three Weasel jets equipped Detachment 5 of TAWC, which was responsible for testing updates to the F-4G's operational flight programs. These aircraft were co-located at George AFB with the main nucleus of the force, rather than at TAWC headquarters in Eglin, Florida. (Frank B. Mormillo)

Incessant shelling and rocketing of northern Israeli settlements by the Palestinian Liberation Organization (PLO), using their enclaves in Lebanon, had claimed the lives of 103 settlers during some 1,548 separate listed indiscriminate attacks between the end of the Yom Kippur War in the autumn of 1973 and the spring of 1982. This was capped by the assassination of the Israeli ambassador to the United Kingdom, Shlomo Argov, by the Abu-Nidal faction of the PLO, which proved to be the final catalyst for Operation Peace for Galilee. Launched on 5 June 1982, its objective was to create and secure an extended buffer zone stretching ambitiously north to the Beirut–Damascus highway, using ground troops and armour, with air force CAS A-4s and AH-1 gunship helicopters in direct support.

By 9 June the ground force was near Syrian lines. If the operation stood any chance of being successfully completed, there was no choice but to engage and neutralize Syrian air defences in the Beka'a, a valley which ran down Lebanon from north to south from Zahla to Mount Hermon along the Syrian border. It was garrisoned by 30,000 Syrian troops, and included nineteen known SAM batteries, comprising a mix of SA-6s (two brigades with six batteries each) providing low-altitude coverage (not counting SA-7/-9 MANPADS), and bunkered SA-2/-3 arrays for medium and high-altitude cover.

Former 'Ha'patishim' Squadron boss Avihu Ben-Nun, who was head of the IDF/AF Attack Branch in October 1973 and who now commanded one of the IDF/AF wings, remained firm in his belief that massed airpower, working in concert, could quickly bring any enemy IADS to its knees – something he saw as a failing in the Yom Kippur War, when too many F-4Es were employed on a piecemeal SEAD basis, and suffered commensurately heavy losses. Chief of the Air Force Gen David Ivri had already authorized combat veterans Aviem Sela and Amir Nahumi to develop an attack plan, and this was in place by the morning of 9 June, using a skilful combination of Elint and photo intelligence, computer-based strike package modelling and a degree of overkill for insurance purposes.

Pre-strike reconnaissance by TV-equipped Mastiff and Scout Elint Unmanned Aerial Vehicles (UAV), which relayed data to ground terminals in real time, showed that the Syrians had foolishly dug in most their SAMs and radars, allowing them to be carefully plotted. The Syrians ignored the UAVs, nudging each other and laughing at the 'toy airplanes'. Phase One of the operation, opening at around 1400hr, slightly later than planned, sent in the UAVs again, but this time including the rather different air-lobbed Samson drone decoys, dropped from high altitude. Each the size of a 500lb bomb, the Samsons glided down into the valley with the sun behind them, their transmitters mimicking individual strike jets, to wake up the Syrian SAMs.

Then all hell broke loose as the Syrians took the bait, launching the bulk of their available SAMs at this onslaught of decoys. They chased them to impact, with others exploding harmlessly out of reach as they approached the end of their flight. Phase Two was concurrent, and initiated the moment a stand-off ESM Boeing 707 orbiting over the Mediterranean confirmed heavy SAM radar activity. It began laying down a noise-jamming smokescreen aimed at blocking Syrian EW and GCI radar, but only at those low frequencies, to mask the ingressing attack force's whereabouts.

By 1414hr the first twelve F-4Es were within targeting reach of the active enemy SAMs and fired their volleys of Purple Fist (domestically fine-tuned AGM-78B/D Standard ARMs) on the heels of the Samsons, resulting in a far higher than usual SAM-kill rate as the radars were remaining active in pursuit of their drone prey. The F-4Es then pressed home closer and launched AGM-65 Mavericks when the SAM batteries were beginning to run dry. Along with the ARMs these were keyed to knock out the acquisition/tracking radars. The next batch of F-4Es then bored in with Griffin LGBs, a domestic derivative of the American Paveway II bomb, 'plinking' more SAM hardware. IAI Kfirs (Lion Cubs) and A-4s swiftly followed them in with strake-finned iron bombs, mopping up the sites.

In less than ten minutes all radars had been silenced, without a single loss to the attackers, and all nineteen SAM units were destroyed before the hour was out. Only three solitary SA-6 vehicles evaded the onslaught, by staying radar silent under camouflage netting during the ensuing hunter operations. As they seemed to be out of the conflict, the search for them was eventually called off.

The lack of enemy GCI coverage, blocked by the jamming, also meant that up to eighty MiGs launched by the Syrian Air Force to intercept the strike package were circling in ridiculous figure-of-eights awaiting instructions that never came, and were pounced upon by waves of the IDF/AF's F-15 Baz (Falcon) and F-16 Netz (Hawk) aircraft which up until now had been lying in wait behind the two mountain chains in Lebanon. Vectored to the MiGs by E-2C AEW as the main strike waves egressed, they shot twenty-eight

MiGs and helicopters out of the sky that day, and some eighty-five had been shot down by the time the Peace for Galilee operation had been completed, for the loss of none of their own.

Follow-on attacks were conducted in July in response to the presence of three new SA-8 SAMs, brought in by the Soviets in an effort to help the Syrians regain possession of the skies, and the F-4Es again smashed them to pieces using Mavericks and LGBs, although at the cost of a post-strike reconnaissance F-4E(S) Oref, felled on 24 July. Its crew ejected but were shot at during their descent, killing navigator Aharon Katz. His pilot was taken prisoner. As the aircraft contained sensitive equipment a strike was launched to destroy its remains, which resulted in the deaths of eleven Soviet engineers busy examining its ECM, sensors and data-link equipment. The Syrian theatre defences in the Beka'a were now all but silent, posing no threat.

With these quick blows the Beka'a operation not only permitted the IDF/AF to exact its revenge, closing the circle by finally stomping on the SAM systems that had caused them so much frustration and heartache only nine years previously, but also provided something of a blueprint for American planners drafting Operation Instant Thunder – the air campaign which would become known as Desert Storm.

An F-4E from Israel's 201 'Ahat' (One) squadron. (Israeli Aircraft Industries)

PACAF's mixed F-4E/G 90th TFS force and companion F-4E-only 3rd TFS 'Peugeots' at Clark AB continued their duties unabated and were re-equipped with PUP F-4Gs; their vanilla F-4Es were replaced by Arnie examples with ALIC HARM capability. Their aircraft, in common with a select number of non-Weasel F-4Es stationed at Seymour-Johnson AFB, were also capable of utilizing the F-111F's AN/AVQ-26 Pave Tack FLIR/laser pod for the autonomous delivery of second- and third-generation laser-guided GBU-10/B-class Paveway munitions; in a separate configuration akin to the 493rd TFS 'Roosters' F-111Fs and other select F-4Es, they could also deploy the GBU-15 electro-optical glide bomb, which used the same TV or imaging infrared seekers as Maverick, but which could be mini-tossed *supersonically* at the target and locked on to it *after* launch, to compensate for the 12-mile stand-off delivery technique.

A centreline-mounted AN/AXQ-14 data-link pod was employed which relayed course corrections and TV images between the bomb and the cockpit, so that the WSO could make targeting adjustments all the way to impact. Thus, unlike with Maverick, the dual-mode TV/radarscope did not go blank when the bomb was released.

Both of these PGMs were based around groups attached to the ubiquitous Mk84 2,000lb hammer (though Mk82-derived 500lb GBU-12/B LGBs also existed), and consideration had been given to marrying a large CBU payload to the GBU-15 for defence suppression taskings under Project Pave Storm, but it never materialized. Rockwell International's GBU-15 cost ten times as much as Texas Instruments' LGB group kit, and that was considered a ridiculously costly way of delivering a cluster bomb to target.[23]

Provisions were also made available for the F-4s to carry the new Raytheon-modified AN/ALQ-184 noise/deception jammer (an updated Westinghouse AN/ALQ-119 pod, featuring a Rotmen lens for increased effective radiated power), though the 52nd TFW continued to use the superior AN/ALQ-131 pod, which offered transponder mode deception-jamming and flightline threat reprogramming. At George AFB, TAWC's Det 5 continued to fine-tune OFPs [Operational Flight Programmes] for the Weasels (which had evolved to OFP 7000 by the late 1980s), and it was in this PUP Phase One format that the force would go to war in the Persian Gulf less than four years later – their first taste of action after over twelve years of intensive peacetime training.

Yet, in a sweeping defence cut instigated by President George Bush's administration, the F-4G very nearly went from cradle to grave without firing a single shot in anger. As part of a realignment effort after the collapse of the Berlin Wall, which signalled the end of the Cold War and the beginnings of the new Peace Dividend, on 30 January 1990 Air Force Chief of Staff Gen Larry Welch announced that all F-4Gs would be retired under the forthcoming budget. PACAF Weasels initiated the wind-down. However, on the other side of the globe, Iraqi leader Saddam Hussein, known to many as the Butcher of Baghdad because of the horrific slaughter of the Iran–Iraq war, unwittingly gave them a major reprieve. They would prove to be his undoing.

S I X

DESERT
STORMERS

O n the morning of 2 August 1990 Iraqi tanks ground their way
through Kuwait City, giving Saddam Hussein what he thought
was a firm grip on his oil-producing neighbour. Advance
indications that something was awry had been noted by US
Sigint satellite sensors, which on 29 July recorded the resumption of Soviet-
built Tall King long-range EW surveillance radar activity near Baghdad,
signifying the first significant military operations since the Iran–Iraq war of
1980–8. The Kuwaiti Air Force was powerless to intercede against such a
mighty foe, and many of its aircraft were flown to Saudia Arabia, from
where they and their pilots could better help prosecute a defensive barrier
against possible Iraqi aggression further south.

International condemnation of Iraq's forced annexation of Kuwait was
swift, and received UN backing. Saudi Arabia, as master of the Arab
world both in wealth and in terms of its hospitality to fellow followers of
Islam, as caretaker of Mecca and other such holy sites, sought justice for
its little neighbour and, concerned about Saddam Hussein's longer-term
objectives, was instrumental in bringing together a Pan-Arab Coalition to
force the Iraqi Army out of Kuwait. Under UN Security Council Resolution 678, force was authorized to expel Iraqi forces unless they voluntarily
withdrew from Kuwait by 15 January 1991. Invitations were extended to
a concerned Western world, which replied with a massive deployment of
air, sea and land forces under Operation Desert Shield, led by the United
States' military might managed by US Central Command (CENTCOM).[1]

Notable dissenters were Libya, traditionally anti-Western; Jordan, which
was another of Iraq's neighbours and concerned about maintaining the
status quo, and successfully maintained a nervous neutrality; and the
Soviet Union – traditional enemy of the West, key supplier of armaments
to its prospective adversaries, and reluctant to stop a gravy train of hard
currency-earning exports. Even France, at the beginning, showed a marked
reluctance to participate in what it saw as a NATO-led operation,
especially as it was sponsored by Saudi Arabia – arch-enemy of some of
France's electronics customers – though the French Air Force had no
reservations about its contribution in the form of Operation Daguet. Italy,
too, by default was enabling the Butcher of Baghdad's scientists to develop
nuclear, chemical and biological weapons.

Israel had recognized this threat a decade previously. On 7 June 1981 the IDF/AF launched Operation Opera, a strike conducted by eight of its new F-16As against the Osirak nuclear power plant near Baghdad. Ironically, it was in response to the complete success of this raid that Iraq, during the eight-year war with Iran, installed a huge, Warsaw Pact-style Soviet IADS as a hedge against such intrusion, with C3 netted by France, which installed the KARI (French for Iraq, in reverse) automated reporting system. The defences in downtown Baghdad alone – some 380 triple-A batteries, twenty-six SA-2/-3s, eight SA-6s, fifteen SA-8s and nine Rolands – were more concentrated than those installed at the Murmansk ship-building and sea port facility in northern Russia, which even SAC SIOP crews treated with some trepidation.

Triple-A pieces were particularly numerous in Iraq, numbering some 7,500 in all, and ranging in calibre from 14.5mm to 100mm, a significant proportion of it radar-directed. KARI itself was headquartered in Baghdad, with the outlying country divided into northern, western, central and southern air defence sectors, the tentacles of the system comprising Sector Operations Centres (SOC) at Kirkuk, H-3 airfield, Taji and Tallil

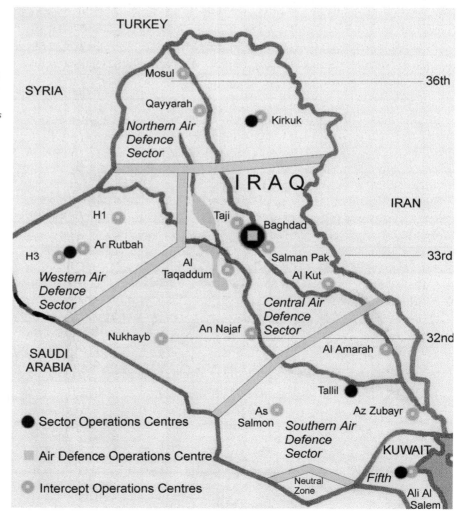

*The Iraqi KARI air defence IADS just prior to Operation Desert Storm. Intercept operations centres were linked to regional sector operations centres, which in turn reported to Baghdad. Kuwait acted as a temporary fifth regional sector prior to the Iraqi's expulsion in February 1991. Iraqi air defences as of January 1991 included 3,679 radar-guided SAMs (not counting 7,380 MANPAD/vehicle-mounted heat-seeking SAMs), 972 triple-A sites with 2,404 guns, and some 6,100 mobile guns linked to this automated reporting system.
(Author)*

TURKEY

SYRIA

Mosul

Qayyarah

Kirkuk

Northern Air
Defence
Sector

I R A Q

IRAN

H1

Taji

Baghdad

Ar Rutbah

Salman Pak

33rd

H3

Al
Taqaddum

Al Kut

Western Air
Defence
Sector

Central Air
Defence
Sector

Nukhayb

An Najaf

32nd

Al Amarah

SAUDI
ARABIA

Tallil

As
Salmon

Az Zubayr

● Sector Operations Centres

Southern Air
Defence
Sector

KUWAIT

Air Defence Operations Centre

Fifth

Intercept Operations Centres

Neutral
Zone

Ali Al
Salem

36th

respectively, with a new SOC under construction at Ali al Salem in Kuwait. Numerous Intercept Operation Centres (IOC), with GCI facilities, co-located or strategically scattered around the country, reported to the SOCs, and in turn to Baghdad.

Just as with Linebacker operations over North Vietnam eighteen years beforehand, SEAD assets were top of the Desert Shield shopping list of air capability. CENTCOM at Riyadh, Saudi Arabia, thus ordered in the big-shooters. The difference was that this campaign, when fought, would be hard-hitting right from the outset – a far cry from the piecemeal gradual-ism of Vietnam. This was reflected in the original choice of code-name, Instant Thunder, devised by a team led by Col John Warden III. Brig Gen David A. Deptula, who was then a Colonel and Warden's deputy at CENTCOM, described the intended strategy as a 'highly integrated plan like the [Israeli] Beka'a operation, but more massive than Linebacker'. It subsequently evolved into Desert Storm.

As Lt Gen Charles 'Chuck' Horner's head of the Central Command, Air Force (CENTAF) Special Planning Group and commander of the 15th AD and its fighter assets, Brig Gen 'Buster' Glosson planned the air campaign in detail, alongside electronic warfare guru Lt Gen Larry 'Poobah' Henry (Ret), a three-tour Vietnam veteran and former George AFB Weasel wing commander, who innovatively shaped the SEAD strategy and got things moving.

BLACK KNIGHTS AND PANTHERS

Col George 'John Boy' Walton II (USAF Ret), then a lieutenant colonel, commanded the 561st TFS equipped with F-4Gs. His squadron was in the

A pair of F-4Gs cruise over the Tonopah Range with wall-to-wall anti-radiation missiles. HARM has been substantially updated, but Shrikes – shown on the nearer machine – had been ousted from the inventory by late 1992. (USAF)

top five for deployment. His recollection of the transit to the Gulf echoes the feelings of other deployed aviators:

Just four days after Iraq had invaded Kuwait, I assumed command of the 'Black Knights' at George AFB. As the squadron had already been alerted, I knew we would be departing town shortly thereafter. We headed east to Seymour-Johnson AFB on 12 August where we waited for our turn in the barrel for the journey across the Atlantic. A single travel pod [MXU-648] was carried between each pair of airplanes and this was filled with the necessary down gear equipment [safety pins, etc.], so we didn't have much space available for personal belongings. The flight suits on our backs and a few changes of underwear was pretty much all we had.

While waiting at Seymour-Johnson AFB, our deployment location changed several times. I was first told we were going to Sharjah, then Dubai (both in the UAE) and then Doha, Qatar. It just kept changing. Finally, on the day of our departure we were told, 'It looks like you're headed to a place called Sheikh Isa' – a place that none of us had ever heard of. We were told that it was on the southern end of the small island-nation of Bahrain, but it wasn't on any map; at least, none that we had. It wasn't until I was crawling into my airplane that I was handed a satellite photo of the base and I'm pretty sure I was the only one to have a copy. The only question I had was 'How long is the runway?' – which was a fairly important question given how heavy we would be when we arrived. The answer was they didn't know! I replied, 'I guess we'll see when we get there!'

Consequently, on 16 August four cells of six airplanes – plus a pair of air spares and chase planes – cranked up not knowing many specifics about where we would be landing. We met up with tankers out of Plattsburgh AFB, New York, with six airplanes on three tankers to start. We'd refuel from the no. 2 and no. 3 tankers until they ran out of transferable gas, after which they turned around and headed back to Plattsburgh AFB and then we'd move on to no. 1 tanker. We were eventually handed off to tankers out of RAF Mildenhall at mid-Ocean. They took us just past the Azores where we met with a third group of tankers. They in turn handed us off once more just south of Sicily. Our final hand-off took place in the Middle East region while cutting across the Red Sea. Each of us hooked up as many as *twenty-one times* during the trip over.

The airplanes were fully armed with weapons when we deployed because there would be none waiting for us on arrival, and we had no clear picture what our immediate needs would be when we got to Bahrain. Half the airplanes carried a travel pod and a HARM while the balance carried a pair of HARMs. In addition, all the airplanes carried three external fuel tanks. There was some concern about transiting the Mediterranean, with Libya already declaring its support of the Baghdad regime, so we also carried a pair of AIM-7s in the aft stations and a single AN/ALQ-184 jamming pod in a forward station. At no time did we have any CAP support – a fact the tanker folks were a little nervous about. Mind you, we didn't see anything on the radar and we were vigilant as we were passing through the 'Med', but it was otherwise a quiet passage.

I can recall it being one of the quickest nights I ever had. As we approached the Straits of Gibraltar the sun was setting behind us. It was pitch-black with no moon for a period of only 4–5hr because we were flying into the rotation of the Earth, which sped up the time we spent in darkness. We could see the lights of Sigonella AB in Sicily, the 'boot' of southern Italy, and even down to northern Africa. As we approached the Nile River Delta, the sun was coming up in our faces.

Having flown 15½hr non-stop, we finally arrived overhead Sheikh Isa AB. It looked absolutely pristine. The reason it wasn't on any map was that construction of the facility had just recently been completed. Upon landing, I noted only a few tyre marks on the runway in front of me. As it turned out, the runway was plenty long enough for our needs. Upon shutting down, we had to put all the down gear on the airplanes ourselves because we were about 24–36hr ahead of the first C-5s that were transporting the balance of the maintenance and support personnel. It was incredibly hot and humid and all of us were exhausted from the long flight, but eventually the aircraft were bedded down.

The US Ambassador to Bahrain, who was accompanied by a US Air Force brigadier general in a flight suit, greeted us. There was also a couple of Bahraini soldiers who helped us by using sandbags to chock our wheels. As it turned out, the brigadier general was Buster Glosson, deputy commander Joint Task Force Middle East, based on the command ship USS *La Salle* in Manama. Not too long after, Brig Gen Glosson was posted to Riyadh and became Lt Gen Chuck Horner's head of the CENTAF Special Planning Group for the air campaign. Brig Gen Glosson had a talent for picking good people to work for him and his staff in Riyadh were all champs. I knew a lot of them and respected them for their abilities as tacticians and flyers. With Lt Gen Horner's leadership as the Air Boss, I knew we were all set for a decent show – and I felt pretty comfortable with it.

We had departed Seymour-Johnson AFB with twenty-four airplanes and we arrived with twenty. Two airplanes fell out *en route* and each took a chase with them to their divert locations. One pair landed in the Azores while the second pair ended up at Sigonella AB. Within three days all twenty-four airplanes were on location. If you look at the other airplanes like the newer F-15s and F-16s, we fared pretty well for an old warhorse of a fighter. The air superiority F-15s had deployed first [7 August] to Dhahran AB in Saudi Arabia followed by F-16s to Al Dhafrah AB in the UAE and F-15Es to Thumrait AB in Oman [both on 10 August]. We were the fourth fighter squadron to deploy, which might have been an indication as to where Lt Gen Horner had fit us into the scheme of importance in the build-up for the air campaign.

The first order of business after our arrival was to get fuel back in the jets. However, there was initially only one refuelling truck available and fuel had to be transported by this one truck to Sheikh Isa AB from Manama on the northern end of the island. The truck would refuel

about one and a half airplanes per trip, so it took quite a while to get the whole fleet filled with JP-4. Logistically, we were really behind the power curve until the rest of the wing support arrived to get the ball rolling. The tents went up to house folks, the maintainers got the airplanes back in business, and it was the 35th TFW vice wing commander, Col Robert 'Tip' Osterthaler [since retired as a brigadier general], who pulled it all together for us. He did an absolutely masterful job and we were up and running very quickly. I was appreciative of all that Col Osterthaler did for us because it allowed me to focus on fighter operations and getting ready for the possibility of war.

I had been a Wild Weasel previously, flying for the 52nd TFW at Spangdahlem AB during the mid-1980s, but in those days our F-4G aircraft were equipped with the AN/APR-38 RAWS. The F-4G had since been upgraded to the AN/APR-47 RAWS, which was a tremendous improvement in capability. As soon as I took command of the 561st TFS, realizing I did not know squat about this new equipment, I exercised my privilege as the squadron boss and designated Capt William 'Bud' Redmond as my Bear. He had a reputation as the sharpest knife in the drawer and I needed some instruction. However, the first opportunity we had to get together for some academics on the system was during the deployment flight to Bahrain. Consequently, during most of that 15hr flight, Bud gave me an academic lesson via the intercom on the AN/APR-47 – back seat to front seat. What I learned was that the system had made a quantum leap in technology, and I also learned that Bud was a tremendous resource both as an instructor and as a leader. From that day, and for the next nine months, Bud stayed with me as my crewed backseater.

As a new squadron commander with a war staring me in the face, I wanted to do all the things I had learned from all of the truly great tacticians and leaders with whom I had served during my twenty years with the US Air Force. In order to build a winning attitude and a capability that would give us the best chance of bringing everybody home, I wanted to create a feeling of camaraderie among the crews so they could learn to trust and rely on each other as never before. I crewed the squadron into four-ship flights, which were to remain together for the duration of our stay in the Middle East. Personalities being what they are, there were occasional hiccups, but eventually everybody settled into these flights. And those flights became inviolate. If I ever attempted to fly someone else in a particular four-ship, I heard about it – 'Don't mess with my four-ship!'

It worked extremely well. Each flight was very close and each individual knew what everyone else in the four-ship was doing, thinking and feeling. Each person had a role in their four-ship and they developed a great pride and identity as a flight, so we pretty much left them alone. I had my own four-ship and treated it just as protectively as all the other four-ship flight leads did. By the time we got into January, the four-ships were pretty much sacrosanct.

On 5 September the first group of 81st TFS crews and airplanes, assigned from the 52nd TFW, joined us. The arrival of the Spangdahlem AB contingent added twelve airplanes, which would expand the ATO [Air Tasking Order] and allow further tasking. As we had already begun planning for the air campaign, the 'Spang' guys quickly established themselves and did a great job folding into the overall plan that was to become the greatest air campaign in the history of aviation. It was tremendous having an extra twelve airplanes onboard, but more importantly they brought their experience and their talent onboard. We capitalized heavily on this.

As we started getting closer to December we began flying longer-duration missions that required more and more air refuellings. Given the distances to our potential targets, we would need this kind of training and would need to be very good at it. A 4hr mission was going to be the norm. Individual capabilities were increasing as we got better and better at the tactics we would need to employ. Initially we did some local training with the limited airspace in and around Bahrain. We expanded into Saudi Arabia, conducting missions that involved a little bit of low-level work, but mostly medium-altitude missions. We also patrolled along the Kuwaiti–Iraq borders to make the bad guys aware we were always watching and eventually we started flying more and more at night, realizing that half the war would be fought after dark.

As time passed, morale became an issue. Were we going to be here through Thanksgiving, or even Christmas? A lot of folks were starting to wonder how long this was going to last. No one knew, but it was clear that this would last somewhat longer than we had envisioned. Finally, during December, President George Bush announced that Saddam had until 16 January to get out of Kuwait. Morale went through the roof as there was finally a definite date that we could hang our hat on. This meant that we now knew when we could get started and knowing that, we knew when we could finish and go home. It was the day after Christmas when the second batch of twelve F-4Gs arrived from Spangdahlem AB, so now we had a total of forty-eight lethal SEAD aircraft. As we rolled into January 1991 it was becoming more and more obvious that this was going to turn into a shooting match.[2]

Training sorties became increasingly exploratory. The key function of Desert Triangle missions, beginning on 29 October 1990, was to unearth the Franco-WarPac air defence system War Modes, as it was known that peacetime training and combat radar frequencies differed. Some border violations ensued – whatever was required to meet requirements – to provoke a response for Elint mapping by back-door RC-135s and other electronic-listening machines. F-4Gs and F-16s did most of the needling, although some stealthy Lockheed F-117A Nighthawks were assigned this task, flying from King Khalid AB in Saudi Arabia with reflectors added to hide their true low-observable characteristics. For example, on 25 September EF-111As, F-4Gs and EC-130Hs were locked in what became known as a voice product network engagement, and on 25 November a combined US Navy package of F-14As, A-6Es, EA-6Bs, E-2Cs and a solitary EA-3B listener garnered similar intelligence to gauge the Iraqi response to a possible carrier strike.

Desert Triangle sorties were carried out on an almost daily basis until 17 December, when Operation Border Look began, committing large numbers of CAP jets and support aircraft to mask the start of an air campaign. Maj Gen Larry Henry explained that 'we had the luxury of planning a pre-emptive strike . . . and we even had the luxury of being able to feint at [Saddam's KARI] several times and watch his reaction'. However, it soon became clear that KARI, unlike the North Vietnamese or Libyan systems confronted previously, was so highly automated that draftees straight from school could operate the IADS warning system effectively, literally by push-button – as long as its lines of communication remained intact. Taking it down would mean hitting all the critical SOCs and IOCs, *as well as* the SAM batteries.

From January 1991 everything became sharply focused, and even Sheikh Isa AB's Weasel Dome (the 35th TFW(P)'s R&R tent) was closed when it became clear that the situation was about to become a real shooting war. Launched on the night of 17/18 January, Operation Desert Storm had two parallel goals: the theatre objective of pushing the Iraqi military out of Kuwait and restoring a legitimate government; and the strategic objective of destroying the Hussein regime's command and control 'centres of gravity' along with his nuclear, biological and chemical weapons facilities. This meant flying into downtown Baghdad and the regional, heavily defended KARI C3 nodes and engaging the solid walls of SAMs and triple-A.

F-4G air and groundcrews enjoyed access to the Weasel Dome during the Desert Shield build-up of forces. (Jim Uken)

POOBAH'S PARTY: NIGHT ONE

There were several new elements in the defence suppression line-up beyond the hard-hitting US Air Force F-4Gs and US Navy carrier-borne SEAD strikers. Opening up Day One's 2,000-sortie air assault was a combined US Army/US Air Force helicopter force code-named Task Force Normandy, its mission to knock out a pair of critical EW radar sites 400 miles west of Kuwait City. Nine McDonnell Douglas AH-64A Apache helicopter gunships, led by three GPS-NAVSTAR-equipped MH-53J Pave Low III pathfinders, dune-hopped across the border and salvoed their Hellfire laser-guided missiles against Squat Eye, Flat Face and Spoon Rest radars beginning at 0239hr (local time), breaking open a hole for EF-111As to set up moderately safe orbit points within Iraqi airspace. This went almost like clockwork, except that one of the sites managed to get off a push-button warning before its destruction, resulting in triple-A sites opening up spontaneously over Baghdad before anything arrived, while Dassault-Breguet Mirage F1EQ CAP aircraft were scrambled in an attempt to engage the EF-111As and ingressing F-4Gs.

Another new defence suppression tool was the use of AGM-86C Conventionally armed, Air-Launched Cruise Missiles (CALCM), derivatives of the Boeing AGM-86B nuclear ALCMs carried by US Air Force B-52s. It was these 2nd BW aircraft that effectively opened the offensive downtown, launching CALCMs at extreme stand-off range at the climax of their exhausting 35hr, 14,000-mile round trip from Barksdale AFB, Louisiana. The nuclear cargoes had been replaced by tactical ones containing unitary penetration warheads and also specialist so-called non-destructive warheads containing wire filaments, the latter designed to short-out electrical grids at power-generating and relay facilities in Baghdad.[3]

Acting in unadulterated provocation were the forty-four Northrop Scathe Mean BQM-74C Chukar decoy drones, fielded and launched by the 4468th TRG, composed of former Ground-Launched Cruise Missile (GLCM) personnel under the command of Col Doug Livingston. This force was top secret: a self-contained turnkey unit nicknamed Poobah's Party after its originator, Lt Gen Larry Henry (at the time a major general), who made the whole thing happen. Having studied the successful Israeli Peace for Galilee SEAD shoot-out over the Beka'a, he convinced Brig Gen Glosson, who was planning the strategic air campaign, that aircraft losses could be cut to a minimum if decoys could be employed to wake up the Iraqi radar defences and thus make them more vulnerable to attack by HARM missiles.

The 4468th TRG trucked into the desert near the Kuwait–Iraq border, set up camps and launched its decoys in time to arrive over the target when the F-4Gs were cocked ready for action and within HARM shooting range.

The other crucial element was the first daring widespread application of low-observable or stealth technology: the Lockheed Skunk Works F-117A Nighthawk. Forty-four of the Black Jets from Col Alton Whitley's 37th TFW, comprising aircraft and crews from the 415th TFS 'Nightstalkers' and 416th TFS 'Ghost Riders', had deployed from the Tonopah Test Range airfield in Nevada to King Khalid AB during Desert Shield. Ten of them flew 900nm to form the vanguard into Baghdad, relying on their third-generation stealth characteristics to mask them from TTRs while dropping GBU-27A/B Paveway bombs (utilizing 2,000lb BLU-109/B penetration warheads) or standard laser-guided hammers on critical telecommunications nodes and command bunkers, which successfully severed the command and control arteries at the heart.[4]

Preliminary targets included the Nukhayb IOC in the Central Defence Sector not far from the Saudi border, to allow McDonnell Douglas F-15E Strike Eagle interdictors and their support package relatively undetected access into Iraqi airspace, followed by attacks on downtown Baghdad itself to shatter the KARI system. Key targets there embraced the Al Taqaddum IOC/GCI node to the south-west of the city, the 370ft high Al Kark communications tower on the west bank of the Tigris River, the Iraqi Air Force command bunker in the Taji suburbs of Baghdad, and the

An F-117A is loaded with a laser-guided bomb. Flown from near Khamis Mushayt under the 37th TFW(P) banner during the Gulf War, fifty examples currently serve with the 'Fightin' 49'ers' at Holloman AFB, New Mexico, not counting an additional aircraft operated by Detachment 1, 53rd Test & Eval Group there, plus another with the 410th Flight Test Squadron at Palmdale, California. (Lockheed-Martin Tactical Aircraft Systems)

twelve-storey International Telephone Exchange (known as the AT&T Building to mission planners).

This first wave of F-117As went in just before 0300hr without any kind of direct electronic support, thereby creating enormous surprise in their attack, but there is no doubt that they were partly masked from outlying EW radars by the sheer volume of observable air traffic mounting around the borders which created a huge and useful amount of background static. Additional targets included in the subsequent waves that night included the Tallil SOC and Salman Pak IOC, and the combined Ar Rutbah IOC/GCI node in the Western Defence Sector, near H-3 airfield. By night's end twenty-nine F-117As in three waves had struck twenty-six high-value C3 targets, isolating Iraq's regional defences from Baghdad.

Those shorter TTR radar waves not rerouted along the length of and behind the F-117A or negated by the aircraft's wallpaper layers of quarter-wavelength Radar-Absorbent Material (RAM) were bounced off the mirrors concept polyhedron and airframe in directions that took them away from the radar source, thus denying the enemy any effective hook-up between radars and triple-A or SAMs. On top of this, the waves of decoys and cruise missiles were precisely interleaved so that the Iraqi triple-A gunners would be pumping shells at unmanned aircraft in ferocious bursts of activity, and would thus be relatively subdued when the waves of Nighthawks were over the target. The barrels on their ZSUs and other triple-A pieces would quickly heat up to dangerous levels whereby rounds would cook off in the barrels, forcing them to cool their guns for several minutes at a time.

Some of this story comprised contemporary misinformation, but other aspects were half-truths. For example, much of the Iraqi triple-A could not reach the F-117As: the eight ZSU-23/4s in Baghdad, along with the numerous pieces ranging in calibre up to 57mm, would have been ineffective above 20,000ft, while some of the heavier 85mm and 100mm guns' rounds, with a reach of up to 44,000ft, were fused for the incorrect altitude and not aimed. The F-117As thus tended to operate above the arcing umbrellas of firearms and hosing small-calibre triple-A, and below the big, lower rate-of-fire, high-reaching artillery. This combination provided windows of opportunity to give the stealth pilots the freedom to laser sparkle the assigned targets for their Paveways with the INS-cued Texas Instruments forward- and downward-looking infrared acquisition and laser designation system, with staggering precision. No big triple-A shells caused any damage.

Times over target (TOTs) were built into the game plan, so as to enable multi-ship attacks: simultaneous attacks by several aircraft, within a time gate of some 1½ seconds, all using different headings and altitudes for deconfliction. There were no constant waves of bombers with vulnerable (and predictable) waypoints, as had been the case during the Linebacker operations over North Vietnam nineteen years previously, the highly observable bombers relying on massive noise-jamming to mask their presence and thus inadvertently furnishing home-on-jam SAM guidance.

Nonetheless, the triple-A fire over Baghdad appeared terrifying during the target ingress, and again when it opened up after the first wave of PGMs began impacting. The bravery exhibited by those aircrew, who at the time were working in an Emission-Controlled (EMCON) radio silent environment, unaware of their colleagues' fate and believing their chances of getting home were at best slim, deserves considerable accolade. Capt Marcel Kerdavid, whose bombs hit the Al Kark Communications Tower and the command bunker at Taji that night, was awarded the Silver Star for his efforts.

The second and third waves of F-117As were supported by EF-111As, once they had broken through a cordon of Iraqi Mirage F1EQs, working on between two and four different bearings at stand-off orbit points, blocking downtown Baghdad's EW and GCI radars, whose longer wavelengths might otherwise have detected the Nighthawks after the initial mêlée was joined. However, the chief reason they were there was to block any TTR radars that might harass a *damaged* Black Jet. Later, Lt Col Ralph Getchell noted that the F-117As were 'low-observable, not no-observable', and that in planning their attack routes they carefully took advantage of the F-117A's strengths to minimize the times during which they could possibly be detected and tracked. This made some use of the trailer-sized Air Force/Lockheed threat-planning computer, nicknamed Elvira (after the legendary 'Mistress of the Night') by Team Stealth, which factored in the F-117A's low-observable characteristics.

However, much planning was conducted in old-fashioned map-and-pencil mode by the 37th TFW's EWOs (more than one of the pilots was a former F-4G Bear who had subsequently earned his wings and transitioned to the Nighthawk), who had access to a constantly updated EOB library, to avoid known hot spots wherever possible. The intended route could then be entered in the F-117As' computers to derive navigation and threat-avoiding flight-plans.

Despite the best efforts of the ground crews at Tonopah East, it was possible that access panels on the Black Jet might become unbuttoned or detach inexplicably because of q-factors (dynamic pressure), or weapons bay doors might fail to close, and this prompted the 37th TFW(P) to request EF-111A jamming support. Red/Green Flag exercise experience over the Switzerland-sized Nellis Range had demonstrated that SAM MUTES operators tended to negate electronic jamming by reducing the sensitivity or gain of their radar's receiver. Any reduction in gain prompted by jamming from the EF-111As would thus cause the small radar blip of a blossoming F-117A to disappear from the scope.

Later in the air campaign Nighthawks were directly employed in the SEAD effort. For example, from 9 February, before the Taji expanse of military warehousing and maintenance facilities could be hammered by B-52Gs, all the local SAMs had to be neutralized. Ten F-117As were dispatched in advance to knock out every SA-2 and SA-3 strategic site positioned in and around Baghdad. Eighteen direct hits were achieved with twenty bombs. This SAM-busting feat was repeated on 16 February when ten F-117As struck seven SAM batteries as part of their strikes against SS-1

Two 390th ECS(P) EF-111A Ravens hug the deck in typical ingress fashion. Pairs of these jamming aircraft were on hand to support Desert Storm operations, working in much the same pattern as the EB-66 Destroyers of the Vietnam war era, but employing the far more sophisticated AN/ALQ-99E jamming sub-system. (USAF)

Scud Surface-to-Surface Missile (SSM) production facilities and aircraft repair depots at Basra, Salman Pak and Batra.

By the end of the conflict, Team Stealth had achieved 1,669 pinpoint direct hits against their assigned targets – a 75 per cent success rate; and although representing only a token percentage of Coalition air power, the F-117As accounted for two-fifths of all key strikes during the first three days of combat. Overall, the 'unit's record of 1,299 sorties without damage argues persuasively that the F-117A was not detected by Iraqi radars in any tactically useful manner'.[5]

WEASELS IN ACTION

Spangdahlem crew chiefs express their sentiments during the strategic offensive period of the F-4G SEAD campaign. (Jim Uken)

Directly in the fray from Night One were the F-4G Weasels, whose conspicuous airborne AN/APQ-120 fire-control radars, beer callsigns and 'Magnum!' missile launch calls soon became synonymous with the presence of lethal SAM-busters in the skies, and proved to be a major thorn in the enemy's defences, silencing battery after battery. It is worth noting the comparative Radar Cross-Section (RCS) of the F-4G: the F-117A boasted an RCS of between .01 and .001 square metres, akin to a hummingbird, whereas the F-4G had a head-on RCS of 6m, several orders of magnitude bigger. In comparable terms, this enabled the F-117A to fly 90 per cent closer to ground radars, and 98 per cent closer to airborne radars, before it was detected. High-altitude triple-A, which might have posed a genuine threat to F-117As with a lucky shot, thus began venturing after the Weasels instead!

The US flag was proudly hoisted over Sheikh Isa AB during the opening night of the campaign, as crew chief Scott Bymun remembers. 'The Bahrain [Amiri] Air Force wouldn't let us fly the US flag on base. The night that the war began, several crew chiefs put the US flag on a pole and posted in on revetment 20 (right at the end of the runway). Being as it was night-time, they also used a light-all to illuminate it. Several Bahraini officers tried to take it down. That was when the security police and several pissed-off Marines got involved. Have you ever seen twenty heavily armed men guarding a flag?'

Col Walton's F-4Gs picked up SAM emissions 100nm from Baghdad. At 0337hr SA-8, triple-A and (captured Kuwaiti) I-HAWK sites came up on the airwaves, and got particularly heavy from 0348hr onwards, as the BQM-74C decoy drones entered the Baghdad conurbation. The BQM-74Cs (and other unmanned distractions) apparently increased the number

A victory salute by the 35th TFW(P). Thanks to their efforts, and skilled 3-D computer modelling of the Iraqi EOB, Coalition losses were kept to an absolute minimum. (Jim Uken)

of active enemy emitters by some 22 per cent, so that some 45 per cent of all F-4G HARM launches caused enemy radars to go off the air, most staying that way.[6] George Walton said: 'We did not observe any hits on the drones by the Iraqi air defence. The 35th TFW(P) felt the drones were highly effective . . . providing a "target-rich" environment for the Weasels.' Once zapped or obliged to shut down voluntarily, the radars became completely ineffective. This continued to hold true for the first week of combat, as a direct result of the presence of the F-4Gs. Innately vulnerable, the Weasels carried their 'big sticks' and orbited the targets in arc form, always on the lookout and selecting prospective radar targets.

The 561st TFS put up the initial twelve F-4Gs tasked to the Baghdad area (with 69-7288 believed to be the first in), followed by jets from the 81st TFS, which were tasked to support aircraft assigned to knock out chemical and weapons storage sites in proximity to Salman Pak on the Tigris River. It was during the latter mission that Maj Bart Quinn and Capt Ken Hanson won their Silver Stars, pressing home their attacks amid a wall of flak.

The southern strike force of F-4Gs fired twenty-two HARMs with ten shots adjudged successful (a 46 per cent success rate). Col Jim 'Uke' Uken, then a lieutenant colonel and Assistant Operations Officer for the 81st TFS, described by Col Walton as 'a masterful tactician', led the first of his squadron's four-ships into Kuwait, covering strikes against the combined Ali al Salem SOC/IOC, and Ahmed al Jaber and Shaibah airfields. The

COLONEL GEORGE 'JOHN BOY' WALTON II

Described by his wing commander as having 'respect for the enemy' but nonetheless 'fearless', US Air Force Fighter Weapons Instructor Course graduate (then) Lt Col George Walton led the 561st TFS into Desert Storm, with his hand-picked EWO Capt William 'Bud' Redmond. He would ultimately fly 29 missions and combat hours. During a thirty-year career, he has amassed approximately 4,500 flying hours, 3,000 in the F-4.

About three days prior to the beginning of the war, I received a call from Riyadh wanting to know what callsigns we would like to use. I had wanted to use some of the more famous F-4 callsigns from the Vietnam period like Buick, Olds, Chevy, etc.; however, they were already taken. 'So what else you got in mind?' asked Lt Col Jim 'Beagle' Keck, our SEAD representative in Riyadh. I thought about it, and asked Beagle if we could use beers. Beagle replied, 'What do you mean?' I answered, 'Beers like Lonestar, Michelob and stuff like that!' Beagle replied, 'Sure, why not!' So he put us on the ATO with beer callsigns. The use of callsigns became very important for mission recognition and it wasn't long before the entire theatre recognized the beers as the SAM suppressors. This was a pretty clever way to do business, but then the theory goes, the Iraqis learned this too.'

On the morning of 16 January, we arrived at what we called Fort Apache, a revetted operations compound. There were swarms of media types hanging around, asking lots of questions – questions that none of us could answer. As the evening rolled around, the crews grabbed some chow and later met for the brief. On the original ATO, sixteen F-4Gs were tasked to go to Baghdad that first night; a mission I had immediately earmarked for myself. The ATO was kind of a living document and as such it was constantly changing as sorties were changed based on need. Finally, I ended up with twelve F-4Gs to take to Baghdad because four were required elsewhere. We were all pumped so by the end of the day, even though we had been up for many hours, the adrenalin kept everyone wide awake and alert. I briefed my twelve-ship about 2230hr.

Bud Redmond finished the aircraft pre-flight without me, while I finally managed to excuse myself from the lingering Press and crawled into the cockpit. Bud was already strapped in the back. I plugged in my headset, selected the airplane's intercom, and attempted to make my initial check-in with Bud. However, he could not respond. It was a dead line. I adjusted the cockpit mirrors so I could see Bud and realized he could hear me, but I could not hear him. As time was running out, I informed him that we didn't have time to make it to a spare, and that there was no way we were going to miss this mission. He responded enthusiastically with a thumbs up so we were a go. We worked out a couple of signals by tapping the stick and the throttle so that we could communicate a little; I had also informed him that I knew my job and was certain that he knew his and together we could get this done. Again, a thumbs up from the back.

At every Coalition air base throughout the region there was a scheduled time when engine start would occur – strict EMCON procedures were in place to minimize warning the Iraqis. With the checks complete, it was time to taxi out so I signalled for the chocks to be removed. At about this time, I think Bud beat on something in the back and the intercom was on-line – we were back in business; a huge relief. As we taxied out into the darkness, there were rows upon rows of our support troops out there saluting and showing their support as we taxied by.

As we came to the last revetment prior to the arming area at the end of the runway, a US flag had been set up and was being illuminated by dozens of portable light stands. It was a beautiful sight there, blowing in the night breeze. Until this time, we had never put up a US flag anywhere on the base, in deference to our Bahraini hosts. So this was something special. It was absolutely the most spectacular thing I think I can ever remember seeing. It got pretty emotional in our cockpit and I doubt there were many dry eyes in any of our aircraft.

Three separate four-ships made up my twelve-ship. The callsigns were Coors 31, Lonestar 41 and Michelob 51, all headed for Baghdad. Hailing from Texas, I had wanted that Lonestar callsign, but a mix up in the paperwork put an end to that! We taxied out without saying a word, then on a specific time hack we released brakes, engaged the afterburner and departed. We headed north then west, passing just south of Dhahran. The other two flights joined in radar trail as we moved west, searching for the critical KC-135 tankers that would provide us with enough fuel to make it to Baghdad and back.

The sky was crowded with literally hundreds of other tankers, fighters and bombers that we could pick up on our radar. Fortunately, we were all located far enough to the south of the Iraqi border that their

Col George Walton climbs into his F-4G (George Walton)

EW radars could not detect us. It took about an hour to get to the Lime refuelling track where we met up with our tankers, callsigns Tuna 64, Tuna 65 and Tuna 66. The track was located just about dead centre of the Saudi Arabian desert.

Our TOT was 0350hr. We carried with us two HARMs and three external fuel tanks with a pair of AIM-7F air-to-air missiles in the aft missile wells and an AN/ALQ-184 self-protection jammer. Missions going to the Kuwaiti Theatre of Operations (KTO) were loaded with four HARMs and one centreline tank. The 561st TFS was targeted primarily at Baghdad in the initial wave and the 81st TFS went primarily to the KTO. Initially, when planning for the air campaign started back in August and September 1990, the Baghdad mission was our first priority. As the guys from 'Spang' arrived, planning expanded to include additional sorties targeted for the KTO and the western part of Iraq in the vicinity of Al Qa'im. After those early missions — which were already preplanned — missions for both squadrons were equally divided throughout the theatre.

After the first wave and not long into the second day of the air campaign, we changed to one universal configuration of three 'bags' and two HARMs. The issue here was gas. We had greater flexibility for ground spares with this configuration and did not have to worry about where we sent one of our aircraft, be it the shorter-duration mission to the KTO, which only required a centreline tank, or the longer-duration missions to Baghdad or the H-2, H-3 area in western Iraq. The longer missions were problematic for the centreline-only aircraft.

We had the AN/ARN-101 which had an estimated time of arrival meter we used to make sure our jump-off point to begin the run to Baghdad was timed precisely. We headed north to the northern end of the refuelling track and dropped off the tanker, with the second and third four-ships delaying their drop-off to provide the spacing we needed between each of our attack four-ships. Each flight executed a preplanned spacing manoeuvre in order to break into a long offset trail formation with 8–10 miles spacing between each F-4G. This would flow each four-ship into a 24–30 mile trail formation. As we fell off the tanker, we began to dim our exterior lighting with the exception of the formation lights — fairly dim green strip lights used for flying formation at night. Although it was a dark night, it was very clear. As we crossed into Iraq, we turned off the remainder of our external lighting.

As the lead aircraft of twelve, my F-4G was to target a specific SA-2 and HAWK site known to be located on the eastern side of the city. The no. 2 in my flight had another set of specific targets, as did no. 3 and no. 4 in sequence. Each of the twelve aircraft on this attack had specific targets identified and located with back-up plans if, for some reason, their target was not on-line and emitting radar energy when it was time to attack. We knew very well where these systems were located on the ground and the plan was to individually target these preplanned assignments; and if we couldn't shoot our primary assigned target, we'd take out the next logical threat in a preplanned sequence in order to deconflict from others targeting threats in the same area.

In addition to the lethal SEAD capability of our F-4Gs, EF-111As and EA-6Bs were busily jamming search radars that forced the more critical TTRs to come on line independently, so that we could locate and shoot them. A number of drones, launched from within Saudi Arabia, were also out in front of us and had set up orbits, thus providing the Iraqis with targets to chase. Also along, and flanking us to the east, was a flight of F-15Cs out of Dhahran AB, led by Capt Steve Tate. They had escorted us to a distance far enough south of the city that they were not exposed to the SAMs and from there they established a BARCAP to protect us on egress.

Our ground track took us up the eastern side of Baghdad so that we could get as close as possible to our assigned targets. The ground track of the flight was roughly south-west to north-east, with the last airplane in the string of twelve shooting at targets on the south and south-east side of the city. It was a logical, easy targeting scheme that made sense and was easily understood by all who participated in this first-wave attack. The Iraqis were surprised and cooperated very well, coming on-line with their various radars at exactly the right time for us to employ our twenty-four HARMs.

This was a joint attack mission, with the US Navy being assigned threats in the western quarter of Baghdad. Coming from the Red Sea Battle Group [CTF-155] with F/A-18Cs carrying HARMs and EA-6Bs jamming from the west, it was a perfectly executed initial attack against what was arguably the most heavily air defended city anywhere in the world. Additional US Navy strike aircraft launched Tactical Air-Launched Decoys [TALD] to give the Iraqis something to shoot at.

As the first bombs began to explode in Baghdad, we were just entering the perimeter of the populated area in the southern suburbs, and the Iraqi triple-A came on with a vengeance. Almost immediately, Iraqi radars began searching for us to return fire. We looked for and found our preplanned targets and Bud quickly located and targeted the first threat, and a missile was fired shortly after. I was somewhat startled by the blinding bright light from the missile motor as it came off the airplane, and I blurted out an expletive that got Bud's attention. He asked what was wrong, and I told him that other than being blind, everything was cool! My night vision was gone for a few seconds but recovered in time for me to notice our first HARM going straight up. My first thought was that we had a wild rocket, but I quickly recalled the missile was in its bias up for energy. The HARM goes up for energy and then comes back down, converting all that altitude into a downhill acceleration for speed, all the while opening its magic eyes and looking for the threat we told it to target.

Not long after the first missile was away, Bud found a second target and we launched the next missile. As soon as this one was gone, we made an immediate turn to the right, pointed the nose to the south toward our egress location, and went as fast as a three-bag airplane could go toward the Saudi border.

Because fuel was so critical and using the afterburner would highlight our position at night, we did not use the added thrust and acceleration that the afterburner provided unless absolutely necessary. Meanwhile, behind us, the rest of my twelve-ship was busy finishing up the targeting scheme we had planned, and egressed south. As we were operating pretty much as single ships in the dark, we each had our own programmed egress to get us back to Saudi Arabia, where we would rejoin as three four-ships for our post-strike tanker rendezvous.

As we were about 20–30 miles south of the city and going south, there was suddenly an explosion that appeared off to our left and only a few miles away. It was a huge fireball that I thought at first must have been a SAM exploding. However, there were no indications of a SAM launch, so Bud and I wondered what it might have been. We later found out that this explosion was an Iraqi Mirage F1 that Capt Tate had targeted from the stern and fired at from long range, destroying it. To this day, I feel certain that Mirage was targeting Bud and myself.

We crossed the border just about the time the sun was starting to come up. It was a hazy morning, but one at a time, without anyone saying a word, my Coors flight joined up with me as we found our way to the refuelling track and the next two four-ships joined us as well. All twelve had made it out! I was very relieved and elated. We completed our first mission with no losses. We took our fuel and headed home. Upon recovering at Sheikh Isa AB, hot pit refuelling was the norm. Once on the ground, with one engine still running, we would refuel prior to taxiing back to our respective reveted parking locations where ordnance would be loaded for the next mission. The media was waiting for me, as expected, and before I could break free to have breakfast and prepare for the next mission, I had to spend a few minutes speaking with them.

[Lt Col Walton's notable comment that 'Baghdad was lit up like a Christmas tree' was aired around the world the following morning. During the 79 F-4G sorties launched on the opening night, 125 SAM sites were engaged and approximately 56 radars knocked out.]

As for the beer callsigns, they became pretty famous during the Gulf War. It's been said that when the 'beers' showed up, Iraqi radars shut down. And there may be some truth to that. Nonetheless, I received a call one day from an F-15 unit asking if we'd be willing to swap callsigns, so I said sure. The next day we went into an area using their Exxon callsign [originally assigned to KC-135s during Desert Shield] and they in turn used our beer callsigns. They didn't encounter any radar threats that mission, while we were able to shoot quite a few radars while masquerading as F-15Cs for a day.

SEAD forces were tiered, with the F-4Gs opening up the initial corridors before handing off to supporting US Marine Corps F/A-18Cs, which in turn hooked up with US Navy/Marine Corps aircraft hitting Al Basra airfield; this freed the F-4Gs to go after other strategic radar defences, as Col Uken recalls: 'The actual number of HARMs fired in the KTO was approximately 200 in the first 24hr. The 81st TFS spent two-thirds of its time over the KTO, flying with a centreline "bag" and wall-to-wall HARMs underwing. The Baghdad-bound strikers launched with three "bags" and two HARMs. However, those lines of distinction soon evaporated when we became more "reactive" and were scheduled on a daily basis.'[7]

The F-4Gs operated initially at around 20,000ft and then began increasing altitude by 2,000–3,000ft a day until, by the end of the first week, they were routinely cruising at 28,000–30,000ft, out of range of all but the SAMs and 100mm triple-A. However, these sometimes found their mark, inflicting some damage. EWO Capt Kevin 'Grince' Hale was watching the AN/APR-47 RAWS scopes during a racetrack pattern between the south-east and north-west of Baghdad one night when enemy gunners walked 100mm fire across his flight path, severely concussing the aircraft. 'We flipped upside down with about 120deg of bank and lost about 8,000ft of altitude,' he later recorded. His pilot instinctively blew off the wing tanks, recovered the aircraft and pulled it up to 32,000ft, to get out of reach of the guns. They recovered safely at Sheikh Isa AB with the aircraft's port lights, part of one of its hydraulic systems and the AN/ALQ-184 ECM pod completely shot-up.

The SAMs also very nearly found their mark. Mike Kadlubowski was overflying what he thought was an innocuous training radar when suddenly the site turned out to be an SA-3, which promptly attempted to engage them. With hindsight he reckoned the incident seemed funny – but it was not quite so hilarious at the time though. On Day Three of the air war, Maj Steve Jenny and his EWO Capt Mark 'Bucci' Buccigrossi had six SAMs shot at them in less than 3 minutes. Escorting some B-52Gs on a bombing run against Republican Guard positions dotted along the Kuwait–Iraq border, the RAWS suddenly lit up with some new threats posing a serious danger to the B-52Gs. Two SAMs started climbing at the F-4G's ten o'clock position, prompting the pilot to yell, 'Get the pod! Get the chaff!'

During the defensive break a further two SAMs gave chase, but all exploded harmlessly out of reach. However, the hard gyrating had cost the crew a great deal of speed and height – and then the fireworks began. Steve Jenny had no choice but to push the stick forward to build up some speed, placing them well within the triple-A pocket, but they gained sufficient momentum just in time to evade a third pair of missiles. Distracted away from the B-52Gs by the cavorting F-4G, the Iraqi gunners did not inflict even a scratch on the bombers.

Shortly after recovery and de-suiting, Jenny and Buccigrossi were told to take off again 35 minutes later, without a formal briefing – they were tasked to provide SEAD for some forty F-16Cs striking a nuclear facility on the south-east side of Baghdad. As things turned out, they possessed the only fully functional AN/APQ-120 radar in their flight. Already exhausted, they found themselves acting as pathfinders for their colleagues. Both men were awarded the Silver Star for their gruelling efforts.

The only F-4G loss occurred on 19 January. Capt Tim Burke and EWO Capt Juan Galindez of the 81st TFS (in 69-7571) were seriously low on fuel at the close of their mission against H-2 airfield near the Jordanian border, but bad weather prevented them from executing a successful AAR plug to top up their tanks and they were vectored to King Khalid Military City airport by an AWACS. Suffering from electrical problems, the aircraft failed to touch down through the 400ft thick fog over the airfield and on their fifth approach the fuel-starved J79 turbojet engines finally gave in, forcing the crew to punch out on short final. Galindez landed in the middle of the busy runway! Both men returned to duty two days later. Washington put the loss down to hostile fire, the wreckage revealing a hole in the fuel tanks. However, the Weasels ascribed it simply to bad weather and fuel starvation.

After the first three days, following the initial barrage of HARMs, the enemy operators remained relatively mute, as Col Walton recalls:

> By Day Three, HARM expenditures were somewhat high and I was a little concerned. I informed the guys to employ them at legitimate targets and that there was nothing wrong with bringing them back home. After Day Three, it was not atypical for a four-ship to go out with eight HARMs and come back with them still on the pylons.
>
> After having flown more than a dozen more missions, there was one trip to Baghdad I recall as it was somewhat humorous at the time. We were on a run with B-52s against a missile factory at the Taji complex, north of Baghdad. It was a night mission, and a beautiful clear night at that. It was so clear you could see all the way to Kuwait from Baghdad. The lights in Baghdad were totally out, either because we cut the electricity or because they were trying to hide, or both. I had four F-4Gs and the twelve B-52s to escort. The B-52s flew in from the west at about 40,000ft. Their bomb run would take them from south-west to north-east, passing north of the Al Taqaddum airfield on the west of Baghdad where we were to join and escort them. Our goal was to flank them to the south and east so that they were protected from any SAMs in that quadrant as they concentrated on their target. As we flew from west to east, flanking them at 20,000ft, we stayed far enough south that we didn't have to worry about their bombs falling on our heads. Our job essentially was to flow through the area as they released their weapons on the Taji facilities.
>
> The twelve B-52s flew their attack with us paralleling their flight path to the south. As soon as the first bombs impacted the ground, every gun in the city of Baghdad started to shoot – there was 100mm, 57mm and 23mm triple-A. All were shooting. The gun operators were probably just sitting at their emplacements, heard the explosions and just started pulling the triggers. There wasn't anything to shoot at, they just started hosing off their guns. There was one ZSU-23/4 that was approximately 3 miles south of the Taji complex that joined the fight even though the bombers were well beyond its effective range. He would shoot for about five seconds, stop for one. He'd shoot for another five and pause again. From our vantage point it looked just like an out-of-control fire-hose spraying bullets back and forth. I thought the shooter was going to melt the barrels.
>
> Each stick of bombs kept pounding the Taji facilities, one after the other after the other. The final B-52 in the cell – the twelfth – must have seen the same -23/4 gun site that Bud and I were watching because the pilot adjusted his vector slightly and his final stick ripped right through that triple-A site. For a few seconds it was quiet, and

then suddenly one final tracer bullet came out from where the site used to be. I recall thinking [that] it looked like the last defiant act! We chuckled about this one gun emplacement that went up against the B-52s the entire way home that night.

The radar network similarly threw up one dramatic final protest on 10 February, late into the air war, as Col Walton explains:

It was rather bizarre to us at the time. Eight of us were escorting some F-111s to Baghdad. It had been quiet for the past couple of weeks, with very few SAM radars to shoot at. Either they had been destroyed or we had scared them enough that they did not turn them on. As we approached Baghdad, every radar in the city came on. This surprised us all, as it was like shooting fish in a barrel. We expended all sixteen HARMs within 1½ minutes. There was never any threat to the F-111s because no missile-guidance radars were associated with any of the threats that came on-line. Only search radars and TTRs were up for us to shoot at and all were good solid targets.

It wasn't until a few days later that we heard Saddam Hussein had gotten angry with his Air Force Chief of Staff and the head of the air defence force and had them executed. That was a good night for us because whoever replaced those two didn't want to suffer the same fate. I'm guessing the new commanders ordered their operators to turn their radars on and start looking! The end result was that we shot quite a few radars that night.

Col Jim Uken recalls a change in tactics after the initial strategic offensive:

We began flying what we called direct support or area suppression. Direct support missions were where we were tied to a strike package, using four or six F-4Gs. Area suppression was as it sounds: we got to a particular area and provided support for any given number of flights, firing against targets of opportunity. Ten days into Desert Storm, this evolved into what we called 'Weasel Police' tactics. The wing tasked two-ship flights to cover all of Kuwait and south-eastern Iraq over a radius of about 100 miles at a time, using AWACS coordination to cover a particular sector while strikes were going on. Any threat that popped up in that area we would neutralize with the HARM missiles.

In reality there were many different attacks going on, and quite often we would not be in a position to support both packages at the same time. What we would end up doing, if a threat popped up in proximity to a package we were not able to support, was to give them a radio call and tell them what the nature of the threat was. [Weasel Police sorties typically tasked six F-4Gs, split into sections of two.] Each would loiter in the target area for half an hour, with two ships inbound and two outbound for aerial refuelling replenishment. After 4–5hr on station, another six-ship would take over.

Spangdahlem's most successful SAM-busting crew comprised pilot Maj Vinnie Quinn (seen here) and EWO Ken Spaar. They zapped a dozen sites. (Jim Uken)

This system furnished 24hr coverage over the KTO (the F-4Gs configured with two HARMs each) and endured until the close of hostilities in late February 1991.

To the north at Incirlik AB, in Turkey, Brig Gen Lee Downer's 7440th CW (P) was testing the new Superwing concept under Operation Proven Force. The 23rd TFS F-4Gs and Block 30 F-16Cs provided SEAD support in slapshot fashion, while the bombers bored in on their targets; from Night Two, these included attacks on EW radar sites at Basiqah, Machurah and Sinini by F-111Es using principally Mk82 air-inflatable retarders (Ballute, high-drag versions of the Vietnam-era Snakeye, first used during the raid against Libya) and new CBU-87 combined-effects munitions, 'who flew through the holes in the triple-A,' according to Capt Greg Stephens.

However, the lack of PGMs or night-time targeting sensors reduced accuracy, and success only became commonplace once digitally upgraded Avionics Modernization Program F-111Es began arriving, to act as pathfinders for purely ballistics-based weapons drops. Also, because of concerns about fratricide, the firing of HARMs was suspended in mid-February for several days, resulting in the F-4Gs employing some seven Shrike and fifty Maverick rounds in anger.

The 23rd TFS typically employed three four-ship elements for daytime strikes and two four-ship elements for night-time work. The lead element(s) comprised a pair of F-4Gs with HARMs, with slapshot F-16Cs adding to the armoury, while the second element employed two F-16Cs with HARMs while the two F-4Gs toted high-drag, short-range Mavericks. Several of the latter were employed against fixed targets such as bridges and dams and 'made a nice bang'.

Overall, in just forty days of combat, the 81st TFS claimed 142 radar kills during 1,167 combat sorties, their highest scorers being Capt Vinnie Quinn and his EWO Maj Ken Spaar, who fired thirty missiles and claimed twelve sites. Lt Col Ed Ballanco (unusually, flying with four different EWOs) came a close second with eleven radars knocked out. High-scoring F-4Gs were 69-0250, credited with twelve sites, and 69-7232 and 69-0286 with eight apiece. High-shooter in the 561st TFS was 69-7263 *#1 SAM-Slammer*. Its dedicated crew chief Sgt Alan Martin claimed it fired thirty-seven HARMs, two Mavericks and a Shrike during the war.

However, individual crew SAM kill scores were not kept by the 561st TFS, who felt the AN/APR-47 RAWS BDA was not sufficiently reliable. Their sortie tally was 1,176, with most crews logging 100 combat hours. Maj Robert C. Shwarze noted that altogether the Sheikh Isa AB F-4Gs shot 905 HARMs for 254 radar antennae believed destroyed.[8] The kill statistics, however, do not reflect the more significant fact that the mere presence of F-4Gs kept the Iraqi defences quiet, allowing strike aircraft to go about their business unmolested.

Col George Walton, boss of the 561st TFS, was both rightly proud and immensely relieved at the Weasels' performance:

We came out of the conflict having not lost a single person. From the beginning, I was worried we would lose a few. It's pretty obvious that we benefited from those Wild Weasel guys of the Vietnam era – the aviators who started this business in the old F-100s, F-105s, and the F-4Cs. Weaseling is like playing a game of chicken with a bunch of really nasty surface-to-air threats. It was extremely dangerous. Sort of like going after a rattlesnake with your bare hands. Today, however, with technology and tactics developed from the lessons learned by our Wild Weasel predecessors, and with the creation of the AGM-88 . . . by the time Desert Storm came around, the mission – although still a game of chicken – was now more like going after that same rattlesnake but with a 10ft machete.

We benefited greatly from the courage and the professionalism of those early crews who passed on to us a legacy of bravery and

The US Marines' Hornets and Prowlers were co-located at Sheikh Isa, alongside the Weasels. They provided sterling SEAD and jamming support over the KTO. Here, a two-seat Hornet cruises over the oil derricks' crude extraction points, set alight by Saddam Hussein's forces as a last-ditch act of vandalism as they retreated from Kuwait. (McDonnell Douglas)

dedication that is unlike any other in tactical aviation. We can't thank them enough for what they did to get us where we are. And I am so very proud of the job the 561st and the 81st Wild Weasel squadrons did during Desert Storm. If there was a Weasel supporting a strike package into either theatre, no aircraft was shot down by radar-guided SAMs.'

The co-located US Marine Corps MAG-3 EA-6Bs from VMAQ-2, which had deployed twelve of their eighteen aircraft to 'Shakey's Pizza', provided support jamming for Coalition strike packages alongside F/A-18s working in the KTO and fired their first HARM on 13 February. The exploits of their US Air Force companions obviously caused a stir. Overall, US Marine Corps EA-6Bs and F/A-18s fired 233 HARM missiles.

'SWAMP FOXES'

While some derided the all-digital F-16 as inferior to the F-4E (which it had almost completely replaced in US Air Force service by early 1991) because of its (then) lack of beyond visual range air-to-air engagement and PGM delivery capability, it was undoubtedly in the thick of it throughout the war, mostly conducting daytime 'harassment bombing' of Republican Guard positions, or providing slapshot ARM shooting support for Proven Force F-4Gs.

One unit stood head and shoulders above the others, mostly as a result of a rather extraordinary command decision to task early Block 10 F-16As, rather than later production Block 30 ALIC/HARM aircraft, on important SEAD missions. F-16As from the 157th TFS 'Swamp Foxes', South Carolina Air National Guard (SC ANG), operating from Al Kharj AB, rose to the challenge and earned considerable praise throughout the US Air Force, even from the normally critical F-111 community, who often derisorily referred to the F-16 as the Lawn Dart.

Col George 'Jet' Jernigan, ANG (Ret), then a major and flight commander in the 'Swamp Foxes', was told to report to the air staff headquarters in Riyadh just before Desert Storm began brewing:

I had concerns prior to going to CENTAF headquarters. I was a little concerned that we would be relegated to secondary missions and roles. However, I was informed that when the President gave the order to execute the war, Kuwait would be left basically untouched during the first night except for a few cruise missiles. But when the

The South Carolina ANG's F-16s lined-up at their home-drome, McEntire ANGB. Col George 'Jet' Jernigan led a flight of twenty of these aircraft against SAM sites in the KTO during Desert Storm, using only iron bombs! (LMTAS)

sun came up a few hours later, the game plan was to take out the Al Salem [Ali al Salem] and Al Jaber [Ahmed al Jaber] airfields as CENTAF was concerned that the Iraqis would employ these airfields to fly strikes against Riyadh.

The SC ANG was to take twenty F-16As and attack ten of the highest-priority SAM sites so that the bombers could come in to attack the runways. I was stunned to learn that the US Air Force considered the ANG Block 10 F-16As [to be] their most lethal SEAD asset, because our total capability included an AN/ALR-69 RWR, an old Singer INS that would drift about 1½ miles every hour or so, and unguided Mk82 and Mk84 munitions.[9]

To its credit, the all-up F-16A offered an uncanned automated daytime visual bombing system using the HUD, INS and radar. The Westinghouse AN/APG-66 multimode radar could be used to derive target slant-range to a gunsight-designated target in Dive Toss for automatic weapons release (a continuously computed release point, offset-based, radar-assisted bombing mode was also available), much like the venerable F-4D/E/G; but perhaps its greatest virtue was the A-7D/E-style CCIP mode for dumb bombing and strafing, which computed airspeed, dive angle, weapons ballistics and height above ground level to automatically derive a manual firing reference on the HUD. The pilot rolled in on the target, and released the bombs when the fall line marker intersected it. When employing guns or rockets, he was furnished with a continuously computed aiming ring-like pipper for accurate shooting. Failing that, he could use 'rack of the eye' methods, based on experience.

It was this system which enabled the F-16 crews to achieve such high scores during Gunsmoke air-to-surface shooting and bombing competitions at Nellis AB. In 1989 the 157th TFS won Gunsmoke against seventeen competing US Air Force teams, including many active-duty participants. George Jernigan was team chief for that competition, and fourteen months later he found himself at Al Kharj AB as one of forty deployed pilots, along with twenty F-16As with World Champions painted on their tails. He remembers how the squadron's F-16As were put to use in the SEAD role:

While the Block 10 F-16A is still a superb visual condition bomber as far as accuracy goes, I was just amazed to find out that this was how they wanted to use us. When I told the guys back in the squadron what the plan was, I said I had wanted [the ANG] to be an equal partner with the active US Air Force, but not quite *that* equal! [Jernigan ended up commanding the mission, leading his twenty F-16As as SCAB 01, plus the strike and support package. The threats] were all visual targets and we had their geographic co-ordinates. The SA-2s, in particular, were very easy to locate – a big Star of David on the ground. The SA-3 is pretty easy, but the SA-6s were much more challenging targets. I had one SA-6 out of my ten SAM sites and the rest of them were -2s and -3s.

We had trained for a European war at low-altitude ingress and this was our first foray into the medium-altitude arena, so all the defensive manoeuvres required to negate the SAMs were theoretical.

Chiefly, I was dissatisfied with the fact that I had only twenty airplanes to attack ten SAM sites. The minimum survivable number of airplanes is four. If you have got four airplanes per target then you have a lot of options, but I had to allocate only two airplanes per SAM site. We took the force and split it into two groups with myself leading one group into western Kuwait, and Dean Piddington, an excellent F-16 pilot, leading the group over to eastern Kuwait.

We were 12 miles in front of the other aircraft in our group. The game plan was that he and I were going to simultaneously attack an SA-2 site and an SA-6 site about 10 miles over the border, which were blocking the way into Kuwait. But once we attacked and dropped our bombs, our two-ships were going to come off still in front of the package and lead the way in, hopefully having the other SAM systems look at us, while the other two-ships were able to get in and drop their bombs. [Jernigan had been allocated six F-4Gs and two EF-111As to suppress the radars, so] I was particularly concerned about the number of triple-A sites and felt like I would probably lose some airplanes.

[The force took off in the dark and rendezvoused at 45 minutes' flight-time from the border.] As the sun started to appear on the horizon, visibility was about 100 miles – you could see everywhere. When we got to about 12 miles south of the border, I split the flight, called for a fence check, and we descended from 28,000ft down to 25,000ft to get some extra speed. About 10 miles south of my SA-2 site we actioned off about 30deg to the left so that we could see it out of the right canopy and there was no resistance; we were getting no RWR indications. As I rolled in to a 45-deg dive to attack the Star of David, with my wingman at my left eight o'clock passing through about 12,000ft, I crossed the target and hit the button, immediately making the airplane about 4,000lb lighter. I came off to the left going deeper into Kuwait and checked left seven o'clock.

My wingman had released his bombs and he was following me with afterburner, trying to get back to altitude, and that's when my RWR started to go off. It indicated an SA-2 launch at left eight o'clock. I looked out of the canopy and had a big telegraph pole coming through the sky, riding a smoke trail. We checked about another 45deg to the left, put the missile at left nine o'clock and made sure the ECM pod was still on, and started putting out chaff. As the missile continued to track the aircraft, I started to barrel roll into it and it missed by a couple of thousand feet, and blew up behind us. We rolled out and once again had depleted energy and airspace, and started to climb back to altitude when we got an SA-6 launch indication from right four o'clock. Once again, another missile was coming up. We checked and executed the same manoeuvre in the opposite direction and were able to negate it.

As scary as it was, I still felt like my wingman and I were in control of our situation, but by now my flight of twenty airplanes was split down to individual two-ships and it sounded like every two-ship was engaged. The guys were screaming over the radio: I heard break calls, I heard one of my lieutenants screaming that he was hit.

With one turn of my head I could see the entire nation of Kuwait and I saw between *forty and sixty* smoke trails streaking through the sky, and massive black explosions all over the place! I didn't know whether each one of those was a downed aircraft or not.

We continued to fly deeper into Kuwait because I was leading the last two-ship. They were about 6 miles behind me, and had an SA-2 site about 8–10 miles north of Ali al Salem airfield. From that site, we ended up getting an SA-6 launch indication, but I felt it was out of range so called for afterburners, and we drove away from that missile and outran it as they had launched out of range. I directed the two-ship to negate and blow off their SA-2 attack, and go back to hit the original site that I had hit, to finish it off.

About that time I checked the time on the clock and it sounded like we were in total disarray, and that I probably had a few airplanes down in Kuwait. I gave the command to abort because the bombers would be coming in about 5 minutes. We climbed up to 30,000ft – my wingman and myself – and accelerated right up to supersonic speed. We had a couple more threat reactions, but nothing dramatic, and we coasted back into Saudi Arabia.

I went back to the administrative frequency I had set up to check the flight in and I waited about 2 minutes before I could bring myself to do it, as I didn't know how many guys were gone. One of the most special moments of my aviation career was when I finally gave the command to check-in and, one at a time, *all nineteen* F-16A wingmen checked-in! It was probably the quietest flight with that number of guys that I have ever been on, as we reflected on what we had just been through.

What I didn't mention earlier is that, about 20 minutes from crossing the border into Kuwait, the AWACS told me that the F-4Gs were weathered-in at Sheikh Isa AB and they would not be coming; and then the EF-111A guy – I was in contact with him over the radio – said one of them had aborted and that his [solitary jamming] orbit had been redirected 60 miles south [of the package], and he wasn't sure how much good that would do me.

As a solo ship, it was felt by higher authority that the EF-111A was too vulnerable in the intense KTO. George Jernigan okayed the situation with his second element, and they decided to press ahead. It later transpired that, over a period of 7–12 minutes, Jernigan's F-16A force had had more SAMs launched at them than any other flight in the history of aviation. 'The aircraft that came in after us got some RWR "cuts" but did not see a single smoke trail. Post-attack BDA revealed that we destroyed three out of the ten SAM sites, and damaged two others. It turned out to be very effective suppression of enemy defences but our feelings were that it was more a *depletion* of enemy air defences.' The strike waves on their heels took out the runways before the SAM launchers could be reloaded.

'We landed, and went through refuelling, and before I had the motor off there was a Mk84 already attached to the right wing. I shut the airplane down as they were beginning to load the left wing, and as I walked towards the squadron tent the next guy to fly it passed me by, ready to

head back north. "Hot pit" refuelling and rearming immediately after recovery was common practice for US Air Force fighters during the Gulf War, allowing rapid reaction if required.'

For nearly six straight weeks the 157th TFS flew combat bombing missions. 'We got shot at almost every time we went north by the triple-A or SAMs, and it was a very intense period in the KTO. The first seven to ten days where the "McEntires" [157th TFS] were tasked for SEAD, we were going after SAM sites each day, and got a little better because the sites were forced into autonomous modes.' Jernigan flew fifty combat missions during Desert Storm. 'I had two Code 2 write-ups [minor problems], and we were using the aircraft beyond the original design concept of the F-16A. It was a small, lightweight fighter loaded up with stuff and we really abused it. In a hostile environment they performed beautifully.'

Not long after the conflict, the stressed-out F-16A/Bs were all but withdrawn from the US Air Force inventory. The 157th TFS began converting to fresh Block 52 SEAD, HARM-toting F-16Cs during 1994, payback for their efforts. George Jernigan appreciated the upgrade: 'The first seven days of Desert Storm convinced me that, since we were going to be doing SEAD missions anyway, I would prefer to be in an aircraft that has the capability to do something besides drop dumb bombs, where my pilots had to put their butts a mile over the target to be able to destroy it. It was a fairly unpleasant experience, but at the same time a valuable lesson.'

Hot pit replenishment. Returning F-4G crews ambled to the refuelling area, post-mission, where they would be topped-up with kerosene and HARMs before returning to their parking spots, ready for the next mission. This avoided the need for copious AGE (Aerospace Ground Equipment) in the new armoured parking areas under construction by the USAF Red Horse teams. (Jim Uken)

NAVY IN THE STORM

US Navy seagoing assets were divided between Carrier Task Force Yankee (CTF-155) in the Red Sea and Carrier Task Force Echo (CTF-145) in the Persian Gulf. Backbone of the Gulf-based aircraft carriers were the eighty-eight multi-role F/A-18A/Cs, which were deployed in no fewer than nine squadrons, not counting the four squadrons on station on USS *Independence* and USS *Dwight D. Eisenhower* during the Desert Shield phase of the air effort, flying strikes and SEAD missions but chiefly providing top cover for the Fleet and longer-legged A-6E and A-7E strikers. They scored the only US Navy air kills of the war, VFA-81 'Sunliners' downing two Iraqi Air Force MiG-21s on the opening night. After splashing the MiGs, they proceeded to deliver their iron on target, thus validating the F/A-18 strike-fighter concept.

Despite its heavy tanking requirements and problems with its laser spot tracker/strike camera pod, the F/A-18 behaved well mechanically by demonstrating a 90 per cent Fully Mission Capable (FMC) rate. Overall, US Navy F/A-18 squadrons logged 4,449 sorties, including 217 strikes on enemy airfields for the loss of only one pilot and his aircraft to hostile fire – the very first Desert Storm Coalition casualty. On the first night of the air war Lt Cdr Michael Scott 'Spike' Speicher from VFA-81 was flying Sunliner 403 (BuNo. 163484) on a SEAD mission from USS *Saratoga* when he was shot down, probably by a MiG-25, 29nm south-east of Baghdad. Some controversy still surrounds this loss, including the whereabouts of Speicher himself, who has since been relisted as MIA.

Cdr Mark Fitzgerald, leading the first A-7E package into Iraq, saw a MiG-25 pass overhead with afterburner engaged and heading towards the F/A-18Cs. Pilot Cdr Michael Anderson, who also spotted the afterburner trail of the giant steel MiG, was attempting to get AWACS clearance to fire on it when Speicher's aircraft suddenly disintegrated, suggesting a possible mid-air collision. It appears that this was the only Coalition loss to enemy aircraft throughout the entire war, despite initial reports of the aircraft being destroyed by a SAM. Post-war evidence, based on examination of the aircraft wreckage by Iraq, indicates that Speicher most likely ejected, but had no radio, and did not survive his ensuing evasive sojourn into the harsh desert.

'BORN IN COMBAT, AND DIED WITH ITS BOOTS ON'

Very impressive were the US Navy's A-7Es of VA-46 and VA-72, the last two seagoing A-7E squadrons in the Fleet, which logged 722 missions and over 3,000hr, operating exclusively from USS *John F. Kennedy* in the Red Sea. They 'came in during Vietnam and went out the door a hero of Desert Storm: the A-7 was a wonderful slice of naval aviation history – born in combat, and died with its boots on', according to former VA-72 XO and veteran pilot Capt John Leenhouts, then a commander.

VA-46 and VA-72 fired 152 HARMs against SAM and triple-A sites, and dropped 1,033 tons of iron bombs on bridges, airfields and military industrial complexes. They also delivered over 20 per cent of all Rockeye CBUs dropped by Coalition aircraft. Iron bombs were also employed in the SEAD role, as John Leenhouts recalls:

We went up north of Al Asad and took out SA-2 acquisition and tracking radar with Mk83s. We could carry four Mk83s; we later switched to eight Mk82s. Most of our HARM suppression work was done for [US] Air Force F-111s, British Tornado GR1s and A-6Es from both carrier battle groups.

When Desert Shield kicked off, VA-72 was in the midst of its transition to F/A-18s. We had already given up most of our A-7Es. About one-third of our maintenance people had left and we had turned in most of our related tools and publications. Everyone was in the relaxed mode. I was actually on a nearby beach when the recall went out on a Friday afternoon. We were quickly informed that we'd be departing for the Gulf. The first question was when, to which the answer was Tuesday.

We called guys back from all over the planet, rounded up additional airplanes from two of our co-located sister squadrons (VA-37 and VA-105) at NAS Cecil Field, as these were the only other active-duty A-7E squadrons remaining (in fact, they took our F/A-18 transition spots while we went to war). We also called back the maintenance people, gathered up the necessary tools and publications and we were on the boat by 15 August as ordered – all within four days – and never looked back.

As I figured that we'd be going low, I thought we should acquire the appropriate paint and camouflage the airplanes. We ordered water-soluble brown and tan paint and in no time, tons of it showed up – during this period, anything and everything that we had ever wanted showed up! However, upon obtaining a brief from SPEAR [Naval Intelligence Command's Strike Projection and Anti-Air Warfare Research] group, we were informed that the Iraqis had well over 7,000 anti-aircraft muzzles out there, so going low wasn't a good idea and we might want to rethink our tactics.

We quickly decided to abort the low-level plan and give ourselves some distance between the threat and us so that we could react to it. We'd get above the anti-aircraft fire as best we could and then employ our HARMs as well as [using] jamming and tactics to defeat whatever missiles they shot at us. So we thought we had a safer margin to operate in. You could see the mapped-out area of where a SAM site was established. They may have moved the radar control van somewhere else, but the sites were similar to a Star of David, although they were not necessarily as symmetrical as that; but they were spawned tentacles in the general area. When you got there, you could tell what it was.

Although the A-7E was in the midst of retirement when Desert Shield was initiated, just the same it was selected to deploy to the region because it was a great HARM-shooter. In addition to having excellent Elint files associated with its RWR system, it was a very easy airplane to reprogramme. It also had amazing endurance, and

A-7Es, flying from the Red Sea, sported a trio of HARMs for Desert Storm operations – two for shooting and a spare for threat analysis or self-protect firing. Maximum 'trap' limitations imposed this limit. (US Navy)

could also carry a lot of ordnance – in all, A-7Es employed nine different types.

We started from Night One, going all the way to the outskirts of Baghdad and the surrounding areas – a 6–7hr mission. Samawah, Al Qa'im, Al Asad, Al Qurnah, Al Khafi, Tallil, H-2 and H-3. We visited all the major bases and numerous other strategic targets as well. Initially HARMs were employed, then Walleyes as we went after command centres, bridges and radar sites.

On 19 January, somewhere around 0200hr, I was leading a flight of six A-7Es tasked to provide SEAD for a strike package of six A-6Es that were going after a headquarters building at an airfield just west of Baghdad. We were out in front of the EA-6B Prowlers, with the A-6Es following closely. Our A-7Es were loaded with three HARMs apiece, and no external fuel tanks – the airplanes had been basically cleaned up to reduce drag. Three HARMs was the maximum load carried. You could always expend one, but you didn't want to throw two away. You never wanted to carry more than you had a high probability of using. We would recover with one or two HARMs, but not three. Each one equates to about 1,000lb of fuel. Although you *could* actually recover with three, you had to be really low on fuel, and that wasn't a good idea.

During Desert Shield we had conducted numerous training sorties uploaded with a FLIR pod and a single external tank. However, before hostilities began it was decided to drop wing pylons 3 and 7 –

a centre and inboard pylon – while the opposite inboard was maintained in case we wanted to carry a tank. The AN/AAR-49 FLIR pod was more weight than it was worth. By dropping this FLIR pod and the two pylon stations, the jet was able to maintain over 525kt on the deck, and required very little in the way of air refuelling.

After getting off the boat, the plan called for the strike package to rendezvous with Air Force KC-135 tankers, as most missions averaged 690 miles each way. There were usually eight aircraft assigned to a tanker and refuelling was conducted continually along the entire refuelling track, which was about 400–450 miles. During this leg of the flight, you would probably hook up as many as five times, taking on approximately 3,000lb per refuelling. As soon as the eighth aircraft had completed its refuelling, the first would be back on the drogue for a top-up. And just before the push, which was usually about 50–75 miles from the Saudi Arabia–Iraq border, everyone took a final top-up, which for some could amount to as little as 300lb. We then raced to the targets, after which we'd only have to tank once and this provided more than enough gas to get us home.

During the first two nights Iraqi radars were very active, therefore PB HARM launches were employed. However, by Night Three they had started 'blinking' their radars – they got smarter – so the PB method was no longer practical, thus the TOO mode was the order of the night. I was working at my assigned altitude block of 23,000–24,000ft. I was slightly off axis, and was coming in at 30–40deg off the strike axis; you never wanted to be overtop the strike aircraft, which in this case were going to conduct a multi-axis attack.

On this particular night we had tail winds upwards of 130–160kt, and unpredicted. I was setting up my EOB orbit, which is more or less an oval racetrack circuit, while attempting to establish a precise timeline so that we could cover the A-6Es. They were strung out in a long stream at medium altitude, slightly above 20,000ft, and we were tasked to cover them while they were within the various SAM engagement rings. I planned to arrive at the forward edge of my assigned threat ring at approximately the same time the strikers were going through this ring and others that overlapped. The SAM sites were to the west of the city, and we were going to be kept quite busy working the various sites as the A-6Es ingressed and then egressed the 30–45 mile engagement area. A lengthy, 15–18 minutes window of protection was required to cover the strike.

The expectation was that the SAM's tracking, and then acquisition radars would light us up, at which point we would hopefully be provided an opportunity to pick off the radar sites. When the radar tracking system illuminated your aircraft, that meant they were looking at you and fixing to fire before they got their fire control on you. You had to wait about 3–7 seconds, or however long you felt good about before unleashing a missile – the plan was to unleash the first salvo of HARMs at this point. All we were working with was the aircraft's AN/ALR-45F. The HARM's seeker head also provided additional EW information. As such, you were somewhat reluctant to get rid of one until you had something locked up.

However, as we were hauling the mail to the target, those horrendous winds came into play. I had worked out a precise timeline in my mind to get me to the edge of the SAM engagement envelope, but I had not calculated those trailing winds that were now driving me. The end result was that I didn't realize until I got into the heart of the SAM ring that I was in it. I was mentally trying to keep myself out of its lethal envelope, while waiting for the SAMs' tracking radar to light me up. The tactic to be employed was to shoot, then turn out so that I'd have room to manoeuvre and to give myself the SAM evasion timeline should a launch occur. You needed to be able to observe the initial tell-tale trailing inferno of the missile – this was how you determined if you were the target. If you saw the missile streaking across the sky, it wasn't coming for you, but if you saw what looked like a black dot in the night sky, this usually meant the missile was headed straight for you.

Nevertheless, as I was going in, a SAM site's radar locked me up, so I shot and the HARM headed straight for the target – which was a good sign. In the TOO mode, the missile heads straight for the radar source, while in the PB mode, it goes up, and then comes back down seeking out an active radar emitter. Of course, the site's radar was in a 'blinking' mode so I didn't know if the operator knew that I was shooting or not. I'm not sure if my initial missile hit the target, but it was working as advertised and I was happy. I now turned 180deg while punching out chaff as I continued on the outbound leg of the racetrack, so now I was flying into the head winds. Consequently I was having difficulty getting away, and I was getting a really sick feeling!

As I continued on the inbound leg of the racetrack, the site was still up. So it was obvious the operator must have shut down soon after my launch. Although a HARM will continue to home in on the location of the radar source even after the emitter is shut down, the missile's accuracy starts degrading rapidly upon shutdown; consequently it has to be dead-on, or it's not going to do any damage. On this second run in, the site just tickled me, and wouldn't lock me up long enough for me to take a shot. On my way out, I again punched out chaff.

During the next orbit the site locked me up once again and I was able to squeeze off another HARM, and again this one went straight. By this time, I was certain the operator had figured out that I was shooting at him. I was now down to my last missile, but I'd really like to have saved it so that I could maintain as much situational awareness as possible. Ideally, you always wanted to have at least one HARM onboard during the egress as it provided you with much better Elint.

In my cockpit I was trying as best I could to maintain good situational awareness of the threat profile. I knew where the radar emitter was, and I was aligned against its SA-3; the site never put its SA-6 on me, nor its SA-8 that was known to be in the area. However, an earlier event may have taken the SA-8 down and the Intel may not have reached us. So on my fourth run in, I took it all the way in to about 4 miles – meaning that I was in the heart of the SAM's envelope. At that moment, I'm certain that the operator thought he had me, as he came up with not only the tracking, but also the fire-control radar as well – we were in business now. Although I didn't witness this, I'm sure he launched and was hoping to track on me, but I let go with my third and final missile.

Not knowing if in fact a SAM had been launched, I punched out a cloud of chaff and opted to make a diving descent below it. I descended to around 10,000ft, which was going to break any lock – even that close – rather than turn away and being held up in the head wind. A SAM was launched, but never tracked me, so I'm relatively certain that the radar operator most likely shut down yet again at the last second. I'll never know if I killed that site. All I do know is that it didn't get me. None of us ever really knew. The only HARM-shooters who knew were the EA-6B guys – and it was still about an 80 per cent presumption.

Incidentally, whenever we fired a HARM we were required to broadcast in clear voice the word Magnum to alert the other Coalition aircraft to the fact that a HARM was in the air. Once the Iraqis figured this out they started shutting down their radars when they heard it, which sometimes worked to our advantage. Therefore we started changing code words. One of our favourites was CandyGram, from the movie *Blazing Saddles*. Every little bit of humour helped!

Now I was down there, and had violated the rule – don't change your altitude – because there are airplanes out there everywhere. So as best I could, while fighting those head winds, I made a slow methodical climb while keeping my speed up as I knew I couldn't climb very fast. When I was about 14–15 miles from the radar site, I knew I was outside the lethal envelope of the SA-3. I was still in the envelope, but outside the lethal range.

While heading back to the boat, a call came from Bulldog – the on-scene AWACS – warning that there was activity over Mudaysis, which was an Iraqi airfield just south-west of the border. This particular airfield had been utilized regularly as a sort of dumpsite. Everyone seemed to go there to expend any unused ordnance that couldn't be brought back to the boat. The inhabitants had had enough, and were getting a little perturbed about this and now a nearby SA-2 site was going active.

I had been duelling earlier and in doing so had expended all my HARMs. Consequently, my RWR situational awareness had been degraded somewhat and now I was flying through a hot SA-2 threat ring while still fighting 130kt head winds. I thought to myself, 'This really sucks!' Well obviously I made it, but that third night of the war was the worst night of my life.

Don't get in too close. Don't duel with them. These were 'don'ts' that had evolved from the Vietnam War, yet I still ended up deeper in the heart of the threat than expected. This was partly due to the winds and because of the desire to protect the strike group. I could have easily thrown away a perfectly good jet, not to mention my own life while trying to do the right thing because the lives of fellow aviators were at stake. The goal is to successfully suppress the threat by setting yourself up as the bait, driving right at the source of the radar, making yourself the more lucrative target. And during this strike, as was the desire, the SAMs targeted A-7Es solely.

Countermeasures systems were supplemented by impromptu field modifications.

During a strike mission we always took our EA-6Bs along with us, sometimes to within approximately 20 miles of the target, from where they provided great jamming support. The Iraqis would know that we were in the vicinity due to the EA-6Bs' jamming, but they couldn't get any kind of fire control on us. They wouldn't know if they were the intended targets or if we were just passing by until the bombs started to detonate, after which they'd then have a pretty good idea as to where we were or at least where to look for us. They could then attempt to pinpoint us as we rolled in from high altitude and if conditions allowed and they could visually sight us, after which they'd attempt to employ their radar to range us.

In the A-7E we only had two AN/ALE-39 chaff/flare buckets located in the tail section, which accommodated some sixty rounds. We usually didn't carry flares, as they would have highlighted us against the night sky. However, upon returning from our initial strikes we were all complaining that we didn't have enough chaff. One of the air wing ordnance guys resurrected the idea of simply getting an empty coffee can, filling it with chaff, plugging the open end with an oversized sponge with a piece of wire attached, and then wedging it upside-down into each pylon housing. The wire was then attached to the bomb lug of an uploaded bomb and when jettisoned, it would pull out the sponge thus releasing the chaff. This method was only employed when carrying Mk83 or Mk84 general-purpose bombs mounted directly to the parent.

As we rolled in from altitude and upon weapons release, we filled the sky with chaff so the Iraqis couldn't put a fire-control radar on us. I think this impromptu method of dispensing chaff had been practised during the Vietnam War when a similar concept placed the can under the tailhook of an A-4, which upon lowering dispensed the chaff. I had heard that on those occasions when the chaff wasn't employed and the pilot forgot about it, they'd wipe out the carrier's radar-controlled approach after lowering the tailhook on finals, and this was made even more interesting during night landings.

Of the twenty-four missions flown by Capt Leenhouts, seven were deemed worthy of decoration. The awards included a pair of individual Distinguished Flying Crosses, four individual Air Medals, two Strike Flight Air Medals and an individual Navy Commendation with a Combat V.

During the final days of hostilities, I made another (although somewhat unplanned) after-dark visit to H-2. Due to its significance, I had been there on Night One. During tonight's visit, fourteen

*John 'Lites'
Leenhouts by his
Corsair II. By the
time of his
retirement, John
Leenhouts had
accrued some 1,645
traps on sixteen
different aircraft
carriers.* (John
Leenhouts)

aircraft (twelve A-7Es and a pair of A-6Es) were dropping by to finish off some MiGs that had been detected by satellite imagery parked in open revetments. The weapons of choice for tonight were Mk20 Rockeyes and Mk82s. I was the flight lead, and the plan called for me to lay down a string of eight 2 million-candlepower LUU-2 parachute-retarded flares to shed some light on the target.

The weather was clear and there was a full moon, hence the airfield was clearly visible and we were able to acquire our aimpoints from far out. I figured the flares wouldn't be required. Upon voicing that suggestion to the strike group, the skipper of VA-46, who happened to be flying with us that night, replied that since we've got them, let's go ahead and use them. He then added that the flares should make the task that much easier, thus allowing the group to achieve some good hits. I dropped down from 25,000ft to 10,000ft to execute the run, popping a flare every 15 to 20 seconds in a zigzag pattern. After the last flare had been dispensed, the plan of attack called for pairs to roll in, in trail at 30-second intervals. I was to climb back up to 25,000ft, rejoin the group and be the last one in.

No sooner had the last flare come off, and the first pair of aircraft rolled in, when this target unexpectedly came alive – and this was a place that had been pounded numerous times since Desert Storm kicked off. The air defences were unbelievable. There was a steady barrage of triple-A fire coming out of there, in addition to some rocket-assisted artillery that was reaching altitudes of 22,000–23,000ft. And there were also lots of SAMs, albeit unguided. As I was climbing up, the group was rolling in. In the hail of fire, panic set in and I was screaming over the radio in an effort to make sure we were deconflicted as I made my way towards the back end of the formation. I couldn't see them and needed to know where everybody was.

Upon joining up at the rear of the formation, I rolled in, selected a triple-A site as my aimpoint and delivered my Rockeyes – each one containing a couple of hundred armour-piercing bomblets – putting that site to sleep. We finished off the MiGs, and inflicted additional damage to the airfield. Ironically, on this night H-2 was our secondary target. It was supposedly thought to be a milk run and as such we were probably somewhat at ease – maybe too much so.

Due to limited visibility in northern Kuwait our primary target, which would later be known as 'the Highway of Death', was weathered out. Consequently we were looking for work. We knew that the MiGs were there and figured that since this place had been pounded repeatedly since Day One, it would be a relatively low-threat target. We were dead wrong – they were going full-out as if it was Night One. It turned out to be one of the highest threats I'd encountered during the entire war. [Capt Leenhouts' SEAD force had already fired twenty-one HARMs on Night One, silencing SA-6, SA-8 and Roland SAM batteries at the base.]

It was interesting in that Gen Horner didn't seem to know that we were participating in Desert Storm until about the third night. As he viewed the daily mission reports, he noticed that A-7Es seemed to be dropping bombs everywhere. The thinking was that there was to be no old technology involved. With that thought in mind, CENTCOM had turned away A-7Ds from [the] Iowa ANG just as they were set to deploy for Desert Shield.[10]

Commander of the Red Sea Battle Group (CTF-155) Rear Admiral Riley D. Mixion (a former A-7E pilot who flew more than 250 combat missions during the Vietnam War), noted the squadrons' accomplishments: 'On two occasions they had nineteen A-7Es on a strike. That's amazing considering we only had twenty on ship and that only one was broke.' On 27 March 1991 he personally directed the final Corsair II cat launch. VA-46 and VA-72 returned to NAS Cecil Field that month, with the airframes being distributed between museums and the boneyard at Davis-Monthan AFB. The only war casualty was BuNo. 158830/AC-403 of VA-72, which was damaged in a barricade landing on 26 January. It was gutted of essentials and shoved over the side of the ship.

SPEAR, which John Leenhouts mentioned earlier, was instrumental in the success of the air campaign. The US Navy had originally created SPEAR to help its carrier air power deal with Soviet and other potential adversaries following the embarrassing 1983 mission over Lebanon, when they lost an A-6E and an A-7E, one crewman killed and another captured. In December 1990 Vietnam veteran Capt Michael Johnson headed the SPEAR group, aided by analysts from each of the armed services, and explored ways for the Coalition forces to breach the KARI air defence shield. They concluded that radar-guided SAMs, not interceptor aircraft, were Iraq's 'logical choice as the primary air defence weapon'. Accordingly, emphasis was placed on SAM and radar suppression.

The SPEAR group also gave Commander US Naval Forces Central Command (COMUSNAVCENT) and his air staff the clout they needed to argue that the Coalition should not use the ageing A-6E in the initial strikes against downtown Baghdad, as Brig Gen Buster Glosson's Black Hole team had originally planned. COMUSNAVCENT was not prepared to accept high losses among aircrews when UAV and air- or submarine-launched cruise missiles were available.[11]

ANOTHER FINE NAVY PEDIGREE

Even though they did not venture to downtown Baghdad, the Fleet's seventy-eight A-6E TRAM and seventeen newly updated A-6E SWIP aircraft, on the cusp of retirement, continued the type's Vietnam tradition as bomb-hauler, minelayer and SEAD platform *par excellence* throughout Desert Storm, as well as undertaking an ancillary SEAD function, dropping expendable TALDs. Originally developed for use by the IDF/AF as the Samson decoy and produced for the US Navy by Brunswick Defense, the 10ft long, 400lb AN/ADM-141A TALDs glided to the target area after release, using pop-out wings to sustain their flight momentum for up to 70nm if dropped from high altitude, and radiated RF-spectrum repeater-type signals to generate the characteristics of US strike jets. Their chief contribution was to wake up the Iraqi defences, effectively doubling

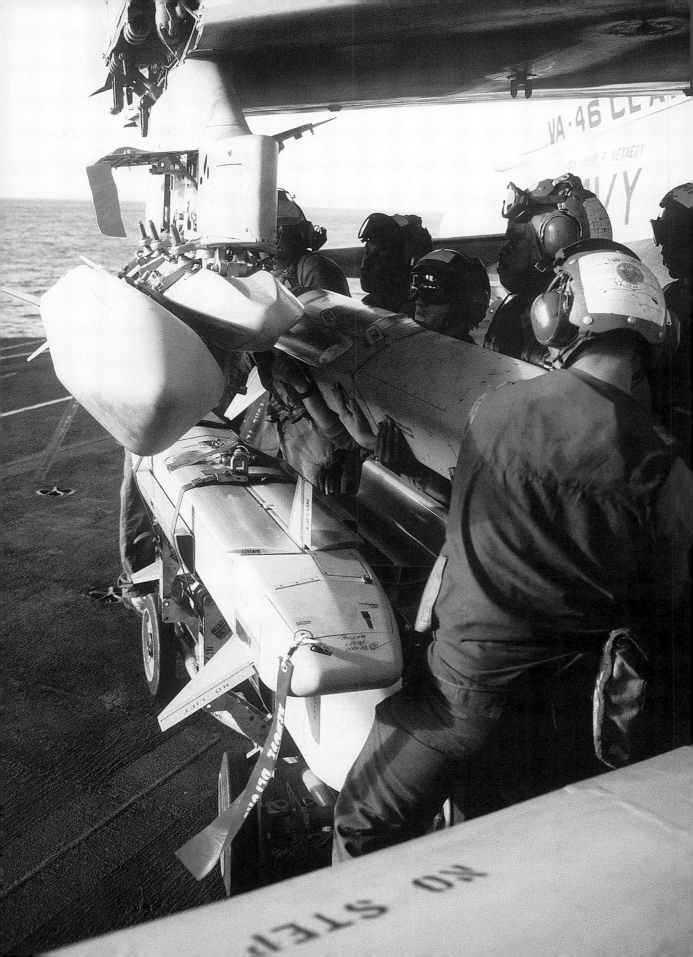

the effectiveness of PB HARMs from 15–25 per cent to 25–50 per cent, according to Brunswick Defense. A total of 137 TALDs were expended, most during the first three days of Desert Storm, though they were employed by VA-75 as late as 10 February during ongoing deep interdiction strikes against H-2 and H-3 airfields in western Iraq. As with the 4468th TRG's ground-launched BQM-74C decoys, they saturated the enemy defences with false targets and having expended their energy and tumbled to earth, accounted for a great many of the air kills claimed by Iraq.[12] During the opening US Navy SEAD strikes against Baghdad and Al Taqaddum, A-6Es dropped 25 TALDs within the space of 20 minutes.

TALDs were in fact dropped by several different carrier-borne aircraft, even anti-submarine warfare Lockheed S-3B Vikings getting in on the act as Elint mappers, using their onboard ESM gear and dispensing AN/ALE-181 Air-Dropped Rapid-Blooming Onboard Chaff (AIRBOC) to help add to the general confusion caused to KARI while air raids were in progress. VS-38 'Red Griffons' was the first S-3 unit to employ TALDs, making the most of all available carrier aircraft as the S-3s were not always required for tanking duties.[13] Typical A-6E load-outs included six or eight TALDs on two MERs, usually mixed with one or two HARMs.

But it was in the bombing, anti-shipping and radar suppression roles that the A-6E crews really left their mark. During January 1991 Lt Cdr Chris 'Snax' Eagle was a lieutenant and an A-6E B/N assigned to VA-145 onboard USS *Ranger*. VA-145 was a vital element of CVW-2, which was otherwise known as the All-Grumman air wing because of its sharp end make-up of A-6Es, EA-6Bs and F-14As.

Having been designated as the inaugural West Coast squadron to acquire upgraded A-6E SWIP airframes, VA-145 achieved its operational certification during 1988. Along with improved ECM, the A-6E's stand-off weapons capability was greatly increased with an enhanced AGM-84A Harpoon anti-ship missile, laser and IR AGM-65 Maverick, the AGM-84B Stand-off Land Attack Missile (SLAM) and a HARM capability. Lt Cdr Eagle explains how the A-6E SWIP was used:

The SWIP upgrade to the A-6E made HARM delivery possible by adding an Integrated Missile Panel (IMP) into our centre console, as well as an entirely new computer programme for our weapons system computer. The standard A-6 Armament Control Panel was used to set up missile release, but the IMP was used to communicate with each of the smart weapons that SWIP allowed us to carry. In the case of HARM, we could choose to fire in PB mode where we actually designated a specific target emitter via the IMP, or TOO mode where target selection was made by the B/N scanning through HARM seeker head-detected targets displayed on the B/N's infrared indicator.

Once a target was selected and designated, the pilot could choose to fire the missile via his commit trigger on the control stick. We also had an SP firing mode available in which the target is actually selected and designated via the AN/ALR-67. On some bombing missions we carried HARM for use in this mode but never had occasion to use it – meaning we brought the missiles back to the ship on those particular missions.

Opposite: A VA-46 'Clansmen' SLUF is loaded with Tactical Air-Launched Decoys for Desert Storm ops. (US Navy)

The Stand-off Land-Attack Missile (SLAM) was based upon the AGM-84 Harpoon anti-ship missile and is now used with devastating precision as a stand-off replacement for the Vietnam era AGM-62 Walleye. It was trialled during the Gulf War. (McDonnell Douglas)

CVW-2 began launching coordinated night strikes at 0400hr on 17 January, only some 36hr after arriving on station in the Persian Gulf.

At VA-145 we were assigned twelve aircraft of which eight were A-6E SWIPs and the remaining four were A-6E TRAMs. We had no [KA-6D] tankers but we could fly the tanker mission if required employing the [D-704] buddy store and we did do some of that. However, we had S-3 tankers assigned to our air wing, and since we didn't have F/A-18s, there wasn't a huge tanking requirement. Everyone on squadron was SWIP-qualified, which basically meant that we had mastered the new weapons.

At VA-145 we focused primarily on the HARM because the other three weapons were not likely to be employed. However, there were only four of us that were qualified on the SLAM; even so, we were never tasked to exercise this mission. Nonetheless, during this period the SLAM software wasn't very user-friendly anyway. Unlike VA-75, which was the only other A-6E SWIP squadron, and flying off the USS *John F. Kennedy* in the Red Sea, we at VA-145 had the necessary [AWW-7] data-link pods and mission-planning capability and could guide our own weapons autonomously – they hadn't acquired this capability as yet.

Of the thirty-eight combat sorties I flew, only one was a dedicated SEAD mission. It occurred during the second night – 18/19 January – while air ops from USS *Ranger* were still being conducted at low-level.

The target on this night was the Iraqi port city of Umm Qasr, which housed a naval base that supported SSM-firing patrol boats and storage facilities for CSS-N-1 Silkworm SSMs that were employed for coastal defence. As such, CVW-2 had visited this location on the opening night – with great success. CVW-2 was tasked to revisit Umm Qasr on this second night to mine the mouth of the Khawr Az-Zubayr River in an effort to bottle up the harbour and thus keep any surviving Iraqi Navy vessels out of the Gulf.

Displaying the all-weather capability of the Intruder thanks to the unfavourable weather conditions, Eagle and his pilot Cdr (now Rear Admiral) Denby 'Heels' Starling, the squadron CO, were to provide SEAD coverage for a flight of four A-6Es that were tasked to deliver forty-two Mk36 Destructor mines. Flying in trail at 500ft, this was the first aerial mining operation since the Vietnam War.[14]

Our load-out was a pair of HARMs and a centreline tank – typical of a dedicated SEAD mission. As we were out over the water, air defences were minimal, but the closer you got to the beach the more intense it became. Upon reaching the launch area, we basically loitered and timed ourselves to arrive at the first shot point at a specific time. From there, we then had a specific amount of time to get to the next shot point. We took our two shots, which would hopefully keep the Iraqi heads down as the strike force ingressed the target, and then returned to the boat.

A few weeks into the conflict, the powers that be decided that the only Navy HARM-shooters would be the EA-6Bs. I think the reasoning was that certain shooters – and I won't name the aircraft type – were hosing off HARMs at an alarming rate based on false indications. Nevertheless, I know for a fact that it wasn't my squadron; we never went out on that sort of mission. As far as I know, every missile that our squadron fired was a PB shot, meaning we targeted a particular location and programmed the missile to look for a very specific threat. We did not take any shots that relied on the HARM seeker or our AN/ALR-67 as a sensor [in TOO mode].[15]

VA-145 lays claim to having fired the first naval aviation shot of Desert Storm – a HARM on the opening night. This was also the first HARM fired by an Intruder in combat. VA-145 also has claim to the first firing of four HARMs from a single A-6E during one mission. Apparently this had not even been attempted previously, even during testing. By the end of the conflict the 'Swordsmen' had expended thirty-three HARMs. During the course of Desert Storm VA-145 flew 681 combat missions and was credited with destroying (among numerous Iraqi Army pieces) forty-one naval vessels, twenty-three munitions bunkers and seven communication sites, plus numerous other vital targets.

LIEUTENANT PETE HUNT

*D*uring January 1991 A-6E Intruder pilot Lt Pete Hunt was assigned to VA-145 on USS Ranger. He would fly forty-five combat missions including one dedicated SEAD mission, and launched five HARMs during the 43-day air war.

Pete Hunt: I flew my first Desert Storm mission on 17 January, when my B/N, Lt Cdr Rivers Cleveland and I launched at about 0415hr. The initial plan tasked five A-6Es to execute a low-level strike against the Umm Qasr Navy Base, which was just north of Bubiyan Island. The Iraqi Navy had based its Soviet-built fleet of SSM-firing Osa IIs and captured TNC-45 patrol boats here and these vessels posed a serious threat to the Coalition armada that was operating in the confines of the Persian Gulf.

As one of our A-6Es was forced to abort, there were now only four aircraft – in trail – 1 minute apart and headed for the target. We were no. 3 in the formation as it ingressed at about 450kt at 400ft above the water. At approximately 15,000ft a package of support aircraft, which included a couple of EA-6Bs and a couple of SWIP A-6Es carrying four HARMs apiece, was ready to unleash a barrage on the targeted SAM sites. At the last minute, Intel had advised of a new SA-2 system that had become operational. As a result of this, there would have been a gap in the SEAD coverage. Since our squadron was SWIP-capable, it was decided to upload a HARM on one of the strike aircraft and attempt to take out the site during the low-level ingress to the primary target. The reasoning behind this was that there were no other assets that could be dedicated to this SAM site in particular, other than jammers which on their own were still very effective. Consequently, in addition to twelve Mk20 Rockeyes, our A-6E carried a single HARM.

Ironically, the whole concept of carrying a HARM on a strike-dedicated A-6E had actually been discouraged – strongly discouraged – by the expert tacticians at the Medium Attack Weapons School, as it was thought that the mission would become so complex that it would adversely affect the bombing mission. The SWIP was an add-on to an existing weapon delivery system and, as such, things had not been exactly streamlined. You had an old armament control panel that had been wired to the SWIP computer with its new exotic missiles. At that time, there were about thirteen steps involving switches and/or dials that had to be worked in some fashion to cycle back-and-forth between the bomb delivery mode and the HARM launch mode. It was nothing like in an F/A-18 where you flip a single switch on the stick – it was a very laborious process.

Chris 'Snax' Eagle: SWIP provided an extension to our weapons delivery capability, not a total upgrade. So even though the IMP was somewhat MFD-like, it only allowed us to programme missiles, not fire them. In addition to configuring the weapon via the IMP, we still had a (somewhat antiquated) mechanical switch and push-button armament control panel to deal with in order to actually fire them. There was no single air-to-air/air-to-ground mode switch like the F/A-18 has. So unlike modern cockpits full of MFDs, the B/N had to contend with at least four separate weapons select switches, each protected by its own rotating collar, and a couple of different push-buttons to change over from a missile attack to a bombing attack.

There were also eight switches that we call Interval, Quantity and Time, which had to be rolled over from HARM settings to Rockeye settings. A B/N may or may not have handled some of the switchology, but would also have been busy retargeting from their HARM target to their Rockeye target. The need to fire the HARM would have required the B/N to temporarily suspend his target acquisition efforts for his Rockeye target until the HARM was away. All that the SWIP panel (the IMP) really did was allow the HARM options to be programmed prior to launch; it did not make attack switchology any easier. In summary, if you only had one kind of ordnance to deliver on a given mission, things were not so bad, but if you had to deliver more than one type, the A-6 did not make it easy.

Pete Hunt: As I guided the aircraft through the low-level ingress, there was heavy triple-A and numerous SAMs launched, but I don't think any of them were guided. We were within the envelope of our targeted SA-2, but still outside that of the SA-6. We had a near constant SA-2 missile acquisition warning, indicating that we were being looked at, but there was only one very minor missile tracking (indicating a guiding missile in the air) that went away quickly. We used our full load-out of chaff; we didn't carry flares, as IR missiles are usually ineffective at night.

During the last 7 miles or 45–60 seconds from target, we were executing constant 3–4g turns to avoid the heavy streams of triple-A in the area and would ultimately pull 5g coming off target. However, anything over 2g and we'd lose our Terrain Clearance radar and radar altimeter. Added to this was the fact that it was night-time so we were pretty much task saturated. Consequently, it was standard procedure to run a chaff programme wherein chaff was dispensed automatically, say several times a second, pause for a period and then repeat. Mind you, I don't think we would have overlooked the expendables – the operating switch was right there on the throttle quadrant and every time you pulled g, chaff was instinctively dispensed.

As I was keeping a watch out for SAMs, Rivers was making the final preparations for missile launch. As both targets – the SA-2 radar and the port facility piers – were within minutes [approximately 23 miles] of one another, Rivers was very much engrossed during this leg of the ingress. Upon reaching our shot point, we launched our PB HARM from an altitude of just 400ft. This launch turned out to be the first by an A-6 in combat. We then quickly descended to about 250ft to avoid the triple-A because the arches seemed to meet the higher we went. Of course, it would have been a lot better in hindsight if we would have just been a lot higher!

Just seconds after our HARM shot, our supporting EA-6Bs and A-6Es unleashed their salvoes on the targeted SA-6 sites. About 3 miles from target, we climbed back to 400ft to allow for a better Rockeye dispersal – we could have delivered them at the lower altitude, but this would have provided less dispersal time. Rivers was still head-down as he surveyed the pier on the FLIR; initial target acquisition was accomplished with the radar with a hand-off to the FLIR. However, he quickly discovered that the boats we were after had sortied out. In fact, during our ingress we had observed several of them shooting at us prior to going wet-dry.

Since the boats weren't there, we flexed to our secondary target, the port facilities' communications and supply buildings, and scored a direct hit with our Rockeyes. And we acquired some indication from a supporting EA-6B that the targeted SA-2 radar signal did go down at about the time of the HARM impact – other than this, we had no other hard evidence. As for the boats, we eventually did get them all. As for

Lt Chris 'Snax' Eagle (now a lieutenant commander) and VA-145 'Swordsmen' CO LCdr (now rear admiral) Denby 'Heels' Starling (right). (Chris Eagle)

Lt Pete Hunt (left) and Lt Cdr Rivers Cleveland. (Pete Hunt)

whether or not the weapons school was correct in their assessment, the answer was simply stated, yes and no – as we were able to manage. Rivers and I, independent of the squadron, had actually been perfecting the arduous cycle process between missile mode and bomb mode during our transit to the Gulf. By coincidence, and because we had actually lobbied to get in on the initial strike, we found ourselves in a position to test our technique. When the SEAD element was added to the strike mission, everyone kind of looked at each other in a perplexed manner. However, having practised for this, Rivers and I stated without hesitation that we could do this. And although we had practised intensely, we still found ourselves mentally rehearsing the procedures while in the ready room just prior to walking out to the jet. There was a lot that could have gone wrong.

About 20hr after our first mission, we were at it again. However, this time we flew a dedicated SEAD mission. The flight was made up of three A-6Es uploaded with four HARMs apiece. We were supporting a strike against CSS-N-1 SSM sites in Kuwait. Our three-ship was tasked to launch twelve PB HARMs at precise times at an SA-2 and three SA-3 sites. We were loitering out over the water at high altitude and launched our missiles at 90-second intervals. The shot point for each launch was the same. Consequently, due to the limited amount of time between the four launches, I had to execute a constant 4g S-turn to get us back into firing position as expeditiously as possible. During the manoeuvring, Rivers was working the necessary switches and inputting the new data to set up the next shot. As said previously, this was a very challenging process to complete under normal conditions and carrying it out while executing a 4g turn didn't help matters any.

Although it was still a discouraged tactic, a single HARM was occasionally carried by our A-6Es. Rivers and I flew one more mission with the missile during early February because of a specific threat that was imaged and because there was no available SEAD. We carried the HARM in the SP mode for a quick reaction strike. However, the perceived threat didn't come up and consequently we brought the missile back to the boat.

Both Lt Pete Hunt and Lt Cdr Rivers Cleveland were awarded the Distinguished Flying Cross for their 17 January low-level strike against the Umm Qasr Navy Base.

As for radar site kills, Lt Cdr Eagle recalls that 'unless an EA-6B states that the target is active and boom, all of a sudden it shuts down and is not heard from again or you acquire corroborating imagery, you just didn't know if your HARM attack was successful. The fact that the emitter shut down really meant nothing – all the operator had to do was flip a switch. It was very difficult to confirm.'

Capt Joe 'Killer' Kilkenny, former A-6E pilot and VA-75 ops officer during Desert Storm (at the time of writing, he is CAG of CVW-3 onboard USS *Harry S. Truman*), notes that 'We typically fired more HARMs during the day to allow our A-7E squadrons to visually bomb and they shot more at night so we could radar/FLIR bomb.'

Altogether, US Navy A-6Es flew 4,824 combat sorties during Desert Storm, more than any other carrier aircraft. The ninety-six airframes involved averaged just over fifty missions each.[16] However, Desert Storm also turned out to be the A-6E squadrons' last shot. Post-Cold War budget cuts imposed by the Clinton administration meant that the A-6E fleet was quickly slated for retirement, despite SWIP and an aggressive carbon composite-based re-winging programme already under way to extend their fatigue lives.

The squadrons turned in their beloved reworked aircraft only to watch many being stripped down and dumped in the sea to help generate an artificial reef off the Florida coast. At the dual retirement ceremonies for the last two A-6E squadrons at NAS Oceana (VA-75) and NAS Whidbey Island (VA-196), held on 28 February 1997, a stupendous 1,700 A-6 pilots and B/Ns were present at Virginia Beach, and more than 1,000 in Oak Harbor, to toast their sad farewells.

BLOCK 80'S PROWLING

The A-6's Grumman stablemate the EA-6B provided essential electronic combat support throughout Desert Storm and is still the heart of the Fleet's electronic combat capability. In addition to twelve EA-6B ICAP-IIs operating on the beach with the US Marine Corps' MAG-11 at Sheikh Isa AB, support was furnished by six US Navy Electronic Attack squadrons (VAQs) which flew twenty-seven EA-6Bs, split between the veteran ICAP-II/Block 82 and newer Block 86 models. The latter had only entered service in June 1988 and were still very much in the work-up phase.

The force had begun reintroducing a COMJAM capability via the Rockwell-Collins AN/ASQ-191, and both models of the EA-6B could make full use of the Tactical EA-6B Mission Planning System (TEAMS) to programme the AN/ALQ-99 systems for individual mission needs, enabling more sophisticated cooperative jamming as well as being able to react to unexpected or pop-up threats more swiftly. It also permitted greater use of HARM, and this rapidly became the case in the EA-6B community which used it as a sensor as well as a weapon.

With some sixteen years' experience as an EA-6B ECMO, Lt Cdr Chris 'Quiver' Burgess is definitely an expert on the subject. During 1991 Chris was a lieutenant assigned to VAQ-131 onboard USS *Ranger*. During Desert Storm he flew thirty-five missions in support of CVW-2, and explains how the mission had progressed since the Vietnam era:

In a way the Gulf War was somewhat of a revival for the EA-6B community because prior to this, we had always been looked upon as the unwanted stepchildren of the air wing. What we did was pretty much intangible. However, after the initial strike of 17 January, all that changed – at least from my experiences. Soon after this first strike – a low-level strike – the strike leader, who happened to be the XO of one of the air wing's A-6E squadrons, approached me and shook my hand while asserting 'Thank God you guys were there', and continued to praise us for the great job we had done. He reported that the strike group had witnessed numerous missile launches, but said that none was tracking.

In essence, that was the first time for a majority of the guys who were dropping the bombs to actually witness tangible evidence of what it was we provided [for] the air wing. And this sort of adulation continued throughout the war. Nonetheless, VA-155, which was assigned to our air wing, did lose an A-6E; although heavy anti-aircraft fire was encountered, to this day no one really knows if it flew into the surface or was actually shot down.

The EA-6B was designed specifically for electronic warfare or tactical jamming, which the US Navy has now termed Electronic

An ES-3A Shadow electronic-surveillance machine on deck. These aircraft were assigned to VQ-5 'Shadows' and VQ-6 'Black Ravens' for ship- and shore-based surveillance during the 1990s, supplementing the EP-3E ARIES II fleet. S-3 Vikings performed TALD dropping and even bombing during the Gulf War. (Frank B. Mormillo)

An EA-6B on detachment to NAS Fallon, Nevada, demonstrates the EA/ES mix of football receiver, underwing jammer and HARM missile. The Prowler remains the most flexible HARM targeting platform flying today. (Frank B. Mormillo)

Attack (EA). This mission was once called ECM, but we don't call it this anymore – ECM is now just EA. In addition, we also conduct Electronic Surveillance (ES), which was ESM. Consequently, what we do in our dogma, so to speak, is deny, degrade and deceive – not having touched upon the fact that we can also shoot missiles. These are the types of activities we employ to bewilder a radar operator who is attempting to acquire a tracking solution to prosecute a target.

In addition to EA and ES, the EA-6B also has a hard kill capability by way of the HARM. However, as for going out and hunting for targets like the dedicated Wild Weasels of old, we don't really play that game. This is not what the EA-6B was designed to do. The Wild Weasels had equipment that was much quicker and much more accurate at finding the locations of radar sites. However, with that said, we do have the ability to react to pop-up threats.

Essentially what we are attempting to achieve is to buy a window or umbrella of protection of 3–4 minutes by employing all our capabilities, which should allow a strike package to get in, prosecute their targets and get out again. During that 3–4 minutes, that's when they would be flying through the lethal threat area; and what we're talking about is primarily the SAM threat. Realistically, there is nothing that can be done about triple-A – which is more deadly than missiles – except for maybe avoiding it. Nonetheless, depending on what the threat is, we still practise low-level ingress techniques.

Your generic integrated air defence system functions something like this: you've got a big picture EW radar that sweeps 360deg or possibly 180deg, but either way it's a big slice of the pie. Generally speaking, the EW radars will hand off a track solution to a TTR, which is a smaller sector, say 10–15deg wide, which will sweeten up the solution with information such as airspeed, altitude and other variables.

The ultimate goal is to hand off the track to engagement radar, which is best described as a pencil beam illuminating the target with very high energy. This is what's employed to guide the missile to the intended target. What we do, what's our bread and butter, is to take away that EW picture. You sort of force everyone into an autonomous mode where they are looking at the world through a straw. This makes it very difficult and very time-consuming for them to pick up good targeting solutions on aerial targets, and this is where the deny or degrade capability comes into play.

Generally, the old way of thinking is the use of brute force as you try to put snow on their radar screens. Typically, radar returns are not real strong signals anyway. So if you raise the threshold of the noise around the target, it's real easy to drown out the real return and this kind of jamming is relatively easy to counter. In order to see through this kind of jamming, the stuff that the victim radar can do to accomplish this is very unsophisticated. Consequently, we now employ other techniques that are somewhat more deceptive.

Such techniques include using two or more displaced EA-6Bs coordinating their noise- or angle-deception jamming, blocking the separate co-located antennae at the same time on different frequencies; and in the event of a SAM launch, alternating their output between them in the tracking frequencies, even mimicking any enemy radar blinking, so that enemy SAMs are given a target to chase that appears to shift about the sky, making them constantly change course and run out of energy more quickly.

Lt Cdr Chris Burgess explains the new edge the HARM has provided the EA-6B Prowler:

Basically what makes the Prowler unique as far as employing the HARM [is that] we can fire the missile in *all* of its modes – we are not just working from a pre-programmed DA number; we have the ability to programme the missile. We can monitor the environment in real time and create a specific DA number as warranted; we can also modify an existing one. It has been stated in a complimentary, and in an uncomplimentary, manner that the Prowler fires its HARMs by committee. With a four-person crew, there are more brains working at figuring out what's going on.

Although the ECMOs rotate through the three seats, I preferred to be in the back, because from there you're pretty much running the show. It is ECMOs 3 and 4, in the back seats, who are the warfighters as they intercept, analyse and identify the threat in real time and then tailor the missile to seek out a specific signal or signals. No other aircraft can do that. The backseaters then send the information to the HARM control panel, which is located up front with ECMO 1, who also works communications, navigation and countermeasures. ECMO 1 then throws a couple of switches, thus passing on the information to the HARM, and then the pilot completes the process by pulling the trigger.

As we were operating out of the Persian Gulf during Desert Storm, we were able to generate a greater number of sorties; and since our

HARM DA NUMBERS
ECMO LIEUTENANT COMMANDER CHRIS BURGESS

EA-6B Prowler ECMO Lt Cdr Chris Burgess explains how the aircraft offers a far more flexible launch platform than the routine US Navy attack jets by being able to flex through Direct Attack (DA) numbers and reprogramme the HARM in-flight in response to changing threats; something it has grown ever more capable of doing since Desert Storm with the fielding of more capable Blocks of the HARM and the EA-6B.

When we conduct operations, it's usually preplanned. There is a standard list of what are termed DA numbers, which are pre-programmed commands for a PB HARM strike. The data for a DA number is usually acquired by way of the various Elint platforms that monitor and map out the EOB of an enemy air defence system. The precise location of a SAM site would be pinpointed, and it would also be classified by its radar emission characteristics. A programme for the HARM would then be written and assigned a DA number, which would specifically target the known frequencies of the radar emitters associated with the targeted site. For example, an SA-6 is a semi-active, guided SAM. It's linked with a specific illuminator radar, a specific TTR and a specific acquisition radar in addition to a couple of other items that are part and parcel of the overall weapon system – each emits its own distinct signal. Therefore, if operating in the area where the aforementioned SAM system is radiating, the appropriate DA number would be inputted into the HARM control panel, which would forward the data to the missile. The HARM can be then programmed to seek out the acquisition radar first and, if not found, then the tracker radar. If the first two were not found it could then move on and target the illuminator radar. In essence, we can set up a flexing logic for the missile in countless numbers of ways. We can have missile flex from one signal to another and in any order or priority we want.

In an F/A-18 [with the later Blocks of HARM], the pilot inputs what is referred to as a Pre-Brief number into the CLC and the HARM is provided with the particulars of the perceived threat radar(s) that may be encountered in the target area. And that's about the level of sophistication. When working from a pre-programmed DA number, it's very canned. Upon launching a missile, if the weapon system programmed into the missile is up you'll probably hit it. On the other hand the Prowler can employ its receivers to find out what's actually out there and *then* target it. This aspect makes the Prowler more capable with the HARM because we can monitor the environment in real time and create a specific DA number, and we can also modify an existing one.

missions were somewhat shorter than those operating from the Red Sea, we typically flew with three jamming pods, one missile and a drop tank. We had organic tanking from our air wing's A-6Es [equipped with buddy stores] and S-3As. If we needed additional gas there were all kinds of Air Force refuelling tracks up there as well; there was pretty much gas everywhere. I even remember plugging off a Canadian CC-137-cum-Boeing 707 tanker one night. With that said, tanking is a real inconvenience, so if we don't need to do it – we don't. We almost without exception had enough gas to go on a 1hr 45 minute cycle during which we'd support our mission and return without having to tank – which was nice. It's a great capability, but no one enjoys it.

As USS *Ranger* was designated as the night carrier within our carrier battle group, our situation was somewhat unique in that nearly 80 per cent of our missions were conducted at night, which I really liked because you could see if you were being shot at. During the air wing's first strike, which commenced at approximately 0430hr on that January morning, every HARM launched by our squadron was on a timeline – meaning they were pre-briefed.

There was no mystery to going out and executing a timeline. You just had to be on your game to get the airplane pointed in the right direction at the correct airspeed and altitude so that the impact of the missile coincided with the arrival of the strikers in the SAM threat rings. It didn't matter if we observed that a radar we were targeting wasn't emitting. We put the missiles in the air. They were all pre-briefed – there were HARMs raining down on the enemy with the intention of achieving a hard kill. However, if the radar operators were afraid that missiles were inbound and shut down their radar, thus denying the HARMs guidance, this in essence helped us achieve our goal.

During the first few days of combat, we had one Prowler return to USS *Ranger* with a missile and our skipper was not impressed over the fact that the crew couldn't find *something* to shoot at! The mind-set within the squadron was: we're at war, let's be at war, let's employ these weapons. We expended a number of HARMs – quickly – during the initial days of Desert Storm; in total, VAQ-131 fired twenty-four during forty-three days of combat. However, not long after the shooting began, maybe 7–10 days, the Navy became somewhat restrictive with regards to what was required to launch a HARM. Some thought we were going to run out of them if we kept expending them at the current pace. [By 20 January about a thousand HARMs had been launched by US Navy, Air Force and Marine Corps shooters.] Consequently, the criteria, or ROE, for a HARM launch were elevated slightly.

For a Prowler to shoot a HARM, we had to intercept a signal; we then had to have an external source verify that signal. The best source out there was the RC-135 Rivet Joint, which is a much more capable ES platform. We would contact the RJ via a secure radio and advise them that we had what we believed to be a particular SAM designation at a particular bearing from our present position, and enquire as to what they had observed. They'd take a couple of seconds, and then concur that they too had an identical signal radiating from the same location. That's all we needed; this was deemed a second verification, so we were then cleared to engage the site.

Although it sounds simple, this was hardly the case. In the cockpit, there was another radio going, in addition to cockpit conversation, so it did get pretty hectic. The whole concept was pretty interesting.

During one of the few day missions I flew, we were supporting an F-14A conducting a tactical reconnaissance mission as it flew along

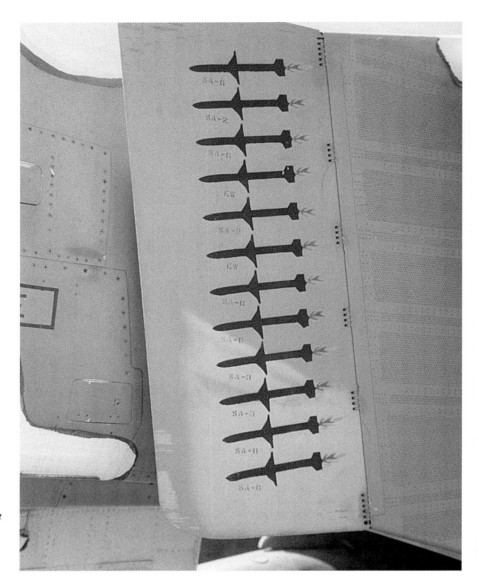

This jet proudly bears a dozen radar kills, half of them SA-6s, but including early warning radar and SA-2/3 from its Gulf War days. (McDonnell Douglas via John J. Harty)

the Kuwaiti coast in search of CSS-N-1 Silkworm SSMs. Our mission plan called for us to basically fly out over the Gulf, abeam the Tomcat. We were not jamming, but listening for any engagement radars that came up to threaten the Tomcat. In this case, we were sort of in the reactive HARM mode, where we were going to react to the environment – there was nothing pre-emptive going on here.

Somewhere in the middle of this south-to-north track, we intercepted an SA-6 signal. I was the mission commander, sitting in my favourite spot – in the back. ECMO 1 got on the radio with the Rivet Joint in an effort to acquire verification and as soon as he did, we launched the missile. Employing the aircraft's receiver, we can programme it to lock on to the frequency. So as soon as the HARM came off the rail, we were provided with a countdown to impact. If at the impact time, the signal goes dead, you then had a pretty good indication that you'd hit the source of that signal; this is what's termed an electronic BDA. But this doesn't always work, as there are various issues that will affect this procedure.

If jamming, the Prowler's ability to receive is degraded, because our own jamming will interfere with our receivers. So if that's going on, it's tougher to accomplish this. The other issue is that it's very difficult to be 100 per cent positive that you are 'slued' to what you think you're slued to – that is, you're listening to what you think you are listening to. Mind you, you got really good at it after being in theatre a while. We had another method of achieving a secondary verification wherein we could actually verify the target ourselves without assistance from another platform. By utilizing the HARM's seeker head while it's still on the rail, we were able to accomplish this task. Although it was kind of a gray area, just the same we had two different sources confirming a radar source. The first source was by way of the aircraft's receiver suite through the ECMO's interface and the second source was the missile identifying it as the same signal – and that was good enough as these were two completely independent systems.[17]

On 28 February 1992 all Coalition operations were suspended to give the Iraqis an opportunity to sign a cease-fire agreement. The war was over. During an intense six-week campaign Coalition air forces had flown more than 116,000 sorties for the loss of thirty-seven fixed-wing aircraft to hostile causes (twenty-eight of them US), not counting twenty-three helicopters and a further fifteen jets stricken by operational causes. Iraq's IADS had been dealt a severe blow, and (according to US CENTCOM figures dated 7 March) the Iraqi Army was decimated.[18]

While the air war was a huge success and achieved its original objectives, it merely marked the beginning of what has evolved into a constant patrolling of large sectors of Iraqi airspace, with both sides taking pot-shots at one another. The process began on 6 April 1991 with the formation of Task Force Provide Comfort, initiated to furnish protection and humanitarian relief for the Kurdish refugees who were being persecuted by the Hussein regime. Operation Provide Comfort (restyled Operation Northern Watch on 1 January 1997) introduced a No-Fly Zone (NFZ) north of the 36th Parallel, using air power operating from Incirlik AB in Turkey.

It became formalized under UN Security Council Resolution 688, which came into being during 1992. This simultaneously called for the enforcement of a NFZ south of the 32nd Parallel, both to protect Iraq's Shiite Muslim minority, the so-called Marsh Arabs, and to prevent a build-up of Iraqi ground forces in the south of the country. It was later extended to the 33rd Parallel, a mere 24 or so miles south of Baghdad.

From 26 August 1992 the mission became Operation Southern Watch, known to the crews as SWATCH. CENTAF was duly reorganized after Desert Storm during the Desert Calm wind-down, with the principal SWATCH SEAD assets comprising TDY EF-111A and F-4G units under the local command of the 4404th CW(P) at Dhahran AB. Both north and south NFZ forces worked with naval aviation, and a sizeable contingent of British and French aircraft.

A 561st F-4G patrols the Iraqi No-Fly Zone, brandishing AGM-88 HARMs, three fuel bags, and a long AN/ALQ-184 jamming pod. Note also the inner-wing pylon AN/ALE-40 chaff/flare modules. The shiny Hill Gray II monochrome camouflage scheme (named after Hill AFB, Utah, where it originated during Phantom maintenance at Ogden) was introduced in 1987 and stayed with the Advanced Wild Weasel right through to retirement. (Mike Pietrucha)

PHANTOMS PHOREVER!

Capt Mike 'Starbaby' Pietrucha, US Air Force (Ret), the last ever EWO to graduate from Wild Weasel school and the last to accrue 1,000hr on the F-4G, explained its mission capabilities from the backseater's perspective – what he called Fighting from the Pit – during the type's climactic final years of service in the Gulf region:

It's no secret that one of the reasons for the success of all the Wild Weasel variants was the fact that they were all two-seaters, with an EWO in the back. In addition to having another set of eyes and brains, the EWOs had a good deal of specialized training that gave them a solid knowledge of enemy radar systems. The back seat of the F-4G was designed to provide the EWO with the information needed for effective targeting of the threats. As the last of the 'Baby Weasels', I never flew with either the AN/APR-38 or the steam-driven LN-12 INS – I was lucky to see only the AN/APR-47 and the AN/ARN-101 INS.

When I went through the Weasel school in 1991, we had just received OFP 7000 software for the -47, which was a major upgrade for the system. The software added a bunch of new features, and made the system entirely software programmable. We continued the upgrades with OFPs 8000 and 9000 before the F-4G Wild Weasel was retired, which not only kept the system current, but also advanced the capabilities beyond anything else on the planet.

The Phantom II was an ergonomic nightmare, and the F-4G was no exception, although some efforts in that area had been made. There was no forward visibility from the back, although some jets later received the RCP visibility mod, which repositioned some instruments and allowed the EWO to see some cables, and pass a granola bar or piddle pack to the front seat. Most of the work was done between the knees, on the radar scope, or right up at eye-level on the AN/APR-47.

The AN/APR-47 was both a traditional RWR and an Elint package all rolled into one. The PPI scope presented a threat display from one to fifteen symbols, which could be sorted by type (i.e. non-threat radars could be filtered out) and displayed on a variable-range scale. The PAN [panoramic] scope presented the entire electronic order of battle – every radar beam that was out there – and was a great help in counting beams (some radars have up to six). The attack scope was rarely used, and the oscilloscope feature on that scope almost never. Numerous other lights and read-outs allowed the EWO to view specific parameters of any given system. The pilot got a smaller-size repeater version of the PPI, and nothing else.

Often overlooked is the audio analysis feature. EWOs generally listened to the threats one at a time. While the computer does most of the threat ID, there are many radars that overlap parametrically; that is, they have similar fingerprints. In many cases, the computer cannot tell the difference, but the EWOs (and many experienced pilots) were able to ID the threats by listening. The SA-2's Fan Song radar, for example, often appears like an air traffic control radar. However, the Fan Song's distinctive rattlesnake sound makes the difference immediately obvious. In some cases the EWO could not only ID the radar, but tell which mode it was in, gaining valuable warning time when a radar switched into a threatening mode.

The AN/APR-47's great benefit from the offensive point of view was its unique ability to locate threats geographically. It was able to get very precise azimuth and elevation definition. As time went on, the system would automatically triangulate multiple cuts as the aircraft moved, thereby determining location. Obviously, the more arc that the F-4G flew (both horizontally and vertically) relative to the target emitter, the faster the system would range. I have seen solutions come up so fast that the symbol first appeared on the scope with a range solution already determined.

Of particular note was that the system could be entirely programmed from the cockpit. Any function, from the threat tables, which listed the threats that the system would scan for, to the display symbols could be entirely reprogrammed from the cockpit in a timely manner. This gained the F-4G the instantaneous ability to flex while airborne, without the need for depot-level reprogramming or even mission support system assistance.

As is the case with all fighter missions, the briefing sets the stage. The crews are briefed on the enemy threat array, on any other support, and on any strike package that they are tasked to support. Package details include number and type of aircraft, attack axis, altitude, weapons, TOT and egress plan. Times are important, for they determine when a flight of strikers will become vulnerable to the threat. The lead EWO will brief the targeting plan, which generally includes criteria for taking a HARM shot, and a target sort, in which the no. 1 aircraft accepts primary responsibility for some threats and passes responsibility for others to the wingmen.

The sort is crucial to prevent Weasels from double-targeting a single system in a time-critical environment. Sort could be by system type, location, or any other method; one EWO at Spangdahlem AB assigned the following priorities: 'Old EWO, old SAMs; new EWO, new SAMs'. Programming changes to the Weasel's baseline software are also briefed, as are system settings and the plan for working with degraded equipment.

Weasels generally practised reactive SEAD; that is, they reacted to the presence of threats active in the target area. The great advantage of this was that the EWO was able to take advantage of the AN/APR-47 to get maximum effect out of his (generally) two HARMs. We only planned on using them against threats that were actively radiating, thus increasing the probability of hitting the right guy. The trick was determining which of the potential targets was a threat to the strikers, and was therefore worth a shot. A short-range divisional air defence system like the Roland was no threat to guys dropping from 24,000ft, and a Fan Song 30 miles away from the strikers could radiate all day for all the good he was going to do.

HARMs had a 360-deg footprint and could be shot against a target in any position relative to the shooter, but large turns used valuable missile energy and burned up time. HARM shots were generally made from the back, as the pilot could not hand off data to the HARM. Pilots got a veto over any shot, which was important if the flight lead was out in front, or any other condition that was not immediately obvious from the back. We really employed the HARM in two modes: Range Known (EOM mode) and Range Unknown (SP mode).

Range Known shots were by far the better option, and allowed very precise targeting at longer ranges. Range Unknown shots, while less specific, might be taken where somebody was in danger and there was no time to wait for a range solution. PB shots, taken against a non-emitting target, were rarely taken and even more rarely successful. When a PB shot is taken, the crew is betting that the threat is where it was briefed to be, and that a threat will be on the air during the HARM's flight; they are long odds for a betting man.

While I've emphasized the AN/APR-47 and HARM, it's worth noting that the AGM-65 Maverick was employed during the Gulf War. The HARM outranges about 90 per cent of the SAMs in the world today, the Maverick is outranged by about 90 per cent. Still, it doesn't need an emitting target, and it does kill what it hits. The radar scope served a dual purpose and could be used to display the Maverick seeker. Mavericks could be controlled and shot from either cockpit.

The AN/APR-47 was not the only important piece of equipment run from the back. The radar, ECM, chaff (and sometimes flares) and INS controls were all resident in the back seat (not to mention some 250 circuit-breakers). Recalling the Phantom II's legacy as a US Navy interceptor, the radar was run from the back, as the pilot's controls were limited to an auto-acquisition switch and a cage button. The auto-acquisition generally didn't work worth a damn, and a good pilot could talk the EWO on to a target quicker than the auto-acquisition could find one.

The AN/APQ-120 was a Vietnam-era pulsed radar with a one-bar raster scan and less computing power than my digital watch, but was an absolute necessity for an aircraft that used the AIM-7 as its self-protection missile. The ECM pods, either an AN/ALQ-184 or AN/ALQ-131, were mounted in the left front missile well with the control unit in the back seat. Three switch positions and eight buttons made for up to twenty-four possible combinations. The -184 wasn't particularly smart, and the EWO had to dial in the jamming technique that he wanted. The -131 was pretty bright, and had two automatic modes that only required selective use of the ON/STBY/OFF switch. The AN/ALE-40 chaff/flare dispenser controls were in the back, but the pilot was normally given control of the flares while the EWO handled chaff.

With such a demanding mission and a busy cockpit, crew coordination was crucial in the fight; the pilot is not just a bus driver, although that joke was often made. While the EWO selected the victims, the pilot had to get the weapons system in position to support the strikers while simultaneously avoiding hazards. The mission was not to avoid the threats, but it never paid to discount them either.

Some crews worked better than others did simply because some personalities meshed. I flew best with Dave 'Santa' Lucia and Dennis 'Malf' Malfer because of our respective personalities, but they were not the only excellent pilots in the F-4G. After a little time, you got to know your crewmate pretty well, and then a little situational awareness goes a long way. In some cases communication between Malf and I consisted of an exchange like 'um', 'yeah' and we were on our way. I also knew always to carry an extra piddle pack for him, and a spare granola bar (because he was difficult when hungry).

All things considered (including the rotten visibility), the F-4G was a fun office. The mission was demanding, but Weasel squadrons and crews were something else, and I'm afraid their like will not be seen again.[19]

Rotations of F-4G crews came from both the 561st FS and 81st FS, the Tactical prefix having been dropped in October 1991 as a result of the merger of SAC and TAC into the new, unified Air Combat Command (ACC). However, on 30 June 1992 the 561st FS was deactivated as part of the closure of George AFB, leaving the 81st FS, under the command of Lt Col Dan Shelor, as the only active-duty F-4G squadron in the US Air

Force inventory. In place of the 561st FS, the 190th FS, Idaho ANG at Boise Air Terminal (Gowen Field), traded in its RF-4Cs for F-4Gs, with some thirty-one examples passing through its hands.[20] Between them, the two squadrons continued to provide crews and aircraft on rotation in support of Provide Comfort and SWATCH, until yet another switch came about.

On 29 December 1992 HQ USAFE formally announced that the 81st FS F-4Gs would transfer to Nellis AFB and the newly reactivated 561st TFS, which was formally resurrected on 1 February 1993 under 57th Wing control. Aircraft and crews were reassigned to Nellis AFB on return from TDY in South-West Asia, and the squadron eventually had some twenty-nine F-4Gs on strength. That same February the 81st FS reacquired F-16Cs. Finally, on 15 January 1994, Spangdahlem AB hosted its 'Pharewell Phantom' ceremony. Command baton of the 561st FS, initially under Lt Col Dave Constantine, had passed to veteran EWO Col Jim Uken, who continued to hold the fort for a further three years until 9 January 1996, when he led the last F-4G SWATCH mission, symbolically flying 69-7232 – the first F-4G to have entered Kuwaiti airspace during Desert Storm, and credited with five SAM kills when flown by Uken and his pilot.

For the 561st FS's farewell to the Phantom ceremony in April 1996, F-4G 69-7295 wore this unique shark's mouth. The F-4G is missed by many and represented the last true Wild Weasel in USAF service. (McDonnell Douglas via John J. Harty)

When the F-4G finally bowed out of active service eleven weeks later, Col Uken led the last eight of the unit's F-4Gs to the Aerospace Maintenance and Regeneration Center (formerly MASDC) at Davis-Monthan AFB on 26 March. On 20 April, in subsequent ceremonies, the 190th FS bade a sad farewell to the venerable F-4G, closing its own illustrious eighteen-year chapter and the US Air Force's thirty-three year front-line relationship with the McDonnell Douglas do-it-all fighter.

On 25 June 1996, two months after the retirement of the F-4G, and entirely unrelated to it, a massive terrorist truck bomb demolished the Khobar Towers apartment building in Dhahran, killing 19 airmen and wounding some 500 other US personnel. As a result, by October SWATCH HQ and aircraft were redeployed to the remote, high-security Prince Sultan AB (P-SAB) at Al Kharj, which had evolved from its early 'Tent City' origins into a fully fledged complex with extensive amenities, with operations coming under the jurisdiction of the 363rd AEW. Today additional facilities exist at Eskan Village, near Riyadh.

As its current commander Gen Allen G. Peck noted, Southern Watch maintains a routine through randomized scheduling of operations, varying day and night flying, the number of days in a row that flying continues, and other procedures to guarantee that 'there are no patterns Saddam Hussein could use to anticipate . . . where we'll be'. Liaison is maintained with Northern Watch at Incirlik AB via a hotline between the two HQs, established by Brig Gen David A. Deptula during his command tour there in 1998–9. Aircrews are now hooked into the system through secure communications and can get clearance to fire on a reactive basis within seconds of reporting hostile enemy activity.

The proof of the pudding came during Operation Desert Fox, a four-day punitive campaign against Baghdad's military and outlying Republican Guard facilities by US naval aviation and long-range bombers and cruise missiles. Orchestrated by Marine General Anthony C. Zinni and initiated on 16 December 1998, the operation was launched as a result of continued Iraqi intransigence in preventing UN personnel from performing their weapons inspection duties. The SEAD supportive effort closely mirrored the opening sequences of Desert Storm, but on a much smaller scale. Eighteen communications and EW radar nodes were struck, along with sixteen SAM sites, including SA-6 units and hybrid, modernized SA-2/-3 Tiger Song radar systems which used a mix of Vietnam-era and modern Western computer technology. The new Tiger Song radar system had gone undetected until RC-135s tuned into them.

34 AD targets in Desert Storm

As was expected, the only robust challenge came from Iraqi triple-A, which fortunately inflicted no casualties. The key SEAD elements comprised two EA-6B and six F/A-18C squadrons flying from the aircraft carriers USS *Enterprise* and USS *Constellation*. Although a limited action in its own right, Desert Fox effectively initiated an ongoing aerial offensive against the Iraqi IADS in the NFZ sectors which has witnessed Allied aircraft becoming embroiled in a series of DEAD (Destruction of Enemy Air Defences) actions, and a litany of successful SAM kills.

Between Desert Fox and late 2000, Iraq fired triple-A and SAMs or committed other violations against patrolling aircraft on more than 700 occasions. One particular Iraqi tactic became known as the SAMbush: the

Iraqi Air Force would launch Mirage F1 or MiG-23 interceptors against patrolling aircraft only to turn away, but in the direction of a newly positioned SAM or triple-A site. With 110 sites and a not insignificant number of interceptors to employ, Iraq has had plenty of leeway to continue conducting this nuisance game. A total of 221 provocative acts were recorded in 2000.

The latest major round of action at the time of writing, conducted during a 3hr raid beginning on Friday 16 February 2001 in response to some sixty-five threatening actions by Iraq since the beginning of the year, including fourteen SAM firings, took twenty-four US and British aircraft to the edge of the 33rd Parallel. These struck five separate Command, Control, Communications and Computing (C4) targets, including Tall King and Volex long-range surveillance radars linked by new fibre-optic communications. C4 and SAM radar facilities were struck at Al Taqaddum, Taji and in downtown Baghdad, along with control stations at An Numaniyah (within the SWATCH area) and As Suwayrah.

Four RAF Tornadoes flying from Kuwait hit Al Numaniyah with Paveway LGBs, whereas the US aircraft employed stand-off weapons, including new GPS-NAVSTAR-guided AGM-154 Joint Service Stand-Off Weapon (JSOW) glide bombs, to reach their more northerly targets. Launched by F/A-18C Hornets operating from USS *Harry S. Truman*, thirty still-experimental JSOWs were dropped, two of which went astray while a further twenty-six missed the intended aimpoints by tens of feet because of slightly incorrect pre-flight mission profiling, but nonetheless still inflicted damage by means of their cluster submunition warheads, which punched holes in soft targets such as radar dishes, control vans and launchers.

Stand-off Land Attack Missiles, Extended Response (SLAM-ER) derivatives of the Harpoon ASM hit their targets bang-on. F-15Es flying from Ahmed al Jaber AB in Kuwait employed AGM-130s to hit the harder command nodes with pinpoint accuracy. SAM and triple-A opposition was completely unguided, and supporting EA-6Bs and F-16CJs fired no HARMs.

For diplomatic reasons the Saudis have insisted on strict rules regarding how P-SAB and its other facilities may be used in support of NFZ activity, so as not to appear too heavy handed to other Arab nations. This has meant only AAMs and HARMs can be employed from Saudi soil, along with jammers and tankers as they are considered purely defensive. If US or British units require the use of GPS-aided fourth-generation J-series weapons, or third-generation LGBs, they must operate from Kuwait instead.[21] Similar restrictions have been imposed by Turkey regarding Northern Watch activities flown out of Incirlik AB.

The net effect of NFZ activity is that the US has firmly shifted its attention away from Northern Europe for the time being, and will continue to focus on Africa and the Persian Gulf for the foreseeable future, alongside that traditional potential trouble-maker North Korea. One other theatre has recently caught its attention: the Balkans, in which it has provided continued SEAD, EA and ES support as part of its commitment to NATO.

S E V E N

SIXTEEN-SHOOTERS

B y the late 1990s the US Air Force's leading-edge theatre SEAD capability had became refocused on a trio of fast-reacting platforms. Central to this new electronic triad is the Boeing/Raytheon RC-135V/W Rivet Joint, which furnishes real-time Elint from stand-off orbits using its 'vacuum cleaner' electronic surveillance equipment, and hands off targets for the kill to the Lockheed-Martin F-16CJ via an <u>improved data-link modem (IDM)</u>. Grumman E-8 JointSTARS radar-mapping aircraft are also in the process of being intranetted via IDM, capable of plotting mobile triple-A and SAM pieces by means of synthetic aperture radar technology and MTI processing, and directing strikers on to them before they can scurry for cover.

While outwardly similar at first glance to its limited-capability Desert Storm Block 10–30 predecessors, the new F-16CJ – the fighter element in the triad – represents the pinnacle of LWF development. The Wild Weasels no longer officially exist since the disbandment of the F-4G community, yet the crew chiefs of the 35th FW at Misawa AB replaced their MJ tailcodes with the famous WW in June 1996, in recognition of their SEAD

The majestic RC-135V Rivet Joint banking away from the tanker, post AAR top-up. (USAF/TSgt Donald McMichael)

tasking. Even a brief glance at the 35th FW's squadron buildings will remind anyone who knows the time-honoured *Cave Putorium!* and other Vietnam-era Wild Weasel mottos, that this tradition thrives among the F-16CJ squadrons. Between 1994 and July 1997 ten F-16CJ squadrons formed at five bases:

20th FW, Shaw AFB, South Carolina
55th FS 'Fighting Fifty-Fifth'
77th FS 'Gamblers'
78th FS 'Bushmasters'
79th FS 'Tigers'

35th FW, Misawa AB, Japan
13th FS 'Panthers'
14th FS 'Fightin' Samurai'

52nd FW, Spangdahlem AB, Germany
22nd FS 'Stingers'
23rd FS 'Fighting Hawks'

169th Wing, McEntire ANGB, South Carolina
157th FS 'Swamp Foxes'

Misawa-based F-16CJs perform a formation break for the camera. (LMTAS)

366th Wing, Mountain Home AFB, Idaho
389th FS 'Thunderbolts'

F-16CJ 'Fighting Hawks' taxi from their revetments at Spangdahlem, Germany. (USAF)

The squadrons employ F-16CJs from one of two slightly different production blocks fitted with whopping <u>29,000lb class Increased Performance Engines first delivered in May 1993</u>. The Block 50D is powered by the GE(USA) F110-GE-129, and can be distinguished by its larger air inlet to 'optimize the performance of the higher airflow GE engine,' according to a press release dated June 1999, while and the Block 52D, with the standard F-16 engine air inlet module, is powered by the Pratt & Whitney/United Technologies F100-PW-229. Although equipped with the Loral AN/ALR-56M RWR, able to give a cut on a threat of just a few degrees, the true heart of the F-16CJ's SEAD avionics is the inlet-mounted Texas Instruments AN/ASQ-213 HARM Targeting System (HTS) pod – sometimes called the Weasel in a can – which offers automated forward hemisphere radar-targeting that is sufficiently accurate for Range Known HARM attack.[1]

First in the series was the HTS R5 model, which provided a basic capability. This achieved IOC during 1994 and got its first taste of action the following year, when Spangdahlem AB's <u>23rd FS flew SEAD patrols from Incirlik AB</u> in support of Operation Provide Comfort. That August, ten of the squadron's F-16CJs were redeployed to Aviano AB, Italy, as part of Operation Deny Flight over the Balkans, the aim of which was to keep primarily Bosnian-Serb forces at bay in an effort to quieten the region, ravaged by civil war since 1991. Deny Flight dated back to <u>12 April 1993</u>, when the UN passed Resolution 816, establishing a NFZ over Bosnia in support of the UN Protection Force; as attacks within the safe havens continued, so Resolution 836 was passed to sanction the use of force, principally air power.

SEEN AS A PRECURSOR TO USE OF GROUND FORCE

However, on 29 August 1995 Deny Flight quickly erupted into Operation Deliberate Force in response to a Bosnian-Serb mortar attack on a civilian market in Sarajevo. The punitive counter-strike was planned by Maj Gen Hal Hornberg, director of NATO's 5th ATAF at the Combined Air Operations Centre (CAOC) at Dal Molin AB near Vincenza, in northern Italy. Immediately after midnight on 30 August the leading strike package, code-named Dead Eye Southeast, engaged fifteen targets in the Serbian IADS, from Neveslaje, near Mostar, to Bijeljina, near Tuzla, including radars, SAM sites and command bunkers. The first NATO wave comprised fourteen SEAD jets from USS *Theodore Roosevelt*, plus backstage EC-130-Compass Call. This package was followed by LGB interdiction attacks and CAS strikes by Strike Packages Alpha–Echo.

29
Aug
1995

The raids were a complete success, the only loss being a French Air Force Dassault-Breguet Mirage 2000N, hit by an SA-7 MANPAD, its two-man crew ejecting and being taken prisoner. Launched throughout the day, bombing was completed by 1910hr. It is believed that US Marine WSO Capt Troy 'Tonto' Ardese, flying in a fast-FAC HARM-toting F/A-18D from VMFA(AW)-533 'Hawks' based at Aviano AB, helped achieve the first successful HARM radar kill in the Balkans.

The F-16CJs of the 23rd FS soon began flying daily missions in support of ongoing NATO strike packages, inheriting the SEAD job from USS *Theodore Roosevelt*, which was in the process of departing from its station in the Adriatic. Interdiction attacks by then were focused on Serbian ammunition depots, command bunkers and Udbina airfield. Enemy radar activity had long since reverted to sporadic transmissions, but on 8 September the squadron achieved its first F-16CJ HARM kill in response to being locked on to by a Serb radar. The following day the squadron took on the Serbian IADS around Banja Luka, in north-west Bosnia, while providing cover for F-15Es sent in to destroy a communications facility with GBU-15 E-O glide bombs.

Nine HARMs were expended by the F-16CJ pilots during the course of some 160 sorties against Serbian radars provocatively illuminating NATO aircraft, with most firings occurring on 8–9 September. The results remain unknown, but there were no losses to SA-6s or to strategic SAMs. By the end of the month the Serbs began pulling back their armour and heavy guns from the exclusion zone around Sarajevo, and air action ceased on 5 October. A four-year lull effectively ensued.

Keeping busy elsewhere, F-16CJ squadrons assigned to the Air Expeditionary Force system, including the 13th FS and 14th FS in the Far East, have flown TDY assignments in support of NFZ activity over Iraq since 1995. Success there has been more unequivocal, and has helped the F-16CJ establishment develop new cooperative tactics with RC-135s and EA-6Bs, helping to make things work. A notable clash occurred on 4 September 1996, when a 35th FW F-16CJ operating in support of SWATCH knocked out an SA-8 near Mudaysis, just north of the newly extended southern 32nd Parallel.

According to the official press releases the F-16 pilot 'got strobes' (actually alphanumeric and aural warnings) that the SA-8's Land Roll radar was attempting to lock on. A patrolling RC-135, listening to the Iraqi radar voice transmissions, confirmed their hostile intentions and the pilot was cleared to attack. 'The pilot performed a "funky chicken" manoeuvre, which involves violent jinking with rapid changes of altitude to break lock, and shooting out chaff to confuse the SAM radar. The F-16 then fired a HARM missile at the [Land Roll], which went off the air at the missile's impact. The entire engagement took less than a quarter of an hour.'[2]

'Funky Chicken' is an apt description for the new, agile solo Weasel's ability to cavort, because of its innate high performance. Despite its otherwise extraordinarily well-behaved habits, pilots can pull significant *g* in the F-16, making this type of manoeuvre very dangerous, precipitating black-out because of Gravity-induced Loss of Consciousness (G-LOC), and possibly resulting in a crash or SAM strike if the pilot does not recover consciousness quickly enough as the onset of heavy *g* in the F-16 is so rapid. Old-fashioned high-*g* breaks during training and exercises were apt to increase the frequency of such events.

After a number of peacetime training losses, the US Air Force has introduced more discriminating F-16 pilot selection and specific training and equipment – new G-vests and breathing techniques – to counter this potentially deadly phenomenon. A further consideration in developing new techniques for breaking radar-lock is to prevent the AN/ALR-56M and HTS receivers from tumbling and generating erroneous displays during an attack run, which they were originally prone to do during aggressive manoeuvring.

NEW-GENERATION HARMS

AGM-88C. The Charlie variant entered operational service in <u>1993</u> and added an all-new WGU-2C/B warhead that introduced just over 12,800 tungsten-alloy fragments and a revised explosive charge, giving more bite. New software became synonymous with the **Block IV** AGM-88C the following year, allowing the missile to completely self-guide in the TOO mode commensurate with the doubling of its seeker range sensitivity.

Because of the rapid depletion of stocks during Gulf War combat, the US Congress directed that the weapon be opened up to further competition in an effort to provide a low-cost seeker, and this resulted initially in two concurrent versions, the Texas Instruments **AGM-88C-1** and Loral Aeronutronic **'C-2**. With a fat post-war order book, it was felt that everyone would be a winner, but in the end the Pentagon elected to buy C-1 models only, largely because of Texas Instruments' automated manufacturing facilities which guaranteed the desired reliability and homogeneity for ease of logistics support. Loral's low-cost alternative was only test-flown before Texas Instruments won the contract for 2,041 AGM-88C-1 rounds to replace those expended during Persian Gulf combat.

The next development, on the heels of numerous threat library upgrades for the various users, was some years in the making and based upon the **Block V** seeker, which completed its live-fire tests in October 1998. This introduced home-on-jam guidance software. With so many GPS Navstar-aided navigation and weapons guidance technologies depending on the Navstar constellation remaining reliable, HARM's homing spectrum was expanded to include GPS jammers. These may be employed by enemy forces in time of conflict to disrupt all the new smart bombs and navigation aids.

An Edwards test F-16CJ lets loose a HARM missile. (LMTAS)

The NWC and Falon Inc. have also created a pylon-mounted receiver working in the A–D Bands to detect sources of GPS interference, so that they can be handed off to the HARM on lesser-equipped aircraft. Block V also permitted the AGM-88C to be safely powered up, tested and reprogrammed at sea (a feature retrofitted to the AGM-88B model also using new Block IIIA software for that variant). The facility was first demonstrated on USS *George Washington* in July 1999 while on deployment to the Persian Gulf.

AGM-88D. In direct measure, HARM is also incorporating its own GPS guidance and inertial navigation sensor under the HARM Precision Navigation Update effort, so that it has what is curiously called 'geographic specifity'; i.e. it is less likely to go ballistic and cause undesirable collateral damage in the event that it loses radar-homing, as its guidance keeps it confined to a limited box. The German and Italian companies BGT and Alenia are heavily involved in this effort with the intention of equipping their Panavia Tornado Electronic Combat/ Reconnaissance aircraft with the derivative.

Block V software can be installed in any US-deployed AGM-88C, if required, for use in conflicts where the enemy plays dirty and sites its SAMs and associated radars close to schools, hospitals or other politically complicated locations – the Achilles' heel of the missile during Allied Force combat – or where the concentration of defences is extremely high and Day One attacks need to be extremely judicious.

COLL AT. DAMAGE

A Phase III **Block VI** effort, in progress since 1994 exclusively for US use, marries a HARM broad-band seeker with GPS mid-course guidance, while also adding high-end active Millimetre Wave (MMW) active radar guidance, which employs automatic target recognition algorithms during the terminal phase of the weapon's flight path. In essence, the tiny MMWs can differentiate actual ground targets — what aircrews from their grandstand view term creepy crawlies — so that HARM will use the enemy's radar dish for preliminary homing, but then switch over to its MMW templates and search out the SAM site's actual command vehicle or control cabin and zap it.

MMW also allows the Advanced Anti-Radiation Guided Missile (AARGM) to compensate for differences in dish and terrain height if the antenna, rather than the control van, is the primary target. Increasingly, prospective enemy EW emitters are being installed on plinths or mobile extendable towers which tend to defeat HARM's proportional guidance, which has always assumed that the target is at ground level. If Raytheon are entirely successful, a completely new, stealthy AARGM will emerge from the effort. Block VI, nonetheless, will reach operational status within the existing HARM airframe, re-equipped with a new form-fitted radome for the diverse seekers, which will be interchangeable.

The latest hit expression is 'In your face from outer space', with HARM targeting aided by space-based intranet sensors. On 22 April 1993 a VAQ-209 'Star Warriors' EA-6B fired the first successful over-the-horizon HARM using space-based targeting fed directly into the cockpit. Observable aircraft employing target flexing will thus be able to employ stealthy HARM derivatives with equal efficacy.

As the original 1969 design is proving too cumbersome for modern stealth aircraft designs relying on internal carriage to preserve their low RCS and to maximize surprise, a tail-steered ramjet-powered AARGM configuration will be available for use by both the Block 10 Lockheed-Martin F-22 Raptor and the JSF. The stealthy launch platform and the missile should be invisible to S-300/400-series SAM systems until it has already closed to within kill distance. Range will be approximately 150 miles.

While much testing has demonstrated that the F-16CJ is capable of launching with four HARM missiles, pilots have always preferred to stick to the swing-role configuration of a two-band centreline jamming pod (either the short AN/ALQ-184 or the shallow AN/ALQ-131), inboard drop tanks, two HARMs mid-wing, and outboard AIM-9 Sidewinders (employed during daytime missions) and two or four AIM-120 Advanced Medium-Range Air-to-Air Missiles (AMRAAM). CBU-87 CEMs canisters are sometimes employed in lieu of, or mixed with, HARMs. As Desert Storm veteran pilot Col George 'Jet' Jernigan explained: 'We are training using HARM and CBU-87 embedded mixes within a flight so that we have an inherent DEAD capability.'

Routine flying training mirrors their swing-role mission. According to Lt Col Pete Costello, deputy commander of the 77th FS at Shaw AFB in 1999, the F-16CJ training sortie mix is approximately 60 per cent SEAD, 30 per cent air-to-air and 10 per cent air-to-ground. Pilots entering the programme at Shaw AFB come from all backgrounds, as Lt Col Costello explains:

A four-HARM load was experimented with and the F16-CJ is certified to fly in this configuration; however, pilots prefer mixing two HARMs with four air-to-air missiles. (LMTAS)

When they come out of Luke AFB, Arizona (the chief F-16 RTU base), there are two different courses they emerge from. The B course is for youngsters brand-new to the F-16. They go to Luke AFB right out of pilot training and spend about six months there learning how to fly the F-16 in all of its roles, except for SEAD. The other course is what they call the TX course, and there are different tracks within that depending on what aircraft you've flown previously. It's a shorter course of two to four months. They get qualified or requalified on the F-16, then they show up at Shaw AFB, where we put them through vocation training which is, for a B course brand-new youngster out of Luke AFB, about an eleven- or twelve-ride programme. For someone who has previous experience on the F-16 we will modify that number down to about five or six.

The back part of that mission quali-
fication training is where we get them
SEAD-qualified. We spend time in the
weapons and tactics trainer. They have
a basic switchology and avionics ride
where they practise using the HTS and
the HARM missile itself, against simulated threats at the two electronic warfare ranges we have access to: nearby
Poinsett, and the mid-Atlantic range up
at MCAS Cherry Point. Then they do a
tactical ride after that, and then a night
SEAD ride because it's a little bit
different doing it at night. Then we give
them a certification checkride. Once
done, they are certified combat mission
ready.[3]

Night-time operations are gaining greater prominence and during 1999
the 20th FW commenced training with ITT industries' AVS-9 Night Vision
Goggles (NVG), qualifying everyone in the 20th FW by the following year.
The prospect of pilots peering through these eerie green imaging devices,
on the lookout for mobile SAM sites, seems a little bizarre given the
F-16CJ's HARM capability, but the system does permit low-level target
ingress and can prove useful for visually spotting SAM sites. Apparently,
the trade-off from having to sport a heavy 'bone dome' and the removal of
the RCS-reducing Indium Tin Oxide gold canopy coatings (which have
been discovered to compromise NVG performance) is more than offset by
increased pilot situational awareness during night-time aerial refuelling
operations in a lights out, communications silent environment.

What the F-16CJ community consistently demands is above-average
F-16 aviators. While Lt Col Costello and many other experienced pilots
view the F-16CJ as only an interim capability pending the advent of the

*The 22nd FS 'Stingers' participated
in Red Flag 00-1 exercises, carrying
a mock combat load of Sidewinder,
AMRAAM, HARM missiles, HTS
pod, ACMI instrumentation device
and AN/ALQ-131 ECM. In
combat, the ACMI pod would be
replaced by an additional HARM
missile. (Frank B. Mormillo)*

*A 22nd FS F-16CJ on finals. (Frank
B. Mormillo)*

(still in development) stealthy F-22 Raptor Air Dominance Fighter, which in Block 10B configuration is scheduled to assume a SEAD tasking, the aircraft has steadily grown in prowess with further improvements to the HTS. The limited-reception R5 system has been superseded by the R6, which one pilot described as 'providing better cockpit displays, faster processing, and much greater accuracy when locating and defining threats. If you turn on your radio this thing will find you!' The HTS system includes a steerable antenna that searches and acquires threats, then attempts to triangulate their position as the pilot plies his course, allowing it to deduce range and discriminate between two different threats on the same bearing. Lt Col Costello explained that because the F-16CJ community are shooters and have no ES function, the system was very much made to meld with the F-16's HOTAS capability:

The HTS is passive and it searches for electromagnetic radiation throughout the spectrum of the expected threats. It will collect all the signals that it sees and over the course of time will give you geo-specific data as to the location of the threats. You look at the multifunction display and see what threats are presented [in icon form], and select which ones you want to engage [using the appropriate throttle switch], just as you would an air-to-air threat using the radar. It's very intuitive, as it works the same way. Once selected, the HTS hands off all the relevant data to the HARM missile prior to launch. It's extremely automated, which it needs to be in a single-seat aircraft.

Threats are sorted and prioritized automatically. Typically, two two-ship elements of F-16CJs cover each others' vulnerable areas, and those of the strike package they are supporting, while receiving radar target updates from ES platforms such as the RC-135 and EA-6B, by means of IDMs. Exchange of information between the F-16CJs themselves is also possible, thus enabling them to swap threat information and deconflict HARM shoots.

ALLIED FORCE

The F-16CJs' real call to arms came in 1999, once again in the Balkans. On the night of 24/5 March NATO embarked on Operation Allied Force (OAF), in an effort to compel former Serbian President Slobodan Milosevic to make peace and cease his ruthless ethnic cleansing pro-grammes, which by early that spring had extended into Kosovo and the merciless slaying of ethnic Albanians. To the US contingent, the effort was appropriately titled Operation Noble Anvil. A build-up of US electronic combat capability in preparation for this was heralded with the redeployment from Spangdahlem AB to Aviano AB of Lt Col Mike 'Boe' Boera's 23rd EFS, which arrived on 21 February, the same day that F-117As touched down after crossing the Atlantic. (This force initially came under 31st EAW control, managed by the CAOC near Vincenza, but later reverted to 52nd FW jurisdiction at Spangdahlem AB, when the TDY

96215

F-117As and F-16CJ reinforcements deployed there during June.) Joining them at Aviano AB on 15 April just prior to the outset of OAF was Lt Col Steven 'Yahoo' Searcy's 78th EFS, deployed from Shaw AFB.

Maj Bob 'Festus' Egan, assistant operations officer for the 77th FS in October 1999, and with over 2,000hr in the F-16, takes up the 78th EFS story:[4]

The 20th FW got the word to send over a larger squadron to Italy to support the Allied Force mission. We ended up sending a full squadron plus extras, with more pilots than we actually needed so as to have some reserves and also to be able to do 24hr operations. We arrived and picked up with the Spangdahlem AB group over there, doing primarily the SEAD mission – every sortie that we ended up flying over there as a wing was direct SEAD support for Allied Force, both night-time and in day-time.

Most of the southern-type sorties we flew in direct support of Kosovo, and from Aviano AB this was about a 6–7hr mission. We were flying out of Aviano AB, hitting a tanker for refuelling, going in and doing about an hour watching Kosovo as a four-ship, coming out after that hour's worth of time, refuelling again and going in for

The 389th FS 'Thunderbolts' fly a SEAD support tasking as part of the composite intervention 366th Wing, based at Mountain Home, Idaho. (LMTAS)

265

another hour. We were rotating two four-ships at a time. Length of time out to station was about an hour, hour and ten; and the same back to Aviano AB, coming back home exhausted on autopilot at high altitude. Most of the interior missions that we flew were a little bit shorter than that usually, but we still had two VULs [excursions into enemy airspace, or vulnerability time] that we did as part of the strike package support over there. Then there were the night-time ones with one or two VULs as well, the time of missions lasting anywhere between 2½–3hr all the way up to 5–6hr.

Finally, we provided cover after if there were any shootdowns. The basic threat was the SA-6 and the SA-3 along with various MANPADS and triple-A pieces. They were running basically the old Soviet systems, but even the old Soviet systems are still good enough to be able to shoot down aircraft.

Serbian air defences were considered moderate because of their concentration in such a relatively small country (compared, for example, with the vastness of Iraq). Guns included pieces ranging in calibre from 20mm to 57mm for low-altitude defence, backed up by several types of infrared-guided SAMs, including MANPADS and the mobile SA-9/-13 Gaskin/Gopher. Some sixty-eight SA-6 launcher systems were also operational in the Federal Republic of Yugoslavia. Most were situated in and around Belgrade, with additional systems dotted around command and control nodes and important military headquarters. These included strategic systems, including sixty each of the SA-2 and Perchora-M SA-3A.

Curiously, despite their close ties with Russia, the SA-3As lacked any kind of state-of-the-art night-vision devices, and so were wholly reliant on radar for guidance. Reluctant to employ the radar for fear of being struck by a HARM, the operators launched SAMs blindly, hoping for a lucky shot. Particularly heavy barrages were noted on 12 and 26 May, when the enemy shot some thirty-six and thirty-three SAMs respectively, none of them finding their mark. The main danger to NATO aircraft was at low-level, from the triple-A and infrared-guided MANPADS. As Maj Bob Egan explains, there was no *ab initio* effort aimed at taking down the enemy IADS, as had been the case during Operation Desert Storm:

The plan of the war was political to begin with, but after the first week it was found this wasn't going to bring about a solution, so they went more into the military end, and we started taking out their IADS in a systematic fashion. What was interesting, and what made it difficult for us, was that a lot of the doctrines that we had anticipated via experience in Desert Storm and Deliberate Force, as well as what we knew of the old Soviet Union, did not always hold true. Firstly, they were very mobile and very conscious of our efforts to take them out. It made our job very difficult and also made most of the missions throughout the war very sporty! There was never one time, like in Desert Storm, where we owned the sky, if you will, from the SAMs and the triple-A pieces.

They had just as much capability to do harm to our forces at the end as they did at the beginning. They may not have had as many

missiles or as many missile sites because we did take out quite a few, but they had the same capability as they did at the beginning with the SA-6 and the SA-3. They learned a lot of valuable lessons fighting us, and as soon as they started getting hurt they changed their tactics. Now that also saved a lot of our own flyers because there were a lot of times when they didn't come up and engage us, which is a success in itself. Our job is to go in and get them to actively engage us so that we can take them down; and if that doesn't work, we do direct support with our own packages.

In terms of an analogy, if we were looking at a soccer match, we wouldn't necessarily be the forwards, we'd be the midfielders waiting for that ball to come back, and then putting it back into play. We were always there when the packages went in. If we didn't go, nobody else went. It was good to be well appreciated. There were several nights though that we did see quite a few SAMs shot at us. I'd say there wasn't a single sortie where I went across the fence that I'd say I felt comfortable on.

I had three SAMs shot at me the first night going across the fence, which opens your eyes and gets you thinking about what you're actually doing and what your job's all about. I'm lucky in the fact that the training and the systems worked the way they did. It was a night-time hop, we were flying as no. 3 and no. 4 on a SEAD support mission going into central Yugoslavia just south of Belgrade, going in with a two-ship of 23rd EFS instructor pilots from Spangdahlem AB leading and our two-ship from the 78th EFS doing familiarization. We were genning ourselves up.

After that point in time, we did our own night-time missions. So, we took off, hit a tanker out over the Adriatic, went lights out (doing that for the first time was pretty interesting!), set up in a tactical formation and flew across. We were supporting a NATO package that night consisting of British Tornadoes, Spanish EF-18s, as well as American F-15Es and F-16CGs out of Aviano AB. With all the support assets such as EA-6Bs it was a fairly large package – probably in excess of thirty aircraft.

We were hitting three DMPIs [Desired Mean Point of Impact] and then flowing off of that particular strike, going back to a tanker, then going back in again with another set of strikers to do a DEAD mission, where we were going to try to take out a couple of sites. This was a coordinated attack between the package and ourselves. During the first push in, I was no. 4. We had a two-ship in front of the package, sweeping out and trying to sanitize the airspace of any kind of SAMs, followed by the package itself, and then my flight lead and myself bringing up the rear, covering the tail end. As we flew in, we were going through several known SA-3 and SA-6 rings that evening. The initial push in did not elicit any action from the SA-3.

Some triple-A came up at them as they pressed into the target area, and that was when my wingman and I ended up crossing the fence, and got engaged by an SA-3 site just south of Belgrade. Being the tail-end Charlie guy, the controllers were either waiting for me or had everything set up by the time I came across. I got lit up by an SA-3

Later model SC ANG F-16CJs in-flight. The South Carolina ANG is one of a dozen F-16CJ operators, and one of the most experienced, its pilots having previously cut their teeth flying vanilla Block 10 F-16As in a combat SEAD role during Desert Storm. (LMTAS)

site. I employed some countermeasures and chaff, tried to manoeuvre away from the site, and then got an SA-3 launched at me. I defeated that one. The missile initially guided on me but then went aft and exploded high, probably a mile away.

Coming off that, we pressed into where the package were dropping their ordnance around another SA-3 site, and then, still in the tail end Charlie position, had two more SA-3s shot at me. One of them was a ballistic launch, where they were just shooting them up to see if they could knock anything down; the second one was actually engaging my aircraft. I repeated the evasive manoeuvre, a level S-type manoeuvre at altitude with chaff, and defeated the missile.

At that point in time we egressed out from the target and hit a tanker again, and I was not feeling exactly like I wanted to go back across the site. Our flight had already shot off a couple of HARMs from the front element. As we went in on the second push, the new package we were supporting consisted of some F-16CGs and some F-15Es as well as the four of us. We were actually going in to take out the SA-3 site that initially engaged me. But it never came up again, so we spent about 35 minutes inside the threat range just south of Belgrade. Whether they'd had their fill or shot their missiles for the evening, or just knew what we were trying to do at that point in time, who knows, but no one engaged us at all.

They were moving around a lot, the SA-6s especially because they're a tracked vehicle. The SA-3s were broken down and moved almost every night. We knew the general area and we knew basically how far they could go, and where good areas of approach for them would be, but we didn't always know where the specific sites were, and when we did we would send up alert aircraft to try to take them out. We did a lot of alert during the daytime as they are easier to spot.

At night you can see everything, even the triple-A that only comes up to a couple of thousand feet, and my secure sense of being a fighter pilot was probably shaken slightly. It gave me a keen awareness of what the job entails and it was good to have that done and over the first evening, and not be lulled into a false sense of security and end up getting shot at later on when maybe your wits weren't about you. It's not as difficult the next time, although you're probably more apprehensive. But once you get your concentration going it was very easy to focus in on your job.

Col George 'Jet' Jernigan performs the pre-flight walk-around of his F-16CJ at McEntire, South Carolina. (Kevin Jackson)

A few missions into the conflict I wouldn't say it got more comfortable, but we were certainly more confident about the way we were doing our business and the tactics we were employing. Later on I did get one more SAM shot at me, but it was more of a ballistic-type launch that was not guiding on me. But I was out there during several instances in Kosovo when we had MANPADS launched at A-10As, and having seen those and reacted to them at night it was a little bit easier to do the job. You knew exactly what to concentrate on at that point in time and the other things in your world went away fast, and you focused exactly on your job.

Obviously, being the guy who's protecting everyone from the SAMs, we had to really have our head on a 360-deg swivel. We had to know exactly what's going on when we supported CAS operations going on throughout the Kosovo region. From tip to tip Kosovo was about 90 miles, and about 130 miles across – a fairly small chunk of airspace. So it was a constant, roving type of patrol, making sure you kept an eye on everything that was going on, because we might have A-10As dropping bombs on one side, British Tornadoes dropping on the other, Navy packages flowing in, all at the same time. We had to try to support everyone and know where they were in relation to the threats.

The air-to-air threat was fairly low. Sombor, Obrva and Sjenica airfields all got hammered early on by NATO. However, HARM fratricide remained an issue throughout Allied Force, resulting in strict ROE as Bob Egan recalls:

I did twenty missions over Kosovo and over Yugoslavia, but I never fired one even though I had three opportunities. Because of the direction I was pointing in at the time, and where the shot was going to be taking place, I was precluded from actually firing the HARM. There were several instances where we had HARMs going into Bulgaria, and because Kosovo was in close proximity not only to Bulgaria but also to Macedonia and to Albania, where we had friendly forces and their radars, we had to be very conscious of how we were employing that weapon. So there were a lot of times where if you were pointed in the wrong direction, even though the site came up, you simply couldn't fire.

That went also for any of the ordnance we were dropping. If that bomb goes astray because of smoke obscuring an LGB, or if a HARM flexes off into space, we know the implications behind it – that some innocent person may end up dying.

Nevertheless, the two F-16CJ squadrons at Aviano AB fired some 150 HARMs during the course of Allied Force.

In my formations I had several wingmen shoot HARMs and in my four-ships I had several flight leads shoot HARMs, and in each one of those instances we had good information on where that site was and pretty good Intel. So we did the job. We may not have hit the site, but we brought the site down. It made them think twice about coming up again and tangling with us. If we went and didn't shoot a single HARM and we never had a SAM site come up and shoot, we had done our job. I'd be very happy if that were the case. It is a miracle we only had two aircraft shot down, in my personal opinion. We forced them not to use their radars, so a lot of SAM launches were unguided shots. Once again, that reduces their stockpile and helps us out.

Only two aircraft, and no fixed-wing pilots, were lost to 673 SAM firings during the course of 38,000 OAF combat missions – a significantly lower loss per sortie rate than in Desert Storm.[5]

When the war kicked off, based on their own propaganda and the way they saw us, they probably were very well motivated and they were very aggressive in the way they employed their SAMs. I will say that if you take a look and ask anyone involved from the beginning of the war to the end, that aggressiveness went downhill toward the end of the war. They weren't shooting a whole lot; in fact, they weren't coming up a whole lot because they knew that if they did they were going to die. There were several operators though, who were more aggressive than others and stayed that way throughout the war. We had one in around the Obrva area, in central Yugoslavia just south of Belgrade, and we called him a 'Weapons School' operator, because he was the most tenacious and we never were able to get him, in terms of taking his site down.

Other operators that became aggressive we ended up seeking out and successfully taking out. I'd say there were several SA-6s down in Kosovo that were very assertive to begin with, but once we started to concentrate on the Kosovo operations and on taking them out specifically, we never did see them come up again during the entire remainder of the war. So we were fairly confident that they either met their end or went somewhere else to hide the war out.

Another factor was the way the Serb forces flagrantly disregarded international codes of conduct, such as the Geneva Convention.

There were several instances where their SA-6 SAM sites, their triple-A pieces and their radars were put up against churches, hospitals and residential areas. This limited our tactics, restricting our run-in headings because of the political aspects and problems of collateral damage, and put us more in harm's way than if we had been able to do our mission in a true tactical fashion. There were a lot of SEAD missions that I went on which, because of the political aims to minimize collateral damage and casualties in the civilian population, caused us to work even harder. Several times we had to come right through a threat instead of around it. That, obviously, is doubly hard when you have the whole strike package come through a threat area, as you've got more people in harm's way than just yourself and your wingman.

Even the 'HARM target isolate' mode on the venerable F-4G would not have coped with such contingencies.

During Allied Force the F-16CJ pilots did not employ NVGs, and Bob Egan remarked jocularly that 'There were a lot of airplanes out there at night; 36–40 airplanes coming off various tankers. If you have NVGs, now you see 'em all! Maybe it would be better just not to see everybody!' As for day versus night flying difficulty:

A night mission is a ten, a day mission a five. We can employ a lot more flexible tactics in the day because you have that visual option. At night you're restricted, especially if you don't have NVGs. You've got to use your radar a lot more, you've got to use your air-to-air TACAN, you've got to use various things to keep you orientated. AWACS, communications, everything is more intensive at night than during the day. You can't use visual signals; you're lights out so there isn't a light drill to be able to go through; you're not going to see your wingman and his strobes at night, and obviously to fire a flare at night to get a tally-ho is not a good idea. I saw that one night, when someone else popped a flare off and immediately that drew *everyone's* attention, including the enemy. SAMs are going to get shot at that area, triple-A is going to go up to that area. So a night mission is worlds different, a lot harder than the daytime. Night is an unknown. It's not natural for a human to be out in the dark.

F-16CJs taxi to the EOR prior to take-off for another Allied Force effort. The aircraft served in a purely reactive role; there was no ab initio *effort to take down the Serbian IADS, as there was against Iraq's KARI during Desert Storm.* (USAF)

I had four night missions before I flopped over to daytime, and then had sixteen day missions. We found out we needed more day supervision, so being one of the squadron supervisors I ended up flowing into the daytime operation. We basically kept our supervision in the day and supervision in the night the same. However, pilots flopped day and night depending on what missions were tasked. We'd keep them on a routine, a couple of weeks, maybe three to try to get their body acclimatized, and then once they were done in that point of time we'd try to roll them slowly to daytimes and vice versa, so that each section got a chance, night to look at the day, day to look at the night.

So we developed a balanced group because at the time we didn't know how long it was going to go on, and we wanted to make sure that no one person was specifically either nights or days.

Most of the wingmen got twenty OAF sorties and most of the flight leads anywhere between twenty-four and twenty-six. Most of the supervisors like myself had the chance to go and have two weeks at the K-Op on the command structure to help out the generals and everything else on the planning aspect. We probably got around the twenty-sortie mark; the squadron commander and operations officer the same as they didn't fly as much as a normal flight lead did.

Although exhibiting a 95 per cent reliability, physical HTS pod shortages presented some problems. There existed a requirement for 218 pods in 1999, and with only 146 available the inevitable shortfall affected a third of the F-16CJ force. New production will ensure aircraft/pod parity will be achieved during 2004, with approximately 230 units in the inventory.

ALLIED LOSSES

Back into combat went the F-117As, operating initially from Aviano AB (having arrived there on 21 February), and then, from 4 June, during the final stages of the campaign, from Spangdahlem AB, following the deployment of reinforcements from their home at Holloman AFB, New Mexico.[6] Updated since Desert Storm operations with newer ring-laser-gyro based SNU-84 INS and with access to more portable Air Force Mission Support System computers for flight-planning, which had replaced the poor old worn-out Elvira, everything seemed to be going like clockwork – until the fourth day of operations. On 27 March F-117A Vega 31 (82-806) was brought down over Budjanovic, some 25 miles west of Belgrade, creating a Russo-Serbian public relations feeding frenzy and a hiatus at Lockheed-Martin's Skunk Works.

The negative forces encountered by the pilot were enormous. He remembers 'having to fight to get my hands to go down towards the [ejection seat] handgrips. I always strap in very tightly, but because of the intense g-forces, I was hanging in the straps and had to stretch to reach the handles.' Suffering only minor abrasions from the ensuing punch-out, he landed in a freshly ploughed field, made for a culvert 200yd away, and dug himself in to evade sniffer dogs. In a remarkable counter-coup, the rescue teams (a pair of MH-53J Pave Low IIIs plus MH-60G Pave Hawks from the US Air Force Special Operations Squadrons, guided by an MC-130P Combat Shadow) plucked the pilot to safety just under 6hr later, right from under the enemy's noses. Another F-117A was allegedly seriously damaged by shrapnel from an SA-3 launch on 30 April, the aircraft managing to recover safely.

The unexpected stealth loss caused a considerable stir. What seems to have happened is that inadequate jamming support by EA-6Bs, which were overstretched supporting observable aircraft, allowed the Serbians to plot F-117A flight tracks through their occasional glitter and blind-launch salvoes of SAMs in their path, creating debris that could damage the airframe, compromise the RAM coatings and also be hoovered up by the intakes, resulting in catastrophic engine failure. No official report of the loss has been released, though some accounts suggest that the pilot dropped below cloud to get a good target lock for his Paveways, and might have been tracked visually.

The duty RC-135 Rivet Joint in-theatre, which could have relayed a warning call, was topping up its fuel and thus was temporarily absent in a nose-cold condition, while F-16CJ support had been recalled to different co-ordinates before the F-117A had exited the target area. In any event, a combination of these factors caused 82-806 to tumble. Somewhat surprisingly, the wreckage of the F-117A was not struck, and Russian advisers were seen poring over it after daybreak, particularly eager to examine its RAM coatings and EO bomb-nav-laser suite. The official explanation for not destroying the wreckage was that it would take at least ten years for a prospective enemy to capitalize on the technology and build something comparable to third-generation stealth, by which time the United States would be two or more generations ahead in the game.

On 2 May, in effective reprisal, F-117As began undertaking operations with new soft bombs to black out the enemy's power supplies. The CBU-102(V)2/Bs each scattered 202 BLU-114 sub-bomblets, which sprang open to disgorge spider's webs of wire filament spools that shorted-out electrical transformers, taking 70 per cent of Serbian commercial electrical supplies off-line. A repeat attack on 8 May kept the Serbs busy cleaning their wires, with significant effects on the country's land-line telephone system and the mobile-phone transmitters used by some SAM operators. There were no further F-117A losses after this time.

In the aftermath of the campaign, the F-117As are receiving a number of important upgrades under the Single Configuration Fleet update. The wallpaper RAM coatings are being systematically replaced by new, robotically sprayed polymer-based coatings built up in layers, which are more effective while also easing maintenance requirements into the bargain. Block 2 capability is endowing the F-117A with GPS-aided Paveways (such as the EGBU-27/B) to permit higher-altitude accurate drops through cloud cover, including newer J-series weapons capability.

Block 3 and 4 improvements will replace out-of-date cockpit displays and add new Link 16 modems, for passive in-flight target updates. The aircraft may also carry a combined HARM and bomb payload for certain missions. Experiments during the mid-1990s over the White Sands

Obscura and Red Rio Ranges demonstrated that an F-117A could close to within lethal shooting distance undetected while a SAM site was engaged in tracking a far-off observable jet. Ironically, the bait during these trials comprised Block 30 F-16Cs from the 27th FW at Cannon AFB, New Mexico. F-117As flying with Ninja callsigns were reported to have broadcast 'Have a HARM launch, missile away', whereafter the range controllers would relay each missile's accuracy against the simulated SAM site.

The only other Allied Force fixed-wing casualty was F-16CG Hammer 34, lost on the night of 2 May after a strike against Serb SAM sites near Novi Sad. Battered by an SA-3, the pilot got out a 'Mayday! Mayday! Mayday!' before successfully ejecting. Two MH-53Js and an MH-60G scrambled from Tuzla, only to become the targets for four MANPAD launches, two of which missed them by less than 200ft! The rescuers homed in on the pilot who was steering them via his radio, his instructions based on the swirling blades of the approaching helicopters.

In an act of incredible bravery, the armoured MH-53Js acted as a protective sandwich, laying down suppressive fire on either side of the pick-up point, while the MH-60G crew's PJs extracted the pilot amid the intensifying triple-A and small-arms opposition as the sun rose. Fortunately, no friendlies were hurt. The 22nd FS at Spangdahlem AB, aiding the rescue effort with F-16CJ SEAD top cover, ended up flying almost 9hr missions in support of the rescue forces. The squadron logged some thirty-seven SEAD missions from its home base during Allied Force, all conducted under Spangdahlem AB's 52nd AEW banner.

Flares are effective against old generation MANPADs and AIMs, but less so against newer heat-seeking or imaging-infra-red-homing missiles. (USAF)

There had been one previous F-16C loss over the former Yugoslavia. On 2 June 1995, in support of Operation Deny Flight, Capt Scott O'Grady was downed by an SA-6 his systems apparently couldn't see, paralleling Israeli experience twenty-two years earlier. O'Grady, probably suffering some disorientation after his ejection, decided to work his way back to the centre of the bull's-eye before convincing himself to return to near the crash site, where he was rescued five days later by a US Marine Corps SAR effort.

Puzzled by the loss, the Air Force Electronic Warfare Environment Simulator (AFEWES) swung into action to determine how the event came about. O'Grady's aircraft featured the Loral AN/ALR-56M RWR (manifested as two 'beer can' lumps on the wing's leading edge) while his lead carried the older ATI AN/ALR-69 system. AFEWES, using available Elint tapes, simulated a number of different scenarios and eventually determined that the SA-6 batteries were linked to both Straight Flush fire-control tracking and Long Track acquisition radars, at odds with what was thought to be current Soviet operational philosophy for the SA-6. The RWRs were thus reprogrammed so that they would recognize the new emitter signal patterns and prompt adequate jamming responses. The updates arrived in time for Allied Force operations, and no F-16s were lost to SA-6s during that conflict. However, this anomaly underscored the need for better ES, particularly for ACC's RC-135V/Ws on constant patrols in any troublespot. Dealing with what was akin to two Major Regional Conflicts plus routine global peacetime monitoring had led to some gaps in their coverage, including the Tiger Song system in Iraq.

One of the most fundamental lessons to emerge during Allied Force was that HARM missiles alone were not able to permanently shut down the enemy IADS, especially if no systematic SEAD campaign was initiated until well after horns were locked with the enemy. The popular US military rhetoric was that 'Nobody wanted to eat a HARM missile for Slobodan Milosevic' or, as former Secretary of the Navy John Lehman Jr more eloquently put it: 'They did not react the way we thought they would. We thought they would make every effort to shoot us down, but they chose to shoot unguided missiles that were not very effective.'

Essentially, electronic combat was far too dependent on the enemy fully utilizing their defences, in order to make weapons like HARM effective, and locating mobile defences for more conventional attack methods. Relative Serbian-Montenegran inactivity, on Russian advice, preserved their IADS, allowing them to take unguided pot-shots at random, at their own choosing. As Gen Michael E. Ryan, US Air Force Chief of Staff, told the Senate Armed Services Committee during March 1995: 'When it is turned on, when it attempts to target us, it is destroyed, so what [Slobodan's air defence operators] have tried to do is conserve it by using it sparingly and when he uses it we strike back and take it out.' This quick-reaction philosophy had become known as DEAD, and was trialled more successfully as part of NFZ enforcement against Iraq, beginning the previous December following Desert Fox operations.

Over Yugoslavia, one of the chief problems facing such reactive measures was that Serbian air defence troops were communicating with one another by mobile phone, allowing them to link up radar with MANPADS and take brief looks, just sufficient to cause a major nuisance. Moreover, the mobile SAM sites were cloaked by weather, and often simply could not be located if they decided to stay mute. The CBU-102(V)2/B attacks by F-117As took out portions of the communications system, but the sites themselves went largely unscathed and ambush still remained a serious threat from beginning to end because of their mobility. The E-8 Joint-STARS was not yet properly hooked up into the system like the E-3 AWACS and RC-135 Rivet Joint.

Nonetheless, a key success was the demonstration of the value of IDMs. Aviano's Block 40 F-16CG strikers fitted with Sure Strike modems were capable of receiving target co-ordinates relayed by F-16CJs and RC-135s, and on 27 April two two-ships successfully pummelled an SA-6 site. As a spin-off from this, the latest F-16CG/CJ configuration, designated 50T5, permits the carriage of J-series weapons, and these have made their service debut with the 20th FW at Shaw AFB. F-16CJ groundcrews in South Carolina initiated training with AGM-154 JSOW shapes on 10 April 2000, and flight operations began in May.

The next upgrade in the series, the R7 HTS enhancement, will endow the F-16CJ with greater precision-locating capability and permit the pilot to hand off targets to DEAD weapons like JSOW and the (still in development) AGM-158 JASSM, and make use of more advanced Blocks of HARM employing back-up GPS guidance as a fail-safe. These weapons will enable crews to accurately target inactive radars, based on new in-flight intranetting of target data.

A parallel, wider-sweeping effort called the Common Configuration Implementation Program (CCIP) is under way to give nearly 700 serving US Air Force Block 40/42 F-16CGs and Block 50/52 F-16CJs a look-alike core avionics suite and displays, allowing some swap-around of equipment and assignments, to spread the burden and allow more flexibility. In addition to a new modular mission computer, colour MFD set, advanced IFF, common data entry electronics unit and off-boresight AIM-9X Sidewinders linked to a joint helmet-mounted cueing system, the aircraft are being equipped with the crucial new Link 16 Multifunction Information Distribution System (MIDS) data-links.

Current F-16CJs possess a first-generation version of this so-called intranetting of threat data by means of their IDMs, but using the new Link 16 capability (a spin-off from the CAP fighter community's or Joint Tactical Information Distribution System) will enable the F-16CJs to connect with a plethora of air, ground and seaborne friendlies. Pilots will see the threats generated by their HTS (and correlated with RC-135 and other data) superimposed on a colour map display overlaid with flight plans, target symbols, friendly and enemy aircraft whereabouts – and threats struck-out if another flight is already engaging them, to ensure target deconfliction. They will also be able to swap target images.

The impact these new data-links are having on modern air combat should not be underestimated, as a Symetrics Corp representative explains:

The IDM is becoming the primary method of transmitting data. You can't beat the reduction in transmission time; it sends all the information directly to the HTS so the pilot does not have to manipulate anything, thus reducing the risk of error. It also integrates the Photo-Reconnaissance Intelligence Strike Module (PRISM). This allows you to capture frames of video imagery – anything, such as FLIR pod imagery, TV, or national source information. You can capture an image, compress it and send it either backwards or forwards.

A pilot is always provided an Intel brief of what the assigned target will look like; however, the situation may change while en route, so he can be sent an update, or reassigned to a new target. Also, if a two-ship flight is assigned a target, the first pilot will be able to transmit an image of what the target looks like to his no. 2 after his initial attack.

The first MIDS-equipped CCIP-reworked aircraft will roll out following depot-level maintenance at Ogden ALC in early 2002. Further intranetting of airborne sensors, already under way, will increasingly make use of space-based sensors looking down at the target area, fused by air-breathing platforms such as the developmental C-135-based Speckled Trout, and conveyed directly to the cockpit. The concept has been demonstrated in tests already, under the Talon Sword effort.

COUNTERMEASURES FOR THE 'NOUGHTIES

NATO's eleven-week Operation Allied Force was suspended on 10 June 1999, its objectives having been largely met. Overall, it was adjudged to have been a successful campaign, and one in which the F-16CJ, RC-135V/W and EA-6B made a significant contribution in the support SEAD role. Moreover, NATO destroyed 79 per cent and 30 per cent of the Yugoslav MiG-29 Fulcrum and MiG-21 Fishbed fighters respectively, along with two-thirds of the strategic SA-2s and three-quarters of the SA-3 sites.

However, the reactive nature of the SEAD effort lacked the gusto of Operation Desert Storm, relatively few enemy radars were hit, and crews were being targeted three times as often by Serbian SAMs than during Desert Storm, because of the inability to do anything more than degrade the Serbian IADS into isolated lethal pockets of resistance. As a result, a significant proportion of aircraft were tied up in SEAD and defensive taskings instead of being able to swing over to strike or air-to-air operations, as was supposed to happen, effectively lengthening the campaign significantly. Ten years after Desert Storm, many veterans still feel that the overwhelming success of that campaign, followed by the wholesale disbandment of dedicated electronic combat forces, has lulled the United States into a false sense of security.

Another crucial lesson to emerge from Desert Storm and Allied Force combat experience was the continued vulnerability of traditional jets to infrared heat-seeking weapons, as pilots seldom knew the missiles were attacking them unless they sighted them visually or could pick up a co-located radar transmitter used for initial target tracking and missile cueing (such as the SA-8's Land Roll radar, or an interceptor's AI radar). Even if spotted, SAM microcircuitry could more easily filter out the target aircraft from the flares it ejected to continue their business unabated. Part of the solution has been to match the pyrotechnics' heat signatures and trajectory more closely with the aircraft pumping them out, but additional measures are in development.

The first comprises Missile Approach Warning Systems (MAWS) working much like RWRs, but in the ultraviolet and infrared parts of the electromagnetic spectrum, so that they can pick up the missiles' often smokeless rocket plumes and alert the pilot to initiate evasive manoeuvres and eject flares or other decoys in a timely manner. Further developments have been aimed at producing a Directed-energy Infra-Red Counter-Measures (DIRCM) device employing a laser and xenon lamp to send out a disruptive beam of energy back at the SAM or AAM to fox its terminal guidance seeker. Draggy, bulky and built into prominent blisters and turrets, these devices (such as the Northrop-Grumman AN/AAR-54 MAWS-based AN/AAQ-24) have so far proved credible only for use aboard slow-movers such as Special Operations MC-130 transports. However, they are already proving to be far less prone to false alarms than pioneering Vietnam-era devices like the old F-111's tail-mounted cryogenic AN/AAR-34 CMRS (Countermeasures Receiver Set), and are able to provide full 360-deg coverage, offering much potential for aircraft undertaking CAS and just-behind-the-lines BAI (Battle Area Interdiction) taskings.

It is simply a matter of time before miniaturization makes them feasible for use aboard jet fighters, including overlapping infrared and ultraviolet to further reduce false alarms and provide all-altitude missile detection: ultraviolet is better able to discriminate missiles against ground hot spots and see through haze at low level, while infrared is still the preferred method at medium and high altitudes to keep track of missiles' hot motors in the ozone, especially once the rocket motor has expended its propellant and the missile is flying solely on kinetic energy.

The principal innovation for smaller fast-movers has been the Lockheed-Sanders Common MAWS (CMWS), in development since 1995 (to replace a hotch-potch of systems) and flight-tested aboard a USAF Block 40 F-16 beginning in early 1997, using relatively crude fore, aft and sideways-looking sensors embedded in its wing pylons. Adding all-up DIRCM capability to fighters is the next logical step as soon as tunable broad-band lasers become available, offering a lightweight system capable of handling multiple heat-seeking weapons working in different IR bands, but it remains several years away from fruition.

Current DIRCM projects include a small pyramidal Sanders Agile Eye IR sensor and laser with all-round vision through its seven apertures, that juts out of an aircraft by a mere 3½in. The US Air Force, meanwhile, has been investigating the feasibility of adding DIRCM capability to its LANTIRN FLIR/laser targeting pods, used by the F-15E and F-16CG in the DEAD role. Current lasers can be retuned to disrupt SAMs' optical tracking devices, but there has been opposition to this on ethical grounds as the systems would also be inevitably employed to blind triple-A gunners – and not necessarily temporarily.[7]

More worrying has been the burgeoning sophistication of modern radar-guided defences: Electronic Counter-Counter Measures (ECCM, or the ability to see through jamming); modern radars' ability to employ rapid frequency hopping across multiple radar bands, with complex target data quickly processed by state-of-the-art netted computers for timely missile updates, paralleling the pace of domestic personal computer processing speeds (but up to three generations ahead of what most people are familiar with); and the general proliferation of former Soviet hardware overseas. Worse, multifarious local updates in countries such as Iraq, North Korea and Serbia which have mated CIS and Western SAMs, radars and computing have in turn created SAM/radar hook-ups with few common denominators, unlike the Cold War era when a given Soviet-produced SAM and its radar were near-standard and specific strategies could be devised to counter them relatively cheaply and quickly.

Each IADS now has to be monitored and its *modus operandi* carefully examined virtually constantly – the job of the US Air Force RC-135V/W Rivet Joint and similar US Navy EP-3E ARIES II – with ECM programmes recatalogued on an almost weekly basis. Late Vietnam-era time-honoured jamming methods are lapsing into obsolescence, and are ineffective against newer track-while-scan and monopulse radars. At the same time, SARH SAMs such as the battle area and local defence SA-6 and its successors, the SA-11 Gadfly, and SA-17 Grizzly, are proving potentially capable of using home-on-jam and other ECCM fail-safes, based around new target acquisition radars such as Snow Drift (which is replacing the first generation Tube Arm), and the Fire Dome illumination radar to paint the target, using discriminatory MTI techniques.[8]

New angle-deception jamming techniques are constantly evolving in response to these, and the method of transmitting them is changing even more radically. Instead of merely radiating directly through the ECM pods or the aircraft's built-in jamming antennae, which point to the jamming aircraft if things go awry, the signals can be transmitted via a Fibre-Optic Towed Decoy (FOTD), such as the Sanders AN/ALE-55, being developed by the US Navy under its Integrated Defensive Electronic Counter-measures (IDECM), which also includes an AN/ALQ-214 traditional jammer. Jamming signals are routed from the aircraft ECM through the tough fibre-optic cable to the trailing decoy's own TWT amplifier. If the jamming proves ineffective because of home-on-jam ECCM, the missile will home in on the decoy, not the aircraft, which switches over to transmit a signature emulating the tower autonomously. The decoy can be extended or ejected as the SAM nears it, creating a safe blast clearance.

An interim AN/ALE-50 towed decoy is already in US service, current contracts including fitment for 437 F-16s, contained in four rear wing pylon 'doghouses'. The AN/ALE-50 made its service debut in 1995. It cannot transmit complex jamming and simply repeats the enemy radar signals for enemy SAMs to home in on, luring them away from the aircraft, but it has already been successfully combat tested, with no losses in a scenario which felled one invincible F-117A and seriously damaged another. It was combat-trialled first on the US Air Force's SEAD F-16CJs deployed from Shaw AFB and Spangdahlem AB to Aviano AB, along with Rockwell B-1B Lancer bombers operating from RAF Fairford and the

American Midwest. AN/ALE-50s are also being installed on a select number of Raytheon ALQ-184(V)-9 jamming pods, for fitment to US Air Force F-16s lacking the relevant pylon arrangement, so that they can quickly get the system onboard if called to combat.

The cucumber-sized towed decoys are cut loose after they have done their job, but doubtless some of the more sophisticated FOTD models in development will be reeled back in. The US Air Force has already acknowledged that it would have lost several B-1Bs during Allied Force operations without the devices in trail, and increasing sophistication means future versions are less likely to be dumped, being available for re-reeling. General John P. Jumper, commander of ACC noted that:

> the first night that the B-1Bs were deployed [in Allied Force], they came straight from the test world at Nellis AFB. On the first night, they came down south over the Adriatic Sea in a formation. AN/ALE-50 towed decoys were deployed and we watched the radars in Montenegro . . . track the B-1Bs as they came down and turned the corner around Macedonia and up through and into Kosovo. We watched the radars, in real time, hand off the targets to the SA-6s, and the SA-6s came up in full-target track and fired their missiles. Those missiles took the AN/ALE-50s off of the back-end of the B-1Bs just like they were designed to do. The B-1Bs went on and hit their targets.

The TRA-developed ADM-160 miniature Air-Launched Decoy provides greater IR and RF spectrum protection for its droppers. Its size belies its capabilities to mimic accurately a full-sized fighter aircraft. These sorts of countermeasures, alongside FOTDs and stealth, are at the forefront of today's electronic arena. (LMTAS)

An infrared decoy version is also being developed as a counter to heat-seeking missiles, burning pyrophoric material at a ferocious 900°C with no visible-spectrum emissions. The material is extruded from the decoy by a small piston and stops burning if extrusion is halted, so that it is not merely a one-shot defensive system. It has not been bought yet because of one lingering problem: the inability to counter imaging infrared missiles, which only high-energy DIRCM may be able to counter satisfactorily. Imaging infrared and ultraviolet seekers, at either end of the visible spectrum as insurance, are appearing on overseas teenager SA-14/-15/-16 MANPADS. The SA-16 Gimlet simply ignores flares altogether. The best counter is to fly above 20,000ft to avoid these and triple-A fire, and rely on older PGMs or newer J-series weapons in a first-pass lob well away from the target area. But such tactics place observable strikers within prospective shooting range of the SA-11 and SA-17, as well as new strategic SAMs being offered for export by Russia.

SUPER HORNETS, GROWLERS AND PROWLERS

If that were not enough of a worry for mission planners, repeated concerns about the inability of the latest generation of US-designed RF-spectrum ECM systems to cope with the new radar/SAM threats in the BAI and interdiction scenarios has resulted in Congress paranoically mandating several project cancellations or restructurings over the past decade, some of them quite short-sighted. A specific case in point was the Joint-Service ITT/Westinghouse AN/ALQ-165 Airborne Self-Protection Jammer (ASPJ), which began development in the mid-1980s and was in low-rate initial production when the project was terminated in 1992, after ninety-five packages had already been produced. They were mothballed instead.

Following the loss of Capt O'Grady's F-16C over Bosnia three years later, and at the behest of the US Marine Corps, twelve of the systems were taken out of storage to replace the by then antiquated AN/ALQ-126B aboard the Corps' F/A-18D Fast-FAC Hornets operating over Bosnia from Aviano AB, which had suffered too many near-misses. Its remarkable success quickly led to 150 Fleet F/A-18Cs being reconfigured for the system (alongside the Grumman F-14D Bombcat), coincident with provisions for the improved ALR-67(V)-3 RWR. However, as the ASPJ was out of production and the packages in short supply the US Navy has been obliged to repeatedly strip them out of F/A-18Cs and F-14Ds following their deployments and reinstall them on combat-bound machines. Northrop-Grumman's former Westinghouse Division has since built thirty-six more AN/ALQ-165 units, to relieve the strain, but the lack of adequate ASPJs is causing wear and tear on the avionics racks with each installation and gutting, while aircrews have nothing to train with prior to a deployment.

The F/A-18C/D's successor, the enlarged, partly stealthy F/A-18E/F Super Hornet, is entering multi-year production as the mainstay US Navy Fleet all-rounder to replace both the F/A-18C/D and F-14A/D. Powered by GE F414 engines and equipped with an AN/APG-73 multimode radar, with provisions for both ASPJ and the AN/ALE-50, as well as HARM

Opposite above: The US Navy's latest SEAD platform is the highly capable, long-legged F/A-18E/F Super Hornet, which is gradually ousting the F/A-18C/D from the Fleet. It is easily distinguished from its predecessor by its enlarged dimensions and stealthy parallelogram intake lips. (Boeing)

Opposite below: A proposed replacement for the EA-6B Prowler is this jamming pod and HARM-toting spin-off from the two-seat F/A-18F Super Hornet, known appropriately enough as the F/A-18G Growler. Further miniaturization of yet faster electronics is making this aircraft possible. (Boeing)

capability, the aircraft garnered top scores during its 850-sortie operational evaluation and, at the time of writing, has logged over 7,000 accident-free flying hours. Authorization has been given for production of 222 examples through Fiscal Year 2004 (over sixty funded already), with an eventual production goal of 548.

So far, it has not suffered any of the problems of its shorter-ranged forebear, while continuing its proven tradition of high FMC strike-fighter, able to conduct both SEAD and strike on the same outing, and it is slated to receive the all-up IDECM, which will eventually include DIRCM and FOTD countermeasures as well as traditional RF-spectrum jamming. It is currently equipping VFA-122 'Fighting Redcocks', the training squadron, and is scheduled to make its first operational deployment with VFA-115 'Eagles' on USS *Abraham Lincoln*. A proposed derivative, the F/A-18G Growler, may be deployed when the EA-6B becomes too long in the tooth for any further upgrades.

The EA-6B is, nonetheless, already the subject of a key Block 89A/ICAP-III update offering much quicker reaction time, or reduced mean time between signal intercept and jam, based around Litton Industries' Amecom Division LR-700 ESM receiver which is two generations ahead of even the sophisticated F-4G Weasels' now retired AN/APR-47 RAWS. The new LR-700 system, in conjunction with improved jamming pod coordination across the RF spectrum, permits the ECMOs to provide spontaneous, very finely tuned jamming against the latest Russian strategic SAMs' radars, including those of the new Almaz NPO S-300 Favorit family. Although they have not as yet been encountered in combat, they are mature systems first deployed as long ago as 1978 in prototype form and which, today, in more advanced configurations, are being forward-located and offered for export in exchange for much-needed foreign goods and currency, making them a very real threat in any future conflict.

The SA-10 Grumble possesses a reach of some 45–105 miles, depending on the model, with radar guidance principally coming from associated F-Band CW pulse-Doppler Clam Shell, tower-mounted Big Bird or 3-D Tombstone long-range surveillance/EW radars, with I/J-Band Flap Lid phased-array radar used for target tracking.[9] The companion SA-12A Gladiator, developed from an anti-ballistic missile SA-12B Giant SAM system and its target-locating High Screen radar, has more recently been associated with the mobile, frequency-agile F-Band Bill Board for long-range initial target acquisition, backed by the Grill Pan phased-array radar for aircraft target tracking, able to track up to twelve targets and control six SAMs against them, simultaneously. This achieved full operational service in Russia as long ago as 1986.

Defeating the SA-10 and SA-12A's quick-thinking, frequency-hopping acquisition and tracking radars at those ranges requires massively increased response times at very precise frequencies, as these SAMs are theoretically capable of intercepting HARM missiles fired their way, making jamming crucial. Furthermore, a battery of them can network target data, taking turns to transmit, and thereby avoid being hit by HARMs relying solely on anti-radiation homing. The jamming modes that the EA-6B ICAP-III will provide are thus two-fold. The first is known as

Following, whereby the EA-6B spontaneously emulates the enemy emitter's change in frequency to block it. The second is Trailing, which is very similar but the pods maintain jamming in the radar's last used frequencies as well as following newer ones, on the basis of the time-honoured adage 'what goes around, comes around'.

A key feature of the ICAP-III is full Link 16 MIDS data-link compatibility, so that two or more EA-6Bs can work together for a more accurate targeting fix, either for precision mutual jamming or a HARM shoot. Following the flight-test phase, of the current inventory of 124 EA-6Bs all surviving useful airframes are expected to be brought up to full ICAP-III configuration beginning in late 2003, at the rate of twenty-two conversions annually. This will permit the United States to field a combat-capable cadre of twenty reworked EA-6Bs by early 2005.[10]

The urgency of these resurrected efforts reflects new Russian SAM capability. Time-honoured defensive tricks such as terrain masking and defensive high-*g* breaks simply would not work against S-300 class SAMs, even if the pilot was G-LOC-immune: these weapons utilize gas-dynamic control systems for super-manoeuvrability during the closing stages of interception, allowing a 20*g* acceleration in under 0.025 seconds in response to such antics, as well as the ability to engage targets down to treetop level (assuming adequate line-of-sight for a tower-mounted tracking radar). As one pilot put it, 'You have to *hide* from them until you can *kill* them'. New fourth generation stealth designs in development, such as the Joint-service Strike Fighter (JSF) F-35 and F-22 Raptor, relying on golfball and marble RCS respectively, aim to do precisely that – hide, not evade, and right over the enemy's noses.

What makes the new radar threats so different, and these stealth aircraft so important, is that, since the end of the Cold War, top-drawer Russian strategic SAMs have become increasingly available for export: the S-300PMU/PMU-1 and longer-reaching S-300PMU-2, the SA-20, are specifically designed for export and are likely to be operational soon in North Korea, the Balkans, the Indo-Pakistan border area and the Persian Gulf – all ongoing troublespots. It is only a matter of time before even newer SAM systems follow in their tracks.

One pivotal new sensor to be integrated on these revolutionary aircraft is the envisaged Raytheon Advanced Tactical Targeting Technology (AT3) system, under development since late 1998 for US Air Force-wide application eventually. A recent US Air Force news bulletin described the system thus:

> [AT3 is] planned to be a part of the resources of air vehicles in a combat theatre, whether they are dedicated to the suppression of enemy air defences or dedicated primarily to other missions. The AT3 programme is designed to allow [them] to detect, identify and locate precisely enemy air defence systems from ranges of up to 150nm. The accuracy of the location of the systems is intended to be within 50–165ft and to be completed within seconds of the first electronic transmission made by the enemy system. AT3 will employ techniques that integrate separate simultaneous information about an individual enemy air defence system to allow weapons to be targeted on the system.

Looking like a rocket from this perspective, the F-22 Raptor is tomorrow's air dominance fighter. Block 10B versions are destined to employ HARM derivatives and J-series weapons, and will use their inherently stealthy RCS – allegedly 'the size of a marble' – to sneak in close and knock out S-300 and S-400 class Russian SAM radars. Vietnam-era systems would be easy prey for this world-beating design. (LMTAS)

The idea is that strikers, with help from the RC-135V/W Rivet Joint, can pinpoint and destroy enemy air defence systems 'catastrophically immediately after they are turned on'. And not a moment too soon.

The Russian Almaz S-400 Triumph family of SAMs presents a new set of problems. These deadly devices, undergoing field trials since 1999, employ the same baseline systems as used for the S-300 series: the GAZ-66 and MAZ-543 6x6 or 8x8 chunky-wheeled self-propelled launchers, which can disperse from the central radar nervous system along with survey, mess, dormitory and power generator modules fielded on MAZ-543 chassis vehicles, allowing them to pop up at remote, unexpected locations. Although the SA-6 battle area class of SAMs has been doing this for decades on caterpillar-tracked AFVs, true self-contained mobility has only become a phenomenon of weapons with longer reach in much more recent years. Even telescopic radar towers are transportable, allowing for detection of low-flying aircraft and cruise missiles.

Moreover, the newest SAMs offer an intercept speed of up to 14,770ft/sec, but with the ability to track simultaneously double the number of airborne targets than the slower S-300 family. Stand-off jamming, pushing back the IADS' effective detection range, would allow the new generation of stealth jets to sneak in and toss new lattice-finned small smart bombs at their targets, with each bomb self-guiding to a specific target using GPS guidance for mid-course steering, allowing the JSFs to break away and head for home. Nearing the target, the lobbed weapons will employ terminal sensors such as imaging infrared- or millimetre wave-based target recognition templates, with the ability to flex to alternate targets prior to release. High-altitude attack at up to 40,000ft would help them to avoid the clutches of infrared SAMs and triple-A, and drop the weapons at Mach 1.3–1.5 up to 40 miles from the desired impact point.

However, cold-blooded objectivity suggests that, before long, Information Warfare (IW) is likely to be just as important as a dedicated D/SEAD force, and a Hercules-load of semi-renegade white-hat hackers more capable of initially bringing down an enemy's IADS, by means of accessing and disrupting communications systems, in conjunction with interdictors employing soft bombs (even including filaments designed to short-out a city's worth of desktop PCs) deposited by stealth strikers and cruise missiles targeted on key power grids and communications nodes. Demonstrated during Desert Storm and Allied Force, the forerunners of these are considered by some forward-thinkers to be the proper direction.

For example, Serbian MANPADS and SAM radar operators in the field were often discovered to be using up-to-date portable telecommunications-based technology during Allied Force, non-dependent on land-lines, making isolated pockets of mobile SAM resistance far more dangerous than was originally projected, and forcing SEAD supportive air power to assume a constantly reactive posture, wherever aircraft operated. This effectively thwarted the use of CAS/BAI aircraft such as the A-10A, Harrier GR7 and F-16C in an anti-armour and artillery hunting campaign below 15,000ft where they would have been most effective, because of fears of high losses, however well the strategic campaign against the Serbian infrastructure in Belgrade and other nodes was executed by more well-protected interdictors.

Hitting communications effectively is almost certainly the dominant feature of any future major conflict, and one that will involve IW guile as well as hardware. Even more revolutionary IW methods are being devised. During Allied Force, Gen John P. Jumper stated that:

The world of IW is one that is difficult to talk about in any detail. I will tell you that we did more IW in this conflict than we have ever done before, and we proved the potential of it. In my view, the future is very bright in this regard. Instead of sitting and talking about great big large pods that bash electrons, we should be talking about microchips that manipulate electrons and get into the heart and soul of systems like the SA-10 or the SA-12 and tell it that it is a refrigerator and not a radar. Those are things that we are capable of doing today. That is a world I think that we can get to sooner rather than later. And we need to pursue those things. These are light, lean and lethal alternatives to many of the things that we do today that take up big spaces on aircraft to bash electrons. But IW is one that we are just starting to get our arms around. We pay a lot of attention to it at the strategic level, but I submit that we don't pay nearly enough attention at the operational and the tactical level. We need ways, in my opinion, to get into the command-and-control system, to the SAM systems, and to take those things down in ways that would not require putting in a strike force or a HARM missile force to take those things out.

It could be that Iron Hand is an adventure that has come and gone in only two, at best three, generations of skilled flyers. If programmes like the F-22 and JSF flounder, or stealth is rapidly rendered obsolete by new counter-technology, the lessons learned in Vietnam may have to be re-experienced all over again – the hard way. Like it or lump it, another epoch of electronic combat has already begun, and it is not certain yet whether it is the cat or the mouse that has gained the upper hand.

ABBREVIATIONS

AAM	Air-to-Air Missile	CAS	Close Air Support
AAR	Air-to-Air Refuelling	CBU	Cluster Bomb Unit
ABCCC	Airborne Command, Control and Communications	CCIP	Continuously Computed Impact Point, or Common Configuration Implementation Program
AC	Aircraft Commander		
ACC	Air Combat Command	CEM	Combined Effects Munitions
ADI	Attitude Director Indicator, or artificial horizon	CENTAF	Central Command Air Force
		CENTCOM	Central Command
AEW	Airborne Early Warning; latterly, Air Expeditionary Wing	CI	Control Indicator
		CINCPAC	Commander in Chief, Pacific Fleet
AFC	Airframe Change		
AFSC	Air Force Systems Command	CINCSAC	Commander in Chief, Strategic Air Command
AGL	Above Ground Level		
AGM	Air-to-Ground Missile	CLC	Command Launch Computer
AIM	Air Intercept Missile	CRT	Cathode Ray Tube
ALC	Air Logistics Centre	CTF	Carrier Task Force
ALIC	Aircraft/Launcher Interface Computer	DA	Direct Attack
		DEAD	Destruction of Enemy Air Defences
AMA	Air Materiel Area		
AMTI	Airborne Moving Target Indicator	DECM	Defensive Electronic Countermeasures
ANG	Air National Guard	DIANE	Digital Integrated Attack and Navigation Equipment
ARM	Anti-Radiation Missile		
ARREC	Armed Reconnaissance	DIRCM	Directed-energy Infrared Countermeasures
ASM	Anti-Ship Missile		
ATI	Applied Technology Industries	DLA	Dual Launch Adaptor
ATO	Air Tasking Order	DMZ	Demilitarized Zone
Atkron	Attack Squadron	EA	Electronic Attack
AWACS	Airborne Warning & Control System	ECM	Electronic Countermeasures
		ECMO	Electronic Countermeasures Officer
BAI	Battle Area Interdiction		
BARCAP	Barrier Combat Air Patrol	EFS	Expeditionary Fighter Squadron
BDA	Bomb Damage Assessment	Elint	Electronic Intelligence
B/N	Bombardier/Navigator	EMCON	Emission Control
C3	Command, Control and Communications	EOB	Electronic Order of Battle
		EOM	Equations of Motion, or range-known
C4	Command, Control, Communications and Computing		
		ES	Electronic Surveillance
CAG	Carrier Air Group commander	EW	Early Warning radar
CAP	Combat Air Patrol	EWO	Electronic Warfare Officer

FAC	Forward Air Control	PAT/ARM	Passive Angle Tracking/ARM
FFAR	Folding Fin Aerial Rocket	PB	Pre-Brief
FLIR	Forward-Looking Infrared	PGM	Precision-Guided Munitions
FMS	Foreign Military Sales	PJ	Parajumper rescueman
FS	Fighter Squadron	POL	Petroleum, Oil, Lubricants
GCI	Ground Control Intercept	PPI	Plan Position Indicator
GE	General Electric (USA)	PRF	Pulse Repetition Frequency
GPS	Global Positioning Satellite	PUP	Performance Update Program
HARM	High-speed ARM	QRC	Quick Reaction Capability
HAWC	Homing and Warning Computer	RAM	Radar Absorbent Material
HOTAS	Hands on Throttle and Stick	RAT	Ram Air Turbine
HTS	HARM Targeting System	RAWS	Radar Attack and Warning
HUD	Head-Up Display		System
IADS	Integrated Air Defence System	RCP	Rear Cockpit
ICAP	Improved Capability	RCS	Radar Cross-Section
IDF/AF	Israeli Defence Force/Air Force	RESCAP	Rescue Combat Air Patrol
IDM	Improved Data-link Modem	RHAWS	Radar Homing and Warning
IFF	Identification Friend or Foe		System
IFR	Instrument Flight Rules	ROE	Rules of Engagement
INS	Inertial Navigation System	RP	Route Pack (sector in North
IOC	Initial Operating Capability, or		Vietnam)
	Intercept Operations Centre	RPV	Remotely Piloted Vehicle
JASSM	Joint-service Air-to-Surface	RTAFB	Royal Thai Air Force Base
	Stand-off Missile	RTU	Replacement Training Unit
JCS	Joint Chiefs of Staff	RWR	Radar Warning Receiver
JSOW	Joint-service Stand-Off Weapon	SAC	Strategic Air Command
KTO	Kuwaiti Theatre of Operations	SAM	Surface-to-Air Missile
LLLTV	Low Light Level Television	SAR	Search and Rescue
LWR	Launch Warning Receiver	SARH	Semi-Active Radar-Homing
MANPADS	Man Portable Air Defence	SEAD	Suppression of Enemy Air
	System		Defences
MCAS	Marine Corps Air Station	SIDS	Shrike Improved Display System
MIDS	Multifunction Information	SIGINT	Signals Intelligence
	Distribution System	SIOP	Single Integrated Operations Plan
MR	Military Region (in South	SOC	Sector Operations Centre
	Vietnam)	SP	Self-Protect
MTI	Moving Target Indicator	SSM	Surface-to-Surface Missile
NAA	North American Aviation	STARM	Standard ARM
NARF	Naval Air Rework Facility	SWATCH	Southern Watch
NAS	Naval Air Station	SWIP	Systems, Weapons Improvement
NAVSTAR	Navigation Satellite Timing and		Program
	Ranging	TAC	Tactical Air Command
NFZ	No-Fly Zone	TACAN	Tactical Air Navigation
NVG	Night Vision Goggles	TACOS	Tanker, Countermeasures or
NWC	Naval Weapons Centre		Strike
OAF	Operation Allied Force	TALD	Tactical Air-Launched Decoy
OAP	Offset Aimpoint	TARCAP	Target CAP
OET	Operator Enters Target	TAWC	Tactical Air Warfare Centre
OFP	Operational Flight Program	TCTO	Time Compliance Technical
PACAF	Pacific Air Forces		Order

TDY	Temporary Duty		TWS	Track-While-Scan
TFS	Tactical Fighter Squadron		TWT	Travelling-Wave Tube
TFTS	Tactical Fighter Training Squadron		UAV	Unmanned Aerial Vehicle
			USAFE	United States Air Forces Europe
TFW	Tactical Fighter Wing		VA	Attack squadron
TFW(P)	Tactical Fighter Wing (Provisional)		VAQ	Electronic countermeasures squadron; latterly, electronic attack squadron
TI	Texas Instruments			
TIAS	Target Identification and Acquisition System		VDI	Vertical Display Indicator
			VF	Fighter squadron
TO	Technical Order		VFA	Fighter-attack squadron
TOO	Target of Opportunity		WESTPAC	Western Pacific combat cruise
TOT	Time Over Target		WSO	Weapons Systems Officer, or 'Wizzo'
TRANSPAC	Transiting the Pacific			
TTR	Target-Tracking Radar			

CONVERSION TABLE

1 ft	=	0.31 m
1 mile	=	1.61 km
1 nm	=	1.85 km
1 kt	=	1.85 km/hour
1 US gallon	=	3.79 litre
1 lb	=	0.45 kg
1 (short) ton	=	0.91 tonne

NOTES

CHAPTER ONE

1. J.T. Smith, *Rolling Thunder – The Strategic Bombing Campaign, North Vietnam 1965–1968* (Air Research Publications, 1994). Rolling Thunder actually began with RT 5 on 2 March 1965, earlier RTs 1–4 having been cancelled. With stop-go pauses, the campaign endured through to RT 58, which concluded at the end of October 1968.

2. T. Clancy with Gen C. Horner, *Every Man a Tiger* (Sidgwick & Jackson, 2000). The frustration imposed by Rolling Thunder's gradualism and the strict Rules of Engagement caused some crews to ignore the rules when the situation dictated, and deliberately bomb short or long to strike a lucrative nearby target.

3. Commander in Chief Pacific Fleet (CINCPACFLT) Staff Study 10–66 (4 August 1966), which examined losses attributed to triple-A and small-arms fire and terrain/weather.

4. S.J. Zaloga, 'Soviet Air Defence', *Janes' Defence Data 1998*; B. Nalty, 'Wild Weasel Bares its Fangs', *Tactics and Techniques of Electronic Warfare* (Office of Air Force History, August 1977).

5. The Eye series included the Mk82 Snakeye bomb, a standard 500lb general-purpose iron bomb or mine fitted with a high-drag tail unit that popped open into a steel cruciform after release to avoid the dropper being caught in the bomb blast during low-level deliveries, provided deliveries were at or below 500kt airspeed. Other members of the Eye family used extensively by the US Navy, and in limited numbers by the US Air Force, included the Mk20 Rockeye II cluster bomb and AGM-62 Walleye TV-homing smart bomb, the latter baptised in combat by Cdr Homer Smith, CO of A-4E-equipped VA-212 'Rampant Raiders', flying against enemy barracks at Sam Son from USS *Bonne Homme Richard* on 11 March 1967, representing the first of the new generation of so-called smart bombs.

6. The US Air Force's initial encounter with SAMs during July 1965 (and their response) is aired in the next chapter.

7. Repeater Mode jamming, along with other active countermeasures techniques, is explained more fully in the ensuing chapters.

8. CINCPACFLT Staff Studies (1 March 1967 and 14 May 1968).

9. Cdr J.B. Nichols USN (Ret) and B. Tillman, *On Yankee Station, The Naval Air War over Vietnam* (Naval Institute Press, 1987).

10. *A-7 Configuration Comparison* (LTV, March 1983). LTV produced 199 A-7As and 196 A-7Bs. The follow-on A-7E's digital systems are described in Chapter Three. The first 67 A-7Es produced under Blocks I–III were redesignated A-7C as they were powered by the A-7B's TF30-P-408 rather than the Rolls-Royce/Allison TF41-A-2. Block IV thus initiated the production of what eventually amounted to 529 A-7Es.

11. B. Gunston, *Fighters of the Fifties* (PSL, 1981). Douglas built 28 F3D-1s and 237 F3D-2s for shore-based night-fighter duties through October 1953, and

35 of the latter were subsequently converted to the F3D-2Q configuration. The aircraft were redesignated EF-10B in October 1962, as part of the US-wide simplification of weapons system nomenclature.

12. A concurrent programme saw 85 A-3Bs converted to KA-3B tankers, with 34 of these subsequently being adapted to the more versatile EKA-3B configuration.

13. These were the origins of today's AWACS. EC-121Ds AEW aircraft fitted with ventral and dorsal radar began flying Vietnam combat missions on 17 April 1965, using the callsign Disco, and providing warnings over the radio on Guard frequency (to be received by everybody), calling 'Yellow Bandits' for MiGs airborne and 'Red Bandits' for MiGs within 10 miles of US strike waves. 'Bluebells' was used for active SAM sites, and position provided relative to the Hanoi bull's-eye. The callsigns were later changed to different colours for the different types of MiG, i.e. 'Blue Bandits' for MiG-21s, 'White Bandits' for MiG-19s and 'Red Bandits' for MiG-17s. EC-121s worked with US Navy Red Crown radar picket ships and carrier-borne Grumman E-1 Tracer and E-2 Hawkeye AEW aircraft, forming part of the Navy's Positive Identification Radar Advisory Zone, which controlled and monitored US aircraft movements in and out of North Vietnamese airspace as well as providing warnings of enemy fighter and missile activity.

14. The original A-6A pen-aid devices were similar to those of the A-7A, comprising AN/ALR-15 receiver, AN/ALQ-51 gate stealer and AN/ALE-18 chaff dispenser. The ATI AN/APR-25 and Magnavox AN/APR-27 were added later, along with the AN/ALQ-100 jamming and AN/ALE-29 chaff-dispensing systems. The Iron Hand mission really became the bailiwick of three subvariants of the A-6B, which are described in the next two chapters.

CHAPTER TWO

1. Maj W.A. Hewitt, *Planting the Seed of SEAD* (1993).
2. A.R. Seefluth, 'Birth of the Pods', *Air Force Magazine* (February 1992).
3. The seven F-100F WW-I conversions were 58-1221, -1226, -1227 and -1231, followed by 58-1206, -1212 and -1232. Two were originally selected for conversion under an informal contract dated 15 September 1965, followed by another pair contracted on 19 October, then three more were added on 7 January 1966.
4. The first ever Weasel combat loss occurred on 20 December 1965, when Capt John J. Pitchford and his EWO Capt Robert D. Trier flying F-100F 58-1231 were shot down by triple-A during an attack on a SAM battery 5 miles southeast of Kep airfield. Trier went down with the aircraft. Pitchford ejected, was taken prisoner and survived captivity. F-100F 58-1212, flown by Capt Clyde Dawson and Capt Don Clark, succumbed to triple-A on 23 March 1966, both men being listed as KIA. The third F-100F loss was an accidental one and involved 58-1221 on a theatre familiarization flight on 13 March: the aircraft crashed approximately 20 miles east of Ubon at 1330hr (local time). Tuttle and Clark ejected successfully after the engine developed a series of severe compressor stalls followed by a flameout, and could not be restarted. *Misc sources.*
5. D.R. Jenkins (with M. Roth), *F-105 Thunderchief, Workhorse of the Vietnam War* (McGraw-Hill Publications, 2000).
6. Based on correspondence with the author and extracts from Mike Gilroy's article 'First in, Wrong Way Out', *Journal of Electronic Defence* (October 1999).
   F-105F WW-III losses during July and August 1966 comprised: 63-8286, Maj Roosevelt Hestle and Capt Charles Morgan, brought down by triple-A

over RP V and captured on 6 July; 63-8338, Maj Gene Pemberton and Maj Ben Newsom (POW, both dying in captivity), hit by a SAM over RP VI on 23 July; 63-8361, Capt Robert Sandvick and Capt Thomas Pyle III, downed by triple-A over RP VIB on 7 August to become POWs; and 63-8308, Maj Joseph Brand and Maj Donald Singer (MIA), hit by triple-A over RP V on 17 August. *Misc sources.*

7. Based on correspondence with the author and an interview conducted by photographer Frank B. Mormillo on the author's behalf with both Kim Pepperell and Gerry Knotts.

8. F-105F WW-III losses in 1967, with respect to survivors and their families for any errors or omissions, included: 62-4420 over RP VI on 29 January, Maj Larry Biediger and Lt Claude Silva both KIA; 63-8286 downed by a SAM over RP III on 18 February, Capt David Duart and Capt Jay Jensen becoming POWs; 63-8277 downed by a SAM over RP V on 27 April, Maj John Dudash being killed and Capt Alton Meyer taken prisoner; 63-8330 hit by a MiG-21 over RP VIB on 6 October, Capt Joseph C. Howard and Capt George L. Shamblee nursing the aircraft out to the Tonkin Gulf prior to ejection; 62-4430 over RP V on 5 November, Maj Richard Dutton and Capt Earl Cobeil ejecting to become POWs (though Cobeil died in captivity); 63-8295 downed by a MiG over RP V near Phuc Yen airfield on 18 November, Maj Oscar Dardeau (KIA) and Capt Edward W. Lehnhoff (MIA); and 63-8349 on 19 November, Maj Gerald Gustafson and Capt Russell Brownlee ejecting over Laos and being rescued.

F-105F Ryan's Raiders included 62-4419 and -4429, 63-8263, -8269, -8274, -8275, -8276, -8278, -8293, -8312, -8317, -8346 and -8353. Three remain unidentified. Three were lost during 1967: 63-8269 on 12 May over RP I, Capt Peter P. Pitman and Capt Robert A. Stewart both KIA when their aircraft hit the ground (probably as a result of becoming disorientated at night with failed instruments); 62-4429 succumbed to triple-A on 15 May over RP VI, Maj Ben Pollard and Capt Donald Heiliger being taken prisoner. The third loss occurred on 4 October during a mission to Lang Con railroad bridge; Maj Morris L. McDaniel and Capt William A. Lillund were listed as MIA. *Misc sources.*

CHAPTER THREE

1. Theoretical maximum range was approximately 75nm if the Standard ARM was fired directly at the target from 40,000ft, but attacking jets invariably flew at half that altitude or lower, thus reducing range to 30 or 35nm. Off-axis launch reduced range considerably.

2. A-6A BuNos 149949, 149957 and 151558–151565 inclusive. All had originally been manufactured at Grumman's New York plant between late 1963 and 1964.

3. The ER-142 was first fitted to the F-105F WW-III Thunderchief, as a replacement for the IR-133 system, from September 1966. See Chapter Two.

4. In correspondence with Peter E. Davies and the author, 1985–7. Throughout the first half of this book, use has been made of both the earlier (VHF, UHF, L, S, C, X etc.) and later (A, B, C etc.) banding systems and readers are referred to the chart in Chapter Five for comparison (see page 161). It should be noted, however, that the older banding system changed during the Vietnam years, in accordance with manufacturers' specifications and security clouding.

5. TRIM's cupola (known as the Optical Sensor Platform) featured both TI

LLLTV and FLIR sensors linked to the A-6's standard DIANE avionics through a new P-7B TRIM computer programme. This permitted the crews to locate targets by night on IARM, which replaced the radar-only DVRI. Typically, sensors were slewed to targets or offset aimpoints acquired first using radar, 'with the sensors being used to correct the radar solution if imagery was recognized', according to the VA-165 report. The weather precluded use of the sensors on about two-thirds of strike missions, but optronic target aids had arrived – precursors to today's LST/SCAM and LANTIRN pods, used in the DEAD role. See Chapters Six and Seven.

6. The third Line Period was 21 July to 3 August. 'Due to brief in-port period at Cubi Point, 15–19 July, the narrative and statistics are inclusive of both Line Periods 2 and 3,' wrote Cdr Zick in his VA-165 end-of-year report.

7. After their tenure with VA-52, the A-6B PAT/ARMs went on to serve with VA-95 'Green Lizards' and VA-115 'Arabs', the latter seeing action during the Linebacker offensive. See Chapter Four.

8. A-6A BuNos 149944, 149955, 151591 and 152616–152617.

9. Further F-105F Wild Weasel losses in 1968 not mentioned in the narrative, other than Ryan's Raiders, claimed 63-8356 *Miss Molly* and its crew Maj James C. Hartney and Capt Samuel Fantle III on 5 January, shot down by a MiG-17 during a mission to Dong Luc railroad bridge. Night-time precision bombing then became the exclusive province of the F-4D-equipped 8th TFW at Ubon RTAFB. Many of their aircraft were later equipped with ARN-92 LORAN under the Pave Phantom project, and worked the night-shift along the Ho Chi Minh Trail. Unlike the Ryan's Raiders, which were hybrid night attack-cum-Weasels, the F-4D employed no specialist radar-receiving equipment and were used primarily for sensor-sowing and target strikes along the Trail.

   There also were three known Ryan's Raiders losses during 1968: 63-8293 was hit by triple-A over Laos on 18 February and abandoned by Maj Michael S. Muscat and Capt Kyle Stouder over Thailand, who returned to fight; 63-8312 *Midnight Sun* was felled by a SAM over RP VI on 29 February, Maj Crosley J. Fitton Jr being listed as KIA and Capt Cleveland S. Harris as MIA; and 63-8353 on 15 July, downed over RP I, Maj Gobel James being captured and Capt Larry E. Martin listed as KIA.

10. Maj W.A. Hewitt, *Planting the Seed of SEAD – The Wild Weasel in Vietnam* (1993). In July 1968 the US Air Force embarked on several Wild Weasel studies based around the ubiquitous, multi-role F-4 to carry Standard ARM and replace its already war-weary F-105s.

11. L. Davis, *Wild Weasel: SAM Suppression Story* (Squadron Signal Publications, 1985); and Maj Gerald Stiles USAF (Ret) in correspondence with the author 1984–5.

12. Material courtesy of F-4 historian Alan Howarth, in correspondence with the author.

13. V. Flintham, *Air Wars and Aircraft* (Arms & Armour Press, 1989). A US Navy Lockheed EC-121M Super Constellation monitoring aircraft from VQ-1 on patrol from Atsugi AB over the Sea of Japan was downed by North Korean MiG-17s on 15 April 1969 (local time), with the loss of all 31 crewmembers, further inflaming US–North Korean relations. A further 21 Americans were killed in border skirmishes with North Korea along the Korean DMZ that year.

14. Refer to Don's Dirty Dozen and Crew Chiefs in Chapter Four, for an account of the 67th TFS's combat exploits during the Linebacker II offensive. William McLeod's extensive account of the F-4C WW-IV Weasel-related squadron chops and changes in Japan, South Korea and Okinawa is included for

posterity because official records still reflect the original masterplan which actually did not take place as specified in those documents, causing some confusion among unit historians.

CHAPTER FOUR

1. 'Air War Vietnam, Part III, The Battle for the Skies over North Vietnam', ed. Lt Col G. Nelson and Maj N. Wood, from *Air War Vietnam* (Arno Press, 1978).

2. Window, initially dumped at one minute intervals from RAF bombers, and dispensed automatically later in the war from the aircraft using new hoppers, was first employed in quantity by Avro Lancasters on night-time raids against Hamburg in late July 1943, to confound German EW/GCI radars such as Freya and Wurzburg, which were responsible for vectoring the enemy's deadly night-fighters on to the bomber streams.

3. Electronic warfare special report, *Aviation Week & Space Technology* (McGraw-Hill Publications, 27 January 1975).

4. Another unfortunate incident involving Shrike occurred on 15 April that year, when two AGM-45s fired from an F-105G guided to the superstructure of the US Navy frigate USS *Worden*, killing one man and wounding everyone else on the bridge.

5. According to Barry Miller, 'crews often found the calls annoying and so commonplace they were often ignored. In one case, I recall a 17th WWS crew (I believe it was Capt Dobbs and Capt Haines) on a night mission, at first disregarded the call, but upon checking the SAM call location and their own, were shocked to find them the same, and promptly reacted'. The volume of enemy SAMs was overwhelming at times.

    The EA-3A pure eavesdropping variants flown by VQ-1 and VQ-2 had been flying Elint from NAS Cubi Point since early in the war. VQ-2 maintained its two-aircraft Detachment Bravo at Da Nang AB from 1965–9, and operated from the Philippines during 1972–3. Two Elint EP-3Bs entered service with VQ-1 in June–July 1969 and operated from Da Nang AB, with the first of ten EP-3E ARIES joining them in 1971.

6. J. Ethell and A. Price, *One Day in a Long War* (Greenhill Books, 1990).

7. Regular Skywarrior deployments ended on 10 October 1974 when Det 4 of VAQ-130 completed its last WestPac cruise on USS *Ranger*. The aircraft was replaced by the EA-6B Prowler for carrier-based jamming duties.

8. VA-35 repeatedly hammered SAM sites in the Haiphong complex with Mk83 bombs and Rockeye II CBUs on 19, 20 and 26 December 1972. Kien An and Cat Bi airfields also received bombing treatment.

9. *ATKRON 146 Annual Report for 1969*. VA-146 was first to receive the A-7C and A-7E models during 1969. The pilots described the TF-41 as an immense improvement. By the end of the year VA-146 was exclusively A-7E-equipped. Most of the sixty-seven A-7Cs built served as trainers with VA-122 'Corsair College' (from 1972 known as the 'Flying Eagles') at NAS Lemoore and VA-174 'Hell Razors' at NAS Cecil Field, Florida, the Fleet's West and East Coast A-7 RAGs respectively.

10. DoD News (14 March 2000). As of November 2000, 2,011 American servicemen – many of them flyers – remained MIA from the Vietnam War. However, another 572 have been identified and returned to their families for burial since 1975. Mitochondrial DNA forensic testing has made this possible, laying many ghosts to rest. Cdr Hall was one of the more recent MIA cases to be resolved.

11. B. Nalty, 'Wild Weasel Bares its Fangs', *Tactics and Techniques of Electronic Warfare*.
12. J.T. Smith, *The Linebacker Raids* (Arms & Armour Press, 1998).
13. A story related to the author via Maj Kim Pepperell USAF (Ret). Sam Peacock retired as a lieutenant-colonel and was one of the first EWOs to command an F-4G Weasel squadron, during his final days at George AFB in the early 1980s, where he was affectionately known as Papa Bear by his juniors.

    The S-125 Neva, or SA-3 Goa, was designed as a low- to medium-altitude partner to the SA-2 to cover the lower skies. It relied on Low Blow radar for target tracking and missile command guidance, but certainly North Vietnamese Flat Face radars could have been used for target acquisition.
14. Karl J. Eschmann, *Linebacker: The Untold Story of the Air Raids over North Vietnam* (Ballantine Books, 1989).
15. The early work-up and deployments to South Korea are discussed in Chapter Three, when looking at initial F-4C WW-IV operations.
16. In his 1973 end-of-year report, VA-35 boss Cdr Hesse recorded the stop-go nature of Mod 1 A-6B TIAS training: '22 May: Formal lectures began for three pilots and six B/Ns in A-6B TIAS system. The squadron was further tasked to restore three A-6B aircraft to full TIAS system status. Despite numerous obstacles this difficult feat was to be accomplished by the time VA-35 commenced its first embarked Type Training. 25 June: TIAS training in A-6B discontinued. 12 Oct: MATWING directs resumption of A-6B TIAS training. 23 Oct: A-6B training terminated for second time.'

    The 561st TFS F-105Gs and crews were also placed on alert in late 1973 because of Arab–Israeli tensions in the Middle East. Lt Col Barry Miller said: 'Arab SAMs were proving particularly effective in the war's early stages, and there existed a real possibility US air forces would become involved.' See Chapter Five.
17. The superlative AGM-88 High-Speed Anti-Radiation Missile (HARM), described in Chapter Five. The STARM pod programme was terminated when EA-6Bs of VAQ-131 became HARM-capable, allowing them to use the new missiles for intelligence-gathering.
18. The AN/APR-25/-26 sets were first upgraded to AN/APR-36/-37 standard. The new AN/ALR-46 RWR combined both RHAWS and LWR functions of the 36/-37 in a more integrated fashion, and so there was no longer any separate designation for the LWR subsystem. In the early days of the AN/ALR-46 the LWR remained strictly omnidirectional, and thus if working alone could alert the crews to a bigger panoply of dangers but could not give them a threat bearing.
19. The 39th TFTS F-4C WW-IV school was activated on 1 July 1977, replacing the 563rd TFS. Vietnam War electrocapital displays invariably added new tubes, several of them based on small Sony TV sets inset into the consoles.
20. The ensuing account is based on correspondence with Lt Col William C. McLeod II, who kindly discussed the operation with Col Jack R. Suggs USAFRes (Ret), and provided additional details on the author's behalf.

CHAPTER FIVE

1. Israel had received a grand total of 204 F-4Es and 18 RF-4Es under Peace Echo I–V, Peace Patch and Nickel Grass deliveries by the end of the 1970s, which allowed more squadrons to form, including 107 Zanov Katom ('Orange Tails'), 69 Atalev ('Bats') and 105 Akrav ('Scorpions'). The units operated from Hatzor, Hatzerim, Ramat David and Tel Nof air bases flying

strategic strike, air defence and defence suppression duties. In all, 114 F-4E/RF-4Es were operational at the outbreak of the Yom Kippur War in October 1973 with three squadrons, with a fourth in the process of converting from Mirage IIIs. *Misc sources.*

2. Col E. 'Cheetah' Cohen, *Israel's Best Defense, The First Full Story of the Israeli Air Force* (Crown Books, 1993). The first Israeli F-4E casualty occurred in mid-September 1969, during an attack on a Jordanian radar station at Ajaloun. The crew ejected and were rescued. Hankin was brought down in October 1973.

3. 'Cheetah' Cohen, *ibid*; M. Halperin and A. Lapidot, *G-Suit, Combat Reports from Israel's Air War* (Sphere Books, 1990).

4. Courtesy of Mike Metz, who kindly relayed this account to the author after contacting his former *Rocketeer* and *Squid* squadron mates from Seymour-Johnson AFB, and Torrejon AB, who supplied some of the anecdotal background information quoted. The word jammer in this context refers to the MJU-4 diesel-powered bomb-loading fork-lift used by munitions personnel.

5. Anecdotal information on Maverick courtesy of Stan Goldstein, former EWO of Wild Weasel F-105F *Crown Seven*, flown by John Revak. Following his Vietnam tour, Stan Goldstein was posted to George AFB and was part of the team that trained the initial Israeli crews on the F-4E. All other information contained in this chapter on the IDF/AF comes from open published sources and those listed elsewhere in these endnotes.

6. Deliveries of the swing-role General Dynamics (now Lockheed Martin) F-16 began in October 1978, initially equipping the 388th TFW at Hill AFB, Utah, and the 56th TFW at MacDill, Florida. Select F-4s, too, also received the AN/ALR-69 RWR mod, including F-4Ds which sprouted a grotesque cluster of receivers on the phallic nose radome appendage, colloquially known as the 'Herpes mod'!

7. These included the AN/AAQ-123 as well as AN/ALQ-132 and -140 Multibrick IRCM pods and IR 'blow holes'. The only known operational application of these devices has been on US Air Force Special Operations AC/MC-130s and HH-53/60s, which since the late 1980s have taken on the ARRS rescue role for downed airmen.

8. Interestingly, it was the United Kingdom which first fielded RHAWS/RWRs in combat, when a small number of Hawker Typhoon tank-busters were equipped in 1944–5 with Abdullah receivers designed to detect German EW radars. However, in the jet age, RAF fighters flew naked right up until 1974, when RWRs and ECM began to be introduced on its jets.

9. A contemporary air-to-air ARM project dubbed Brazo (Spanish for 'arm') married a passive seeker to an AIM-7E Sparrow III missile airframe, for use against AEW/AWACS airborne radar command and control posts. In 1974–5 tests were conducted over the White Sands Missile Range in New Mexico, using an F-4D from the Holloman-based 6585th TG firing Brazo against radiating Firebee drones, with the weapons destroying the target or passing within a lethal distance, as planned. Brazo was terminated in 1977.

10. Courtesy Alan Howarth. F-4D 66-7635 later served with General Dynamics and Westinghouse for flight trials of the F-16's AN/APG-66 multimode radar, once gutted of its APR-38 systems. F-4D 66-7647 spent most of the remainder of its career as a regular trainer with the 31st TFW at Homestead AFB. The original proposal called for ninety F-4Ds to be converted to the Advanced Wild Weasel configuration. The US Air Force eventually obtained 134 of the much better F-4G, under two separate batches.

McDonnell Douglas papers written by John J. Harty cite the first flight of the F-4D Advanced Wild Weasel testbed (in its early aerodynamic and 'jerry-rigged' configuration) as November 1972. The same papers mention 1 May 1975 for contract go-ahead for the F-4E/APR-38 combination.

11. In correspondence with the author, 1984–5 and 1989–90, and with subsequent papers and articles produced by Jerry Stiles and in the public domain.

12. Deliveries of 793 F-4Ds had been completed in 1968, while the F-4E remained in production for the US Air Force (993 examples) until December 1976. Overseas sales saw the F-4E in production until 1981, allowing for easy access of basic spare parts.

13. The initial batch of 116 F-4Gs converted from Blocks 42–45 between 1975 and 1981 were all Fiscal Year 1969 F-4Es drawn from the serial range 69-0236 to 69-7588. The follow-on batch of eighteen attrition replacements, converted and delivered in 1987 and 1988, comprised remaining candidates in the Blocks 42–44 serial range 69-0244 to 69-7557.

14. The 39th TFTS became the 562nd TFTS on 9 October 1980, retaining its RTU duties. With the retirement of the F-105Gs at George AFB, the F-4Gs were realigned under the 561st TFS, 562nd TFTS and 563rd TFS.

15. Jerry Lynn flew the Tech Orders over to England for the RAF's Black Buck missions by Shrike-armed Vulcans against the Falkland Islands as part of Operation Corporate in 1982. The missiles came out of the weapons storage area at Spangdahlem AB.

   The first ever F-4G loss was 69-7213 (81st TFS) on 13 March 1980, which crashed on Mount Moncayo, 36 miles west of Zaragoza AB, en route to the Bardenas Reales weapons range.

16. The sixteen aircraft converted embraced four ex-HC-130Hs and twelve C-130Hs. Equipment in the definitive Block 35 configuration eventually included three UHF radios (including secure Have Quick), VHF, KH-58 SATCOM, two KY-75 HF systems and the Tactical Radio Acquisition and Countermeasures Subsystem (TRACS-C).

17. A similar HUD/FLIR system was later made available to US Air Force F-15E and F-16 strike jets by means of a Marconi HUD and Martin Marietta LANTIRN navigation pods, turning the Block 50 F-16Cs into the F-16CG configuration. This also employed terrain-avoidance radar to generate pull-up/nose-down steering cues on the HUD, for low-level terrain-following flight. The LANTIRN targeting pod, the companion device, introduced a movable FLIR and boresighted laser which was used for heads down target tracking and lasing, akin to the A-6E TRAM and the F-111F's and F-4E's Pave Tack system.

18. The first operational unit to equip with all-up F/A-18As was VMFA-314 'Black Knights', at MCAS El Toro, California, in January 1983. A new training unit exclusively for the Marines, VMFAT-101 'Sharpshooters', formed at El Toro in March 1988, so that VFA-125 became Navy-only thereafter. US Navy F/A-18As were all retired from seagoing duties by 1995, so that today's carrier air wings fly only the C/D models, and latest E/F Super Hornets.

19. The warhead was relatively modest given the SAM's size, and in practice these conventionally armed models were thwarted by jamming and poor manoeuvrability in the thin upper air when attempting to intercept an SR-71A. In North Korean use the command and control battery employed Big Back and Side Net surveillance radars, while the SA-5 was operational with three battalions, each employing six SA-5 launchers, ten trailers and six transporter tractors, plus a Bar Lock and a Square Pair radar. It is likely that the Libyan system at Sirte was similar in composition. For Soviet strategic home defence use, more sinister and deadly nuclear-armed versions were apparently available.

20. Lt Cdr J.T. Stanik, *Swift and Effective Retribution, The US Sixth Fleet and the Confrontation with Qadaffi* (Navy Historical Center, 1996).

21. Phase Two of PUP, which was not funded, was to have added a new E-Systems Directional Receiver Group with new steered receiver and phased interferometers, and later a modem for in-flight threat data-transfer to slapshot hunter/killer HARM-toting companions. Sadly, this never went ahead.

22. The fresh conversions were drawn from the same production Blocks as the original batch, as noted in Note 13. These aircraft had been identified earlier as prospective candidates for upgrading to the F-4G configuration and were, as long ago as 1978, prospective FMS F-4G exports to Iran, which had been seeking to purchase twelve of them on the heels of its big new-build F-4E buy. The prospective F-4G buy was effectively terminated after the Shah was deposed from power. The F-4G was never even contemplated for export after that time.

23. Fortuitously, just such a payload forms one version of the AGM-154 JSOW, described in the ensuing chapters, and was employed for the first time on 16 February 2001 against radar sites near Baghdad. Earlier efforts at marrying radar-trashing CBU canisters to PGMs included the Paveway I/II-era Pave Storm, tested but never fielded.

CHAPTER SIX

1. US CENTCOM replaced the Rapid Deployment Joint Task Force originally created by President Jimmy Carter on 1 March 1980. It was formed to handle contingency crises in the Middle East, on the heels of the Iranian Islamic revolution and the Soviet invasion of Afghanistan. President Ronald Reagan recast it as CENTCOM on 1 January 1983, with its area of responsibility widened to include Africa. Air components for CENTAF were furnished as part of Vigilante Warrior deployments, which were effectively replaced by new Aerospace Expeditionary Forces (AEF). Active-duty, Air National Guard and Air Force Reserve units were later reorganized into ten deployable AEFs that could be assigned, in pairs, for ninety-day TDYs over a fifteen-month rotational cycle. The first AEFs began their deployment cycles on 1 October 1995, in support of Southern Watch activities, described later in this chapter.

2. Quotes in the narrative and accompanying box are by courtesy of Tony Cassanova, who interviewed Col George Walton II on behalf of the author for this book. Only the 561st TFS deployed from George AFB, while the 562nd TFTS remained in California. The 563rd TFS had been inactivated on 25 September 1989, with the 561st TFS absorbing its aircraft.

   The mixed F-4G/F-16C squadrons under the 52nd TFW at Spangdahlem AB went through some important restructuring at this time. The 480th TFS stayed in Germany and handed back its F-4Gs to the 81st TFS to bolster its numbers for the Sheikh Isa AB deployment, the 81st TFS in turn relinquishing its F-16C/Ds. The 23rd TFS remained as a mixed F-4G/F-16C unit and deployed to Incirlik AB.

3. A new SEAD weapon that did not make it beyond the test stage was the Northrop AGM-136A Tacit Rainbow cruise missile.

4. D. Hollway, 'Stealth Secrets of the F-117A Nighthawk', *Aviation History* (March 1996); and *Aviation Week & Space Technology* (misc. issues).

5. Quote: *Gulf War Air Power Survey* (Government Printing Office, 1993). Earlier statistics are taken from *Nighthawks Over Iraq, A Chronology of the F-117A Stealth in Operations Desert Shield and Desert Storm, Special Study:*

37th FW/NO-91-1 compiled by SM Sgt Harold P. Myers (Ret) (Office of History, HQ 37th FW, 12th Air Force, TAC, 1991).

See also Dr C.J. Bowie, 'The Stealth Revolution in Aerial Combat', *Air Power History* (winter 1998). Bowie cites the need for only twenty F-117As to hit thirty-seven targets, whereas an observable 'dumb' strike package hitting a mere three targets (the Q Package mission, launched in daylight on Day Three of the air war) required a Vietnam-style ensemble of up to ninety mutually supportive jets, including seventy-two F-16s, eight F-15 escorts and ten F-4G and EF-111A SEAD aircraft. Such comparisons, widely toted after the Gulf War in support of stealth, are somewhat misleading as observable F-15Es and F-111Fs using PGMs achieved enormous damage.

6. *Gulf War Air Power Survey, Vol II* (Government Printing Office, 1993).

7. In correspondence and interviews with the author, 1991–4.

8. Maj R.C. Schwarze *The SEAD Campaign of the Persian Gulf War: the F-4G in Combat*. Maj Schwarze flew 31 combat missions with the 35th TFW(P).

9. Quotes are by courtesy of Kevin Jackson, who interviewed Col George Jernigan and supplied material for this book.

10. Quotes in the narrative are by courtesy of Tony Cassanova, who interviewed John Leenhouts on behalf of the author for this book.

11. *Shield and Sword* (US Navy Historical Center publication). COMUSNAVCENT/ Commander of the US 7th Fleet during Desert Shield was Adm Henry H. Mauz Jr, who was replaced by Vice Adm Stanley Arthur during December 1990.

12. The TALD has since evolved into more sophisticated versions which can conduct jamming or real-time ESM, relaying critical EOB data to friendly Elint aircraft, while a turbojet-powered model (the Improved TALD or ITALD, based on the Israeli Delilah) can be launched at sea-level and offers a range of up to 150nm when released at altitude. The US Air Force has since begun development of its own TRA-built Miniature Air-Launched Decoy, already in flight-test.

13. *The Hook* (spring 1991). In another 'first', S-3Bs from VS-24 'Scouts' launched from USS *Theodore Roosevelt* and dropped Mk82s on a triple-A site in southern Iraq; location/date unknown.

14. On 18 January an A-6E (BuNo. 152928) from VA-155 'Silver Foxes' was lost after delivering its mines. The crew, Lt William 'TC' Costen and Lt Charles 'Tuna' Turner, were declared MIA. This loss prompted Vice Adm Stanley Arthur, COMUSNAVCENT, to cancel further mine-laying missions. Altogether there were five A-6E losses, including a VA-35 aircraft (BuNo. 161668) from USS *Saratoga* on 17 January. Pilot Lt Robert Wetzel and B/N Lt Jeffrey N. Zaun ejected and became POWs. A second VA-35 A-6E (BuNo. 158539) was hit that night but returned to USS *Saratoga*, its crew safe. It was struck off charge. On 2 February a VA-36 aircraft (BuNo. 155632) was lost; Lt Cdr Barry T. Cook and Lt Patrick K. Connor were killed. The fifth loss (BuNo. 155602) occurred as a result of hydraulic failure during recovery on the deck of USS *America* on 15 February. The aircraft lost brakes coming out of the wires, the crew ejected, and the aircraft was left hanging over the side of the ship. With the rest of the air wing awaiting recovery, the flight deck crew speedily removed the AN/ALQ-167 jamming pod and pushed the aircraft into the sea. These training pods had been reconfigured for tactical operations and hastily deployed to the Gulf to provide additional jamming self-protection. This event thus became 'an act of salvage' and not a mishap.

15. Chris Eagle interview by courtesy of Tony Cassanova, on behalf of the author for this book.

16. *Gulf War Air Power Survey, Vol V* (Government Printing Office, 1993). As opposed to 89 Navy F/A-18s that averaged just under 50 per jet.

17. Chris Burgess interview by courtesy of Tony Cassanova, on behalf of the author for this book.

18. Those figures cite Iraqi losses as 42 aircraft shot down, 81 destroyed on the ground and 137 fled to Iran. Some 3,700 of 4,280 tanks were destroyed, as well as 2,400 of 2,870 assorted other AFVs and 2,600 of 31,110 artillery pieces. Iraqi Navy losses were 19 ships sunk and 6 damaged; and 42 Iraqi Army divisions were rendered combat-ineffective.

19. In communications with the author, before and just after his retirement from active duty.

20. A second ANG unit, the 192nd FS 'High Rollers' at Reno, Nevada, was also slated to convert to F-4Gs, but only ever painted-up one 'tail' before its re-equipment programme was suspended in favour of continued active-duty operations. After Desert Storm, Congress had authorized the funding of just two F-4G squadrons, hence the complicated unit juggling that ensued.

21. The J (Joint-service) series of weapons embraces a number of new, fourth-generation PGMs featuring autonomous guidance based primarily upon GPS-NAVSTAR guidance, which gives them a theoretical 3ft targeting accuracy. These weapons embrace the 2,000lb class AGM-154 Joint Stand-off Weapon (JSOW), equipped with either cluster bomb or unitary warheads; the AGM-158 Joint Air-to-Surface Stand-off Missile (JASSM), not yet fielded at the time of writing; the GBU-31 Joint Direct Attack Munition (JDAM); plus the Wind-Corrected Munitions Dispenser family of cluster bombs: CBU-103 Combined Effects Munition (CEM), CBU-104 Gator and CBU-105 Sensor-Fused Weapon (SFW), *inter alia.*

    The F-16 and F/A-18 are now qualified to employ the JDAM, which is currently receiving a Diamond Back JDAM-ER pop-out winglet which trebles range to 24 miles from a 21,000ft drop height. Compare that with Vietnam-era pilots depositing Mk82 iron bombs on top of a target in a dive or Dive Toss manoeuvre!

    JSOW and the rocket-assisted JASSM offering a longer reach are destined to employ a host of payloads, including unitary warheads, cluster munitions, non-destructive configurations, and even CSAR payloads which may be deposited near downed airmen. *Misc sources.*

CHAPTER SEVEN

1. *DOT&E Annual Bulletins.* F-16 production for the US Air Force totalled 670 (of 1,432) F-16As and 122 (of 312) F-16Bs manufactured. The US Air Force has since received over 1,400 F-16C/Ds, which remain in low-rate production. HTS is plugged into the existing electronic warfare system. The F-16 was fitted originally with the ATI AN/ALR-69 RWR, but as early as 1980 a requirement identified a need for it to be replaced with a newer system. Loral's AN/ALR-56M, based on an updated version of the AN/ALR-56C equipping the F-15 Eagle, was selected, and tested on F-16s beginning in January 1991. By December 1992 it had been authorized for full-rate production for installation on Block 40 and 50 series F-16s. The AN/ALR-56M is tied to improved Tracor AN/ALE-47 chaff/flare dispensers and the Block II AN/ALQ-131(V) two-Band ECM pod, and is being hooked-up to FOTD decoys, described later in the narrative. Early problems with the AN/ALR-56M system were encountered during hard manoeuvres, when the RWR did not quite keep up with the F-16's gyrations and generated bearing

errors and delayed deletions on the cockpit display. The fix was training, making pilots familiar with these shortcomings under certain air combat situations.

Earlier aircraft through Block 30 with the AN/ALR-69 are receiving an advanced crystal video receiver update, replacing the current pre-amplifier, to endow them with greater dynamic range, sensitivity, and the ability to cope with a more saturated signal environment.

2 'Iraq's Mobile SAMs on the Move', *Aviation Week & Space Technology* (16 September 1996).

3. Based on an interview with Lt Col Pete Costello by Kevin Jackson, for this book.

4. Based on an interview with Maj Bob Egan by Kevin Jackson, for this book.

5. Including 266 SA-6s, 175 SA-3s, 106 IR-guided MANPADS and 126 other unidentified SAMs. *DoD Debrief*, July 1999, following Allied Force.

6. In a further change, on 8 July 1992 the 37th FW was inactivated and the F-117As were transferred to the 49th FW. On 30 July 1993 the 415th FS 'Nighthawks' became the 9th FS 'Iron Knights', the 416th FS 'Knight Riders' became the 8th FS 'Black Sheep', and in that December the 417th FS 'Bandits', the RTU, became the 7th FS 'Bunyaps'. In June 1999 the RTU was redesignated the 7th CTS, and absorbed ground academic functions. The 37th FW operates some fifty-three F-117As, including those undergoing depot-level rework or in use in a test capacity with Lockheed-Martin's Plant 42 at Palmdale, California. They are projected to remain in service until 2018. *Misc sources*.

7. P.J. Klass, 'Electronic Warfare Special Report', *Aviation Week & Space Technology* (30 September 1996); other open sources, such as *International Countermeasures Handbook* (Jane's, 1996).

8. *Ibid*. Refer to Chapter Four for a fuller account of Vietnam-era Repeater mode jamming techniques. Latter-day jamming is more dependent on predictive Transponder mode techniques because of the abundance of track-while-scan techniques and monopulse radars, timed to interact at crucial stages with abrupt jamming and which thus do not attempt to gradually introduce angular or ranging errors, as did Vietnam-era Repeater jamming. *Misc sources*.

9 The current panoply of SA-10 systems include the S-300PM, or SA-10B; the S-300PS and export equivalent S-300PMU, or SA-10C; the export version of the S-300PM, the S-300PMU-1, or SA-10D; and the twice-the-range S-300PMU-2, or SA-10E. Earlier domestic Russian and export models are capable of being upgraded to S-300PMU-2 configuration, for a 100+ mile range, creating the SA-20. *Misc sources*.

10. *Ibid*. Also 'Electronic Warfare Special Report: Defeating Modern SAMs' (features by B.D. Nordwall and R. Wall), *Aviation Week & Space Technology* (2 October 2000).

INDEX

Page numbers in **bold** indicate illustrations